Charles Ives And His Road To The Stars

A New Interpretation, Assessment and Guide to the Music and the Man

Antony Cooke

Estrella Books

Copyright © 2012 Antony Cooke

All rights reserved.

ISBN-13: 978-1479187553

ISBN-10: 1479187550

Cover Photography

Galaxy Cluster Abell 1689, courtesy of NASA @ nasaimages.org

1947 Portrait of Charles Ives, by Frank Gerratana, with appreciation

Library of Congress Control Number: 2012916974
CreateSpace Independent Publishing Platform
North Charleston, SC

Contents

Foreword by Johnny Reinhard.. ix
Introduction.. xiii
Preface... xix

Chapter 1 1
The makeup of the man
Ives in his time... 2
Ives in our time.. 3
The psychoanalyst's couch 7
Dashed idealism: Ives' lone journey to the stars 10
The Ives we can know through his music 12
The isolationist 13
A career in music?...14
Life choices 18
Henry Cowell, and the awakening 19
Ives the craftsman 19

Chapter 2 23
Building the road
Danbury Years (1874-1894) 24
Ives the dreamer 26
A respectable career in music...28
The key to the new sounds 31
The developing model 34
Multiple orbits 37
The 'lily pads' 39

Chapter 3 41
Originality, influences and musical makeup
    On the use of musical quotations........................43
    Links to other music 50
    A musical radical...51
    The 'isms' of music...53
    The pioneer working alone 54
    Ives' counterpoint...56
    The makeup of the music 58
    Folk, Popular, Civil War music 59
    Church music...60
    The European model 62
    The experimental model...63

Chapter 4 67
Early symphonic ventures
    The European symphonic model 67
    The First Symphony...69
    The Second Symphony..71
    Listeners' guide 79

Chapter 5 91
The Third Symphony ('The Camp Meeting')
    Timeline 92
    A link to the symphony: Fugue in Four Keys on
        'The Shining Shore'...95
    The music of the symphony 96
    Comparisons with other symphonies of the period 98
    Listeners' guide 99
    The Significance of the Third Symphony.......104

Chapter 6 105
The experimental years
    Music in space and time......................................105
    Early experiments...106
    The experimental timeline..................................107

Experimental miniatures 111
First Set for Chamber Orchestra 115
Paving the road to the stars 118
The Unanswered Question (a Cosmic Landscape) 120
Listeners' guide 121
Central Park in the Dark 125
Listeners' guide 128

Chapter 7 133
Ives in Danbury

The Symphony of Holidays 135
Washington's Birthday 136
Listeners' guide 138
Decoration Day 141
Listeners' guide 144
The Fourth of July 147
Listeners' guide 151
Thanksgiving and Forefathers' Day 154
Listeners' guide 156

Chapter 8 161
The Songs

Selected Songs over the course of Ives' most productive years 167
When Stars are in the Quiet Skies 167
From "Amphion" 169
Tarrant Moss 170
Hymn 172
The Cage 174
Watchman 175
The Indians 178
Like a Sick Eagle 180
So may it be! (The Rainbow) 183
September 185
Afterglow 188

Chapter 9 191
The Concord Sonata
    Listeners' guide 195
    Emerson 197
    Hawthorne 202
    The Alcotts 205
    Thoreau 208

Chapter 10 213
The Fourth Symphony
    Parallel thoughts 216
    Movement 1 220
    Listeners' guide 221
    Movement 2 224
    Listeners' guide 230
    Movement 3 234
    Listeners' guide 235
    Movement 4 237
    Listeners' guide 240

Chapter 11 245
The Universe Symphony
    The challenge for the listener 249
    Why Ives did not finish the symphony, and
        the 'Ives Legend' 254
    The real purpose behind the words 263
    The journey over 263

Chapter 12 269
Resurrecting the symphony
    The sketch materials 269
    Paving the road for the listener 273
    The Three Orchestras 277
    All components together 280
    Realizations of the Universe Symphony 281
    Microtones 286

The story behind Reinhard's realization 288
The Ives sound 289
The difficulties of realization.. 289

Chapter 13 291
A listeners' guide to the Universe Symphony
I: Fragment: Earth Alone (also later: Heavens music 292
II: Prelude #1; Pulse Of The Cosmos 294
III: Section A; Wide Valleys And Clouds........................ 295
IV: Prelude #2; Birth Of The Oceans.............................. 302
V: Section B; Earth And The Firmament 303
VI: Prelude #3; And Lo, Now It Is Night 304
VII: Section C; Earth Is Of The Heavens 306
Is Reinhard's realization the Symphony of Ives'
   imagination? 312

Appendix 1 Revising Ives 315
The 'Ives Legend' 318
Questions of Veracity..319
The dates and other irregularities 320
Putnam's Camp...326
Common sense 327
Issues of mortality 328
Cultivating the new avant-garde in America....................329
A question of deceit..330
Psychobiographies 332
Four years of study with Parker: a controversy settled.....332
Summing up 333

Appendix 2 The Universe Symphony Sketches 337
General notes 337
Section A 339
Section B 341
The 'Lost' prelude & the mysterious Section C 343
Additional notes regarding the succeeding Patches 51 – 54... 350

Index 355

Foreword

Many of us have realized that Charles Ives is a bit of a mystery to practically all Americans. It is said only one percent recognize his name, and half of that one percent know him only as a life insurance innovator. Bumping into his Memos at the North Carolina School of the Arts college music library, and later at the Lincoln Center Music Library, only drove my curiosity further, initiated by several memorable encounters with his music. But curiosity can only flow when unimpeded.

There is so much disinformation to impede knowledge of this great American composer. Ives lived in a different era, difficult to interpret from our 21st Century vantage point. However, besides the usual difficulties of obtaining records and by interviewing those who knew him personally, there has been a societal rejection based primarily on misinformation. We have long passed Rollo's antagonism to challenging listening (Rollo was Ives' fictitious name for arrogant music writers who were deaf to what he hoped to achieve) living at a time in which it is now quite comfortable to listen to 'noise' music served at high decibels.

The *faux* Ives 'redating crisis' is one example, the excessive costs levied by publishers for permission to perform Ives's music is another, and the pretense doubting the existence of a full 'Universe Symphony' is still yet another example of the widespread numbing of curiosity for Charles Ives.

Ives is typically relegated to the right (although he was very generous to the left). He was tarred a cranky Yankee, although he was America's most generous philanthropist in music. The complexity of Charles Ives requires an appreciation of the artist's musical sensibilities, as well as his philosophical explorations expounded in sound.

Antony Cooke was seemingly born to this task. He combines a rich musical inheritance with a life long fascination with the universe. I guess it was only a matter of time before our author enthusiastically grasped the complexity of Ives and set to create a narrative that is refreshingly believable. It is to Antony Cooke's great credit that Ives appears once again a flesh and blood human being, quite a turnaround for a man infamously rewritten.

Working through unfinished music compositions had been a particular focus of mine over many years. Solving puzzles necessary to finish compositions that 'ask' to be finished, such as *Psalm 51* by Mordecai Sandberg, and *Simfony in Free Style* by Lou Harrison, was a regular function of my role as Director of the American Festival of Microtonal Music in New York City (since 1981).

The 'Universe Symphony' is the only piece I know of, throughout the entire annals of known history, that specifically 'asks' for another composer to finish a huge work. Immediately after my realization of the 'Universe Symphony' by Charles Ives was premiered in Alice Tully Hall, Lincoln Center in New York City on June 6, 1996, I believed it to be the composer's *magnum opus*.

It just did not make sense to me to deny Ives his explicit directions, not if one feels that being authentic is a good trait to have. The tempo is the singular tempo indicated by Ives of a quarter note = 30 on the first measure of the first page of the Earth Orchestra; no instrument was exchanged in the orchestration; and all the material you hear, and see in the score is what Ives left for us in perpetuity. It was all one grand plan. Nothing was lost, a position contrary to all the assorted academics. I made certain that I left open all of my procedures, along with a *Finale* score of my manuscript of Ives's sketches, and a book. No 'new' notes were added to the score

But since this flew in the face of what the public had been able to detect, it was immediately deemed 'controversial,' with each music critic focused upon completely different points from one another; displaying a veritable rainbow of next generation Rollos, albeit a much more accepting bunch.

Foreword

The media seemed to enjoy the 'controversy' stew, keeping things perpetually vague. I recall an early morning radio interview on WNYC given by the station head, wherein he lunged into whether or not my realization should be considered Ives at all! (I thought we had already covered that territory before we went to air.) Years later, I understand a bit better the pervasive mire that is our collective inheritance of the genius of Charles Edward Ives.

A century ago, Ives was trying to understand his place in the universe, and he accomplished this mission with both humility and creativity. Who is to say that the 'unanswered question' is not meant to give an eventual answer, but only after a certain life journey is taken? Ives' transcendental imagination was apparently too huge for the industry leading *Finale* notation program to account for in the 'modern' age. The inputting of the 'Universe Symphony' in *Finale* did not allow for its three orchestras - Earth, Heaven, Pulse of the Cosmos – to be set in three different meters, resulting in massive paste-ups, and multiple scannings.

My great idea for the studio recording produced by Michael Thorne (Stereo Society 2004) was to make a connection with the Hayden Planetarium at New York's Museum of Natural History. It always excites me to imagine seeing the universe before me while listening to the Universe Symphony. I had a taste of that when a now defunct Italian website matched the colorful Hubble photos with selections from the recording. It worked fantastically, a visual extravaganza with the music akin to the soundtrack to a silent film, even though the photographed astral bodies did not always correspond exactly with the composer's designations. (Disney could probably work wonders through the cartoon medium.)

Perhaps with the publication of *Charles Ives & his Road to the Stars*, the exceptional human being C.E.I. (Charles Edward Ives) can come out of the historical shadows. Most important to this success was to connect the dots throughout his diverse idealistic endeavors, the fruits of Ives's musical labors. And finally someone has looked deeply into the material with the correct 'prescription lenses,' someone who has effectively dodged the metaphoric land mines of false authorities, and who can explain the good news to the general public about the great wealth of their collective musical inheritance.

Johnny Reinhard
October 1, 2012
New York City

Author's Introduction and Acknowledgements

The idea to write a book about Charles Ives came about by accident – or should we say, by sheer good fortune. Having been long an avid fan and follower (half a century and counting), Ives' music would become a permanent landmark in my life. With so much wonderful music existing in the world, it is difficult to claim any composer as a favorite, but then again, perhaps the term sums him up pretty well.

Introduced to Ives by my close friend of early years growing up in England, composer and conductor Oliver Knussen, my initial impressions of Ives were of utter incredulity. Attending one of the first performances of his *Fourth Symphony* in the mid-sixties at the Royal Albert Hall, London, with the Philharmonia Orchestra under Harold Farberman, at the time I did not appreciate what I was privileged to hear and witness. I remember laughing aloud during the second movement. Perhaps Ives would have approved, because this was, after all, the 'comedy' movement - a romp. However, I am not proud to admit that I was laughing *at* Ives, not *with* him. At that time, I was just another personification of Ives' perennial favorite verbal target, "Rollo," the character he borrowed from Jacob Abbott's popular series of books from the 19th Century, whose predictable, good boy sensibilities were always assured.

But then it happened. I was hooked, even though I did not know it yet. Days later, I *had* to buy the recording. It was the one by Leopold Stokowski and the American Symphony Orchestra, the first and still, in my view, the best.* Before I knew it I was a convert, but that is now over 45 years ago. Just a year or two earlier, in that same venue I had been present at the 1963, 50th anniversary performance of Stravinsky's *Rite of Spring* - with Stravinsky present and Pierre Monteaux conducting. What an auspicious occasion! However, in hindsight I am not sure which one of these two monumental musical happenings was bigger in my life. But it was probably the Ives symphony.

*The concertmaster of the orchestra at the time, Murray Adler, had long moved from New York and been working in Hollywood many years before I entered the same industry. Only recently did I discover that the beautiful solos on the recording were by him. I told him that there is a short clip from the recording sessions on YouTube; Murray looked exactly the same more than 45 years earlier! Showing him my old score of the symphony that Oliver had brought back for me to England from New York, (quite something to have in those days), he memorialized it by inscribing it.

My previous book, about an astronomical topic, clearly is about as far removed from Charles Ives as anything possibly could be; well, it almost is, because both share a common connection to the stars. That's what I would have thought until by happenstance and coincidence I stumbled into writing the present book. Dr. Fred Watson, Astronomer in Charge at the Australian National Observatory and I began corresponding following his kind interest in writing the foreword to that book. We found that we had a vibrant mutual interest. By sheer accident, because my profession in music accompanied my other primary interest, *astronomy*, and Fred's profession, astronomy, accompanied his other primary interest, *music,* we stumbled into something we never saw coming.

Before long we were emailing regularly and sending each other CD's of 'space music,' ranging from the music of William Herschel (that *composer* who ended up an astronomer!), Morton Lauridsen, even, yes....Charles Ives. It turned out that we 'discovered' the *Universe Symphony* together. Despite having been such a long time Ives buff, somehow I had let Ives' magnum opus escape me. The recording of the *Universe Symphony*, long an icon of Ives' unrealized vision, had only come into being in recent years. When first I heard Ives' *Universe* I didn't know quite what to make of it. I remember putting it aside and thinking to myself, "Well, at least I've heard it." Perhaps dear Fred still curses me for pushing him into such an aural hazard zone.

However, it happened again. Once heard, this piece, too, lured me back for 'just one more' hearing, possessing that unique and powerful Ives hook. And so it went. The hearings became addictive; for a period of time I could not stop listening to it.

Author's Introduction and Acknowledgements

Naturally getting my hands on the score, and the book documenting its realization and assembly was next. Understanding Ives' *Universe* became almost an obsession; I scoured every detail of everything I could find. By then it had become abundantly clear what it was all about.

Suddenly, I found myself starting the present book; I just knew I had to do it. It was clear that Ives had traveled a musical journey to reach a remote spiritual destiny, of which not even he seemed aware, but it had defined his entire compositional output. It appears he spent twenty years in search of some otherworld idealistic destination where all mankind could live in freedom, peace, openness and caring, free of dictators and ruthless politicians - in short, his transcendental Nirvana. With the *Universe Symphony* he found it, even if he never found its parallel on Earth.

Along my own journey, this book gave me a chance to reflect, and to weigh in on what I have long considered to be some questionable theories and assumptions made over the years about America's true original composer, and perhaps, the most interesting in all 20th Century music. For many Ives enthusiasts, perhaps this writer, too, adding 'greatest,' even 'America's 20th Century Beethoven,' seems increasingly appropriate, even mandatory. But unlike Beethoven, Ives still is not a household name. Many concertgoers remain perplexed by Ives' music, because they do not know how to respond to music that neither soothes the ears nor explains itself easily. As in the best things in life, some effort is required to access it. And the fact remains that most concertgoers still have not yet accepted music from much beyond the 19th Century.

More serious is the deterioration of awareness today about higher cultural things; most people are completely unaware of the world of so-called 'serious' music, and even if they are, regard it as something stuffy and snobbish - more akin to the Emperor's new clothes, or strictly for elitists and academics 'in their ivory towers.' Ives' earlier hopes for an increasingly elevated state of culture from the population were dashed even during his lifetime. It is hard to know how he would react to things today, but we can only imagine!

An amusing anecdote experienced by the writer recently illustrates the situation well, as well as two parallel realities. In a discussion at a coffee shop with an acquaintance about the once dominant European musical culture, and how it had dissipated during the 20th Century, as well as the degeneration of western culture in general, my acquaintance struggled to name a composer from that great era, whose music he told me he had just heard on the radio.

"His name began with an M, I think."
"Gustav Mahler?," I inquired.
"No, something like Monti...something."
"You mean, Monteverdi?
"No, Manfredi, Manatini, or something........"
"Can't place it, I'm afraid."
"It was real pretty music."

That was my clue.

"Mantovani?"
"YES, that's him; wonderful! There's nobody like that anymore!"

Of course I should have expected this. In almost rapid-fire succession, the same person followed up to chide me for not realizing that Roger Williams was a classical pianist. Humorous as this is, it would have made Ives sad. His worst fears came true; culturally, things may be worse now than they were in Ives' time. Although there is a following for contemporary 'classical' music, the actual number of enlightened members of the public seems to be falling. We can witness this by the disappearing orchestras and recital series, victims of lower concert attendance and often-imperious management, only to be replaced by surviving organizations and featured 'social media' events, which recycle the same old chestnuts to an increasingly unsophisticated musical public. However, many of us will continue to persevere, in the hope that the kind of society that Ives dreamed about could still come to pass. Our fingers are crossed.

Special thanks are long overdue to Oliver Knussen, for having started it all (and whom I know recently had what I would imagine to be a near out-of-body experience having actually *played* Ives' piano in his West Redding homestead studio), Fred Watson for having fired me up about all things connected to 'space music,' and Johnny Reinhard for bringing Ives' ultimate musical destiny into the bright light of day, along with all his generous contributions to this book. But mostly thanks are due to Ives himself.

Preface

A galactic supernova (at bottom left)
Image courtesy NASA/ESA, The Hubble Key Project Team
and The High-Z Supernova Search Team

Near the beginning of his book, *Essays before a Sonata,* Charles Ives remarked that his transcendentalist hero, Ralph Waldo Emerson, had traveled a road looking for his star.[1] Through a musical extension of the same philosophy, Ives would travel down that road to find his own star amongst the myriads of others claimed by the souls who had preceded him. Over the course of an astonishing creative period that flared up like a supernova in the New England 'skies' - a prolific explosion of fast evolving musical language and composition - it shone brightly and then it was gone. Charles Ives would stop writing forever, leaving his greatest masterpiece unfinished and in disarray, but not before he had found his star - a place of inner peace, where he could reconcile himself to a changing world and walk in the company of those who had helped to pave his way.

Despite many attempts by some to rationalize the entire phenomenon, did they miss the clues?

Charles Ives' America

Charles Edward Ives was born in 1874 in Danbury, Connecticut, a typical country town of its day steeped in New England tradition. The influences of its quaint provincial culture would retain a pivotal force in Ives' view of the world throughout his life. Although he would leave Danbury to embrace a new century, a far larger world, ultimately even the cosmos, and pioneered some of most radical musical futurism along the way, he clung to his old world upbringing and values. It was a curious *apparent* contradiction, since effectively he had his feet firmly planted in two centuries and two ways of life, though pointed towards a distant destination that would transcend them both.

A product of the post-Civil War era, Ives was an independent spirit belonging to his moment in time and space. The cessation of war and America's booming emergence was expected to bequeath its survivors the promise of a new land of freedom and opportunity. In Charles Ives' America, that survivor was his father, who instilled his own thoroughly 19th Century outlook and culture in his son. However, Ives would build on his father's legacy through the transcendental philosophies that had emanated from its protagonists in Concord, Massachusetts to provide a grand new vision for that new society. Uniquely American, Ives' music spoke to the evolving culture of his country, its unique voice authentically reflecting a spiritual foundation free from the old world domination of the European empire states. Immensely appealing to Ives, transcendentalism created further contradictions in his philosophical outlook, as he determined to bridge the divide between it and his father's special brand of provincial religiosity that he had witnessed and experienced firsthand at revival meetings.

Thus, diverse and sometimes opposite, Ives' passions thus were preordained largely by his surroundings, but nevertheless they came together at a unique time and place in history to pave what we can more appropriately symbolize as *Charles Ives' Road to the Stars*. If he were to be satisfied merely with following tradition in the footsteps of those who had come and gone before, then his search for the fulfillment of his vision of the New World would have come up empty handed, and resulted in just a continuation of the old order. Thus, to reach his destination would entail a journey through personal experience, an American journey that was largely instrumental for his unique perspectives and creativity.

That Ives' own vision for America and the world did not turn out the way he had dreamed drove him ever harder to find the ultimate realm in eternity, where he could keep his lost dreams alive in the distant place he glimpsed ever-clearer in his mind. We can summarize the key influences in his life:

George Ives

The leading figure and influence in Ives' early years, his father's role grew ever larger over time in his son's eyes. Ives later would credit him for anything good that he had done in music.

{{PD-Art}}

It is probably fair to say that George Ives had much more talent than ability to find employment - that is, beyond eking out a living in a small country town as bandleader, miscellaneous musician and teacher. However, what turned out to be an undistinguished musical career had begun shining brightly during the Civil War, when apparently he was considered one of the foremost bandsmen in the Union Army, reputedly having played for Lincoln. An unfortunate incident, when he destroyed his cornet and asked to be discharged from the band, then went absent without leave, to bring a degree of shame that his son would try to rewrite by elevating his memory.

Sharing his father's traditions, musical knowledge and penchant for experimentation, increasingly Ives would revere his father's influence over the years. Irrespective of the level of George Ives' technical sophistication, and the reluctance of some historians to fully accept that role relative to the much more sophisticated influences he would encounter later, Ives did owe his key foundations to his father. The bond between father and son was so strong that in the years following George Ives' untimely passing - just after the youthful Charles had entered Yale - it seemed he would spend the rest of his life in search of the place in eternity he thought his father might occupy.

Danbury, Connecticut

{{PD-Art}}

The epitome of small town America, Ives' many happy memories growing up there tinged most of his musical output with what appears to be a yearning for something lost. Although Danbury's cultural life revolved around historic traditions, its musical activities were dominated by 'society ladies,' a fact that probably was behind Ives' youthful view that music was too feminine to consider for a career, as well as a lifelong revulsion of 'pretty' sounds in music. His father's own lowly status within that society presumably also had something to do with it.

Camp Meetings

The old time revivalist camp meetings were part of the Ives family tradition, in which George Ives often performed while leading the congregation. The music and passion of these assemblies greatly impacted the young impressionable Ives to play a significant role in his own work, along with a wide range of other church music. Famously drawing upon musical quotations, Ives would turn increasingly towards religious sources, his later most profound utterances featuring these melodies almost exclusively. It seems no coincidence that *Nearer My God to Thee (Bethany)* would feature ever more prominently in his music, and would be the final hymn he would quote in any significant work.

CAMP MEETING!
—AT—
SCHROON LAKE, N. Y.

The Seventh Day Adventists will hold a Camp Meeting on

PATRICK McCARTY'S LOT,
SCHROON LAKE VILLAGE,

August 21 to 31, '90

The location is a fine one, being situated on the banks of the beautiful Schroon Lake. A large tent will be pitched on the grounds, in which services will be held, which, in connection with quite a number of family tents, which will constitute the home of the campers, will cause the ground to present an attractive appearance.

Among the able Ministers who are expected to be present may be mentioned S. H. LANE A. E. PLACE, and E. E. MILES.

Preaching Services Each Day at 10:30 A. M., 2:30 and 7:15 P. M.

The Public are Cordially Invited to Attend these Meetings.

ADMISSION FREE.   THE BEST OF ORDER WILL BE PRESERVED.

BY ORDER COMMITTEE.

ROME REPUBLICAN PRINT.

{{PD-Art}}

The Civil War

The American Civil War between the North and the South provided the historic backdrop to Ives' 19th Century America, relayed through his father's experiences. In Ives' world, it was the defining event of the century. We can see its influence in practically everything that he wrote, especially in the melodic quotations, and projections of heroic fighting for the cause of democracy and freedom.

Charles Ives And His Road To The Stars

{{PD-Art}}

New England

Image by Patrick Breen

New England culture and tradition was as much a state of being as it was a region of the country. Here the ways of the 'old' America were firmly entrenched, supplying Ives with a near limitless resource of deeply held cultural attitudes, traditions and optimism, inspiration afforded by its varied and colorful landscapes, as well as historical associations of the country's founding.

Yale Years

The small horizons of Danbury were far too limiting for someone of Ives' potential. With some influence and help from his more prominent extended family, he was able to attend Yale University. Clearly, such a prestigious education would have been beyond his father's means, and certainly out of the question following his death.

Finding ready acceptance and popularity at Yale in a new environment far from the provincial outlook of his upbringing, Ives enjoyed sports and would come under the strong influence of his peers. Yale traditionally had been a place from which new business professionals emerged, presenting Ives with a conundrum in which it appears he did not feel could be open about his musical ideals; here, it was not looked at as something one would entertain doing for a living, although he gladly relished a new role amongst his friends as a popular 'jack of all trades' in musical applications of his talents. Thus it has been theorized quite plausibly that Ives always harbored thoughts of a career in business, and not music.[2] Eager not to be perceived as an odd-man out - especially with the attitudes he brought with him from Danbury - here, he would actively cultivate an image of one who engaged in music for light-hearted fun, or for practical gain (good business!) as an organist on Sundays. The choice of which university to attend presumably was not lost on his family, and indeed, Ives' decisions following graduation from Yale lend weight to this argument. Further:

- His one real attempt to become a successful professional composer were quickly dashed without much of a fight;
- Upon his graduation from Yale, taking an entry-level professional *business* position with Mutual Insurance had been pre-determined;
- Relocating to New York, Ives quickly became thoroughly entrenched in the business life of the big city and fully a part of its culture and lifestyle, while retaining a musical hobbyist's image for his friends and business associates.

Oddly, being academically somewhat of an under-achiever also was considered part and parcel of being a true Yale fellow; this is well reflected in Ives' record, along with that of many of his contemporaries. However, like so many of the most innovative minds throughout history, probably Ives was easily bored by the formal constraints of academia, something that had never caught his imagination even in his earlier years. Being preoccupied by his duties as an organist and composer of music for church services, as well as taking care of his other studies, it is also not altogether surprising that his attentions might have been somewhat divided. Other possibilities of a more clinical nature for his lackluster academic performance have been proposed, too, such as Attention Deficit Disorder (ADD).

Preface

Horatio Parker

{{PD-Art}}

Horatio Parker, Ives' thoroughly European schooled theory and composition teacher, presented an even stronger pull toward another musical universe. German trained, his compositional style was true to the late romantic European tradition of Brahms and his contemporaries, his best-known work being the cantata, *Hora Novissima*. Today, out of a substantial output, this is all he is remembered for. Although Parker's career represented a perpetuation of a culture from across the Atlantic, this did, nevertheless, demonstrate that it was possible for a native born American composer to have a successful career in music. Indeed, Parker was highly renowned in his day. However, even an acclaimed composer in America needed to supplement his income in various ways; thus, in addition to teaching at Yale, Parker also maintained a busy schedule of performing as a church organist and local orchestra conductor.

Regretfully, Parker - who can be credited with developing and refining Ives' basic homegrown skills - would never recognize the huge talent he had under his tutelage, in many ways acting to suppress it, though not deliberately. To be fair, Ives represented a latent form of musician unknown to him, and more than likely would have escaped notice of almost any other professional musician of the day, too. Regardless, Ives would harbor conflicted feelings about Parker's role in his music throughout his adult life.

A career in insurance

Upon graduating from Yale, Ives moved to New York City. His first ten years in New York were spent living in a form of 'digs,' at an apartment residence building specially allocated to Yale graduates, nicknamed 'Poverty Flat.' Here, he would stay *far* longer than his contemporaries. Apparently reluctant to give up his Yale social life and the life of a happy bachelor, his long stay there also probably reflected a form of limbo in life, in which he was not yet quite ready to embrace the real world, and probably an uncertainty about how to embrace both business and music together. Furthermore, his early health issues and the crisis that almost enveloped the insurance business of 1905 were also likely factors in his apparent indecision with moving forward.

Preface

Ives and Life Insurance

New York Life Building
{{PD-Art}}

With Ives' initial introduction and subsequent career in the insurance industry, it seemed the proper place for a young future professional to begin in the business world, and a common expectation of most Yale graduates. In 1905, the near collapse of the industry from internal corruption almost jettisoned his chances in the industry. Ives would be a prominent player in its redemption, however, and his efforts to rebuild the industry model on a new, almost transcendentally inspired foundation were highly instrumental in its reemergence and staying power to this day. Applying a scientific approach and compassion to human needs, Ives' business model and philosophy for calculating actuarial tables revolutionized life insurance.

Harmony Twitchell

Ives' primary support throughout most of his adult life was his wife and soul mate, Harmony, who cared for him, encouraged him, and always stood by him regardless of joy or adversity. There can be no doubt she was at least partly responsible for his attaining the age of almost 80, despite his multiple physical ailments; she provided the focus for his life, the reason to move on from his circular existence at 'Poverty Flat' into his successful future in business, as well as providing the freedom, space, safe haven and optimism - moreover, the belief in him - to compose.

New York City

Although Ives remained spiritually bonded to Danbury, his childhood home, it was hardly a coincidence that he chose to leave and stay away forever. His ambitions, having outgrown the provincial attitudes of 'small town America,' resulted in relocating to New York City immediately upon graduating from Yale. Here he would taste real success, even if it would not be in music. Since Ives was influenced by his surroundings, many of his compositions reflect city life. It is hardly surprising that he maintained a primary residence near his work, although eventually he would crave peace and solitude, building a country estate in 1914 on a serene 18-acre property on Umpawaug Road in West Redding, Connecticut - later to become his full-time residence. Regardless, Ives juggled two major careers, composing in his spare time away from the office, completely unknown to the larger musical world.

The Adirondacks

Because, in 1905, Ives experienced his first bout of the mysterious illness that would return to haunt him for the rest of his life, he came to treasure his time out of the city amongst the inspirational settings and solace of the Adirondacks wildernesses in upstate New York. It lay within easy reach of his country home. The blend in Ives' consciousness of the vast panoramas and his transcendental visions would inspire many of his greatest works - most notably, perhaps, the *Universe Symphony*, the culminating focus of this writing, and one that never left his thoughts.

Adirondacks mountain and lake scene
Image courtesy GFDL

The Transcendentalists of Concord

Although Ives' tradition-steeped values were strongly identified with 19th Century America, it was the revolutionary philosophical and spiritual values of the transcendentalist movement that had the most profound impression upon him, to become perhaps the largest creative focus of his life. The influence of these luminary figures shows up with regularity in most of his mature compositions, since his entire adult life seemed to encompass a search to find his place in their transcendental universe. Creatively, the philosophies of the Concord (Mass.) 'four' - Ives' transcendental heroes - would carry thus even more weight with him than the religious outlook of his upbringing. With it came the final, critical dimension in his astonishing dash to the stars. It is hardly surprising that Ives' great piano epic, the *Concord Sonata,* would pay homage to Emerson, Hawthorne, Thoreau and the Alcotts, as he sought to find an equivalent in musical sound of what they represented to him. However, it was primarily Ralph Waldo Emerson's philosophies that would act as Ives' predominant spiritual guide.

Ralph Waldo Emerson
{{PD-Art}}

Transcendentalists considered that religion and politics, as well as academic intellectualism (to them, as typified by Harvard University in their day!), were anathema to humanity, and that ultimately these were harmful to the human condition; can it be only another coincidence that Ives would attend Yale? Although transcendentalism is extinct today, as a product of its age it was in many ways a form of the romantic idealism that saw man as central in the cosmos, and at one with it. Transcendentalists would build upon the works of those who came before, but by looking to their own surroundings they would create a newly relevant reflection of their own place in time and space. One could argue that similar movements, at least in part, have sprung up periodically ever since even to this day; unfortunately, none of them has ever had a visionary figure quite like Emerson to steer them.

Preface

Nathaniel Hawthorn

{{PD-Art}}

Amos Bronson Alcott
{{PD-Art}}

Regardless, not only did Ives hitch himself to transcendentalism, but also held on to the essential faith of his upbringing, too, and politically being a staunch Democrat to boot, apparently he had no problem juggling such fundamental contradictions under one tent! With the combination of the religious 'fervor' he had experienced amidst large congregations and the passionate political views he found necessary to put meaning to his own brand of transcendentalism, Ives thus hardly marched lockstep with his heroes. He considered pure transcendentalism lacked the components of publicly affirmed faith, as well as a populist voice. However, his personal interpretation shared a common bond with the Concord transcendentalists' belief in man's fundamental goodness and place in eternity.

Henry David Thoreau
{{PD-Art}}

Although Ives' belief system was essentially his own, cobbling together the best he knew from these sources into a highly personal approach to his purpose and life, it is still fair to say that the larger aims of transcendentalism were able to remain comfortably at his core. The very *'American-ness'* of his music, however, was the result mostly of his application of that philosophy upon the culture and traditional ideals in which he was immersed. Critically, it taught Americans they were mistaken in looking primarily to Europe for cues, when their own surroundings could provide far more authentic resources for their own expression. With this in mind, Ives would spend many hours in contemplation from a lookout shelter he built with his brother, Moss, on Pine Mountain, Connecticut in 1903, absorbing the vast panoramas all around him; true to transcendental philosophies, this was how he contemplated his place amidst the cosmos. He would try to forge *that* in musical sound, and ultimately it would include the very cosmos into which he had stared.

The Stars Align

On the heels of all of these circumstances, we should put to rest the mistaken but popular notion that Ives set out to write nationalistic music. To be primarily concerned with such a shallow perspective would have been diametrically opposite to his larger philosophy. Attaining the means necessary to reflect the culture of his own people, land and spirituality would involve exploring new musical concepts - and a road of his own making. If he appeared to resent European culture, actually this was not so. Rather, he resented his own people's preference to remain unquestioningly within those familiar comfort zones - thus embracing the total dominance of foreign cultures, while rejecting any thought of embracing their own. Ives would experience this attitude personally with astounding regularity and bluntness, receiving nothing in return for his efforts other than the support and encouragement from a few people close to him.

Since Ives chose early on to write as his instincts guided him, freeing himself to use whatever served his needs, throwing out nothing by default, *even if it had European origins,* this was in no way contradictory to the transcendental ideal. Ives chose a good model: Emerson himself built upon the (European) philosophies of Goethe rather than start anew. In fact, what Ives did was completely consistent with Emerson's belief that nothing could come about without having existed before. Because the unique sounds that Ives created sometimes seem to belong to another musical universe, it is easy to overlook the important links to the traditions of Western music that he preserved from its fabric. However, Ives had no compunction to add to or reorder existing methodologies in any way he saw fit, while pioneering many new techniques within them. Significantly, if what he wrote always reflected the world within his own horizons, many of the 'alien' sounds actually were born out of developments of standard practice, often extraordinary combinations of elements previously considered irreconcilable.

Ives' transcendentalism was reflected further after the life insurance crisis; that he was motivated to be instrumental in righting its wrongs is central to understanding him. Having witnessed close-up the collapse of the industry, in order to live under its umbrella and within himself, insurance had to represent more than just business - thus it would become no less a part of his idealistic vision than anything else, a world where free people would be protected from financial adversity and so enlightened that even children happily would whistle quarter-tone melodies as they skipped down the street![3] Many people probably overlook, too, the fact that business probably occupied significantly *more* of his time than composing, and thus, they make no allowance for the fact that a large part of Charles Ives, the person, therefore remains unknown to us.

The rush to the stars

The urgency that we detect in Ives' feverish rush towards the form of musical composition he considered central to his life is increasingly apparent once he entered his fifth decade; his rapidly evolving music reflected his father's early demise, and a nagging reminder that time might not be on his side. As he reached ever higher to his destination in eternity, strangely, even in his writings, he seemed unaware of anything out of the ordinary driving him; or at least he would not admit to it, and certainly no words he left behind reveal any sense of working towards some extraordinary final goal underlying his search to match music with his philosophies. However, if we open our eyes, that goal stares *us* in the face.

Although it is possible to understand elements of his music technically, and analyses of his work reveal some insights into what we are hearing as well as its methodology, exactly *how* he formulated *what* he wrote still is largely a mystery. No one who knew him ever would gain any insight into the unique traits of his musical language, much less take from him his preferred way for others to perform what he had written. In this matter he seemed singularly disinterested, deferring most artistic decisions to the performer.

A universe of contradictions

Ives was an unusual figure. Wildly eccentric, complex but simple, explosive yet gentle, revolutionary but old fashioned, a deep thinker but aficionado of puns (!), idealist but realist, publicity-shy yet self-publicizing, wealthy but not materialistic, forward-looking but longing for the past, grand in vision but modest, chaotic but organized, reclusive (as much by choice as necessity) though friendly and warm - these are just a few of the seeming contradictions and remarkable qualities that sum up a composer who many regard as one of the century's greatest, and an American titan amongst his international contemporaries. Ives' charismatic personality seemed totally at odds with his overt shyness; he had no need to impress anyone. Moreover, many of his friends and business associates did not know of his double life (composer and businessman); they only knew *one* of the two apparently separate persons. Into old age, a quiet self-respect, even more the inner peace with who he was and what he had done in his life remained unshakably within him.

Aside from his manifest contradictions, Ives held humankind in the highest regard, and felt a personal stake in its march towards freedom and elevation. He was an anonymous benefactor, and generous to a fault at a personal level. Carol K. Baron, the leading musicologist, revealed this in ways that never had been fully appreciated before. In *Efforts on Behalf of Democracy by Charles Ives and His Family: Their Religious Contexts*,[4] Baron would properly acknowledge and detail Ives' immense philanthropic legacy, one born of spiritual passion and political idealism.

Despite being one of the most colorful, intriguing and individualistic composers to emerge in the 20th Century, Ives, however, was unknown during his most creative period, his influence on other contemporary composers therefore being nil. Aside from his unique outlook and life, his persona was nothing like that expected of great composers. An utterly down-to-earth individual, he could not identify with the popular image of 'tortured artist in the attic,' something misunderstood in many analyses. Uncomfortable with such a role, we can trace it not only to his perceptions of musicians within his community, but his convictions that great music belonged to all humankind, not the elite. Ives could see nobility in the most commonplace of music and music making, his father having shown him not to judge these by the *sound*, (the superficial), lest he miss the *music*, (the profound).

A destination amongst the stars

The Concord philosophers had shown Ives how to lift his musical experiences beyond the provincial sphere of their humble origins to the loftiest heights, and allow them to coexist amongst some of the most avant-garde and daring concepts of his day. Independent of influences from Europe, Ives would touch upon virtually every 20th Century musical innovation - often in advance of, or at least concurrently with others - but always differently in conception and utilization. Progressing in his music via experimentation, through worldly depictions towards the otherworldly, the journey would lift him to a place in which he could reconcile a rapidly changing society with his treasured vision of the old order. Thus, Ives' evolution was his road to salvation and place in the cosmos. Indeed, this scenario has been proposed before. In his 2005 article,[5] Michael Berest contemplated the real possibility that Ives had been on a path to a distant spiritual destination since 1893 - apparently unconsciously - when he wrote his *Variations on America*.

Ives' journey would lead inevitably to the *Universe Symphony*, his greatest transcendental musical contemplation. Until only relatively recently it remained in a state most had regarded as a mythical monument to a near delusional vision far beyond practicality, impossible to complete, or never intended for completion; it was said to exist variously within Ives' imagination like the shifting sands of the desert. Unsurprisingly, in view of its title, the concept was truly cosmic in scope, a destination that is entirely consistent with Berest's speculation and Ives' philosophical stance. Can it be coincidental that Ives never contemplated a work more ambitious, massive or *less* worldly?

If we look for a precise progression in the timeline to this point we will be perplexed. Although the overall direction of his road to the stars is clear - certainly no one would ever confuse a work from 1900 with one from 1920 - Ives, however, worked on countless works simultaneously, reworking existing music and ideas from one to into another with uncanny flexibility and regularity. Usually when he took an existing idea, it would grow further as it continued to evolve, so the truth is that he often lost track of exactly *what* piece was written *when,* his various attempts to catalog his work being frequently contradictory, standing in stark testament to this enigmatic record. The upshot is that sometimes we have works belonging to apparently different periods emerging at the same time. If Ives' mind clearly was not focused on a chronological flow of development towards his final goal, the destination itself was never in doubt.

The period of Ives' road to the stars also encompasses the years in which he built his hugely successful business, which, in turn, was linked to the same stimulus and outlook that drove his music. Within this compressed two-decade-long time frame, Ives' productivity could have filled several lifespans, his contributions in both fields being similarly wide. However, after the *Universe Symphony* largely had formed in his mind, the prospect of new compositions would rapidly decline, eventually to halt altogether within just a few years, and sadly, before Ives completed a full draft of the work.

Many commentators - historians, psychoanalysts and musicologists - have attempted to provide theories and explanations for the apparent mystery behind the rapid cessation of Ives' compositional activity, and especially in regard to the mighty near-mythical symphony. It seems that most of them indeed *have* missed the likeliest clues - through too *clinical* examinations of circumstances unique to Ives. If looking for complex psychological explanations when other far simpler deductions might be staring one in the face is the reason for this, proverbially speaking, perhaps the answer can be found *yet* - if we look objectively and keep our eyes open to the obvious.

Accessing the music

Far from echoing the European model of classical composer, Charles Ives would emerge as a unique entity, the product of a brave new world in which the general American public's level of musical awareness still was in its infancy. Ives came almost to relish his status as one of music's 'bad boys,' and, in fact, was wary of becoming too comfortably accepted by the avant-garde establishment. That would have meant that his mission had failed, having fallen victim to the same predictability of all that he was trying to escape. Ives said he only wrote what he heard in his mind. Contrary to popular opinion, he was not trying to shock or offend anyone, or to scare his audience away. However, he did not mind doing so if his music had this effect on those who were too close-minded to have their horizons challenged (a reminder of the 'society ladies' of Danbury!). Ives was an explorer of the unknown, hoping to open peoples' ears and minds to new musical territories, and openly scornful of the mindset of the 'lily pads' (C.E.I.) - those who only wanted to listen to that which soothed and caressed their ears - while basking in sounds that never challenged their perceptions or declared anything new.

Although part of his chosen isolation was related to increasing health problems, his personal outlook reflected it more profoundly. Significantly, had he tried to please audiences first and foremost, he could never have ventured into the musical unknown and find a way to express his own ideas. Better that he *not* try to make a living from music, and perhaps time would allow others to join him in what he had done. Ives criticized many other contemporary composers for taking what he regarded as "the easy way out" with the concessions that he perceived they had taken in order to please their audiences, rather than risk breaking new ground. As such, he did not have too many kind words for them. Such comments need always to be taken in the crusty spirit intended - Ives was an ideological purist - and they should not be misinterpreted as arising out of bitterness or anger. Unfortunately, some critics have done so.

It seems one loves or hates Ives' music; it still baffles, mystifies and perplexes. However, with exposure only to his more outlandish and daring compositions, it is probably too much to expect to be able to relate readily to it - especially upon just one hearing. If it appears to fall somewhere in the cracks of 20th Century musical development, this really is not so, although it evolved alone. Some critics, even those who should know better, have made the mistake of assuming that Ives' complex and often tangled musical language represents the incoherent ramblings of a dilettante - one who did not know what he was doing. Such sentiments were expressed by many even after Ives' music started gaining attention; stated harshly, dismissively and worse, frequently they were the words of renowned musicians and reviewers in major journals, and even of his friends. No wonder Ives felt ill-treated by the musical establishment, and was so openly critical of those who controlled it, quite aside from the fact that his vision diverged so greatly from theirs.

As things happened, after a long period of gradual discovery, Ives' music would be greeted by the enthusiastic embrace of the new blood in American music, as well as those in progressive movements abroad. However, the golden period that would see him heralded as a musical prophet was followed by a time of questioning in some circles, which would have been fine had it remained similarly objective as applied to others. Always easier to discredit someone's achievements than elevate one's own, an over-eager inquisition would devolve into outright distrust. Ives' reputation, both in his business and private life, was shredded. Though the same types of analyses from the period of 'trials in absentia' seldom seem comparable to those related to his contemporaries, the damage was done - at least for a time. Thus, the attitudes that had dogged Ives during his lifetime *still* were not about to go away easily.

However, it was not very long before there followed something akin to a rediscovery and reappraisal. Many of the one-sided judgments now have been laid to rest, and perhaps this writing will serve to settle a few of the still larger lingering questions and misperceptions about a 'Beethovenesque' figure who lived in our midst, as well as introduce his music to others. Regardless, Charles Ives now stands well established as an American icon in 20th Century music - perhaps *the* icon, firmly ensconced in his position, seemingly sure to stay, and not so different to the man we all thought we knew before all of the late revisionism started. His music stands defiant, no longer needing justification or reason to exist. But it does need understanding and a willingness to set biases aside in order to access and enjoy it. In that respect, for it to be accepted by a wider span of listeners it has still a long way to go. However, it is very hard to understand Ives' music or what drove him if we listen to it only at face value. Requiring a degree of effort from the listener, as with all the greatest artistic works of the ages, Ives' music is never more sure to be rejected amongst those whose enjoyment of music encompasses only easy listening, or worse its reduction to mere background ambience.

The best of numerous books available about the composer, life and music, feature extraordinary breadth and detail of historical information, if not always coupled with insightful or objective analyses of his music. So the problem for most music lovers - who are not also musicians - is not any lack of books on Ives' music, rather it is the approach. Many texts seem so contradictory within their covers that one wonders what opinion the authors had, one's impression seeming to sway back and forth like a ship on the high seas. It seems in many instances what we see is the result of many of them somehow having foisted their own personalities and issues onto *Ives!* For those readers who are Ives disciples, however, such texts might threaten to shake their fervor, although though they should not. Not *every* author, though maybe an excellent music historian - is, or was a musician of any stripe - necessarily objective, or able to appreciate Ives' great and original genius and unique creative personality. For those who have already rejected his music, these sources will not likely cause them to change their minds; they will not read them anyway.

Through no shortage of information, the layman is, by and large, left out, because most texts require that the prospective reader already be knowledgeable about music. On the opposite side of the coin, those few sources that have been written exclusively for the layman assume a level of comprehension and knowledge that is rudimentary in the extreme; these must be extremely frustrating (dare we say insulting?) for those who can handle more than this, but cannot access more advanced or technically specific texts. There are many musicians, too, who do not enjoy reading books that seem more like academic dissertations. Thus, with no alternate approach generally considered, the difficulties in discussing highly technical concepts, such as those concerning Ives' music, by default, result in *musical analysts* writing materials *for other musical analysts!* These texts, inevitably being loaded with detailed formal discussions, esoteric musical terms, musical score examples, and countless other intimate musical references, etc., will be out of range for most average laymen. It is likely they will not be able to relate to them any more successfully than they can make sense of Ives' music in the first place. Thus, through no-one's intentional design, this does more than anything else to ensure that a unique musical treasure trove remains the exclusive turf of an elite club.

Directly related to this, a recent opinion piece on 'MusicWeb International' by Frank T. Manhein,[6] raised the specter of the continuing contradiction with Ives' music and the disparate levels of appreciation between audiences and music 'experts.' It seems that acceptance - indeed, comprehension and appreciation of the music - remains directly proportional to the level of training, expertise, theoretical/historical knowledge, and so forth of the listener. It further seems that only when the subject of Ives' music comes up do we have this particular kind of discourse! Far rarer it seems, for example, is such discussion regarding many other 20th Century pioneers, such as Schönberg, Webern, or Cage - composers who are similarly far from public favorites or whose music is any more accessible, if indeed even as much.

Manhein further commented on the reactions and receptiveness of current audiences to Ives' music, versus other audiences over the course the time that all of them have been exposed to it (mostly since the late 1940's). Things have not changed very much, apparently. But whose fault is this? The implication is that it is somehow Ives', because his music has not penetrated most peoples' horizons. However, if the shunning of new ideas were the ideal approach for a composer to take, then we would still be listening to plainsong. Many of the greatest works of music were rejected by the public, not only at the time of their writing, but even many decades after their creation. Many still are, even though society slowly might have accorded them a level of respect that surpasses any lack of affection for them that they might still hold. In that light, although few laymen would contend that J. S. Bach was not indeed a musical titan, most concertgoers would probably elect to attend a performance of Tchaikowski's *1812 Overture* rather than Bach's *B Minor Mass*. Thus popular appeal is not the ultimate test. Nor should it be.

Aaron Copland, perhaps the most 'popular' of all America's 'classical' composers posed a similar perspective, but with a somewhat more startling analysis. Because most of Ives' music was written 'in the dark,' his music being formulated in isolation - and irrespective of public reaction, acclaim or rejection - Copland saw this is a key *weakness*. If this seems to be an odd position for a composer to take in regard to the arts, especially regarding a true pioneer such as Ives, and thus, the situation *does* seem right in line with Manhein's position. However, with all due greatest respect and the greatest admiration for Copland, he was not a pioneer of revolutionary techniques. Thus, if we accept his hypothesis - perhaps even more if we consider music in general to be merely another form of entertainment - then we might agree with him. But to embrace such a sentiment allows for little creativity or growth, ensuring an artistic status quo and lack of creativity. The greatest moments in art have never followed a quick and easy path to acceptance, based on immediate comprehension by those rendered ill-equipped by its innovation to do so. Indeed, there are plenty of contradictions to Copland's view; can anyone argue that the disastrous first performance of Stravinsky's *Rite of Spring* would lead him to reject it, or to modify his future work based on that reaction? In fact, Stravinsky embraced his newfound radical image, which allowed him virtually to thumb his nose at an intolerant public.

The movie business provides an interesting analogy. For a movie to be successful means that it must be quickly and well received by the public if it is to make its money back for its investors. Therefore the industry faces a constant challenge to embrace the highest art, especially groundbreaking high art at that, *and* succeed at the box office. If the latter is not achieved, the filmmakers concerned will not likely be rewarded with another opportunity to spend their investors' money. This is not to say that high art cannot exist within the movies; surely it does, and when it breaks new ground as well it is movie-making history. But to expect a public more interested in immediate gratification than new and profound, even life-changing experience is always asking a lot in our entertainment-driven culture.

We must make peace with the fact that most of the public does not go to concerts; the musical community has not yet reconciled the gap between what is truly esoteric and that which is merely comfortable and soothing ('pretty') to listen to. It seems the majority of the public still is unaware, even disdainful, of what all the fuss over 'classical' music is about. Ives knew this this problem well - that most of the public found new and unfamiliar music to be uninteresting, more likely ugly; however, greater familiarity often resulted in greater acceptance and even affection. An optimistic spirit by nature, Ives always held out hope for a time when people would tire of the status quo, and demand more from themselves and their artists. As part of the transcendentalists' vision, one might still hope that indeed the day would come when an increasingly sophisticated public finally will make Ives' aspirations a reality.[2] Of course, to date, it has not worked out that way; some even might argue we have stepped backward.

Thus, should we expect to understand *all* implications in art from the outset it would lead to little room for new developments outside familiar comfort levels regardless of our sophistication. So although Ives' isolation was an extreme case of artistic independence to be sure, this writer would argue that it was, in fact, one of his greatest strengths, freeing him to explore startling new horizons, undeterred by the reactions of those whom would likely reject them, and especially not dependent on his need to capitalize on them financially.

Through another prism

Probably, it would be unhelpful to try to explore Ives' music through cross-references with other music of the time, simply because his music evolved largely as a separate and independent entity, even when his techniques were not necessarily exclusive to him. Since the pioneering aspects of Ives' music were conceived for the most part in a near artistic vacuum, they are best presented on his terms. Indeed, Ives utilized and treated them entirely differently than did his contemporaries.

In tracing his artistic evolution through some works that make Ives' road to the stars easier to see, the many omitted should not be seen as a reflection on their significance. It would also do little good if the text were to be centered on analyses of printed scores couched in technical terms, when the majority of readers perhaps cannot read music! Indeed, nor should they have any requirement to do so, since musical notation is a means of communication, nothing more, representing only what the composer formed in his mind and put on the page for the *performer*. One should not need to be a musician in order to enjoy what is involved to compose or perform. Similarly, understanding music on technical terms also should not be a requirement to its appreciation. In this light, only those literary references beneficial to the discussion have been included (at the end of each chapter); they should not be considered essential to a larger understanding. Thus, the descriptive texts in this book intentionally contain *no musical score examples* - no music reading skills being necessary - in keeping with the stated premise to make it accessible to all interested parties, regardless of musical education or background. Though listening guideposts are supplied plentifully, they are outlined in standard terms to illustrate the steps that Ives trod, so that perhaps the road might be a little better lit. Specifically:

- There is a general discussion to read.
- The listeners' guides promote familiarization of the materials with musical guideposts.
- The listeners' guides, along with sufficient listening to reference recordings should enable identification of the guideposts.

Historical perspectives of this book

And finally, it was not the writer's intent to retread yet another detailed, historic examination and documentation of Ives' life. When Magee's *Charles Ives Reconsidered* was released in 2008,[2] as a relatively new entrant into the field and with a purported new stance, it was surprising that much of what was contained within its covers revisited detail presented exhaustively before. Magee even analyzed, to the near exclusion of other possible choices - and in the greatest detail at that - the *same* work, *General William Booth enters into Heaven*, as had Peter J. Burkholder in 1996.[7]

Although some review of Ives' life and circumstances is unavoidable if the context of what is presented here is to make any sense, rather than revisit information for its own sake, fuller accounts of it will be left to those far more detailed and complete texts already available. Let us now explore further what has been outlined here.

REFERENCES

1. 'Essays Before a Sonata,' Charles Ives, *Knickerbocker Press,* New York, 1920, p. 12
2. 'Charles Ives Reconsidered,' Gayle Sherwood Magee, *University of Illinois Press,* Chicago, Illinois, 2008, pp. 55-56; 'Charles Ives & His America,' Frank R. Rossiter, *Liveright,* New York, 1975, p. 114
3. 'Essays Before a Sonata,' Charles Ives, *Knickerbocker Press,* New York, 1920, p. 82
4. 'Efforts on Behalf of Democracy by Charles Ives and His Family: Their Religious Contexts,' Carol K. Baron, *The Musical Quarterly,* Vol. 87, No. 1, Oxford University Press, 2004
5. 'Charles Ives Universe Symphony, "Nothing More to Say,"' Michael Berest, 2005, www.afmm.org/uindex.htm
6. '20th Century pioneer composer Charles Ives: audiences and critics' opinions over time,' Frank T. Manhein, *MusicWeb International,* 2004, www.musicweb-international.com/classrev/2004/Oct04/Ives_View.htm
7. 'Charles Ives and the Four Traditions,' from 'Charles Ives and his World,' Edited by J. Peter Burkholder, *Princeton University Press,* Princeton, New Jersey, 1996, pp. 23-29; 'Charles Ives Reconsidered,' Gayle Sherwood Magee, *University of Illinois Press,* Chicago, Illinois, 2008, pp. 106–113

CHAPTER 1

The Makeup of the Man

In the cosmos, structures called 'starburst' galaxies host star formation and development at such a rapid pace that they rapidly exhaust their star-making materials. These galaxies are destined to have vastly shortened life cycles.

Messier 82, a starburst galaxy
Image courtesy NASA/ESA/STScI/AURA/ The Hubble Heritage Team

On a human scale, Charles Ives' accelerated development and rapid decline is curiously reminiscent of such a galaxy, in that his entire creative development and output essentially spanned just two decades. Apart from some peripheral works dating from as early as the 1880's to as late as 1927, the vast majority of Ives' output and development encompasses the first two decades of the 20th Century. During the century's third decade, the once-fevered music making from one of its most remarkable figures would fall as silent as the guns of the Great War that had accompanied some of his most remarkable years. By 1927, struggling to keep the fires burning, Ives reluctantly would face the reality that his time as a composer was over; in fact, it had been largely so for some time. But Ives had traveled light years from small town 19th Century America to embrace the cosmos itself.

Ives in his time

Unsurprisingly, there is no place better to get to know Ives than through his own words. *Memos*, mostly consisting of dictated prose, is a collection of thoughts about his music, other composers' music, his philosophical outlook, what he encountered from other musicians, critics and even audiences of the day, as well as countless insights into his personality and life.[1] Full of satire, humor, his amusing perceptions of those with shuttered minds, and frequent self-effacing remarks, this is Ives speaking directly to us. He emerges as a living person - indeed, as if we have been in his company. Very little of the baggage that others sometimes have imposed upon him through their theories and interpretations seem present at all, Ives' own rationale for his work emerging more credible than practically anything else we are likely to read. He is quite straightforward, in fact, and comes across as a person most might wish they could have known.

There are other records that verify much about what we read in *Memos*, so we can know Ives from his words. Between 1969 and 1970 (more than 15 years following Ives' death), Vivian Perlis, formerly of the Oral History American Music Project at Yale University, undertook a unique labor of love. In recording what seem to be countless interviews from every living contact that she could locate - friend, family member, musician, or business associate - Perlis assembled them into a book that provided a most revealing portrait of Ives, from youth through old age. Here was the pioneer composer, businessman, and benefactor as seen by others. One of the earliest books on his life still in print, Perlis' living portrait of Ives allowed us to see him through the two-sided glass of the parallel worlds of music and insurance he inhabited. A *relatively* light volume in a purely academic comparison with many others, the information contained in Perlis' work makes it perhaps the weightiest of all; Ives' world speaks for itself, perhaps more tellingly than we will find in any other source, save his own words.[2]

The Ives that emerges clearly did not crave personal recognition; He was comfortable in his own skin. Certainly he wanted his music to be heard, but not if it meant writing what was not true to his being to gain an audience, and especially ignoring all that mattered to him. Perlis' portrait of Ives is much in line with what we already might have concluded from reading his *own* words, leaving very little room for interpretation, or deep-seated issues that need resolution and specialized analysis. Even more, the complexities that many commentators have devised to try to explain his creativity, why it ceased, even his character and life choices - while trying to shoehorn him into a prescribed stereotype - are hard to find.

Ives in our time

If we are looking for extensive detail on the *historic* aspects of Ives' life, however, there are some remarkable sources of information available. We should encourage some caution, though, for those not yet sufficiently familiar with Ives, the person and composer. As mentioned in the Preface, readers should remain always wary of a lot of these texts, along with the conclusions and inferences drawn in them; sometimes the authors' cases emerge as more important to the text than the composer himself. There is a common tendency, too, to communicate mixed signals leading to confusing impressions about the person and his music. We can illustrate this with two such texts.

One is the massive book by Stuart Feder, *Charles Ives: My Father's Song*,[3] one of the most thoroughly researched books of all. Its encyclopedic vault of information does not come without drawbacks, however, typical of many in-depth works about Ives, life or music. Most *non-musicians* likely will find it heavy going, and overly technical for their level of knowledge. As might be expected, it also comes with its fair share of the author's own interpretative agenda.

The other is the classic 1974 work by Frank R. Rossiter, *Charles Ives & His America*.[4] Slightly different in its approach, Rossiter's was amongst the first of such analyses whereby a reappraisal was undertaken out of the partly unrealistic ('legend') status that had been accorded Ives almost indiscriminately. To the general reader it will be more accessible than Feder's, although both volumes must have represented enormous undertakings to compile and investigate.

In the context of looking for explanations into Ives' remarkable and visionary life, both works leave no stone unturned, discovering many red herrings along the way. Unfortunately, these are not always recognized as such, and might leave the reader perplexed about the very subject who could appear now diminished - the unintended consequence of secondhand analyses of figures considered sufficiently *significant* to have been studied in the first place! Regardless, both books are extraordinary examinations of many aspects of Ives' life.

Of the two, it seems that Rossiter's might be the more valuable for the picture it paints of all that surrounded Ives' life and times. Its perspective seems closer to actuality than most, although it trades specific musical analyses about some of Ives' works for unfortunate generalities; such is the downside of someone other than a musician pronouncing weighty opinions about musical matters. In comparison however, Feder's is far more detailed in laying out the historic aspects of Ives' life, and has the benefit of his considerable musical background, though still likely to prove unwieldy for many readers.

In the opinion of this writer, however, both authors fell into a common trap when attempting to make definitive and subjective judgments, especially when apparently blind to the obvious - akin to not being able to see the forest for the trees. These judgments often seem, quite frankly, bizarre, even ridiculous, perhaps having arisen out of a need to see intellectual or analytical profundity in things that would be seen as straightforward - even normal - by anyone else. However, perhaps the most egregious symptom of these artistic evaluations is the fact that they had been stated gratuitously, as if no serious, studied musician of any stripe would, *or could,* possibly disagree.

There is nothing wrong with looking for greater insights and realities, of course, but this writer takes issue with dissecting the 'Ives legend' to the degree that his unique contribution, character and voice is lost amongst the rubble. Thus we cannot overlook the remarkable book by Jan Swafford, *Charles Ives: A Life With Music* (W.W. Norton & Co., 1996), in which the composer's greatness is increasingly revealed rather than supplanted by another's agenda; yet in detail and artistic objectivity it compares with or rivals any biographical text, perhaps being the best amongst them.

Aside from artistic evaluations, other inexplicable perspectives also can be found in other texts. For example, in *Charles Ives Reconsidered,*[5] Gayle Sherwood Magee found it strange, even ungracious, that Ives would have used a personal connection in order to secure a performance of his music, having already distanced himself from that person. In this instance, the issue was when Magee made the presumption that Ives had utilized the friendship between his teacher at Yale, Horatio Parker, and the famed German conductor, Walter Damrosch, to try to secure a performance of his music. That he did this might well be so, although his motivation is pure speculation. Regardless, what does this mean, however? Ives was a former student of Parker, but they had not had a 'falling out.' In that the connection did not result in a performance of his music, Ives would reflect many years later some resentment towards both figures, which Magee saw as revealing Ives in a bad light.

Even stranger were Magee's remarks about Ives' reactions to Damrosch's position on financial matters over the practical business of funding performances of new music, describing them as "abusive," even "abrasive." Somehow this was seen to be at odds with Ives' perspective on his own later financial success.[5] Noticeable, however, was the absence of comment about Ives' great philanthropy in promoting new music and struggling composers, along with underwriting performances of their work as his financial position increasingly allowed him to do. Always an anonymous benefactor, Ives knew all too well how it felt to be ignored and have financial constraints stand in the way. Magee's attitude to both of these two unconnected situations seems hard to fathom.

Ives' fate of post-mortem revisionism should be recognized as something accorded to almost all of our heroes; America's favorite musical son was not likely to be spared from the rite of passage that has become part of our culture. Luckily the counter-reaction to that - the traditional rebuilding of a wounded former hero - has already taken hold; the well-known portrait of Ives leaning forward on his cane with that glint in his eye seems to tell us that he was smarter than all of us put together.[6] He knew we would come around.

Regardless, however, it seems that even to this day Ives still is singled out for a type of treatment that keeps him from attaining full membership in the pantheon of greats. It is hard to recall any other major composer who has been so frequently micro-analyzed, misunderstood, misrepresented, even falsely accused. His unique message has been lost in action amongst the blur of opinions from those who have always claimed to know better than Ives about things that only he knew. Thus it is still common to hear the same kind of disdain about Ives' music that he himself heard in his day; in this respect, amongst those who still "don't get it" (Ives' own terminology!), nothing much has changed. It seems sad also that much of the hand wringing about Ives comes from his own countrymen, those who one might have imagined would have been his strongest cheerleaders. (See Appendix 1.) In fact, Ives' own words about his struggles in *Memos* seem even more telling, and just as viable today as when he recorded them, 80 years ago.

The psychoanalyst's couch

With Feder's perspective, though, the psychobiographical approach was taken to a new level, his work also becoming a psychoanalyst's case study. The validity of such second-hand, second-guessing years after the fact, of course, is in the eye of the beholder. Those lingering questions and issues that had festered for decades certainly encouraged Feder's research and complex premise. However, the somewhat tormented portrait of Ives that Feder painted is particularly odd on almost every level; did this reflect more the author than the composer? Although the father/son connection that formed the fundamental basis of his book are well grounded, surely close bonds between father and son are far from unusual.

Predictably, others glommed on to the psychoanalytical approach in trying to identify clinical explanations for Ives' extraordinary creativity and unique musical perspective, other than the obvious: he was a genius! We should bear in mind that none of these people had known Ives, nor thus were able to give him the opportunity to discuss or respond to their 'diagnoses.' Ives never had been on the couch, but he might have understood *them* better than they did *him*.

In contrast, figures such as Nicolas Slonimsky, who knew Ives personally, spoke explicitly about Ives' simple take on life, and the very *lack* of inner turmoil in his soul.[7] However, if pent-up frustrations are also easy to understand in one who is physically unable to affect any change - such as with the infirmities that Ives experienced - regardless, no less a figure than Bernard Herrmann commented in 1945 upon Ives' state of mind as being neither bitter or compromised, words we should take in earnest in the context of Feder's clinical and generally unsympathetic hypothesis, generations removed.[8] Again, Herrmann knew Ives. The poet Louis Untermeyer,[9] recalled Ives' commanding presence, one not formed by an imperious persona in need of ego gratification, but by an unassuming yet assured understanding of his place in the grand scheme of things. Untermeyer saw a person who did not require congratulation, or mainstream approval; Ives knew what he had done without having to hear about it from anyone.

In Leon Botstein's scholarly and interesting, but in some ways forced comparison of Ives with Mahler,[10] Botstein tacitly embraced the psychoanalytical approach that had portrayed Ives as just another 'case history,' a term he actually used. Ives' unique genius, musical originality, creativity, even his colorful personality were thus reduced to a bland and dismissive search for routine explanation. Otherwise, notwithstanding Botstein's cogent analysis that both of these composers shared some clear traits and common influences, similar comparisons between other composers from almost *any* period would not be hard to find. Fair enough; perhaps he was onto something. For the most part, though, no one would ever confuse the music of Mahler for Ives.

Unfortunately, Botstein's research came too early to save him from making a false assumption about Ives' later rescoring of *Three Places in New England*,[11] (also see Appendix 2), and we leave the paper with the impression, presumably not intended, in which Mahler emerges standing tall, while Ives is reduced to a psychiatric anomaly (another term Botstein actually used!). And certainly Mahler had *far* greater inner psychiatric devils of his own to deal with than Ives ever knew. However, it must not go without comment that Botstein resorted to the most transparent of apologist's tactics in justifying why Mahler should not have been subjected to the same treatment![12]

Closely related, what about the legendary crankiness that Feder claimed to be key evidence of a changing and unstable personality? Although many others have referred to Ives as being a curmudgeonly New Englander, let us try to find *anyone* who suffers from multiple physical ailments who is *not* cranky at times! Indeed, recent research by David Nicholls *(Society for American Music,* 2009) has pointed to Addison's disease, the ailment that afflicted Ives' mother, Mollie. Long considered to be some kind of invalid, due to Ives' reticence to talk about her, as well as George's late reference to a "new nurse," it seems this was responsible for her untimely death and shaky handwriting. A disease that can be inherited, it might well explain not only Ives' own handwriting "snake tracks," but also perhaps at least some of his sudden mood swings, need for reclusiveness, and increasingly delicate state of being. And regardless, who amongst us, having been the target of public ridicule and rejection on the scale Ives was subjected to, or who continued to face the brick wall of others' negative attitudes, would not feel *something!?* Ives' frequent words of disdain for those of limited vision have been interpreted as bitter and angry by many, but it is a matter of record that the callous assessments, remarks and indifference that he endured were beyond anything normally reserved for critiques, so it is hardly surprising that he would strike back. Apparently some individuals have expected Ives to show qualities normally expected of candidates for sainthood.

When later years had exaggerated Ives' personality quirks to a degree, and his physical infirmities were compounding, his close friend, composer Carl Ruggles, recalled that Ives threw his manuscript of the *Robert Browning Overture* across the kitchen floor in disgust.[13] Ives had lived with it for a long time, and now frustrated with it he had concluded it was no good (or in his terms, N.G.). Wrongly or rightly, he felt that it was enslaved to carefully-calculated formal constrictions - some kind of self-conscious straightjacket - the *antithesis* of Ives' compositional aspirations.[14] Ruggles did, however, comment how ill Ives was at this stage, so the connection with his health and mood is clear.

Apparently Ives' critics cannot see, too, the impish irony and boldness of many of his 'cranky' remarks and irascible behavior evident to a degree throughout his life, even the slight chuckle often evident in their intent! All things considered, for the most part, Ives remained pretty much above the fray; it is remarkable, in fact, that he was able to keep his identity and inner peace intact. Regardless, those who knew Ives did not consider his cranky traits defined him; his flash points were tacitly understood. Feder seemed unable to relate to these kinds of human passion, and Ives emerged harshly, and inaccurately judged in his otherwise remarkably scholarly book; ultimately, it must be seen as one that encompasses an errant case study of an absent patient on an analyst's empty couch.

Dashed idealism: Ives' lone journey to the stars

Although Ives' visions (for the people!) of good politics and freedom (including penning a 20th Amendment to the Constitution in 1920, which was proposed formally) were deep-rooted in his version of transcendentalism, they were overly idealistic for any real chance of adoption. However, they are a window into Ives the man. He had reached his zenith, but must have felt he had traveled alone; both culturally and politically, it seemed to him that society had not evolved in a direction that embraced high ideals. It had gone backwards.

When one takes into account the pressures of functioning between business and music, it is hardly surprising that Ives became increasingly isolated, diminishing further any chance he might propose a practical game plan for his idealism. He surely maintained unrealistic expectations of others, especially since new generations had none of his nostalgia for a time now passed. Most people, busy in the practical aspects of living their lives in a booming new century, probably never paused for a minute to consider a state of higher existence! Feder, in trying to make the case that Ives suddenly acquired his political passions later in life, considered that it somehow replaced his musical creativity. However, Ives held profound political views for most of his adult life, echoed in his own modified transcendentalist philosophies. Increasing financial independence afforded him better opportunities to pursue them; time gave him the refinement to do so and the articulation to express them. We can also see them reflected in many of his compositions; strongly based on concepts of the peoples' freedom (i.e. *The Majority;* the *Second Orchestral Set; He is There!; Lincoln, the Great Commoner*), Ives held strong hopes that politicians would do what was right for society. However, with many of his highest ideals dashed by the end of the century's second decade, the disillusionment led to more passionate outbursts, surely a natural expectation. (Harmony, his wife, would caution visitors not to broach certain subjects - mostly politics, politicians, closed musical minds, bad music and musicians - for fear of inducing a heart attack!)

Ives thus had witnessed the rise of crass commercialism, automation, the elevation and exaltation of the glamorous and superficial, tabloid journalism, the descent of higher aspirations into mediocrity - actually things that we see the fruits of today. He had invested much of his soul into the expectation that he would see his nation's evolution develop along Emersonian ideals, in which a true age of enlightenment would grow in the New World - his country, the place his father had fought for. Instead, he witnessed the beginning of the now-familiar 20th Century phenomenon often termed the 'dumbing down' of the populace. Thus Ives' famous outbursts were just as likely to be triggered by it, as its manifestations within the mainstream musical community, the shortsighted visions of which stood in the way of progress. Even if Ives was unrealistic, who can say he was wrong?

Ives, a staunch Woodrow Wilsonian Democrat, felt Wilson had let him down in failing to deliver the kind of leadership he had hoped for, and especially in giving only lip service to Ives' own 1920 Constitutional Amendment. There is no doubt, too, that he felt his highest aspirations for humanity were crushed by World War I, but the icing on the cake shortly thereafter was Warren G. Harding's victory in the 1920 Presidential Election. All the factors combined took the wind out of him, and certainly were a factor in his declining incentive for composition, or anything much else; his motivation had been impaired. That these events came about shortly before his compositional activities started to wane can be no coincidence, even though this writer believes it likely they are only part of the picture, and the lesser part at that. Ives had reached his ultimate compositional destination just in time.

The author is hardly the first to comment upon the circumstances of the time. Michael Broyles, in an expansive article, commented that musicologists had not referenced newer understandings of the history of the period, leading to incorrect perceptions and conclusions about Ives' motivations, personal philosophy, and the way he conducted his life.[15] To those who truly have absorbed Ives' own words, and not forced their own interpretations upon them, none of this should be a surprise.

The Ives we can know through his music

Knowing Ives through his music reveals the same personality we already know from his words. Not afraid to express his convictions, and aware they would not please everybody, his solitude enabled him to give rein to all of them without external contradictory voices to argue with him, regardless. It was the very factor that enabled his musical explorations, unfettered by public acclaim or disdain, and the kind of idealistic naivety that encouraged exploring. And isolated he was; during his most productive years he was virtually alone in all that he did in music, completely unknown to most musicians or audiences. Here was an American original, one who dared to reach for wider horizons than anyone imagined could exist.

The composer-businessman identified and saw himself in terms of the common man, enjoying the company of practically *anyone* he respected as a "good" person. In his presence there was no outward projection of either his profession or avocation. The spirited creator of such songs as *An Election* and *The Greatest Man* is revealed in them for who he really was, a plain spoken, colorful and authentic human being. If one should listen through the old recorded sound and the aging Ives' modest, even ragged singing (!), his own performance made as late as 1943 of *They are There!* will bring more than a smile to one's face.[16] Ives' wonderfully free spirit and musicality is a marvel to behold, as is the fact that despite his terrible physical condition at the time (including hand tremors, general weakness and poor eyesight), it does nothing to suppress some extraordinarily agile and facile playing, also heard in the numerous other musical excerpts he recorded that day. His playing of *The Alcotts* from the *Concord Sonata*, is highly illuminating, and though not inconsiderable by any standards, is distinguished further by its indefinable fluidity, direct musicality and genuine sentiment.

Remarkably though, in all of his music, Ives' authentic character eventually becomes unmistakable, regardless of which of the wide array of styles, or combinations of styles he used to express himself. Thus, he is hardly a chameleon hiding in the shadows. We can argue about what influenced him, or even who thought of what first, but Ives' unique voice always emerges loud and clear. And more often than not, we find that he was influenced by multiple perceptions and experiences, all playing a role within the musical panoramas he built. Reflecting those very multiple perceptions and experiences, and possibly one of most original musical 'voices' who ever lived, he often spoke through an array of technically complex styles, usually combined in seemingly incompatible ways to function simultaneously. Because they require an awareness of more than one stratum at a time, this might explain some of the music's inaccessibility to many listeners, though no one should expect to appreciate Ives' music instantaneously.

We can understand Ives further by realizing that his mode of expression lay somewhere between the purest manipulation of sound and raw emotion. Believing 'absolute' music to be of questionable value, he considered it should be about expressing *something*, even if just human fervor. On the other side of the coin, pure program music was similarly unacceptable to Ives - why therefore did one need the music?! The place he strived to reach also represented a strange blend of the ultra-modern and the past, an Emersonian 19th Century view of humanity and the world, expressed within a vital and vibrant musical language that *looked forward*. Thus, overall, when roaming the distant, futuristic realms of the *Universe Symphony*, Ives remained nevertheless deeply rooted to a world that was fading from view. Ives' comments about Bach, Beethoven and Brahms - whom he respected as the greatest amongst composers - as not having found that perfect mode of expression (out of the need please their audiences), speak to his quest to find it.

The isolationist

Since Ives would realize early on that there was little place for radical musical vision in American society of the day, and having elected to make a living doing something less dependent on society's approval, his choice would prove to be his liberation.

Goddard Lieberson (composer, music critic and music executive) was amongst those who saw it quite simply and clearly: Ives shied away from the *business* of music, in which one would be forced to sell one's soul in order to ensure one's financial security.[17]

Aaron Copland and others proposed the theory that Ives' music *lost* some of its potential by his inability to reap the benefits of interaction with other musicians,[18] as well as through the modifications of style and substance that public performance would demand. It is easy to see that had he experienced such interaction he would have accomplished little, and that even Ives recognized this. As far as his awareness of the work of other contemporary composers was concerned, he did attend some concerts in which he heard some of the new ideas emerging from Europe. However, he soon became aware that exposure to it would affect his own creativity, and thus learned increasingly to stay away and embrace his isolation.[19]

We have learned, however, that Ives did benefit from some interaction with a small circle of musicians, apparently regularly inviting acquaintances to his house for soirées to play through some of his pieces. The *practical* benefit enabled him to adjust his methods accordingly to ensure his ideas worked, rather than *feeding any need for acceptance or approval* from those who played the music. This answers in large part those who maintained for many years that he was writing in a total vacuum without any awareness of the effectiveness of his ideas. He also had the advantage of being a considerable pianist, and was well versed in reusing and redeveloping his materials extensively; this certainly would have given him wide experience in hearing the effects of virtually everything before committing it to paper.

A career in music?

The prevailing societal view regarding musicians at the time and place of Ives' youth was not encouraging. Ives' father, George, had provided ample demonstration of the life one could expect as an aspiring musician in a 'small town America.' Ill paid, generally not respected, and forced to eke out whatever living his musical activities could provide, these would have been humiliating things for any young person to witness. Despite the remarkable influence his father (who Ives revered) played in his upbringing, the decent basic musical training that he had provided, and the plentiful respect he had earned within his own household, Ives was all too aware of his father's lowly societal status for having chosen music as a career. Musicians who enjoyed lofty perches of public acclaim were able to escape this fate, however, their position being socially acceptable only because the vast majority of them were European, or European trained, and seen thus as emanating from a 'sophisticated' culture far out of the range of small town musical culture.

In the Danbury of Ives' youth, business, medical and academic professionals, lawyers, and enterprising tradesmen - occupations and other 'solid' professions were seen as admirable, the hopes of every parent for the next generation. In such a culture with its pioneering past, even common laborers were likely more valued than musicians - people who found ways to provide for their families through 'honest toil.' If musicians were more the occasional providers of entertainment of genteel social clubs and local ladies' gatherings, as a livelihood most definitely this was not something to be confused with real employment or actual *work*. Traces of this attitude can be seen even to this day, even in developed regions of the country; there can be hardly a professional musician who has not heard the question, *"That's wonderful, but what do you do for a living?"* When up against, say, the sport of football, playing music is still considered 'artsy-craftsy,' even a sissy pastime by many. One can easily see how the young Ives would have preferred not to be perceived in this way, how he wished to do better and be respected more than had been his father. And Ives liked playing sports.

Although a few of the more successful homegrown musicians had escaped this stereotype, these individuals were more likely to be embraced only by the upper crust of society. Charles, regarded locally as a musical prodigy, could for the moment escape negative stereotyping through his tender age and talent.

Society has always seen great charm in a precocious youngster; everyone knew Charlie would grow up and get a real job. Thus one must ask what young man would willingly take on a musician's shabby lot in life within a country bursting with new opportunities amongst the more 'respectable' professions? Some young composers might have dared to venture into these precarious waters; some might even have succeeded. However, perhaps their circumstances were better than those of a small town youngster. If Ives chose not to take on music as a livelihood, who can tell him he was wrong?

Ives also had to accommodate his family's status. Many of his relatives were members of the 'higher set'; from Ives' perspective he would have been acutely aware of being a poor relation as a member of George Ives' family - headed by one who was unable as a musician, or even as a businessman to provide the kind of living that might have gained a degree of respect from the community. Indeed, looking for a way out, George also had been confined to the same humiliating status in business, before *and* after trying his hand at full-time music making. Without acquiring a background in one of the respected 'professions' of the day and age, Ives must have considered his chances similarly doomed. Thus, in Stuart Feder's view, by righting those wrongs done to his father, Ives would succeed *both* in music and business, which is a highly credible supposition.[1] Ives would remain deeply connected to his father throughout his entire life, even more after his father's untimely death at age 49 - within weeks of Ives entering Yale.

Frank R. Rossiter,[20] as well as Stuart Feder,[21] also advanced the additional perspective that music was not seen as a particularly masculine profession. This seems entirely likely in such an environment, despite the rejection of the hypothesis by Leon Botstein.[10] Botstein challenged the notion by discussing the successful career of the 19th Century New England composer, Arthur Foote. At the turn of the 20th Century, because the dominant cultural traditions of Europe still were regarded as the default rulers of the arts in America, and there was no one more likely to be greeted with enthusiasm and success in the concert hall than an artist from the other side of the Atlantic, privileged

American nationals traditionally were sent to study in European conservatories to complete their musical education - something not unlike the higher societal 'finishing schools for girls' in days of old. Somehow, this added an enhanced aura of legitimacy to an American-raised musician's quest for acceptance amongst the famous names from overseas. Charles Ives not only resented the implications of the perceived European superiority, but also stood little chance of having the opportunity presented him to study there.

Foote's career provided a contrary view of a musician's lot in 19th Century America. However, the comparison is not as simple as it seems. Feder pointed to written correspondence by the young Ives that directly raised his discomfort in assuming the life of a musician, as well as many of the reasons underlying it. Ives admitted that, growing up he had felt ashamed (living in a small American town) at the prospect of becoming a musician. Thus, Feder and Rossiter raised a legitimate issue, especially since it was born out by Ives' own words in *Memos*.[22]

It does seem that the kind of success and societal acceptance enjoyed by Foote, and that Botstein offered to substantiate his view, was not the norm. It might have applied more to the larger population centers, where symphony concerts and the arts were more likely to be part of peoples' lives, and an accepted part of the culture. It was also true that most domestic composers of the notoriety of Foote, or Ives' teacher at Yale, Horatio Parker, had enjoyed the advantage and added respectability of completing their training abroad. Nevertheless they still found it necessary to supplement their incomes in many ways, from teaching to taking musical positions within the church. Certainly universal stardom in the manner of one of the European masters, such as Gustav Mahler or Antonin Dvořák, was unlikely for most domestically raised musicians in America.

Thus, contrary to all manner of theories amongst historians about the reason behind his career choice in business, it seems easy to deduce. Ives went into business partly out of sheer practicality as much as anything else, because he did not want to repeat his father's experience in his own life. It is equally clear that Ives did not want to be perceived in a negative light - the lot of most musicians of the time - unless, of course, he could make the break into musical stardom at an early stage of his life. Even then, Ives must have been aware that it was still hard to earn a living as a composer, as demonstrated in the relatively challenging career of someone even as celebrated as his European-trained teacher at Yale, Horatio Parker. Thus, it did not take a lot to convince him early on to make another choice in his professional life.

What is strange, however, are the sentiments that his father raised, and those that Ives related in the same breath concerning a career in music.[23] Ives saw no irony in his father's position that if one tried to make a living from music, with only oneself to provide for, it could be justified. Otherwise, he would be forced to compromise his art, or fail to make a living. But wasn't this exactly what his father had done in failing to provide adequately for his family? It is an odd contradiction, to be sure, one that Ives apparently did not wish to see.

Life choices

Initially after leaving Yale, Ives entered the insurance industry, not through any particular design, but through opportunities presented him through family contacts. For a time, it seems, he was biding his time, hoping to make a lucky break in music. Once that had failed to materialize and he had decided to fully commit to business, it would mean that his passion for music would now relegate him to being a 'part-time' composer (the writer was once told that a disgruntled Mahler used this term to describe himself!). This might have seemed a reasonable solution at the time, but it entailed burning an all-too-short candle at both ends. Ives was passionate about both, and in no way saw his business interests as merely an expedience or means to an end, a point often overlooked by Ives' disciples.

Considering his success in the process of reinventing life insurance and bringing credibility back to it, not to mention building the largest agency in the country, while at the same time producing a musical output that would dwarf that of many full-time composers, one can only wonder how he could have managed such an incredible balancing act. More so, we might ask what kind of personal physical condition must have resulted from many stressful years of life alternately behind a business desk or all day and a piano half of the night, not to mention all weekend long. Such a lifestyle seems inconceivable, but it has become part of the Ives mystique: a near super-human reputation fully earned.

Henry Cowell, and the awakening

Largely credited with having 'discovered' Ives well after he had ceased composing (just before 1930), Henry Cowell was to remain a highly significant force during the rest of Ives' life and beyond. Although others had championed Ives before (Henry Bellemann, Nicolas Slonimsky, Robert Schmitz, and Clifton Furness), no one up until this time made the mission such a lifelong passion, or perhaps had the quite promotional flair of Cowell. As a much younger composer, he was one of a new breed of American avant-garde figures that had become very fashionable amongst an emerging societal 'set' that embraced the alternative arts. He saw Ives as the needed paternal figurehead for the new American music, doing his best to rescue him from oblivion, while endeavoring to make sure he was seen and appreciated as a revolutionary kindred spirit.[24] Although it seems Cowell exaggerated many aspects of Ives' life and work (perhaps more out of sheer enthusiasm rather than deliberate fabrication), something central to much of the revisionism of the late 20th Century, critics would be well advised to cut Cowell a little slack; without him Ives might have again slipped back into the shadows. (See 'Ives Legend,' Chapter 11, and Appendix 1.)

Ives the craftsman

If the sole impression of Ives has been formed by exposure only to his more radical compositions, in the absence of any idea of the succession of events or musical developments that led to them, questions about the composer's expertise might be raised. Even some of those who had a legitimate claim to their own expertise made this ill judgment repeatedly during Ives' day. However, since many examples of accessible, extremely craftsmanly, beautiful, dare we say, relatively conventionally-oriented late romantic sounding music came from the very same pen, this tells us that Ives was no dilettante. In fact, we can see he was a master, and it might be easier to find our first steps along the path to all of Ives' music through these more accessible works. Indeed, we can find common threads running through much of his output, akin to the identifying threads of DNA. In isolating them, we might be able to discover his world as we listen, a sound we will come to identify only with one source, regardless of the degree of radicalism in play.

Of Ives' wildly radical compositions, John Kirkpatrick, the legendary Ives scholar and pianist (who also knew him well), assured us that Ives fully heard in his mind all the complexities and sonorities of his music; nothing was an accident, unless he planned it that way, nor was it the result of anything other than the highest of musical skills.[25] Ives' pace of accelerated development would have been unusual in any time, so, in his eyes what may seem remarkable to us was only what caused him to notate what he heard in his head! For this he received his fair share of criticism, but here was a figure, living to true to his being, who had found the path to his own destiny, not towards that which others would steer him.

Perhaps, however, the most remarkable traits of Ives' work are its symbolic representations and spiritual aspirations, beyond being 'merely' that of the pioneer, experimenter and perceived American nationalist. Ives' greatness also is primarily not about being ahead of his time, but more the unique and extraordinary depths that he plumbed - a transcendental mission in life and music that culminated only when he could travel no further.

REFERENCES

1. 'Memos', Charles E, Ives, edited by John Kirkpatrick, p. 106, *W. W. Norton & Co.*, New York, 1972
2. 'Charles Ives Remembered, an Oral History,' Vivian Perlis, *University of Illinois Press,* Urbana and Chicago, 1974
3. 'Charles Ives: "My Father's Song", a Psychoanalytic Biography, Stuart Feder, *Yale University Press,* New Haven, Connecticut, 1992
4. 'Charles Ives & His America,' Frank R. Rossiter, *Liveright,* New York, 1975
5. 'Charles Ives Reconsidered,' Gayle Sherwood Magee, *University of Illinois Press,* Chicago, Illinois, 2008, pp. 92-93
6. Perlis, p. 44
7. Ibid., p. 155
8. 'Four Symphonies of Charles Ives,' Bernard Herrmann, Modern Music 22 (May-June 1945): p. 222; (reprinted in 'Charles Ives and his World,' Edited by J. Peter Burkholder, *Princeton University Press,* Princeton, New Jersey, 1996, p. 402)
9. 'Charles Ives Remembered, an Oral History,' Vivian Perlis, *University of Illinois Press,* Urbana and Chicago, 1974, p. 213
10. 'Innovations and Nostalgia: Ives, Mahler, and the Origins of Modernism,' Leon Botstein, from 'Charles Ives and his World,' Edited by J. Peter Burkholder, *Princeton University Press,* Princeton, New Jersey, 1996, p. 36
11. Magee, p. 159; Feder, p. 355
12. Botstein, p. 41
13. Perlis, p. 172
14. 'Memos,' p. 76
15. 'Charles Ives and the American Democratic Tradition, Michael Broyles, from 'Charles Ives and his World,' Burkholder, 1996, pp. 118 - 160
16. 'Ives Plays Ives,' Charles Ives, CD recording, *Composers Recordings, Inc,* New York, 1999, track 40

17. 'An American Innovator; Charles Ives,' Goddard Lieberson, from 'Charles Ives and his World,' Burkholder, 1996, p. 378
18. Rossiter, p. 147
19. Ibid., p. 154
20. Rossiter; examples: pp. 23 - 24, 28 - 31
21. Feder, p. 119
22. 'Memos,' p. 130
23. 'Memos,' p. 131
24. Magee, pp. 175 - 179
25. Perlis, pp. 221-224

CHAPTER 2

Building the road

Once Ives began to envisage where the quintessentially American transcendentalism could lead him, he began to formulate new techniques that shared increasingly less in common with the models of his European counterparts and the late romantic German musical tradition. Even when we find direct parallels across the Atlantic with some of Ives' techniques, their use and philosophical incorporation puts them entirely at odds with his music - and a *sound* that could have emerged only from the North American continent - that of the New World. Ives not only had created it virtually single-handedly, and in near total isolation from musicians who might have provided him support, but also in doing so had successfully captured the essence of the philosophies that had guided him. He had traveled his own transcendental journey, taking his place alongside that of his hero Ralph Waldo Emerson.

We cannot proceed meaningfully without understanding the elements of Ives' spiritual journey. Aside from the distinct technical elements that have always gained Ives such enthusiastic attention, there are profound cultural aspects, too. Born and raised in the New England town of Danbury, Connecticut in the latter part of the 19th Century, Ives was thoroughly steeped in old American traditions and folklore. These years also were happy ones it seems, so it ought not to be seen as surprising that their residual effect would feature prominently in Ives' personal makeup and character. Far from the type of upbringing he might have experienced had he grown up in Europe, this was pioneer stuff, plain and simple, with a heavy dose of Civil War culture thrown into the bargain.

Danbury Years (1874-1894)

19th Century postcard
{{PD-Art}}

The road to the stars might have never made it out of in Danbury had it not been for something extraordinary about Ives' psyche and his perceptions of daily life, and the attention lavished upon him by his father, George Ives (the local town bandleader and music teacher). Ives Sr. did his best to give his son a thorough musical grounding, including the primary elements of theory (including traditional harmony and counterpoint), as well as immersing him in the music of the masters, such as Bach, Beethoven and Brahms.

George Ives, though trained sufficiently well to teach the youthful Charles, could only do so in the capacity in which he was equipped. Outside the four walls of the family home, he was not seen as particularly gifted, successful, or accomplished, and in the absence of more documentation, we can only surmise the degree of musical expertise he had. Ives, however, referenced his father's multiple skills on various instruments, including the cornet, French horn, and even violin, and most especially an unusual interest in natural acoustical and other auditory phenomena, and his encouragement of musical discovery. Considering that his son was a genius, would it not be realistic to presume that George would have possessed some of the same latent DNA, albeit most of it remaining untapped through limited opportunity? Significantly, George would bequeath to his son his love of good music, musical outlook and perspective, deep connection with the music of the American War of Independence, even more the Civil War, and no less formatively the passionate revivalist hymns of his faith.

There was a distinct difference between revivalist hymn tunes and those more formal hymns of 'higher' churches; the "fervor" of the people found in the former - that colloquial 'old time religion' - would remain an enduring part of his life. With his wide experience later as an organist in significant church positions around New York, Charles Ives also would have a wide resource of the latter to draw from. However, the hymns of the camp meetings struck the loudest chord, and with exposure to them from the cradle, no amount of transcendentalism could shake them loose. Although he was not religious in the traditional sense, Ives always considered that this eclectically religious musical resource expressed the peoples' highest aspirations, providing a window into their souls. We have referenced that his father had shown him that if something was performed with conviction, its sophistication, musicality, or even its sound (!), did not matter. Specifically, Ives remembered his father's sentiments (about the sound of the local stone mason's rough but soulful singing) that made clear he was more interested in musical communication than overly refined *sounds*. Such 'superficial' qualities as these came to represent for the younger Ives a self-conscious trait of the now-stagnant confinements he considered artificiality imposed by the aging traditional European culture.

Ives the dreamer

However, other influences too would stake their claims as well. At Yale (1894-1898) under his teacher Horatio Parker, he would be thoroughly immersed in that very European musical tradition, gaining considerable skill and breadth of ability into the bargain. Yet during this time, even more so after he had relocated to New York, Ives further would be exposed to another veritable goldmine of musical idioms and sounds: *Ragtime, Tin Pan Ally, Cakewalk,* even *Minstrel* music. These would also be found amongst the growing resource of popular musical styles that would find their place in the pavement along his road. Hard as it would have been at the time for a serious-minded, purely classically oriented musician to appreciate, this wide cross section of seemingly unrelated vernacular musical styles would form the unlikeliest foundation of some truly viable music. In Ives' hands they provided a lasting bond to his formative years, his cultural heritage, and most critically, his transcendentally inspired outlook - one that he kept alive against the backdrop of rapid change in America during its emergence in the new century.

Regardless, for the young Ives, in the absence of some meteoric success, it was unlikely that he would ever be able to make the kind of living as a musician that matched his ambitions - which undoubtedly were lofty. As Stuart Feder already had correctly surmised, Ives aspired to all things that had been denied his father. Regardless, since certainly he entertained for a time the prospect of a career in music, Parker's own meteoric rise to domestic fame provided the model. If similarly successful, Charles' larger family and community might perceive he had attained a worthy livelihood. Four years after graduating, he arranged for a New York premiere in 1902 of his most significant work of the time, a cantata, *The Celestial Country*. It was based not only in the German musical tradition, but also patterned on his teacher's most celebrated oratorio, *Hora Novissma* - the very work that in 1893 had catapulted Parker into prominence and respectability as an American composer, and the year that Ives had left home to attend private school (Hopkins Grammar School in New Haven, Connecticut) for 'cramming' before entering Yale.

Perhaps even in spite of the predominantly conservative language of the music, the very essence of its title showed that Ives might well have had his sights set on a spiritually distant destination from an early time; indeed, we can spot many such possible allusions even in other early works. The text referred to far away visions of a fantastic celestial setting, a shimmering place where glorious spiritual oneness with the creator would be encompassed within one's existence and into eternity; was this something, perhaps, akin to the transcendental ideal? Nathaniel Hawthorne's outlandishly adventurous *The Celestial Railroad* immediately comes to mind, of course, and although that vision was wild and hardly comforting, it should be no surprise that this fictional work later did, in fact, form a mighty inspiration behind some of Ives' more important music during his mature compositional period.

With *The Celestial Country* being a romantic work very much in the European mold, Ives clearly had hitched his star temporarily to a style of composition that he believed might better aid his chances of success at the time, whether or not it was his intention to stick with that idiom in the long term. However, although the performance was relatively well received in the New York Times review, in Ives' eyes it suffered from being damned with faint praise. Couched in positive terms overall, nevertheless the less than ecstatic reception accorded it at the premiere cemented Ives' discomfort - apparently, sufficiently to cause him finally to reject any thought of music as a career. Ives inscribed the words, *"damn rot and worse,"* across the review - either as a reflection of the music, but more likely the review. (He showed crankiness from an early age, it seems! Feder's theory for such temperament developing in later years thus goes out the window.) Regardless, it was time for Ives to rethink his options.

A respectable career in music

It seems quite plausible, as Rossiter argued in his book, that Ives never had a particularly strong bent to pursue music professionally, his brief bout of all he had hoped for with *The Celestial Country* being a temporary pipe dream, and a last gasp of hope for a life that would prove too idealistic. Indeed, the entry-level position he took in a Mutual insurance agency immediately upon graduating from Yale in 1898 was not the typical action of someone determined to find his way in music; indeed, his uncle had *already* arranged for that first job in the business world. Strangely, Rossiter considered that because Ives had made *a little* money supplying eminently accessible music for various functions - notably religious - during and immediately after his college years, somehow this was at odds with his stated reservations about making more esoteric, less commercially-viable music a *career!* What is so improper about just trying to survive during one's early days of independence from whatever skills one has at one's disposal? Indeed, Magee effectively laid this issue to rest.[1] Must Ives be judged repeatedly according to standards rarely applied to others?

With Ives' father deceased, and no desire within his larger family to help with financing the 'final polish' for a musical career from a period of study in Europe, the prospect of becoming a professional musician, in truth, probably never was seriously entertained. Regardless, Ives' self-funded production of *The Celestial Country* undoubtedly was his last-ditch effort to pull a musical career out of a proverbial hat in the absence of a European-pedigreed stamp of approval. Coincident with his disappointment over the premiere, Ives resigned his relatively lucrative church organist position and "gave up" music. Better to let it all go before investing further time and trouble than hold out unrealistic hope. What chance would he have had to make a decent living as a serious composer of *any* kind? Having tried to emulate even Parker had not brought Ives success. He could see that any possibility of being taken as seriously as any of the contemporary European composers (and we are talking about figures such as Brahms and Dvořák) was effectively zero, that the sorry lot of the majority of home grown musicians - and likewise that of his father before him - would also be his. Thus, it was proper to embrace more realistic options, and let music remain an avocation of his own determination. However, his choice cemented his musical isolation.

Freed to write in any manner he wished after the failure of *The Celestial Country,* Ives finally had realized that trying to write in the style of a European-styled composer was not genuine to him. New works began to appear after what seems to have been a temporary drought of substantive creativity. Meanwhile, Ives' world was experiencing some dramatic upheavals, personally and in business, in ways that certainly impacted all that followed; indeed the time was life-changing. By the time it was over Ives had fully developed the technical means to reflect properly his visions - drawing from the past, present, and ultimately the future - he returned to many things that had been the subject of Parker's ridicule and scathing ire; many of these ('vernacular' elements of the New World) were those that he had shared with his deceased father. Thus he had taken this rejection personally. If they were considered impossible to reconcile with high art, Ives would strive to validate them, their significance to him, *and* elevate his father.

Because in the 1890's Ives had already experimented with several unlikely musical concepts, such as multiple keys and chords based on new intervals, clearly his more conventional works were not the sole occupants of his mind in the years before *The Celestial Country*. He was also no stranger to quoting familiar melodies, so we cannot make the assumption that later transcendental philosophies were solely responsible, although surely they confirmed his instincts. And because of what he took to be the rejection of what *he* had written in the European mold *(The Celestial Country)*, this might help further account for his open resentment of the dominant European musicians and composers of the day, along with their models, dictates, and ultimately their limitations. It was as if *they* had rejected *him* too. Some of them actually had, of course, as Ives vividly recalled frequently in *Memos*, getting even with them (!), almost with relish.

There are other indicators for Ives' apparent slight of Parker; he is known to have long harbored resentment of the that fact that Parker required him to write the major movement (the first) of his *First Symphony* in an utterly conventional idiom in order to graduate. Although he conformed nevertheless, Ives incorporated a few unconventional aspects for which he was able to gain his teacher's reluctant agreement. Regardless, he was never happy about it, an all-too-familiar experience learned from Parker's negative reactions to anything less than conventional that Ives ever brought him throughout their relationship.

Beyond the Yale years, the period of development moved gradually from the *secular* via radical experimentation towards the purely *spiritual*. Ives would touch upon virtually every 20th Century musical innovation along the way, often independently of the work of his European contemporaries and frequently preceding them. With no direct references to any specific spiritual goal he had in mind, our only clues are his references to transcendentalism, and Emerson in particular. Thus, the town band and its Civil War culture, the familiar popular melodies and hymns, and his father's values, nurturing and open musical perspective would inspire a receptive mind, and be further amplified by the philosophies of the transcendentalists, the sights and memories of his locale and the awe-inspiring landscapes of the nearby Adirondacks. These would serve to guide him now, rather than the formalities and constraints of his Yale education. Remarkably, through such means Ives would reach out to the entire world to reflect the very universe of which he was part. And even when briefly coveting aspirations to write music in the manner of his teacher, surely he sensed the cosmic horizons eventually he would hold in view.

Curiously, although his first large-scale efforts projected Americana at every turn, they were still built using European styles and forms, confirming once again that he had *not* rejected the language itself, a frequent misinterpretation often still perpetuated. It is common, therefore, to find in Ives' music strong links to traditional musical idiomatic language and methods ('the old school of composition'), running in parallel with his newfound techniques and sounds - a striking (and to some, perplexing) attribute in which his approach differs from most of his contemporaries. And despite the European origins of many of the vernacular melodies Ives quoted, it was the subtle colloquial distinctions slowly grafted on them that provided the necessary variation and nuance to create their new identities. As projected by the ordinary people of his New England world, these melodies commanded Ives' attention to cement the spirit and values of his time and place in eternity.

The key to the new sounds

Although he was fortunate to be admitted to Yale, barely qualifying for entrance, it would prove pivotal to the youthful Ives' eventual 'counter outlook' that Horatio Parker would have none of the colloquial or open-mindedness that were at the very heart of Ives' late father's being. Reactively, if ultimately Ives not only would consciously diminish Parker's influence, but also attribute all manner of forward-looking experimentation to his father, regrettably the record does not provide unqualified evidence of the latter. While some is surely based in fact, there is little that can be reliably substantiated outside the few recollections of those who knew him.[2] Regardless, if actual evidence of George Ives' attitude and interest in auditory phenomena is circumstantial, it is strong, as is his son's testament to it.

Thus, regardless of the degree of sophistication that his teaching had been able to instill, it seems the keys to what set George Ives apart were indeed his unique influence that would cause his young son to question conventional rules and limitations of western music. It provided an impetus that begged *confident* strides into realms beyond age-old accepted practices;

as long as an understanding of the musical process was in place with proper theory and grounding firmly entrenched, George Ives felt practically anything had validity. This may be the single most important aspect amongst all that has been misunderstood, underestimated or overlooked by many, the one factor that caused the younger Ives to credit his father so highly as an influence, while increasingly relegate all others to the basement of his consciousness.

Rather than representing some self-serving ingratitude to others - as sometimes has been alleged - his father, thus, really gave him the keys to everything *significant* he would do. This point still seems lost on many, who do not understand why Ives would appear to slight Parker and elevate his father; it cannot be because he did not believe doing so misrepresented either of them. This is clearly the reason that he was never eager to acknowledge the enhanced technical skills Parker had given him - such 'strictures' only reinforced the Old World formulaic dogma that had stifled his voice. Ives outgrew Parker. If others have misinterpreted this to mean that he rejected every aspect of it while almost hypocritically still retaining its foundations, in fact, he had built upon it and moved it to different ground. This was true transcendentalism.

Before his Yale years, and apparently under his father's guidance, Ives had already written remarkably modernistic-leaning music, these works and other experiments featuring polytonality (music in more than one key at once) were virtually unprecedented at the time. We must not forget that these works emanated within Brahms' lifetime! No less remarkable, however, is at least one movement from the slightly later *Three Harvest Home Chorales* (1902), at the heart of what has been termed his experimental period. Although subject to a later reconstruction and revisions, we can be confident that most (if not, indeed, all) of the utterly amazing groundbreaking aspect of the work belongs authentically to the early date, because some of the original manuscripts have survived.

Further, as Magee inferred - that Ives could not have succeeded without Parker's training - it is clear that had Ives followed Parker's way, he would not have found his own.[3] Early on, since Ives showed considerable aptitude at the piano, and was seen as something of a prodigy, he was able to earn some money during his teenage years as a church organist. Having held some fairly significant positions during and after his Yale years, his father had, in fact, tried in vain to convince the retiring teenager to become a concert pianist. There can be no doubt Ives also acquired a broad knowledge of music from this experience; that it was instrumental in the larger development of his compositional skills, as have similar experiences for many composers throughout history, cannot be in doubt. Ives, thus had access to much great music, and by the mid-1890's would have amassed considerable expertise on the structure and language of the best music of the day.

It is likely therefore that this alone, along with his extraordinary natural talent, ultimately would have enabled Ives to acquire the skills that Parker had bestowed upon him *anyway*. Such would be far from abnormal amongst many of the greatest composers of history. It is not arguable that the majority of them have emerged out of situations far removed from the university system, or indeed any similarly advantageous academic situation, many of these figures having no education at all. Magee's apparent viewpoint does not concur with history.

Regardless, it seems quite realistic to suppose that had he wanted it, a performing career would have been within his reach. His private recordings, admittedly made far beyond his prime when decidedly frail, reveal an extraordinary fluency and freedom of expression, not to mention a surprisingly sizable lingering residue of commanding technique.[4] Even late in Ives' life, composer Carl Ruggles considered he had never "heard better."[5] However, Ives' notorious shyness would make sure he remained uncomfortable with the slightest thought or suggestion of being showcased as a soloist in the public arena.

The developing model

In all of the arts there are many parallels; seldom do they proceed totally out of step with each other. Ives fitted this profile only to a degree. Although his music pioneered virtually *all* of the stylistic 'cues,' *collectively*, of other composers of the time, his use of them usually is far from synchronized with them - most innovations occurring in advance of their developments, others a little later. Usually, early 20th Century pioneers limited themselves to a single innovation at a time, not the multiple entities we find in Ives's music. This is because he saw them only as a means to a creative end, not the end itself, and certainly not the manifestation of any particular theoretical approach or philosophy. Typically, he might have been completely at ease with the simultaneous use of every technique he knew in the very same piece!

For the listener, confusing the issue further was Ives' comfort and ease with composing works not always consistently in step with his musical evolution at any given time. Ives utilized whatever would serve his needs of the moment, regardless of the mechanics, or even the aesthetics that others might have deemed appropriate. When asked why he wrote music that so many people found hard to understand, he replied simply that he heard it that way. Although Ives developed many cyclical and organizational methodologies in his music, those who hope to tie some overriding formulaic approach to his *creativity*, or some other deliberately imposed mechanical prescription likely will be frustrated; Ives would be slave only to the soundscapes of his imagination.

Because Ives' musical evolution followed its full course through a period of less than twenty years, for someone unfamiliar with his development along the way, the end point is so far transformed that it might seem to have come from another composer entirely - despite the characteristic and recognizable traits the more experienced listener can detect throughout Ives' output. Some commentators, who never knew Ives, have claimed that he was influenced by other contemporary figures. Try as they might to link Ives' innovations to those of others, it seems clear that most comparable new inroads occurred independently, if not later. Composer Goddard Lieberson, unable to fathom how Ives evolved his language, remarked that he pursued it in a vacuum, independently of other composers of the time, and completely comfortable with his isolation.[6] Try as some critics might to tie Ives' music to other composers, *Lieberson was well aware that Ives did not seem the slightest bit interested in any of their innovations, let alone wish to copy them.*

In following no rigorous development of any particular philosophy, Ives honed multiple trains of thought over the succeeding years. Because he also sketched and worked on countless compositions at once, this led to all manner of inconsistencies in penmanship and writing style, with numerous related notations, often even unrelated comments all over the manuscript and sketch pages. These pages are an amazing layering of complex thoughts, expressed in both musical notes and words all over, with directions, cross-references, conflicting dates, addresses - even peoples' names and ironic remarks. Ives even had a habit of sketching more than one work on any given sheet of manuscript paper, the order and sequence from one segment ('patch') to the next not necessarily being clear in every case. People close to him remarked on the remarkable inner organization he had, despite the outward appearance of chaos. His mind was a library with everything laid out at all times in perfect order; it would only become a headache later for those who were charged with deciphering it!

Examples of reused and re-worked materials are plentiful, too; in Ives' music we can find examples of prior efforts in almost every work, especially the wholesale reworking of those he had abandoned, perhaps because to him they were *all* connected. Stylistically, thus, he could be just as likely to write something wildly avant-garde one moment and revert to more a traditional idiom the next. Sometimes, stepping back represented only the completion of something started long before, while a later work might have been finished in the meantime - the unique freedom manifested in his writing an unselfconscious cross-threaded, cross-pollinated musical fiber.

We find also instances of multiple periods of Ives' development coexisting in separate places *within* some works themselves. The third movement of the late work, his *Fourth Symphony*, immediately comes to mind; out of the blinding blaze of complexity and modernity of the second movement emerges the serene and utterly orthodox slow third movement, unsurprisingly borrowed from a much earlier time. However, in Ives' hands, not only does its inclusion work in the context, but surprisingly serves the larger purpose of recovery from one musical adventure (the second movement) and preparation for the spiritual journey of the next (the finale). So integral was it to the symphony that it appears he lost track of its earlier origins.[7] During later phases of his output, we find a return to earlier language often in his songs, too, where Ives frequently reused or reworked existing materials, even while engaged in writing more radical large-scale works.

Flexibility of purpose, thus, was a hallmark in all that he did. Seldom content with anything as he had left it, the ideas continued to grow in his mind long after their concepts had hatched and left the nest, typically well beyond the original works' completion. Three related examples, two of them for chorus and orchestra, share distinct musical material; the third is a late reworking of the first. They date from a period that reveal Ives' passions about what was going on in the world leading up to and immediately following World War I. This was a time that saw him give full rein to his transcendental ideals and passions, both in music and social activism, even as the world seemed increasingly broken beyond any chance of his aspirations becoming a reality:

- *Lincoln the Great Commoner,* of c.1914, pays tribute to Lincoln's leadership, as well as the qualities of the country so identified with his era. The almost angular vocal line seems to represent a projection of Lincoln's strength and resolve. The extent of early advancement in the musical language used by Ives has never been clearer, and we hear many things in common with Ives' other mature works of the period.

- *An Election,* written in 1920, set to music Ives' total disenchantment with the political establishment, following his initial disillusionment with Woodrow Wilson, and his subsequent 1920 defeat to Warren J. Harding. Ives effectively poured scorn on all politicians in this musical broadside, and it is clear that the bottom of his idealistic world had dropped out. The music owes certain cues to the earlier work, but its agitated mood in both the choral and orchestral writing sets it apart, and the representations of Lincoln's strength have now been transferred to the voice of the people. The ending and other materials, however, were borrowed directly from *Lincoln the Great Commoner*, something, in view of the later orchestral version of that work that had led to confusion about which actually was the earlier one. Thus the extended development of the material makes complete sense in this context, and illustrates how it had continued to grow in Ives' mind during the intervening years.
- *Lincoln the Great Commoner*, the 1922-1923 version of the song, for chorus and orchestra, though essentially the same music as the earlier song, now includes a few late innovations, not only in its advanced and stark orchestration, but also more especially some dramatic moments in the choral writing - reminiscent of huge crowds. It is worth pointing out that these sounds seem to anticipate those used by György Ligeti in his *Requiem*, some 40 years later. The unison chorus further underscores Lincoln's stern resolve. Dating from near the end of Ives' most creative period, the culmination would be the remainder of the *Universe Symphony* sketches around 1923.

Multiple orbits

It is hard to listen to anything from after 1910 and not be struck by the astounding complexity of textures of the musical universe pulling Ives increasingly into it. Remarkable for more than just the ease with which he blended multiple idioms, the 'jangle' of complex interactions of numerous separate components commands our attention, usually occurring in offset tonalities like the intersections of orbits of distant stars in a densely populated and chaotic star cluster. Once we enter the domain of his most advanced works, however, full rein is given to this characteristic, to include even more multiple combinations of components in play at once. Precise alignments from part to part cannot thus be necessarily expected, so for players of Ives' day not to be affected by their immediate musical surroundings might have been be problematic. They must have wondered what they were supposed to do; some works, such as the mighty *Fourth Symphony* had to wait almost 50 years for a complete performance. Even today, airings of most of his music are not commonplace, the difficulties and complexities associated with them widely known.

However, even Ives' most conservative music sometimes is laced with unusual rhythmic complexities that make this difficult to play, too. His own words in many places in *Memos* show that he was not particularly sympathetic to certain prominent musicians of his day as they struggled to make sense of his writing - all while insulting his work - and he relished the chance to rail against them (usually some European "professor" or some such) for their perceived ineptitude. Rhythmically, his musical lines might look awkward on the page, though they sound deceptively simple; actually, they simulate a level of freedom along the lines of the instinctive flexibilities we hear in recordings of Ives' own playing. Such is the nature of Ives; much of his piano music comes without bar lines, meaning specific speeds or sense of meter were not amongst his priorities. All of this could be considered, perhaps, as the ultimate evolution of the old European tradition of rubato playing, demonstrating how Ives retained some European roots, yet redefined them on his terms.

There are issues, too, with the practicalities and costs relative to Ives' musical ensembles. The *Universe Symphony*, for example, the culminating focus of this book, requires an unusual orchestra of highly specific instrumentation, rendering many musicians present (read "paid") unlikely to be needed for the remainder of the concert program. Sometimes more than one conductor is required, too, because Ives often wrote in multiple speeds. Furthermore, a practical difficulty lies in the problem of attracting audiences when so many music lovers are left bewildered by his music, such that even now the music still is greeted by mixed acceptance and risky concert attendance. The public's level of openness and sophistication, it seems, has scarcely budged since Ives' time.

The 'lily pads'

Critics have attacked Ives for reveling in dissonance, even harshness. They have said that he would use these techniques largely and deliberately just to upset the 'lily pads.' This, too, as in so many other instances, is a misguided analysis. There is no doubt that Ives exerted his resentment of unchallenging, 'nice' music through writing bold, stark sonorities. Certainly he took some 'near-schoolboy' delight in shaking up stuffy and timid listeners, but this was not why he used what may have seemed to them to be harsh sounds. To have any chance of expanding the musical range and language, and to keep it alive and viable instead of merely "massaging the ears" (another of Ives' terms) and restrict it to a long established comfort zone, the task required sounds other than those that were familiar, comfortable or consonant. Regardless, Ives was fully capable of touching upon sentiment without any resulting cheapness. In many ways, one can draw a parallel to Beethoven, who dared early 19th Century listeners to embrace bold, startling new music, while being fully capable of tenderness, too. However, does one *ever* have the sense that Beethoven's music is insipid, mawkish or saccharin? Ives' music is much like this.

Thus Ives believed music could not grow if it fell back on comfortable well-trodden paths, lest it wither on the vine of complacency; in driving to keep its vital force alive, he would bring it into his own new world on a new continent of growing confidence and optimism. His musical vision required that we break down our comfortable musical boundaries and biases, and look to a brave new universe of possibilities. As a product of the great emerging superpower, Ives' brave music does indeed herald the New World, the music of the *first truly avant-garde composer.*

REFERENCES

1. 'Charles Ives Reconsidered,' Gayle Sherwood Magee, *University of Illinois Press,* Chicago, Illinois, 2008, pp. 63-64
2. 'Charles Ives Remembered, an Oral History,' Vivian Perlis, *University of Illinois Press,* Urbana and Chicago, 1974, p. 16; 'Charles Ives: "My Father's Song", a Psychoanalytic Biography, Stuart Feder, *Yale University Press,* New Haven, Connecticut, 1992, p. 49
3. Magee, p. 48
4. CD: 'Ives Plays Ives,' Charles Ives, recording, *Composers Recordings, Inc,* New York, 1999
5. Perlis, p. 173
6. Ibid, p. 208
7. 'Memos', Charles E, Ives, edited by John Kirkpatrick, p. 106, *W. W. Norton & Co.*, New York, 1972, p. 66

CHAPTER 3

Originality, influences and musical makeup

As one of the pre-eminent 20th Century musical pioneers, Ives is often casually credited as being the creator of wholly original music, in and of itself. And because Ives could not let go of the 19th Century, sometimes we hear that he was not quite the pioneer we previously had thought - in the context of the *modernism* of the time in which he lived. But is either of these positions accurate or fair? Regarding the latter position, if we are to understand correctly what Leon Botstein meant in his otherwise positive article,[1] (and certainly he is an enthusiast of the composer), he apparently considered that one needs to embrace all aspects of 20th Century modernism - artistically, technically, culturally and *societally* - to be recognized for being considered 'exceptional' within it. It does not take a very wide leap, however, to recognize that Ives was truly exceptional in the context in which he worked, and that he cannot be defined by such restrictive terminology.

In regard to the former, we should pause to consider what makes up originality in anything. Because the transcendentalists believed in the renewal of existing materials, that nothing was new into itself, their perception was profound. Only when we look closely do we find that nothing exists in a total vacuum; all composers have been influenced by their predecessors, place in history, default culture, and events occurring within their own personal circumstances. If people think that Ives was the only figure in history ever to have functioned independently of all such factors, then they have not thought the premise through. Originality in music is defined by what a composer takes to make it his own. Similarly, modernism in Ives' hands was an extraordinary thing; he achieved a unique and seemingly contradictory synthesis in which he expressed his own experience of the 19th Century, in a totally modern, and ultimately futuristic language and idiom that matched the 20th Century and even beyond. In this respect Ives seems truly unique, which perhaps is why so many analysts have faltered when attempting to sum him up, or assign him a place in the grand order of things.

The raw materials of pitch and rhythm are the same in most western music. Pitch consists of only twelve notes in the scale, and a similarly limited though far wider spectrum of chords built out of combinations of them. The mind also recognizes doubling their frequencies of vibration into successively higher octaves, providing a clear road map in which notes are recognizable as the *same* note with every doubling - except they sound *higher!* Obviously also only a finite number of possible combinations of pitches exists, as well as potential successions of them. Another type of frequency involves rhythm, the instinctive sense of it governed in all of us by innate pulse within overall time. If we were to take a simple click and repeat it at ever-faster frequencies, it, too would take on pitch, so rhythm and pitch are more than casually related. Offering an almost endless variety of groupings and subdivisions, the impositions of these rhythmic divisions upon identifiable pitches produce that phenomena we recognize as music; regardless of intent, the human mind always seeks to establish order and patterns within it. Obviously, rhythm gives music its sense of life and motion and the power to affect us on a physical level.

However, the composer seeks to impose his own order upon these different types of frequency to communicate his thoughts - and amazingly - the human experience. Why certain arrangements of sounds have the effect they do on us, including our emotions and feelings, is one of the great mysteries and miracles of that experience. Such is the art of composition, whereby the powers of the mind reorder and assemble selections from the available raw materials into new and (hopefully) original interplay. By some amazing quirk of consciousness, the result has the power to express many things. But most significantly for this discussion, originality is to a large degree subjective, because all music is built out of the same components.

On the use of musical quotations

Over the years numerous musicians and critics have taken issue with Ives' frequent use of traditional American, popular and hymn tunes. Composer Elliot Carter, Ives' fellow compatriot, roundly criticized it - as if Ives could not create his own.[2] However, Carter only revealed his own shortcomings by failing to understand or recognize how, and especially *why* Ives infused these melodic elements into his music. Some have remarked that over time, these melodies will no longer be recognizable, and thus, Ives' music will lose its unique connection with the listener. However, only the slightest of thought reveals this to be an absurd position. In view of the fact that perhaps a large portion of those tunes in Ives' lexicon are intrinsically tied up with the Civil War era and the strong national identity that formed in its aftermath - and defined the nation - for these strongly hued melodies to fall out of the culture, or even international recognition is hardly likely.

Ives' musical roots showed themselves quite clearly; even in his early efforts at composition, vernacular 'Americana' was incorporated into much of it. Examples of such quoted materials exist, too, in a surprisingly wide range of music from his Yale years. Typically written as extra-curricular works based on hymns for church services, they would not have been subject to Parker's curriculum and possible rejection - likely in view of his contempt for the 'sweet sentimentality' of popular and hymn melodies, something not found in Ives' music nevertheless! This underscored much of Ives' later misgivings of his Yale teacher and the music he stood for, since those very simple melodies that Parker despised were destined to become unlikely building blocks in most of Ives' large-scale compositions. However, Ives' *First String Quartet*, his first substantial work to emerge along these lines, dates from his Yale years (1896) and was written under Parker's guidance. With the hymn melodies at its core, somehow, this and a few other works that quoted familiar tunes from Ives' student years managed to survive, showing that Parker had a tolerant, even kind heart.

Almost by some unwritten design, Ives' instincts and comfort with incorporating music from his own experiences played well within transcendental thought, which encouraged Americans to look first to their own surroundings for a cultural and spiritual identity. Because European philosophies and traditions were trapped within their own lengthy evolutions, Ives eventually would find the formal constraints and age-old thought processes of traditional ways stifling and restricting. (Why did *everything* have to balance and position artistic considerations against the purely mechanical?) Curiously, Parker, though philosophically out of step with Ives at almost every level, had encouraged his student's growing interest in transcendentalism. This might explain his willingness to allow Ives a certain degree of freedom in his choices and treatments of compositional thematic material.

It is important to emphasize that although Ives' music became profoundly immersed in American lore does not mean that some kind of jingoistic nationalism was behind it. Ives referenced such thinking in *Essays Before a Sonata*,[3] whereby some composers had tried to cast their own nationalistic identity into their music. By deliberately and self-consciously incorporating traditional melodic elements of their own native origins into the conventional and dominant German romantic-inspired mold, in these instances, the music had not grown out of genuine experience, its specific colorations simply tacked on for easy identification. Thus, being neither authentic nor personal, its core was artificial and born out of shallow provincialism. Ives, on the other hand, had drawn from his own environment to build his music from the ground up, developing a language in which the rugged

Originality, influences and musical makeup

spiritual values and authentic simplicity of a pioneering people had little in common with his European counterparts.

If Ives' music took on actual nationalistic overtones as the First World War approached, it was in reaction to forces across the Atlantic that threatened to crush and destroy all that the New World represented, rather than an effort to exert patriotism for its own sake. The tunes he quoted were old calls to battle and fighting for freedom, recycled from his life and own experience, rather than jingoism. Ives' own remarks - clearly resentful of prominent German musicians of his time - reflect this sentiment, although we should not try to read too much into them; Germany, after all, was the nation at the center of the fight. Ives was anything but racially motivated, and would come to reject nationalism for its own sake, putting the freedom of all man at the top of his priorities, although he would remain extremely protective of the heritage of his own nation.

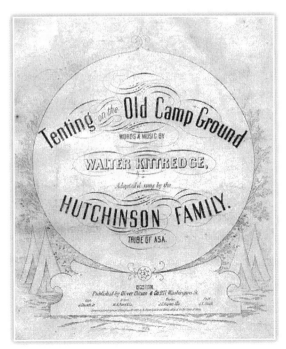

{{PD-Art}}

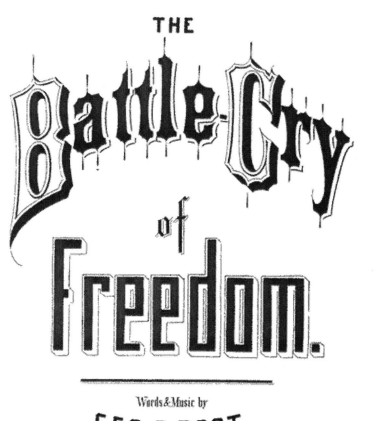

{{PD-Art}}

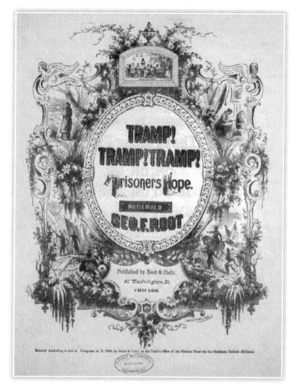

{{PD-Art}}

Although Ives' degree of authenticity was remarkable, still it has been surprisingly misunderstood. In reflecting in no better way the transcendental view that nothing is new, and originality is exemplified by the reuse and reorder of what already exists, it also explains why Ives had no compunction to use small quotations from *European* masters as well, or even to maintain its methods within his musical language whenever he chose. After all, they were part of his experience, too; although this has baffled many commentators, it makes complete sense within the context of transcendental philosophy.

In Ives' mind, quotations in his music were no different than notes, harmonies, rhythms, or even instruments - they were just other compositional building blocks. Failure to grasp this concept might be compared to accusing a 20th painter of being unoriginal because he had used the identical colors, or even similar subjects, to those used by a 19th painter. Ives was not the first composer to quote melodies, even in America; indeed, earlier domestic composers had done so. However, the comparison stops there. In virtually every instance, the works they produced were mere settings of these melodies, not unlike what would be considered today 'arrangements' in popular music. Here, the fundamental identities of the melodies are retained, but essentially they are given nothing more than a facelift, maintaining their former role while providing only novelty. In Ives' music, the use of quotations has other differences, too; not usually more than fleeting references consisting of broken fragments (typically the opening few notes of any tune), and frequently incorporated into unlikely settings, harmonically or rhythmically, they exist in a state of metamorphosis within broader original material.

Furthermore, Ives had a unique ability to combine multiple elements of these melodies at once, horizontally or vertically, according to whatever the circumstances called for. This might have meant blending several parallel fragments in different tonalities *(vertical* combinations), or connecting together individual linear fragments from many sources *(horizontal* combinations). Alternatively, he used just their shapes if not their exact notes, or vice versa, as may be seen in the *Concord Sonata* or the *Universe Symphony* (Section C), both featuring such evolutions of *Nearer, My God to Thee.*

Such usage of materials is unlike almost anything we encounter in all other western music, not least because, within normal European practice, the majority of such vernacular sources would have been considered entirely unsuited to serious artistic composition. The fact that many American melodies had earlier European origins did not affect their new and independent identities, even if their notes were not radically different. Again, this is much along the lines of the transcendental model, because they had become renewed to *sound* different in their new context. (The tune, *America,* must shock many British newcomers to American soil, because it is, in fact, that of the British National Anthem!)

The Ives historian and musicologist, Peter J. Burkholder, wrote a volume that discussed this very phenomenon, *All Made of Tunes*, in which he analyzed and revealed the extent of quotation in Ives' music, together with a detailed examination of the apparent contradiction raised between their ties to the European musical culture from which Ives was trying to escape.[4] Aside from adopting a controversial new dating protocol (see Appendix 1), Burkholder estimated that such quotations applied to approximately a third of Ives' entire output, a figure that might seem too conservative to anyone familiar with even a small part of it. However, if we look beyond the many large-scale compositions and towards smaller forms, such as the extensive song catalog and chamber works, the assessment begins to make sense.

Bernard Herrmann, in his earlier years amongst the new avant-garde in America, but perhaps best known as one of the greatest film composers, (i.e. Alfred Hitchcock's *Psycho*), reflected that the music of Josef Haydn (the de facto 'father' of the modern symphony, string quartet and sonata form), frequently employed similarly vernacular material of its day, and no one had ever found fault with that![5] We might also consider another 20th Century figure, Béla Bartók, whose music is extensively built on Hungarian, sometimes Romanian folk material, especially the unique intervallic nature of its folk music foundation; perhaps this is as close a direct comparison as we will find. This writer cannot recall Bartók's music ever being criticized for the inclusion of such melodic entities; instead it is considered brilliant and inventive. We can find many instances other major composers employing such material, from Vaughan Williams to Percy Grainger. These composers found much of value by incorporating folk melodies or their primary components into their compositions, even though Ives' usage of it is far more diffusely connected to the whole, and more *philosophically* than technically at that.

Leonard Bernstein, a passionate advocate for Ives, famously made the error of confusing this element in Ives' music with American *primitivism*, even likening him to the painter, Grandma Moses. Because some other enthusiasts might not have recognized the purpose of the inclusion of the quotations, they might be blissfully unaware of the extraordinary sophistication and complexity of

Ives' artistic realm - in no way 'folk art' - and at least in as far as its message is concerned, no more 'primitive' than the philosophers who inspired it.

Finally, it is worth commenting again that during the twenty years of his greatest creativity, and while Ives was retreating from the realities of his world to embrace a more spiritual path, quotations from secular melodies gradually would become *less* significant; the religious, *more*. The latter he considered closest to the heart of the people, having experienced their power firsthand in the haunting, impassioned sounds at camp meetings. One other musical fragment of personal spiritual association, (what has been termed the four-note *Fate* motif that opens Beethoven's *Fifth Symphony* - so named because Ives likened this quote to fate knocking at one's door) also occupied a profound place within his music, showing up with uncanny regularity in countless works, in almost every conceivable guise and from very early on.

Similarly, various cosmic clues - 'stars,' 'celestial' themes - merged with the spiritual. More frequent appearances of the *Fate* motif, clear references to the hereafter in the camp meeting hymn, *Nearer My God to Thee, (Bethany),* and others, such as those within *In the Sweet Bye and Bye* increasingly dominated the later stages of Ives' output. The *Universe Symphony* summed up everything, granting a destination for his developing artistic and societal aspirations. By then, however, the quotations were almost completely absent, save one, (significantly, *Nearer My God to Thee);* even this had become scarcely recognizable as he let go his worldly references.

Links to other music

In the realization by David G. Porter of the first movement of Ives' incomplete *Third Orchestral Set* there are moments that sound distinctly like Debussy, a composer that Ives openly criticized; however, the movement, in totality, sounds only like Ives. (Listen to the extraordinary bass and low bell ostinato that underscores that movement.) Similarly, moments in *Scherzo:*

Over the Pavements suggest neoclassical Stravinsky, but the work still sounds only like Ives. (However, this particular composition arrived on the scene many years ahead of Stravinsky's neoclassical developments!) And certainly there are aspects of his earlier works that touch quite openly upon the music of Dvořák, Brahms, even Tchaikovsky, for example - indeed, paying due homage to them - but the music again remains exclusively beholden to Ives.

It has been said also of Ives' piano writing that his choices of idiomatic notation correspond to those found in the works of other composers before him, and thus, reveal his exposure to the piano works of the masters.[5] This is likely so, and certainly fits the transcendental ideal. However, such would be expected from any player/composer who has trained his mind and fingers around optimal ways of utilizing the instrument, a pattern that has developed for all instruments and instrumentalists over the centuries. So it ought not to be seen as so surprising, after all, that others would have trodden some familiar tracks before. Regardless, in every instance the voice of Ives the composer still comes through unmistakably; in other instances, it was Ives who had anticipated the better-known instrumental technique we might be hearing (i.e. the use of tone clusters in the *Concord Sonata*)!

If one listens to *The Celestial Country* it is easy to see that Ives had completely suppressed his own voice. It does not sound like Ives, the music he had written in Parker's language not being authentic to him. Far from forming links to other composers, he almost sold his soul in a deal that turned out to be no bargain. Perhaps he thought that success with that work would have allowed him to introduce audiences to the real musical universe he occupied, indeed a possible explanation. If instead, as a young struggling voice he was just confused, *The Celestial Country* would finally cement Ives' focus to follow the true voice that resonated within him.

A musical radical

The unique combinations of atypical, seemingly unmatched sounds in Ives' music do not have many parallels in other composers' work. Because his compositions were likely to encompass multiple *technically* unrelated components together, this conspires to make him a particularly tricky customer for the uninitiated to un*ravel*. (Pun intended! Ives was an inveterate punner.) Indeed, he seemed to welcome turning upside-down people's expectations and biases, taking a certain delight from sheltered society 'ladies' (the term could be applied equally women *or* men!) reacting in shock at his compositions; this prankster aspect of his personality has been the subject of many analyses. However, those who have looked for hidden or darker meanings should have spared themselves the effort. A humorous person by nature, Ives preserved the lessons instilled in him by his father: his music, thus, would be neither comfortable nor soothing. Rather, it would bring to the listener new and more authentic aural experiences; Ives would thus challenge the listener to be receptive and "use" his (or her) ears. However, in his curmudgeonly old New England ways, he did not mind having fun at someone's expense if he had been the target of their respective scorn and rejection.

Ives compared limited musical horizons to being comfortable with what we already like, beauty often being defined by what we know and have come to accept.[6] What is thought good is considered 'nice,' even though the term communicates nothing other than that it fits our comfort level. "Have a *nice* day!" - a stagnant, never-ending loop that actually wishes us nothing other than to have a kind of day that we like. Pushing the envelope outside that comfort zone will expand the message into territory that is no longer familiar, and therefore less likely to be perceived as 'nice.' Thus if our musical perceptions are to grow it is incumbent upon us to keep an open mind to the unfamiliar. Ives encountered this problem all through his life, so one can only imagine the strength of his unwavering resolve to try to express himself in his own terms in the face of condemnation and ridicule. Though very clear to him, it must have seemed everyone else was blind (or *deaf*). Either that, or as he wondered on more than one occasion, his ears must be "on all wrong."

The 'isms' of music

Since Ives would be slave to no particular idiom, technique, fad, or means of expression, for him, writing music was not about proving the merits of a particular musical system; it was about communicating what he wanted to say regardless of method. The contrast with European composers, who were deeply entrenched in their respective cultures of the time, is striking. Within these cultures they followed, or established particular artistic schools of thought. Over time, these would be superseded by *other* schools of artistic thought that embraced yet another particular philosophy; everything the composer/advocate did would encompass it. There are clear examples in the works of many of the leading creative figures of the time. Debussy, for example, had evolved definitive *impressionism* from Satie's earlier excursions, starkly defining the French avant-garde. Such means of conveying fleeting imagery and senses corresponded closely to impressionistic painting. Schönberg became entrenched in his march towards a system of totally *controlled* atonality - ultimately, his twelve-tone system (*dodecaphony*) emerged as a complete entity unto itself, and dictated the very notation on the page. Such music effectively escapes the sense of key centers.

Stravinsky followed in the steps of the Russian 'Five,' a late romantic movement that encompassed the deliberate efforts of a group of composers, to infuse the ethnicity of their culture into their music, largely absent as an identity during the evolution of Western music, before unleashing a short-lived burst of idiomatic *primitivism*, (and the notorious premiere of *The Rite of Spring* in 1913); *Neoclassicism* came next, in which he attempted to inject his music with some of the artistic purity of the classical period composers. Beyond neoclassicism, Stravinsky's music developed as a modern evolved style that encompassed facets of his previous periods, before moving into a late period based upon *serialism* - an outgrowth and evolution of Schönberg's system - to impose similar logic and order not only on pitch, but also on rhythm, harmony, tone colors, dynamics, and so forth.

Outside music there were numerous comparable developments, too. Picasso's work had certain parallels to Stravinsky's in that both worked through various seemingly parallel periods and artistic identities. His *blue period,* would be followed by the *pink period,* African *cubism, synthetic cubism, classicism, surrealism,* and more; Munch is predominantly associated with *expressionism*; at home in America, the architect Frank Lloyd Wright's iconic contributions include the stylistic cues of the school of *prairie architecture;* in literature, the *modernism* of T.S. Eliot - the list could go on. Thus, as a development of the 20th Century and beyond, artists in all disciplines sought to establish new idioms and techniques in their own image, often seeking to be the recognized pioneers of specific methodologies and philosophies.

In direct contrast, Ives independently pioneered or dabbled in virtually every major technique of the new century almost simultaneously, sometimes within a few years, but often well ahead of his contemporaries; he would, however, remain largely unknown, and 20th Century music would be far along in its evolution before he was noticed. The avant-garde who ultimately would discover him already would have their own methodologies, and though Ives became their 'patron saint,' it was too late for their own language to reflect his remarkable sonic world. Indeed, as true products of the 20th Century, their work imbued elements that reflected more closely the newer, faster paced culture of the times, rather than the old world to which Ives' music speaks so clearly.

Regardless, it is hard not to speculate what his influence might have been in different circumstances, although it is tempting to think that had he been recognized, it would have blocked that very unique spark that his isolation had enabled. During the time of his greatest productivity, he stayed out of the limelight, having chosen not to concern himself with performances of his music. There were none. If he had come up with anything worthwhile, perhaps time would take care of things.

The pioneer working alone

Significantly, since he had foregone the stamp of audience approval, Ives had put himself in a position to write as he chose, to be completely at liberty to use any method or materials that seemed appropriate to his purpose. Thus, totally free from obligation, he could also work and rework his music in any way he wished, unconstrained by finished commissions. For a number of the earlier years, it appears he worked in a total vacuum, only gradually becoming aware of some other contemporary composers' work as the years went on; by then probably he was already well set in his own ways of composition. To the extent that their work might have influenced him therefore it is hard to say, although attempts to link specific characteristics of it to his music have long been made. However, we already know the key to this puzzle because of what Goddard Lieberson told us (see Chapter 2). Since Ives was known to show little interest in anything else that was taking place in music in the outside world, it remains problematic to trace any direct link in his music to any outside influence at all during his most productive and important years, even more to his earlier predominantly experimental period. It is rather like trying to force a square peg into a round hole.

However, Ives *is* well known for his extensive revisions (often multiple), made many years after the first version or edition of many of his works. Whether awareness of other composers' work played a role in this has been hotly contested for many years (see Appendix 1), though once again, his apparent disinterest in such things must be weighed into the equation. Regardless, it is hard to find an instance of any work being altered after its initial incarnation to such a degree that its fundamental identity, pioneering techniques, let alone sound and design, were transformed to render it far removed from the original.

In regard to giving performers insight into his music, Ives was a loner, too, almost casual preferring, as John Kirkpatrick remarked, to enthuse to them about his *latest* musical discovery! However, he was precise about one interpretive aspect, at least, concerning certain pitch 'spellings' normally considered *enharmonic*.* Many a copyist would come up against an irate Ives for having 'fixed' the notes.

---

*Two adjacent notes, otherwise considered identical (i.e. B flat = A sharp) theoretically, are only *almost* the same pitch, because all pitches vary by small degrees from key to key. Ives wanted to 'hear' these subtle distinctions where possible, although keyboard instruments are tuned to an average in all keys. (See also p. 289.)

Ives' counterpoint

There has always been some misunderstanding of Ives' intentions, and the precise nature of what he expected the listener to hear. Although he did not often have the advantage of hearing all of his finished music played (and being able to adjust the instrumentation or dynamics accordingly), we can be sure that he knew what he was doing. There were always things that were intended to weave in and out of the larger musical texture and not stand alone; occasionally a fragmented melody will 'jump' out, just as we might have heard at a Danbury parade - the clash of one of his father's marching bands shifting relative positions with others. With the understanding that we are not meant to resolve *all* of these lines as separate components, clearly different levels demand different degrees of perception and mental awareness. In Ives' case, this makes some sophistication necessary for what we are hearing, since not all the parts of the mix were created equal, or even meant to fulfill what would normally be expected amongst *compatible* and supportive components. Thus, when heard and understood as Ives intended, his objectives gradually become clear. And certainly today's recording technology has helped even further, with its remarkable sonic separation.

Ives' polyphony (the simultaneous combinations of more than one melodic line) is thus a complex matter, since not all of it can be thought of as counterpoint in the traditional sense. If we attempt to force precise vertical alignments of time and harmony upon some of this polyphony (as in characterizing the music of Bach, for example), we will misunderstand the purpose, although Ives' music also does feature or include such types of classically conceived counterpoint in abundance. However, because not all of the linear writing we observe in Ives' scores was intended to stand horizontally independent, its purpose, instead, was to coexist in a *blend* with other individually horizontal entities to create a complex blur. In these instances, Ives was trying to affect *moving* 'harmonic' coloration, rather than demand that we hear in the classical sense the exact relationships of note against note.

But to what degree did Ives anticipate the aural effect of what he wrote? Quite aside from his considerable expertise, ably demonstrated in the orchestration and contrapuntal skills of his earlier more conventional works, in fact, we know, too, that he had benefitted by hearing numerous musicians try their hands at his music in private settings, often his home, long before it started to receive public performances. (It was sometimes at these sessions that Ives would suffer the blunt, and callously indifferent remarks that must have proven very hard to take. Treating him as a businessman, and merely an *amateur* musician greatly wounded his soul.) Moreover, he himself, spent countless hours at the piano working things through, so probably nothing made it to the page having only existed in his mind. It is clear, as well, that he had enjoyed many run-throughs of early century experimental works with small groups of theater orchestra musicians - this being reflected in the instrumentation of the music we have from that time, and often even in the titles of the music itself.

In discussing Ives' music, Goddard Lieberson, who had understood so much about the composer that others somehow missed, slipped himself when he commented somewhat negatively on Ives' *expertise* regarding the practicality of what he wrote. In doing so he misunderstood that critical part of Ives' musical aesthetic completely. In faulting Ives' orchestration and musical complexity he failed to recognize its purpose and design.[7] It seems hard to understand how anyone with a knowledge of Ives' background and writing skills could have made such a judgment, and if Lieberson's remarks and perception's about Ives' music and methods seemed to miss the mark, he ignored Ives' own references to the topic *(Essays Before a Sonata)*.[8] Here, in relation to criticisms that Brahms' orchestration was 'muddy,' Ives believed that if it were less so Brahms would not have been able to express his thoughts accurately. Ives considered it all a matter of proper handling and interpretation of the materials at hand, rather than imposing something upon its composition that would hamstring the intent and communicated thought.

Thus, it is up to performers to recognize what type of purpose Ives had for any given part, and also to recognize those unique spatial balances that were in play; this all requires a fair degree of expertise in itself, along with taking the time to make the appropriate analysis. To have any chance of hearing the precise effects Ives had in mind, we cannot treat all the components equally, or consider them cut from the same cloth. Some minor parts even are symbolic, rather than literal; others are examples of *shadow counterpoint*, not intended to be heard directly, but rather something reflected off the fundamental. (Ives' shadow counterpoint is unique to him - even the term itself - and usually it was assigned to the slightest of instrumentation so that it would not be heard within normal considerations of instrumental balance, or commonly ordained harmonic theory. See Chapter 5.) Alternately, a random clash between equal tonalities and entities was what Ives was striving for; however, there is a difference between controlled randomness and pure chance. In the former, the components usually can be moved around to a small degree and the result is exactly the same, as long as stricter, true contrapuntal relationships between predominant lines (those parts comparable in the classical sense of the term) are preserved, together with the harmonic language.

If Lieberson's perceptions and comments here are reminiscent of Carter's, and to a lesser degree Copland's (in regard to audience reaction concerning Ives' isolation), they seem to typify yet another composer's attempt to impose the constraints of his own limitations, conformities and lesser vision.

The makeup of the music

Ives' work was built on several distinct types of idiomatic foundation that seemingly are incompatible. Peter J. Burkholder memorialized these categories in detail in his article, *Ives and the Four Musical Traditions,* in which he demonstrated his analysis through specific examples. Although we can dissect this overall identification of primary components into even more subcategories,[9] the overall divisions are logical and important to differentiate.

Three of the four primary styles or musical traditions that Burkholder discussed were fully evolved modes of the musical language of the time. The fourth was one that Ives explored independently, and involved techniques sometimes concurrently developed (though mostly later) by others during the early years of the 20th Century. This particular mode of development exerted such a fundamental influence on the other three that it completely dominated them to produce something entirely new in totality.

The assimilation of all four of these idiomatic styles into a large and flexible reservoir of material provided the potential for any or all of them together to be reflected in any number of guises. Ives' unique creative idiosyncrasies generally are identifiable throughout his output, in spite of the dissimilar characteristics of the styles. Significantly, because of the distinctive nature of the harmonic, melodic and rhythmic contours and blends that he chose, the resulting sonic stamp imparted by any of these different components used separately, collectively or in other ways, is usually clearly identifiable. The four styles may be summarized by their key elements and origins.

Folk, Popular, Civil War music

Danbury, as the town of his birth and upbringing, thus by default of providing Ives' earliest exposure to music, would prove to be a lasting foundation and lifelong influence. His immersion in the daily sounds of this little cultural microcosm included the music he heard constantly within his home, that of his father's marching and dance bands, Civil War tunes, popular songs and other styles appearing in a newly reenergized community finally emerging from the receding dark clouds of war. Ives' music would become infused with a broad backdrop of these popular and traditional secular styles, which would stay with him though almost his entire compositional output.

Practically all of Ives' major works were infused with a complex array of fragments from these well-known melodies, reflecting the personal coloration of his life. Sometimes the contexts of these quotations were so altered that it is easy to miss them entirely, the often 'alien' harmonies and crossed or opposing entities serving many functions other than the conventional. Ives was more concerned with the inclusion of the quotations for the realization of his own soundscape, rather than imply the listener need hunt consciously for them - like needles in a haystack - in order to appreciate the music. They are used often, too, in unexpected fashions: sometimes blended with others, in other instances rhythmically or melodically altered, taken from the mid-point, or offset by entirely different tonalities or speeds - frequently only revealing themselves one element at a time, like the peeling back of a curtain.

Sometimes parallel elements of several melodies are set in diametrically opposite ways to create continual reinvention and impact, the resulting exclusively Ivesian sound due to a unique sense for the manipulation of sonic relationships. Even in the context of his more conventional compositions, fragments of familiar melodies are suddenly rendered entirely new by unexpected harmonic or rhythmic settings. Invoking the pioneering spirit of 19th Century New England, or Ives' new life in the big city, we sense their presence through the distinctly idiomatic sound they impart.

Church music

Ives' deep immersion in the hymns from camp meetings, and the great "waves of sound" emanating from these outdoor services, were reflected not only amongst quoted materials, the last to survive at the end of his transcendental journey. Camp meeting hymns were distinctly different to those of church services, their interpretation freer, more direct, and expressed with the authenticity of the people's collective voice, rather than that of the long established formalities of the church. And we know that Parker openly scorned the limited harmonic and melodic language of hymns, so that at Yale, Ives soon learned not to show him his earlier compositions or outside work - since it was laden with many such vernacular references.

Ives also performed as a church organist from an early age, where he learned the more structured forms of religious music. Under the guiding hand of his father, he wrote music based on hymns for use in these services, some of it decidedly radical. Later, with outside influences, notably of Dudley Buck, a leading and highly renowned church musician at the time, Ives' compositional range became increasingly sophisticated. Buck played an instrumental role in gradually introducing to an unenlightened segment of the populace a greater range of musical possibilities. Criticized by the elite for having incorporated numerous popular elements, it cannot be overlooked that he was responsible for elevating the musical appreciation of countless individuals who otherwise would have been left behind.

Because the characteristic style of Buck's music was more refined than that which the majority of churchgoers might have experienced, and featured a ready lyricism and straightforwardness, it was practical for local church choirs to sing. Buck's chromatic harmonies also were more readily associated with the styles of popular music that the public had embraced, and had widely varied forms of presentation to keep the less musically sophisticated listener engaged. In this light, his music also featured the close-voiced chromatic harmonies of 'barbershop quartets' (a readily identifiable feature), certainly considered by the elite to be beneath the great tradition of European classical music. However, the youthful Ives was very enamored of Buck's work, and resented the fact that Parker looked down on it. After all, Buck's approach had provided a means to reach the people by slowly introducing them to a higher level of music, while Parker had shunned them, effectively pushing them away forever. Parker failed to recognize that Buck was a substantial musician, who solved problems of musical communication in his own way. In effect, this had further encouraged the young Ives to entertain the possibility of incorporating elements other than the conventional into his own music.

Buck's approach also solved another problem - that of making a decent living in America as a composer. Ives had the opportunity in the months before he attended Yale to have some instruction from Buck himself. However, even Parker's strict adherence to the broader tradition of the European masters could not dislodge Ives' affection for provincial hymn tunes and the simplicity of their harmonic language - even more the types of influences on such music by figures like Buck. Although Ives modeled his early major work, *The Celestial Country*, on the music of Parker, Buck's influence still can be heard.

The European model

Although George Ives always had taken great pains to instill the music of the great European masters in his son, under Parker, Ives would be schooled further in them, and see his skills blossom and elevated to the degree necessary to write major works, such as the *First* and *Second Symphonies* - large-scale works much in the grand German tradition of Brahms or Dvořák. That he later would credit his father for anything "good" he had done in music, while de-emphasizing Parker's role again speaks more to Ives' auspicious talents in capitalizing on what he saw as his major influence, than it does ingratitude toward Parker. If we accept that Ives likely would have acquired whatever compositional skills he needed with or without his esteemed teacher, indeed his comments about his father really must be seen more in context of his reverence towards him than anything else.

In fact, Parker's influence ultimately seems to have confused the young composer, since for a time he must have thought that the career and musical methods of his teacher were those he should try to emulate. The story of Parker humorously scolding Ives for "hogging all the keys" typified an exclusive adherence to the conventional European model. Had Ives followed that path, he would now be as forgotten as Horatio Parker. Regardless, Parker was undoubtedly a fine teacher and highly skilled musician - certainly, up to this point in time, the most significant with whom Ives had spent extended time. Thus, during the period studying with him, Ives developed a strong background in the compositional language of the late German romantic tradition, enhanced aural skills, and an extremely developed knowledge and technique in all aspects of the established art form of the time. Since in later years Ives had many good things to say about Parker shows that their relationship was far from as strained as many have projected.

The experimental model

This remarkable part of Ives' makeup probably owed more to his father, George Ives' well-known musical curiosity, open-mindedness, and penchant for experimentation, than it does to any other single factor - certainly his time at Yale. Despite little existing in the record to substantiate his father's experimentation, logic tells us that something must have been long in play for Ives to be so comfortably drawn to the unconventional, especially in the absence of similar contemporary work by others. Thus, all alone early in the first decade of the 20th Century, Ives would explore the new techniques that were to become central to his monumental output in the years to come.

Charles Ives was driven by something far beyond mere experimentation, his ideas merely a means to an end in the search for a more personally relevant range of musical potential. Ives' new artistic destination, completely in line with his advancing view of mankind and its place in the universe, somehow managed to stride the highly conservative background existing in music of the day with some of the most radical concepts imaginable. Stravinsky later would refer to Ives as "the great anticipator;" independently, Ives pioneered or peripherally explored even some of the 'isms' discussed earlier. The fact that Ives utilized whatever blend of these experimental elements he deemed appropriate sets him apart; this still causes many to be perplexed in their assessments of his work. Until his most radical compositions appeared, the late romantic language of Parker remained present within it in some form, although we can find its subtler elements still in *most* of the music he ever would write. Ives created his own organization out of the chaos of multiple, contradictory elements.

Whether or not he ever had considered that any other composers might be working along similar lines, Ives' experiments ultimately would include polytonality, some excursions closely related to dodecaphony, polyrhythms, multiple speeds, mixed meters and scales, parallel entities, spatial entities, microtones, tone clusters, aleatoric (chance) elements - he was comfortable with most of them when barely a glint in other composers' eyes (see Chapter 6). However, it is largely within his early experimental works that he could make claim to his priority, rather than in their various incorporations within *later* large-scale works - the former being the proving grounds in and of themselves, the latter their broader and multi-compartmented application. Most of Ives' experiments took place before 1908, that prior to 1902 being more harmonically innovative, and after that, rhythmically so. Regardless, these early efforts, having considerable musical value in their own right, have been incorporated into the general catalog of his performance works.

However, because of the difficulty in determining precise dates from Ives' records (since he did not place a value on recording such details until later in life when his recollections were rapidly fading), in some instances it cannot be proven who was the first composer to use a number of these new techniques. It is also significant that because many of Ives' compositions were handed down in a state of disarray, in short score or just sketch form, in some cases it took years of painstaking reconstruction to produce definitive editions whose dates remain still unclear to a degree. In a few other instances, while Ives was still alive, completion of the more vaguely organized sketches required collaborations with other composers. Because he was old, frail and with poor eyesight by the time many of these were completed, sometimes he was unable to check the final scores, often even inclined merely to trust his collaborator - with good reason, it should be added; Ives was not one to give his sketches to just anyone. Nevertheless, this all conspires to make the job of documentation sometimes not beyond challenge, although disagreement on the majority of the dates of these last stragglers is growing less frequent.

Over a few short years, Ives would assemble the building blocks necessary for all of his future work. Unbeknownst to him, the future road he would travel was already set in place; all he had to do was to build and follow it to a destination probably further than even *he* had ever imagined.

REFERENCES

1. 'Innovation and Nostalgia: Ives, Mahler, and the Origins of Twentieth-Century Modernism,' by Leon Botstein; from Charles Ives and his World, Edited by J. Peter Burkholder, *Princeton University Press*, Princeton, New Jersey, 1996, p. 48
2. 'Charles Ives Remembered, an Oral History,' Vivian Perlis, *University of Illinois Press*, Urbana and Chicago, 1974, p. 145
3. 'Essays Before a Sonata,' Charles Ives, *Knickerbocker Press*, New York, 1920, pp. 92 - 96
4. 4. 'All Made of Tunes, Charles Ives and the Uses of Musical Borrowing,' Peter J. Burkholder, *Yale University Press*, 2004
5. 'Ives's Concord Sonata and the Texture of Music,' David Michael Hertz, from 'Charles Ives and his World,' Edited by J. Peter Burkholder, *Princeton University Press*, Princeton, New Jersey, 1996, p. 114
6. 'Essays Before a Sonata,' Ives, pp. 75-117
7. Perlis, p. 208
8. 'Essays Before a Sonata,' Ives, p. 25
9. 'Charles Ives and his World,' Edited by J. Peter Burkholder, *Princeton University Press*, Princeton, New Jersey, 1996, p. 3

CHAPTER 4

Early symphonic ventures

The European symphonic model

The symphonic model that had developed since the time of Haydn (1732-1809) remained a standard large musical format right up until the time of Ives's early symphonic works. However, everything changed early in the 20th Century, when traditional models would splinter rapidly into newer forms. Although the music of the young radicals from across the Atlantic reflected a dynamically changing world, many 'mainstream' composers continued to cling steadfastly to the traditional format, albeit many steps removed from those of the late romantics.

The traditional model for symphonies typically comprised four movements that followed a carefully organized plan for maximum variety and dramatic focus. The overall working design was so successful that it was also utilized for other major concert works - from *string quartets, trios* and larger chamber music forms, to *sonatas* and *concertos* - although some of these, such as the latter two featured one less movement. Here, the movements corresponded to the weightiest three of the four-movement design.

In all of these formats, the first movement was the most substantial, the second usually slow and no less significant, the third a livelier, more light-hearted relief (in those formats where it applied), to be followed by a spirited and often dramatic finale, which might also be substantial. The first two movements, and sometimes the last, of all these forms usually could be expected to take the standard of all major European formats - *Sonata Form* - probably the most important musical structure to have evolved during Europe's long musical history. Allowing for many variations, the format was a development of three-part *(ternary* ABA) form, in which the same material ('A_1' & 'A_2') was used between a contrasting 'B' section. *Sonata Form* allowed for extended writing and considerable artistic freedom:

- The first theme *(First Subject)* was memorable and capable of extended development of its contours, melodically, harmonically and even rhythmically; it was followed by:
- A transitional section (*Transition*) - sometimes introduced new thematic material, but not in any way intended to detract from the prominence of the first theme; then:
- A second theme (*Second Subject*) in a contrasting key - it, too, might have introduced sub-themes as it worked its way towards the next major section:
- The *Development* consisted of an extended working of all the materials from all that had been heard (collectively known as the *Exposition),* developed in any way the composer chose. It was considered a test of creativity; this section led to:
- A brief concluding portion - the *Codetta* - before the music headed to:
- The *Recapitulation* - a return and restatement of all the materials used in the *exposition,* but usually with an abbreviated transition. Traditionally the *Second Subject* now would be in the same key as the first.
- The concluding portion of the materials of *second subject* propelled the movement into the *Coda,* the final section that brought the movement to a close in the opening key. Sharing features with the *codetta,* it was usually larger in scope, and might have constituted a small development section in itself. However, its character of summation assured the listener that it was leading to the conclusion.

Early symphonic ventures

We could expect considerable flexibility with this plan, since no two works utilizing sonata form tended to be quite the same. Sometimes modified hybrids constituted later movements, such as the *Sonata-Rondo*, often utilized for the finale, or other variations of sonata form. Ives took advantage of the standard formats in both the *First* and *Second Symphonies* (with some differences, though not outside common practice), before developing his own structural formats. However, both of these early works belonged wholly to a late romantic language that set them apart from his later musical evolution.

The First Symphony

The *First Symphony* is generally conventional, cast in the mold of the great European symphonies of the day. There are a few clues about the future that Ives would take, however, not the least of which is the restless shifting through multiple keys at the outset. Far from establishing the predominant tonality, it is as if Ives was trying to escape it. At the point of his life that this symphony was conceived, however, Ives was thoroughly entrenched in the European tradition; his training under Parker had seen to that. Even the departures from the standard model exemplified here were not especially unusual at the time; thus overall, the formal structures remain clearly discernible.

Ives composed the first movement of this symphony under Parker's guidance as part of his graduation requirements, and as such incorporated the fabric of high European art. Parker apparently took issue with the large number of keys ("six or eight") through which Ives had traveled within a few bars of the opening and insisted he make another attempt at it. Less successful in Ives' view, Parker kindly recanted and allowed his student to reuse the original material as long as he agreed to start and end the movement in the same key![1]

Although the symphony is a fine work by any standards, it is a work that reflects other persons' gravities perhaps more than his own, even though it seems that much of it was notated after Ives had left Yale. Presumably he felt the need to complete the train of creative thought he had initiated. Demonstrating a mastery of seamless musical development and flow, and comfortable ease through countless key changes, it is a thoroughly substantial work in the grand tradition. Ives' penchant for borrowed materials appeared even here, the first movement containing references to the hymns *Beulah Land* and *The Shining Shore*, two melodies that feature prominently in many of Ives' later works. If the inclusion of such melodies had not met with Parker's approval, it seems nevertheless he turned a blind eye to Ives' predilection to use them.

Charles Ives in 1898

{{PD-Art}}

The quotations did not stop there. Ives' growing rejection of European musical dominance did not prevent him from including references to some of the old masters. Much has been made of this, but we should keep in mind that Ives retained his reverence of them; his rejection of the easy complacency that allowed ready substitution of another society's culture over one that was home grown was the issue. As such, we can hear a quote from the *New World Symphony* of Dvořák in the second movement, and another from Tchaikowski's *Pathetique Symphony* in the fourth! These inclusions, no more than minor constituents of the whole, might better be seen as reflections of that which had inspired the young Ives. Regardless, in demonstrating the latent talent within him, the *First Symphony* is an early masterwork.

The Second Symphony

Following in quick succession, the *Second Symphony* again would adhere largely to the forms and methods of the European masters. However, it is hardly mainstream in the manner of the earlier work, being marked by a distinctive and conscious American stamp on its foundations through the use of 'paraphrasing' familiar melodies from Ives' Danbury upbringing. Ironically, Ives would continue to adhere to the names and overall large-scale embodiments of the major European musical forms (i.e. *symphony, sonata, string quartet,* etc.) long after he had poured a degree of scorn upon the easy perpetuation of other cultural traditions. However, the language of those later works bore little resemblance to their European counterparts, even though certain technical elements always remained.

Many of Ives' early works echo happy and upbeat memories; some of these were from his college days, where he found acceptance and camaraderie amongst a new group of people. Even though many of these compositions were completed or finally scored well after the time of their original conception and sketching, the spirit of Ives' early optimism remains strongly infused in them, and none more so than in the *Second Symphony*. Interestingly, this work remained dear to him long after he had reached another musical identity entirely, one that was to make a substantial break with the past and all that had been accepted traditionally within American society of the day. Although the symphony remained well within formal constraints, it did, however, represent a clear shift *back* to his musical roots with a vast vernacular foundation, and *forward* in that that he had begun to formulate his own declaration of independence. As such, it is the first substantial work by Ives to announce his personality, loud and clear. Thus, Ives' striking voice emerged, one that pervaded all that he wrote, regardless of the period, musical language or methodology employed. We leave it feeling as if we have come know him; indeed we have.

Title Page of Dvořák's New World Symphony,
with its date of composition (1893), listed alongside
those of his earlier symphonies
{{PD-Art}}

Ives' return to his roots was not accomplished all in an instant. Rather, it would be an evolution based on a gradually evolving departure from one idiom into another from inputs unique to his experience. Quite offended at Dvořák's advocacy that American composers ought to incorporate melodies of spirituals into their music, as he had done in his *New World Symphony* of 1893, Ives took it to be the implication that a European heavyweight would show 'provincial' American lightweights the way to their own culture. Similar attitudes amongst the European musical elite would be partially behind the scathing opinions Ives developed towards contemporary European musical culture in general. Moreover, Dvořák's symphony corresponded precisely to those deliberate attempts he would later criticize for trying to imprint regional color through glib infusions of national folk material upon thoroughly German foundations.

The premiere of the *New World Symphony* coincided with Ives' sophomore year at Yale, and he probably took this as an early cue to think about writing his own work, settling on incorporating developed fragments of simple melodies thoroughly familiar to him. In an article well worth reading, a carefully documented analysis of the symphony by Peter J. Burkholder detailed Ives' authentic incorporation of *these* melodies, of which Dvořák hardly was likely to be aware.[2] Ives would thus answer the Czech composer and determine what would constitute the music of his own culture.

After the premier of *The Celestial Country*, which Ives surely considered a 'debacle,' the concept of the *Second Symphony* must have cemented that conscious choice to chase his roots. Though far removed from the new directions he was already exploring, it was one that returned his identity in the context of a major work. Although it is possible that the symphony might not have been scored until later in the new century's first decade (See Magee.[3]), there can be little doubt, however, that the primary musical content dates from 1898-1902, the years that Ives himself assigned to it. Logically, later dates surely could amount only to final details. In context of the date of *The Celestial Country* (1902), thus, the symphony must have been conceived while he was still writing the *former* work. We can only conclude that it reveals that Ives was far from convinced that the language of his compositional future belonged to Parker's world, and thus it seems that Ives' Danbury roots never really had been put away. Regardless, Ives' dynamic use of certain rhythmic complexities was a harbinger of things to come, although by 1902, Ives had already embarked on numerous avant-garde experiments, which are far from the language found in this symphony. By 1910, Ives' language was at a polar opposite to the *Second Symphony*, again lending no credence to Magee's later dates for its primary composition if we are to take them at face value. Thus, as with everything surrounding the dating of Ives' music, this work is no exception, and we must use our common sense to a degree, knowing that Ives typically spent years refining many works, well beyond the original time of their sketching for their final scoring, or even completion.

Some of the materials of the *Second Symphony* appear to date even to *before* Ives' studies with Parker; according to Ives some of these also had appeared in now lost earlier works. For example, he mentioned that the finale of the symphony was based on the lost overture, *The American Woods*, which dated to his pre-Yale years. Some elements of it had been included and performed in an early piece of 1889 when Ives was just fifteen. The fact that no record of that performance has survived means little, in and of itself, although this has not stopped some scholars to question Ives' date. John Kirkpatrick dated the surviving symphony sketches to no earlier than 1901-02, but regardless, it is clear that the symphony does not correspond remotely to the experiments in which Ives was engaged many years prior to the date that Magee assigned to it. Certainly the cheerful upbeat nature of the young composer and this symphony seems shared, too, in many of his early works, not to mention his preference for incorporating upbeat musical material that was part of his early life, such as in his 1888 *Holiday Quickstep*, (based on a march style that would have been well familiar to him through his father, and specifically its references to David Wallis Reeves' *Second Regiment Connecticut National Guard March*), or the 1895 *March No. 3, with My Old Kentucky Home*, or even *The Circus Band* of 1898, which included fragments of *Jolly Dogs, Marching Through Georgia, Riding down from Bangor* and *Reuben and Rachel*.

Thus, the closer we look at the apparent sudden departure in style from that of *The Celestial Country*, a work Ives claimed to be virtually contemporary with the symphony, in fact, the more we see the probability that the departure took place the other way around. The symphony further reveals another of Ives' compositional hallmarks - that of the endless growth, reworking and incorporation of musical ideas that were ever present within him. The recycling of material - a common trait in Ives' music - reveals how the ongoing creative process ensured that practically everything he ever wrote seldom was put away. From Ives' words in *Memos*,[4] the slow movement (the third) also seems to have origins in another genre altogether (a string quartet for a religious service), before it was developed into a movement for his *First Symphony*. Apparently, Horatio Parker didn't think it suitable for a symphony, even though the surviving sketches place it *after* Ives had left Yale! Regardless, it seems this is likely the essence of a movement saved and later transferred into the *Second Symphony* many years later, especially if the sketches are merely evolutions of existing material. Once again with the dating of much of Ives' music, we may never know the precise timeline for sure. (See Appendix 1.)

It is readily apparent how the telling amalgam of the European romantic tradition of Brahms and Dvořák with the strongly 'accented' thoroughly American content results in a curious but resonating hybrid. Sonically, though, it bears a striking resemblance in concept to both European masters, particularly to Brahms, and the very symphony of Dvořák that Ives seems to have resented. In fact, we can even hear the angst of Mahler sometimes, especially in the slow sections, a composer/conductor with whom Ives was well familiar in New York. Perhaps also in homage, Ives subtly worked references to Brahms' *First* and *Third Symphonies* into the fabric at various places, as well as traces of a Bach *Three Part Sinfonia*, even the *Scherzo* from Borodin's *Second Symphony*, Handel's *Joy To The World*, and *Beethoven's Fifth Symphony*.

In his article and analysis,[5] which differs in some respects from that detailed above, Burkholder concluded that these classical references - always transitional rather than primarily thematic - were suggested by the developing context, rather than by any preconceived plan, since functionally they share much in common with their original usage. This seems reasonable, too, since they had been part of Ives' own personal experience. Perhaps also proving, finally and definitively, that the greatest European composers, at least, still stood tall in Ives' estimation, the symphony makes clear that he was not biased against the artistic expression of the Old World, only its presumption of superiority over that of the New World.

However, the most striking references in the symphony are the seemingly countless popular tunes, folk melodies and hymn tunes that form the mainstay of the primary thematic material. The blending of myriads of these fragments from disparate vernacular sources throughout the fabric - often in subtly characterized snippets, rather than rote statements of complete quotations, would become Ives' hallmark. Designed to infuse their stamp internally in the music, the type of usage that Ives devised allowed for great flexibility and breadth of development. Certainly, this symphony is a personally conceived work of music.

The fact that what he wrote was still umbilically tied to the European model - the norm in music at the time - should not be surprising. If it seems hard to understand about a figure known to be rebellious about accepted traditions, especially in hindsight after so much musical evolution since has taken place, we can understand it if we put ourselves in the shoes of any late 19th Century composer, or indeed, even in Ives' own shoes - and if we take into account that at this time perhaps he still wanted his music to be performed! We ought not lose sight of the fact, too, that Ives' time at Yale coincided with the last three years of Brahms' life; at that time *his* music was considered modern! If the dominant European composers' works became widely accepted almost as soon as they were written, it was because the very concept of alien sonic territory was never considered. It must have seemed that just the continual slow evolution of the western idiom and techniques would continue to define mainstream music forever, something the European composers would continue to dominate. None of the radical avant-garde movements of the 20th Century then existed, much less even were contemplated.

The inferiority complex in America existing in the arts was not about to evaporate; indeed, we still see evidence of it today.

It would take the work of the visual artists to begin the inexorable march towards the progression that characterized all of the arts in the 20th Century, while music lagged behind. *Impressionism* and *expressionism*, especially amongst the French painters after 1880, began to suggest visions in something less than idyllic realism. Because Ives would come to rebel against the mainstream tenets, his brand of music also would set out to stake new territory. However, Ives' revolutionary ideas needed time to form; his evolution would need to gather steam in order to leave the station. Thus, if Ives had not yet quite arrived there with the *Second Symphony*, he was already starting to claim his ground, and if he had not yet reached for eternity, we could argue by the title even of his parallel and totally conventional work, *The Celestial Country*, that the seeds had already been sown.

The *Second Symphony*, nevertheless, regardless of its place in Ives' developmental timeline, remains a time capsule that reveals a distinctive voice and personality. We hear Ives' optimistic and youthful spirit; his father's band, Civil War recollections, barn dances, camp meetings, small town life in 19th Century America, its festive occasions - they are all there, their imprints unmistakable. This was the world Ives inhabited and inherited, one that encompassed the tenor of his evolving voice amongst broader influences. Even the charm of the old Mississippi is there: a Mark Twain novel, a Stephen Foster song - it comes to life again within Ives' vision of a boundless and bountiful land enjoying its rebirth, his America.

Charles Ives And His Road To The Stars

{{PD-Art}}

{{PD-Art}}

Ives' America was one that could not last, since his optimistic joy and sense of aspiring towards a higher ideal eventually would be lost to illness, and the disillusionment following realization that the world he inherited was extinct. Gone too were his hopes for a state of universal enlightenment - the victim of industrialization, commercialization, superficiality, and a brutal world war, and finally, the loss of his political dreams.

In this symphony, if indeed Ives had not yet found a language predominantly his own, his distinctive idiomatic marks nevertheless are all over it. With the uniquely quirky character of its creator lovingly stamped throughout the music, the borrowed skeletal material is woven into its length in a seamless flow of new original invention. Surely we hear the beginning of Ives' manifestation in music of the transcendental spirit. Though hard to hear any trace of the cosmic horizons that already had begun to occupy Ives' attentions, overall, the *Second Symphony* is eminently accessible, a straightforward work needing very little explanation in order to enjoy. If Ives felt he had needed to answer Dvořák with a significant American symphony, no one can argue that with this work - a substantial work by any standards - he did not succeed.

Listeners' guide

In keeping with much of the symphony, the **First Movement** had its origins in earlier music, notably long lost works (the *Sonata for Organ,* and *Down East Overture*). It serves primarily as a lyrical introduction to the second movement, where full rein is given to musical development and orchestral virtuosity, sharing much of the material found in the fourth movement. Both of them act as dramatic introductions to succeeding movements, and in this regard they are transitional rather than primary movements. The first movement also announces *Columbia, the Gem of the Ocean,* and thus connects and anticipates the finale (fifth movement) by placing this material at each end of the symphony much like musical bookends.

- Having decided to utilize a large symphony orchestra for this work, Ives, ever the individualist, chose, however, to feature just the string section alone, entering in fugal imitation, for the first 65 bars, further colored only by bassoons for a few of them. Inexplicably Ivesian in its unapologetic indifference to conformity, it illustrates in the simplest manner the independent creative spirit that set Ives apart from others in his day.
- Ives wasted no time in incorporating his roots, with a fragment from *Massa's in de Cold Ground* ('Down in de cornfield') appearing early, set in counterpoint against the primary melodic material in the upper violins, and again more fully a little later. If this fragment is hard to catch, this is precisely the idea; Ives wanted to infuse the sound of these melodies into the fabric rather than present blatant settings of them. (Listen for the descending line that comprises this quote.) Indeed, the opening theme is loosely based on this same material. There are also some surprising harmonic interactions within this movement that Bernard Herrmann compared to Prokofiev.[6] Interestingly, Herrmann failed to recognize any of the other quoted melodic material until nearer the conclusion of the movement, where he identified a prominent clip of *Columbia, the Gem of the Ocean* appearing in the horns.[6]
- Mid-way through this section, a second primary element is the gentle usage of figurative material from *Pig Town Fling*. Both of these melodies are worked into other locations in the symphony by ingenious manipulations of the material. Burkholder referenced the similarity within this theme to a thematic device in Brahms' *First Symphony*, comparing the close relationships of notation of a dominant part of the line and using the term 'lower neighbor-note' to describe it. Ives might have had the finale of Mahler's *First Symphony* also in mind as he developed the idea; (the similarities appear in later evolutions of this material, most notably in the related fourth movement.

As conductor of the New York Philharmonic Orchestra at the time, Ives would have been well familiar with Mahler's music, and most likely, thus, to the buildup to the coda of the latter's *First Symphony*.)

- Burkholder further demonstrated Ives' remarkable abilities to link thematic elements between portions of disparate melodies; the two elements that Ives used together and separately have some relationships in common.[7] In fact, this is a technique that we will see elsewhere (for example: the *Human Faith Melody* in the *Concord Sonata;* see Chapter 9).
- The music returns to the opening theme material, (including the *Massa* quote); as it builds and develops, we hear a brief allusion to the third movement with a succession of strong, but lush descending chords, (modeled again on 'Down in de cornfield').
- After the brief quote from *Columbia, the Gem of the Ocean*[6] in the horns, there follows a dramatic reference to the 'neighbor-note' figure, now in the decidedly Mahleresque guise referenced earlier (listen for the sharply defined plucked notes in the second violins accompanying it to identify it), and the dramatic build-up conceived in a similar manner to the Viennese master. The music pauses, to continue directly into the next movement.

The allegro **Second Movement,** was again derived from now lost materials, in this case at least one overture *(In These United States)*. As the principal movement of the symphony, unsurprisingly it is the weightiest.

- The movement is ushered in brightly with a *first theme* built on a fragment based on *Wake Nicodemus*, developing until reaching an extended variant of *Bringing in the Sheaves*, utilized here simply as part of the evolving thematic material.
- The *second theme* follows in the form of Ives' version of a lyrical old college song, *Where, O Where Are the Verdant ('Peagreen') Freshmen!*, reflecting the bonds of his college

days still strong (and recent?) in his life. The speed is slower, the melody attractively set, and highly contrasted with the sprightliness of the first theme. The material from this second theme is further developed into new accompanying figuration that becomes dramatic and strident at times.

Ives' abilities to see developmental potential far beyond the limitations and constraints of these simple melodies and other materials is remarkable, as is his talent for finding parts of them that could be woven together with others in a working counterpoint. We see this clearly demonstrated towards the end of the *exposition*, and again up into the final section of the movement (the *coda*), where he included interactions of various unlikely components. Specifically, it might be possible to catch brief glimpses of the following:

- A brief snatch from Brahms' *Third Symphony*, consisting of a short descending chromatic line, culminating by rising like a question mark, underscored with rich chromatic harmony. The passage is also not unlike another to be found in Wagner's Overture to *Die Meistersinger von Nürnberg*, (specifically that leading into Wagner's second theme) - Ives' reference thus enshrining a figuration typically characteristic of late romantic music.
- Concluding the *development* is a luminous fragment of *When I Survey the Wondrous Cross* appearing in the low brass, and evolving much further from that point; technically, it is particularly suited for inclusion since it starts with the same rhythms (in augmentation) as *Pig Town Fling*, introduced in the first movement, and *Long, long ago* touched upon in the last. This illustrates not only some of the careful choices Ives made for extended musical development, but how he linked these across larger musical spans, too. The seamless evolution of *When I Survey the Wondrous Cross* is accompanied by references to earlier subsidiary material, still more sweeping lines in the ongoing string writing that

touches on it, and further coupled to the Brahms fragment used before (now heard in the woodwinds). When the passage reoccurs in the *coda*, the *Wondrous Cross* melody is anticipated several times; in its final grand incarnation leading to the conclusion of the movement the accompanying Brahms fragment is inverted (sounding upside-down).
- A possible further reference to Mahler's *First Symphony* (first movement) strongly comes to mind during the dramatic build leading into the *recapitulation;* the dramatic rhythmic percussion that offsets the rest of the orchestra seems to link the two works.
- In the *codetta*, another reference to Brahms' *First Symphony*, takes the form of dramatic rising triplets; these appear twice as fast in the coda. It is followed by an astounding fragmentary clip seemingly taken from the syncopated second theme of the *Scherzo* of Borodin's *Second Symphony;* this is built from supportive material from that theme, miraculously transformed to clearly indicate its roots. This fragment is strongly confirmed by its even more recognizable final appearance in the *coda*.

The **Third Movement**, originally the slow movement of Ives' *First Symphony*, and based on an organ prelude (#IV), was built in three-part form (ABA). The 'A' section is built primarily around material from two oft-quoted hymn tunes:

- Taking part of the melody of *Beulah Land* from its midpoint as the first part of the primary theme, Ives set it to it emerge from the introductory material.
- This material progresses into the second part of the theme, taken from towards the end of *America, the Beautiful*. The melodic contour that Ives shaped weaves together in seamless fashion both of these unlikely and seemingly ill-matched melodic entities. Again, the character of the music seems remarkably akin to that of Dvořák (the *New World Symphony*), its strong American accent being superficially quite compatible, though in this case born out of genuine experience. The thematic material is

rounded out by a short, sigh-like reference to Brahms' *First Symphony.*

- After a stirring reference to Wagner's *Tristan und Isolde* in a line also characterized by chromatically descending harmonies, a short transition follows. Consisting of material common to other parts of the movement, including another reference based on 'Down in de cornfield,' it is followed a little later by a beautiful restatement of Ives' composite melodic line by solo cello.

- Now having arrived at the 'B' section, numerous discreet references to the four-note, opening *Fate* motif of Beethoven's *Fifth Symphony* are at its core. The motif haunted Ives throughout his compositional career, and it reappears with remarkable regularity, tucked into many of his works with a regularity that denotes its significance to him. In this instance the keen listener might notice that he expanded the motif in most of its appearances by one note.

- Those notes also morph into a fragment of the *Missionary Chant,* first in the horns, then the upper strings, soon after we hear the first quiet Beethoven reference, followed by another supporting rearward glance to the hymn *Nettleton* in the winds. All of this combines to form a unified whole through Ives' careful choice of structurally similar quotes, to the degree that anyone unfamiliar with the materials would never guess their origins.

- Following the return of the primary material, a further transformed 'Down in de cornfield' fragment appears, building and extensively developed; it is accompanied by the *Fate* motif fragmented in the strings. The anticipation within the *first* movement of a passage in the horns at this point might be apparent to the listener.

- The *Massa* material is handed quietly to the strings, growing at times as it develops, to become central to the structure of the middle section of the movement. Significantly, we might also realize that the descending notes characterizing this theme actually have formed a great deal of

the transitional material in other parts of the movement, having been predominant between both of the primary themes.
- With a *recapitulation* to earlier material, ('A$_2$'), the movement works its way to a close, although it is here that Ives scored the *coda* curiously, almost exclusively for strings for a high point into the grand climax. Leonard Bernstein considered this "inexplicable orchestration" - which most certainly it is - but there can be no doubt that it serves its purpose of ending the movement essentially in the same manner that Ives began it, in thoroughly European balance, if not design. Ives was never a slave to convention, even when employing conventional language!
- Note the staggered restatements of the Beethoven *Fate* motif as the movement concludes, uniquely and movingly placed, and in a final transformed apparition.

The **Fourth Movement,** built out of material from another lost overture *(Town, Gown and State,* for band), opens with the same thematic material as the First Movement, along with a supporting woodwind fragment, based also on *Wake Nicodemus.*

- The strong Brahmsian flavor (similar to Brahms' *Fourth Symphony*) is an immediately striking characteristic.
- Becoming slightly faster, the violins and flutes begin a section based again on *Pig Town Fling,* further transformed, accompanied by *Columbia the Gem of the Ocean,* followed by a further reference from Brahms' *First Symphony* as it builds.
- As a short movement, it peaks and falls, serving more as a bridge than an independent musical statement. Along with one last oblique reference to 'Down in de cornfield,' the movement leads to the (allegro molto vivace) *Finale.* The final build to a last statement of the opening thematic material restates part of the first movement (characterized by punctuating, back-and-forth 'stinger' woodwind chords; these are now more pungent and telling than in

their initial appearance in the first movement). Again, it is highly suggestive of that similar dramatic moment of the first movement of Mahler's *First Symphony*, though in Ives' symphony it is also supported by the Brahms 'lower neighbor note' reference, as also in the first movement.

The **Fifth Movement Finale,** the surviving development of Ives' lost *The American Woods* Overture, bursts out of the starting gate with a direct reference to *Camptown Races*, coupled with subtle elements from *Turkey in the Straw*. The movement again is conceived within the tried-and-tested *Sonata Form* of the European masters.

- In the bassoon and celli, soon there are hints of *Columbia the Gem of the Ocean,* which will become the significant feature of the conclusion of the symphony, and most clearly representing the throwback to that part of the original youthful 1889 composition that Ives' had first incorporated into *The American Woods.*
- Note the militaristic piccolo and flute line in the *transition*, strongly reminiscent of a Revolutionary War or Civil War fife and drum; significantly, it is accompanied by snare drum and bass drum. The strings also play four short accompanying chords, rhythmically strongly suggestive of the *street beat* of a marching band.
- The extended *transition* complete, for his *second theme* Ives returned to *Pig Town Fling* crossed with elements of *Turkey in the Straw* in the violins, and a wonderful earthy and lyrical horn solo built out of the harmonic material; significantly, this is also related to the rhythm of *Joy to the World* in a kind of inverted apparition, a melodic fragment directly quoted later. It was here that Ives interjected a touch of *Long, Long Ago* in the flute and oboe, recognizing compatible common ground between themes, in this case both melodic and rhythmic elements.
- Soon comes an actual quote from *Joy to the World,* and its subsequent development, first appearing in the winds.

This melody seems to have been a particular favorite of the youthful Ives, as we find it, too in the slow movement of his *Fourth Symphony* (a reworked movement from his Yale days), and certainly it reflects the optimistic, happy exuberance of the symphony. Soon, we hear it, too, within the texture in the trombones as the section builds around the material before returning to the *recapitulation*.

- As would be expected, the *recapitulation* is laid out in similar fashion to the first part of the movement (the *exposition*), though it is developed far more extensively in order to prepare the listener for the grand conclusion that follows. Leonard Bernstein initiated a cut to the score for the first performance and subsequent recording (a superlatively good, if not an entirely authentically executed version) that shortens this dramatic section. This seems unfortunate, especially if other performers continue to follow this precedent.
- The *second theme* appears in the solo cello, and is a memorable point in the symphony before the final run up to the conclusion; we hear again strains of *Long, Long Ago*.
- The conclusion *(coda)* builds, with increasing references to *Columbia, the Gem of the Ocean*. Henry Cowell cited numerous other melodic fragments, including *Love's Old Sweet Song, The Fisherman's Reel, In the Sweet Bye and Bye,* even *Turkey in the Straw* (interwoven into the violin part), so this climax is a veritable free for all. Along with militaristic rhythmic percussion, and a quote of the *Reveille* 'bugle' call, everything finally leads to a full bore statement of *Columbia* - a rare instance when Ives chose to quote an entire original melody set in the full context of its tradition. This full hearing is, in fact, a hint of Ives' evolving *cumulative form*. (See Chapter 5.)
- With the grand entrance of *Columbia, the Gem of the Ocean* we have reached the part of the movement that dates apparently from far earlier times (1889), the year that Ives mentioned that it first appeared as a short piece his father's orchestra played.[8] Although not verified, the

sudden departure into something so straightforward and delightfully naïve is fully plausible.
- Then, after one last *Reveille* 'bugle' call comes the final shocking last chord - every note but the right one. This is the chord that apparently Ives added as a tribute to his father; remarkably, humorously, and in the most unlikely way, it works. Unfortunately, it has been used against him (see Appendix 1).

The *Second Symphony* again reveals a masterful young composer, who, at a young age had already produced a large-scale, substantive work that is as remarkably conceived, organized and written as anything we are likely to encounter from the period. Exceedingly confident in its manner, it holds its own against virtually any contemporary comparison. Ives' unique world, as expressed through this symphony, is immensely appealing, increasingly more revealed to the persistent listener. In context of what it portends, of course, Ives had barely begun to build his highway, but it is a telling indicator of what was to come, as well as being an insightful guide into the personality of the composer.

REFERENCES

1. 'Memos,' Charles E, Ives, edited by John Kirkpatrick, p. 106, *W. W. Norton & Co.*, New York, 1972, p. 51
2. 'Quotation and Paraphrase in Ives' Second Symphony,' Peter J. Burkholder, from 'Music at the Turn of Century: A 19th-Century Music Reader,' Joseph Kerman, *University of California Press,* Berkeley, 1990; *See also, 'All Made of Tunes,' Burkholder, *Yale University Press*, 2004 for detailed analyses of this concept relative to Ives' entire output
3. 'Charles Ives Reconsidered,' Gayle Sherwood Magee, *University of Illinois Press,* Chicago, Illinois, 2008, p. 175
4. 'Memos,' pp. 51-52
5. 'Quotation and Paraphrase in Ives' Second Symphony,' Burkholder, pp. 48 - 49

6. 'Four Symphonies by Charles Ives,' Bernard Herrmann, Modern Music 22 (May-June 19450, pp. 215 – 222
7. 'Quotation and Paraphrase in Ives' Second Symphony,' Burkholder, p. 36
8. 'Memos,' p. 52

CHAPTER 5

The Third Symphony ('The Camp Meeting')

A 19th Century camp (revival) meeting
{{PD-Art}}

The *Third Symphony* preserves something of the surviving late romantic symphonic model, in which Europe's shadow still is present to a greater or lesser degree, but marks a clear delineation in form and idiomatic language. Here, Ives had moved to a more personally relevant vehicle of expression, rather than impose his ideas onto traditional architecture, as in the *Second*

Symphony. Although the *Third Symphony* falls somewhere on middle ground, again it is dominated by early works, bit it is another step in a developing model. In utilizing American *hymns* exclusively, musically, it is of the new century, but emotionally of the last - an evolving structure in which optimistic youthful vigor suddenly is replaced by a yearning for things lost.

It is also a telling reflection of Ives' growing spiritual thinking; in this extraordinary and introverted masterpiece, it is clear that Ives not only had left his former life behind, he was far along in contemplating the direction of the spiritual journey yet to come, even though this is not one of his more radical compositions. Although the effects of transcendental thinking are present throughout the musical fabric, we can see the direct manifestation of Ives' philosophical break with it, as he could not put aside the deep roots of personal religious experience from his own upbringing. Thus, in maintaining his old religious values *while* immersing himself in his own surroundings and experiences, it was the very essence of his old time religious values fused in a hybrid with Emersonian ideals. Although this symphony retains a firm grip on recognizable musical parameters and tonalities (key centers), the philosophies that had already left their imprint would lead Ives rapidly to the advancement of new horizons of musical form.

The sound is authentic, unique, organic, emotionally tugging, and mostly significantly *no longer suggests anything European*. Ives had penned a reflection of his own experience and country, something at the time no other American had succeeding in doing. Indeed, it seems no one ever had tried, let alone contemplate such a thing.

Timeline

Considerable confusion exists regarding the date of composition for the *Third Symphony*. A preliminary version of the symphony, in complete sketch form, seems to date from no earlier than 1907, with a date given for a final ink score at 1912. However, there would seem to be little doubt that the basic tenets of the music had existed far earlier (during his church organist days) and continued to develop in Ives mind over the years. In what surely can be only the growth of much earlier material, sketches or scores of the symphony itself were most likely therefore the maturation of that process. The unusually wide range of development, and most especially the unconventional, even extraordinary rhythmic intricacies and complexities at times, as well as some truly forward-looking melodic and harmonic writing, seems a testament to the large interval of time between initial concept and final manifestation.

Magee theorized that the primary composition might date more accurately to 1910-1911, following the stillborn birth of the Ives' child and the loss of Harmony's (Ives' wife's) mother. In this sense, the symphony could be viewed as an elegy of sorts, and it certainly would explain its overall somber mood.[1] It should be mentioned, however, that Magee's new re-dated catalog of Ives' works has not met with universal acceptance amongst Ives researchers. The very essence of the musical language involved causes this writer, at least, to challenge whether Ives would regress to such a comparatively conservative musical style in the midst of what seems indisputably to be an accelerating period into the far more radical musical forms of his most creative years. Thus, the loss of his unborn child seems unlikely to have been behind this work, although what Magee detailed in the emotional impact of the Ives' sudden bereavement does makes sense in regard to what might have been a final push to put the symphony into a *finished* form.

Because we know that Ives also was engaged in writing countless compositions simultaneously, the material for many of them often originated in earlier works, to be freshly reworked into something new; this is transcendentalism within transcendentalism! Thus, it should not be seen as inconsistent that the final score of this symphony would emanate from a later time than far more experimental excursions, such as *The Unanswered Question* of c.1906-1908, for example. And certainly the symphony appears to represent a near endless succession of versions, editions, re-workings and re-scorings of previous materials.

Ives composed many organ works for incorporation into church services, having developed a very good sense of what was suitable for congregations, most of these works now being lost. The fact that they are missing in action should not be nearly the mystery, or mark of suspicion that some have supposed. It is more than likely that the young Ives conceived and wrote these organ works rapidly, and viewed them purely as 'music for hire,' never imagining they would have later value to him as they continued to grow in his mind. It is entirely conceivable that immediately after their use he paid little attention to them, and actively discarded most of them at the time, even more likely just leaving them on church shelves. If they still exist, perhaps they are locked up in an attic somewhere to reappear once again far in the future as an extraordinary time capsule.

In reusing his religious materials in new works, typically Ives would add dissonances and layers with each reworking. Saturation of new stimuli and increasing tolerances to them had resulted in his becoming accustomed to an ever-wider spectrum of sounds; therefore, the only remedy was to increase the stimuli! However, in most music he wrote for religious settings, Ives had not felt at liberty to utilize his more radical ideas, being acutely aware it was for occasions in which listeners "could not get out from under" it. Ives was very sensitive about inflicting anything potentially upsetting on conservative congregants who had no choice in the music they would hear.[2] Thus, he found most of his earlier church music insufficiently challenging for use in major compositions, although, in this instance - an expanded development of earlier material - it is a high point in his originality, creativity and artistic growth. Even if far from a radical work, it was written for small orchestra, as lovingly conceived and masterfully crafted as anything in his catalog. The *Third Symphony* is a striking example of Ives' great powers of invention and the expanding applications of his new methodology, in which varieties of coloration were limited only by the resources available.

In the same discussion in *Memos,* Ives also commented on its origins of the symphony, especially in regard to that curious place it occupies somewhere between traditional and experimental.

The Third Symphony ('The Camp Meeting')

It is likely a reflection, too, of the influence of his wife, Harmony, and her traditional religious values and probable favorite revivalist hymns. Ives, thus, set about writing a symphony built on six of them. Originally intending to write a four-movement work, he would change his mind after he had begun to lay it out, realizing that the three movements represented a perfect balance for the context of the materials. In it, he created a style that would have been both comfortable for moderately open-minded listeners, incorporating a certain degree of less than traditional sounds and ideas comfortably nestled amongst the more familiar. Precisely when the main content was conceived or scored, and the degree of compositional daring it flaunts - the musical language of the *Third Symphony* still is well in advance of most other music written even at the latest possible date, at home or abroad.

A link to the symphony: Fugue in Four Keys on 'The Shining Shore'

Although the specific works that Ives used for materials are now lost, we can trace his musical evolution within some other compositions of the time. The *Fugue in Four Keys on 'The Shining Shore,'* provides a direct link to the evolving style we hear in this symphony, not only in the specific musical content, but also in the idiomatic character and sound. The little fugue, only a few minutes in length, immediately tells its tale. First scored for string quartet, it would reappear in 1903 in a version for string orchestra, cornet and flute. Ives referenced such a fugue originating in 1896,[3] but it is unclear if this is the same one, though its placement in time seems about right. If so, the futurist leanings in it are remarkable; once again, this only illustrates how it is hard to determine clear timelines of development.

In sound, the fugue is eerily similarly to the language of the *Third Symphony*, despite the its use of multiple keys at once, and the specific aural relationships from note to note created by those various opposing keys (polytonal writing); as such, this methodology was not incorporated into the symphony. Ingeniously and significantly, however, in the first movement

Ives *simulated* the fugue's melodic and harmonic relationships by use of a flexible motion through transient key centers, as well as duplicating the 'walking' pattern of linear movement between the voices. Additionally, towards the end of the fugue, the cornet solo reminds us of the same yearning, nostalgic elements we associate with the finale of symphony, too, as do the peculiar harmonic entities Ives explored within that poetic last movement. These seem further to simulate many of the fugue's incidental harmonic implications resulting from the interactions of its multiple tonal centers, and as such, the timeline suddenly seems clearer.

It seems no coincidence, too, that the melody of the fugue's primary hymn bears some relationship the opening melody of the first movement of the *Third Symphony*. Though the main melodies of the first and third movements of the *Third Symphony* are built on *Azmon* - not the principal melody that is used in the fugue - these two hymns, *The Shining Shore* and *Azmon*, show a striking mutual resemblance. But the links to the symphony do not stop there. Remarkably, as the fugue proceeds, we hear strains of *Azmon!*

The music of the symphony

If far less radical in design than much of Ives' other music of the period, regardless, the *Third Symphony* was not cut from the same cloth as other late romantic music, as some have stated glibly! Indeed, it contains some offshoots of more radical ideas that hark of compositional developments already extant or still to come. However, the composer, usually characterized as a modern voice in search of the past, appears here as a cautiously modern progressive who has not yet *left* the past.

Although the polytonality of the *Fugue in Four Keys* can be felt in the movement's special harmonic relationships, more notable from a compositional standpoint is a new type of musical form that Ives found more suitable for his large musical structures. Ives realized that *sonata form,* long the established and presumptive architecture of all comparable symphonic works, was too

The Third Symphony ('The Camp Meeting')

constricting for him if he were to be allowed to escape the tidal pull from across the Atlantic. He jettisoned this traditional form in favor of developing one more flexible - Burkholder coined the term *cumulative form* - to a large degree present in many of his works from this moment on. The concept was simple: the primary thematic material is presented initially in fragmentary, even disguised forms, then developed and gradually revealed, only to be stated in its full recognizable form at the conclusion of the movement or work. Generally it shares with *sonata form* the use of two primary thematic components, and likely utilizes sub-themes, though there is no hard and fast rule to any of this.

Interestingly, Ives tried out something else new in this symphony, too. This was what he termed *shadow counterpoint*. Unique in all music, it consists of faintly audible, yet fairly complex subsidiary solo parts that 'shadow' the main lines, almost as if spun off the primary melodic line and existing behind it while adding elements outside the primary harmonic and rhythmic context. Ives regarded these parts as true 'shadow' entities, even in the visual sense, something akin to sunlight darting through the maze of leafy branches of a wooded area on a windy day. Because he floated the idea that they might represent vague realities of the subconscious, they appear to suggest other dimensions, or places in time and space - in fact, they are another incarnation of spatial writing, whereby the 'shadow' exists in another plane. Indeed, these parts are best played in other locations, either off-stage or well separated into the background, and yet an indication that the process of reaching for dimensions outside the merely familiar was part of his thinking process.

Although they were possibly afterthoughts, since he eliminated them from the earlier version for publication, Ives had doubts about including the shadow parts until many years later, after which he intended to restore them, but never did. Fortunately his wishes have been carried out and are present in the 1990 Associated Press edition. These parts add an interesting twist in the sound of the now familiar work (again in reference towards awareness of the spatial element); if played correctly, their effect is to inject subtly poignant nuances from outside the primary sonic dimension, yet they do nothing to alter the fundamental character of the music itself. That the concept works perfectly is another testament to Ives' original voice and vision; within otherwise fundamentally tonal music it is hard to find anything that resembles it sonically in any way. Stylistically, if played with too much definition and forward projection, shadow counterpoint sounds just plain wrong, almost as if the performers are mistaken, or even lost; 'shadow' thus is the operative word. So playing these mysterious-sounding and extraordinary parts just like any other runs contrary to Ives' intent, and results from a lack of understanding their purpose and role.

Today, one is just as likely to hear the symphony with or without these added parts, depending upon the performance edition; the comparison is enlightening, but one would be wise not to judge the music itself harshly should the shadow parts be played in a manner that gets in the way from undue prominence or definition.

Comparisons with other symphonies of the period

Rhythmically and harmonically, characteristics of the *Third Symphony* seem largely absent in many other contemporary works of the time, most of which were post-romantic. Only to a degree does this describe the *Third Symphony*. Ives' very listenable, lovely and charming work, however, is so deceptive that it might cause one to miss its inherent modernity. Overall, though, the symphony bridges the widening chasm between Ives' earlier life and his quest for the stars, as well as being evidence of a long evolving musical process. However, in language, musically and spiritually, it breaks substantially from that of the *Second Symphony*, stylistically landing squarely between it and all that was to follow.

More significant for us, though, aside from the showcasing of Ives' newly developed *cumulative form* and *shadow counterpoint,* it reveals his evolving genius for incorporating, developing and infinitely varying the melodic and rhythmic components, his strong

The Third Symphony ('The Camp Meeting')

sense of structural coherence, as well as his ability effectively to express subtle and personal emotions; then there is the remarkable lack of traditional constraint exhibited by the infinitely varying cadence and flexible counterbalance. Caught in between the old and the new, it expresses something long past through a means that looks ahead, even as it acts as a window into Ives himself.

One cannot fail to be struck, too, by the distinctive, ruggedly 'American pioneer' character, as much due to Ives' departures from the well-worn European footpaths as it is to its basic content. In this respect, we must regard the symphony as one of the most important 'spring board' works, since its foundations lead to the future even if they have not yet left the past. Striking to the listener, too, might be the many musical hallmarks that so personify this composer - the proud, yet profoundly present commentary that speaks to us across time, the strong faith-based religious echoes we feel so clearly from deep within 19th Century America, and the stirring sense of a spirited traditional community Ives knew firsthand, reawakened from its distant slumber. However, perhaps the greatest significance, despite its otherwise earthbound introversion, is the elevated spiritual awareness that pervaded the maturing composer's thoughts throughout - somewhere between transcendentalism and traditional religion - as he began to reach for his eternal place at the end of the celestial road that beckoned him.

Listeners' guide

In the **First Movement,** *(Old Folks Gatherin'),* instead of stating first a *primary theme,* soon followed by a contrasting *second theme* (as found in standard *sonata form),* the movement is dominated by just one theme, the hymn tune *Azmon.* Two other themes are featured also, *Woodworth,* and *Erie,* although they never assume the significance of *Azmon.* Remarkably, throughout the symphony, the character of all of the themes is rendered in a completely new light; the uninitiated might miss the references entirely, especially since we do not hear the sub-themes in their complete and original forms. And true to the concept of cumulative form, even *Azmon* is not heard essentially complete until movement's end.

- The symphony opens in a lyrical manner, tonally restless and built vaguely on *Azmon* in the violins; (this appears similarly again in the *finale,* but is used contrastingly and differently configured.) Clear fragments of the middle of the melody set the tone of the movement.
- Soon after the *Azmon* material has been stated (significantly, in a *fugal-type* entrance), the music develops substantially and continues to build around it, while different instruments take fragments of the melody, and the music becomes increasingly active.
- Reaching a turning point, the announcement of the second theme, *Woodworth (Just as I am),* is introduced in the horns in a similar manner to the second theme in sonata form. However, Ives did not accord his second theme equivalent time or importance here.
- Soon, further *Azmon* material returns, dramatically building in the full orchestra (with a gentle reference again to *Woodworth* in the horns), and leads to a brief hold - identifiable by an actual short silence.
- A complete mood change follows, with material built from *Azmon* accompanying *Erie (What a Friend We Have in Jesus)* in the solo oboe, answered by a solo flute, which develops the material well beyond the original confines of the melody. Moments of unusual rhythmic accompaniment, mostly in the strings, suggest more than one simultaneous speed.
- The section concludes in dialog across the orchestra, until the appearance of a more lively section based on the *accompaniment* to the horns' earlier statement of *Woodworth.*
- This last reference to the second theme leads into a further, brief and lively reference to *Azmon* in the horns,

echoed by the strings, heading into an optimistic, joyous development of it throughout the orchestra, and culminating in an almost ecstatic high point. The music falls off and slows down in an almost prayerful manner.

- Here, Ives saved the loveliest moment of all for the most complete statement of *Azmon* in the violins, fulfilling the purpose and design of his cumulative form. It is accompanied by a rapturous variant by the solo flute of *Erie*, the movement then drawing to a peaceful close. The shadow counterpoint is strikingly effective here, illustrating the principle perfectly.

For the **Second Movement**, *(Children's Day, or Young Folks Meeting)*, Ives chose lively, spirited musical material to suggest happy playfulness. As a reflection of innocent simplicity, Ives chose to keep the structure itself simpler than that of the preceding movement. However, the rhythmic complexities and fast-changing harmonic entities more than engage the ear, and tell us that this is no mere extension of 19th Century romanticism. Clearly Ives found a happy compromise between the old and the new, without abandoning the accessibility of the music's thematic origins. Utilizing some of the developmental principles of cumulative form, it never provides full statements of it, or any of the melodies employed, however.

- Largely built on the opening bars of *There is a Fountain Filled with Blood,* and later, *Happy Land (Far, far Away)* Ives built vigorous motion in the lower strings. Along the way, a fragment of material, derived from *What a Friend We Have in Jesus,* and later used with the second 'theme' of the movement serves to bond the two sections together.
- After a hold and crescendo, the announcement of the second 'theme' takes place in the woodwinds. Built on the latter part of *Happy Land,* the material is developed immediately, variously interspersed or accompanied by a brief descending figure derived from *What a Friend We Have in Jesus* and joined to a fragment of *There's Music in*

the Air. We can recognize these elements as smooth and linear, contrasting with the jaunty rhythmic character of *Happy Land*.
- The music continues to build dynamically, the jaunty rhythms giving way to a return of material based on *There is a Fountain Filled with Blood*, set against a seemingly unlikely, extended quote from *Naomi* in the flute.
- A remarkable final part to the movement gyrates through numerous keys, with the descending lines in the lower instruments echoing, *There's music in the Air*.
- The movement concludes with the only extended continuation of the *Happy Land* fragment, the cumulative concept in evidence, if not quite materializing.

The Third Movement *(Communion)* is built cumulatively from diffuse fragments of the same two primary hymns used in the First Movement. The music is intricately woven together, featuring many diametrically opposite moving lines, as well as unconventional harmonies and conflicting rhythms, to reveal a developing modernity over the period that Ives wrote the symphony. Apparently he was becoming more comfortable introducing advanced elements into the more traditional contexts of his earlier church music. The mood of this movement has an almost tragic quality to it that seems to go well beyond the nostalgic air that pervades the entire symphony. It seems we *can* hear the Ives' bereavement, and possibly this played a greater role in this movement's final form than it did the previous two.

- The first incarnations of the primary material are less directly stated than in the first movement, with the references to *Woodworth (Just as I am)* appearing most diffusely, first (in the cellos) and joined immediately in the higher strings *canonically* (one voice after another - not unlike fugal entrances). A literal reference from the middle of *Azmon* (the descending figure of 'thirds:' notes 1-1/2 or 2 steps apart) appears a little later after an ingeniously devised variant of the first part of the melody.

The Third Symphony ('The Camp Meeting')

- Soon after reaching a high point, the *Azmon* material is taken up again by the first violins, accompanied by a rapidly moving part in the violas.
- This leads to a strong restatement of the reference to *Woodworth* in dialog between the strings and horns, albeit somewhat modified as it progresses.
- A high point that is developed from this material tells us that the conclusion is near, and is accompanied by strong ascending movement in the lower voices. This section seems even more heart wrenching in character than any part preceding it; it is dense in texture, as well as being harmonically transient. This is a pivotal moment; surely it comes close to expressing the 'fervor' of the camp meeting congregants and so personally meaningful to Ives. After the high point the music melts away into a wonderful moment of nostalgic, almost tearful tones in the flutes.
- Moving towards the end of the symphony, Ives placed both primary themes together, with *Azmon* in the violins preceding a bar of *Woodworth* in the flute. Again, it is not a literal quotation of the former, but rather a development of it. As it works its way through, this ingenious setting of *Woodworth* appears to morph into a fragment of *Silent Night*. However, what we really are hearing is the concluding part of the original *Woodworth* melody. Regardless of Ives' possible intentions (to suggest *Silent Night?*), it is an intensely moving moment. The music seems suspended in space and time.
- In fragmented fashion, the strings lead us out of the movement, continuing *Woodworth*, and even further *Silent Night* references, to be joined briefly by what were intended as barely audible distant church bells, in another variant of shadow counterpoint. As the music wafts out into the night in a prayerful cadence, without ever quite completing the hymn melody, this is one of the most profound moments in all of Ives' works, and fully typical of his style.

The Significance of the Third Symphony

Few works provide a better insight into Charles Ives than the *Third Symphony*. Although its technical language barely hints at his final destiny, it demonstrates superlative command of the medium, the small orchestra allowing an intimate glimpse into his inner thoughts without the physical bombast that larger scale works impart, by default. One would have presumed this wonderful little symphony would be performed with regularity; the fact that it is not is as perplexing as it is a sad reflection on the commercial domination of the arts today, where anything that is not already well trodden and familiar remains challenged to succeed at the box office. Indeed, Ives' worst premonitions about where society was going have not been allayed.

REFERENCES

1. 'Charles Ives Reconsidered,' Gayle Sherwood Magee, *University of Illinois Press*, Chicago, Illinois, 2008, pp. 97-99
2. 'Memos', Charles E, Ives, edited by John Kirkpatrick, p. 106, *W. W. Norton & Co.*, New York, 1972, pp. 128-12
3. Ibid., p. 38

CHAPTER 6

The experimental years

Music in space and time

Just as Ives had not sought to write nationalistic music, he had not set out to write 'modern' music for its own sake either. Having found that being confined to existing musical language made it possible to express neither his view of the world nor his creative philosophies, trying to accommodate them in existing methodologies had only resulted in their obliteration. Furthermore, attempting to perpetuate what had long been the language of others would mean that music as an art form would stand still, and effectively, it would die, lost in the interest of soothing undemanding listeners. Thus, Ives would not compromise between being true to himself, and pleasing audiences who wished to hear only what fell within their comfort zone. Most significantly, though, there was nothing existing within the musical language of the day that was capable of touching the celestial destinations that increasingly were entering his consciousness and propelling him towards them.

It is fair to say that Ives held that musical evolution in general had been compromised, with most composers striving to find acceptance rather than face rejection and starvation; in America one could not combine making a living in music with breaking new ground. Thus, by allowing himself to be guided by his vision instead of expedience, the result was that his music became 'modern.' It was his uncompromising convictions that allowed him to continue to brush off the increasing assaults he would endure from listeners, critics, other musicians, and amazingly, even some of his closest friends and family members. He learned to be comfortable within himself; not chasing anyone's approval, he realized that receiving it would make his music neither good nor bad.

Despite some predictive flashes from a few similarly lone creative figures of the period, and the efforts by some revisionists to deny him the legitimacy of his priority in 20th Century music, again, it needs to be emphasized that Ives indeed was the first truly avant-garde composer - and by more than a few years. By the end of the new century's first decade Ives had tried, formulated and used effectively and extensively most major 20th Century techniques in his experiments. This was while musical culture still was dominated by the late 19th Century European tradition, as defined by Dvořák and Brahms.[1] Furthermore, Ives differed from his later European counterparts, not only in this early use of such innovations, but also by his approach of not actively seeking to replace one system of musical expression with another: instead, Ives sought to expand the musical vocabulary.

Regretfully, Ives' discoveries and developments influenced and affected no one; he was completely disinterested in announcing them to the musical world, being at ease with his own quiet search for new ways to lead him closer to his personal goals. Perhaps he rationalized that if his music had any worth eventually it would be played. Thus he had no need for outside confirmation of the rightness of what he had done. If not, he could live with an indefinite lack of acceptance, or being consigned to irrelevance.

Early experiments

As a youngster, Ives would try to duplicate the 'street beat' of his father's band on the piano, with a rhythmically divided tone cluster consisting of low, close intervals, one hand playing slightly ahead of the other. His father had done nothing to discourage such curiosity of unconventional note combinations. (We can hear this recreated in the 1914 song, *General William Booth Enters into Heaven.*) We know, too, that Ives' early experimentation pitted different tonal centers (polytonality) together, in which the settings in different keys of otherwise conventional melodic lines resulted in new harmonic consequences. As early as 1891, Ives had delved into this type of experimentation in portions of his youthful *Variations on America*, confirming George Ives' influence. Demonstrating, too, that indeed Ives knew how to do things the 'right' way, according to his father's strong admonition, this iconic little work also shows an early comfort with the unconventional. We have already seen a later example of such polytonality in the little *Fugue in Four Keys on The Shining Shore*, detailed in Chapter 5. We can find early examples of Charles' polytonal exercises, too, in his father's copybook.

Thus, even before his time at Yale, Ives had questioned the orthodoxy of accepted protocols of tonality. Even more notably, the remarkable *Psalm 67* demonstrates what the future would hold, a work that he initiated also under the guidance of his father, apparently completing it sometime in his last year at Yale. Once again, we can see that he was anything but settled on Parker's traditional approach, having far from abandoned more radical ideas while under his tutelage, even as he flirted with that predominantly European musical path. As both father and son had been intrigued by the effect of the conflicting sonorities, Ives would try to simulate these in his music, especially in recreating the more interesting harmonies that had resulted from chance alignments.

The experimental timeline

After graduating from Yale, Ives would explore melodic and harmonic combinations previously unknown in conventional tonality, building structures from intervals other than found in normal usage. Gradually, he grew bolder, increasing the number and blend of different elements to produce some startling new sounds. His harmonic experiments in multiple simultaneous keys thus concern the organization of sounds within vertical *space* rather than within horizontal *time;* melodic writing concerns both (see below).

Ives' more organized experiments along these lines *(vertical space)* began in earnest at the time of his appointment as organist and choir director at Bloomfield, New York, and even more following his more prestigious appointment at the Central Presbyterian Church in Manhattan (1900 to 1902). His experimental works sound ultra-modern in their tonality, but rhythmically, their logic and musical apportionment remain largely intact, reflecting other music of the time. Many of these works were for organ and choir, even exclusively for organ. Although many of the more radical sounding compositions were unlikely to have been performed in the conservative environment of church services - especially in light of Ives' own sensitivities toward inflicting such sounds on captive audiences[2] - it is entirely reasonable to assume that he would have taken every opportunity to elicit the cooperation of church musicians to try them out. Surely he would have wanted to know how these new ideas worked in practice. It is significant that at this point of time it is hard to find remotely comparable polytonality by any other figure.

After Ives' abandonment of music as a career, the shortage of large-scale or finished works during the four-year period between 1902 and 1906 would suggest that he refocused his life for a time around his business interests. But musical innovation was never far from his thoughts. It was at about this same time that he would see the potential of structured forms in *rhythm*; this aspect of music, including melody, thus is related to ongoing processes *(horizontal **time**)*. Ives recognized that multiple independent divisions and cyclic/sequential entities could be made to interact even with *other* simultaneous entities in new and novel ways. This experimentation included dividing known units of time (pulse) by seemingly unrelated parallel mathematical formulae, such as divisions of 3, 5, & 7 together, effectively creating multiple speeds. Further, *regularly* divided pulse could be expanded with *irregular* divisions, along with the many potential interactive combinations of harmony and melody. As always, both types of experimentation frequently can be tied to real life phenomena that Ives had known. He just happened to be highly attuned to the potential they offered.

Benefiting from run-throughs of experimental works with friends, Ives had a chance to judge the effectiveness of his innovations in real time. By securing readings of many of these early experiments and 'inflicting' them on fellow residents, Ives was able to test the waters by portraying them as jokes or party tricks. During his ten-year tenure living at 'Poverty Flat' (the apartment housing in New York in which newly employed Yale graduates often resided - 'bachelor pads') he had a captive audience, and thus could gain their reaction, and even better, their participation. Thus, since we already know that he had more opportunity to hear his music than legend has passed down, his new methods became second nature long before he incorporated them into large-scale compositions. Although the shortage of large-scale finished works during this period is striking, Ives' experiments flourished while he continued to compose songs, and other works now scattered and lost, together with the beginnings and sketches of many others. Ideas were formulating in his head for future works, and for the reuse of existing materials he had written previously for organ. Even taking into consideration the type of musical processes that were so natural to him, and confirmed by his numerous novel excursions into experimentation during this time, perhaps even Ives still had no inkling of the explosion in his creativity that was about to take place, or the magnitude of its reach.

Late, too, in this period of apparent compositional semi-hibernation, Ives' business prospects began to feel the pinch, as the scandal of 1905 in the life insurance industry closed in around all him, ultimately resulting in the demise in 1906 of the Raymond Agency where he worked. For a time, he must have felt that the ensuing fiasco and investigation would embroil him too. This stressful period affected his health badly, the first of his many well-known incidents having occurred in 1905, to be followed by another even worse scare in 1906. Without the benefit of modern diagnoses, it is hard to be specific about the nature of his illness, all manner of fanciful, even absurd speculation having been proposed over the years, Magee's notwithstanding,[3] but it was sufficient to sideline a young man of only 32 years of age. Having been sent to a Virginia health center to recuperate, Ives began to feel stronger physically and mentally, and his former optimism began to return. However, now he became engaged on what appears to have been a near-frenzied search for increasingly better means of reflecting his evolving vision.

With new business prospects beckoning in the aftermath of the insurance industry debacle, Ives formed a partnership with his old colleague (Julian Myrick, his associate from his former company) to create a new agency, Ives & Co., opening its doors in 1907 at the beginning of the year. This new venture was short lived, however, because its parent company, Washington Life, would be absorbed into Pittsburgh Life and Trust, a company that had no New York agencies. However, the formation of another new venture with Myrick at the beginning of 1909 returned the pair to the Mutual Insurance Co. fold. The company of Ives & Myrick would evolve to become the dominant life insurance agency in the country and the key to both partners' considerable financial successes, both partners having unique talents and roles within it.

This encapsulated the key to Ives' life identity; having already connected transcendental philosophy to music, it would be connected now also to business! Redefining its structure, again using mathematics, Ives matched clients' likely future needs with specific formulae, melding 'scientific' principles of sound business practice with community responsibility. Providing long-term security for families, while ensuring that their provider could perpetuate itself indefinitely, Ives devised a 'socially aware' actuarial system. The essence of Ives' tables remains in existence to this day, his revolutionary approach making him perhaps the most significant player in the re-emergence of the life insurance industry, and causing a quantum shift in the way it functions to this day.

Suddenly, a new spark had been ignited, and Ives' musical experiments increased and expanded to include ever more radical and innovative ideas. His spare time composing accelerated with increasing energy, and substantial works began to emerge. Ives must have known all too well the growing commitment to two full-time occupations would impel him to spend all of his time working, one way or the other, although he probably reasoned he could balance everything together. If the creative energy required to build his new agency had fueled his musical activity and outlook, probably he never considered the long-term consequences and toll it would take, physically, socially, and even emotionally. It was not as if he had not experienced the warning signs.

Regardless, further innovative principles were hatched in these years, especially, as Philip Lambert so artfully illustrated in his 1997 book, *(The Music of Charles Ives)*, Ives' usage of cyclical rhythmic, harmonic and melodic elements in his music.[4] By manipulating and transforming textures, or entering and leaving them according to prescribed waves or series, Ives' new systemized methodology provided a rich new creative foothold for his most expansive ideas. The connection with the grand design of the universe is easy to see - just as stars orbit their galactic cores, and planets orbit stars - consciously or not, it was hardly surprising that Ives would be drawn to cosmic order. In the grand design of his ultimate musical destination, the *Universe Symphony,* this very element would be fundamental to it throughout its length, as *The Pulse of the Cosmos.* (See Chapters 11 - 13; Appendix 2.)

Experimental miniatures

A demonstration of rhythmic waveforms may be heard in the miniature experimental work, *From the Steeples and the Mountains* of 1901, (though possibly written as late as 1906); one of the earliest such examples, potentially it dates thus to <u>before</u> *The Celestial Country*. Amazingly, this little work is also striking for its use of multiple keys and rhythmic divisions, but *also* cycles - characteristics of Ives' later music, even hinting at some of the sounds of the *Universe Symphony*, some 15-plus years later. The overall waveform is large at about 3-1/2 minutes, and evolves through multiple sub-cycles built upon the simple peeling of church bells (in different keys and speeds) with four separate sets of bells and two pianos; a trumpet and trombone expound upon a canonic fragment from *Taps* - or is it *Columbia, the Gem of the Ocean*?

The miniature for a small instrumental group, *Scherzo: All the Way Around and Back*, c.1907, illustrates a large cycle in a near-perfect palindrome. About a baseball game in which the base runner has to return from 3rd. to 1st. after a foul, the scherzo's up-and-down waveform occupies some 50 seconds, or so, (aside from its noisy conclusion), and it seems we hear a less than reflective derivative of *Taps* once again in the bugle.

Ives found he could expand his cyclical concepts in multiple ways according to orderly principles, even in the continuous evolution of harmonic and melodic structures. This could cause their formulae and intensities to function variously in relative proportion, or new harmonic progressions to be realized within a new systematic context. Further sub-cycles within the whole could compound these interactions in new and novel ways, with unconventional melodic lines often offset against opposing rhythmic elements.

Ives' little tone poem, *The Pond* (1906) reveals another novel idea: as an early example of 'spatial' writing (see later), the undulating impressionistic patterns and sustained harmonies paint a visually serene outdoor setting. If the vast landscapes that often had inspired him could be limitless and open, why not musical landscapes, too? Ives referred to it as an *"echo piece,"* which indeed it is, using a solo trumpet to introduce an aural effect that attempted to recreate his father's experiments playing an instrument over a body of water.[5] In a scene presumably cast at night, at the conclusion the sound of a lone piccolo floats across the pond through the mists, again with a fragment of *Taps* in the piccolo. With that brief reference to something Ives would have heard his father play on many occasions, and fearing that he might become drawn into the insurance crisis and scandal, perhaps he was yearning for his father's reassuring presence. Certainly, the depiction of something he had witnessed his father do fits the analogy. However, Feder considered that Ives had a darker emotion on his mind: early death.[6] This analysis is quite possible, of course, maybe even likely, especially considering the date of the work and Ives' health concerns at the time.

The Pond, Central Park, New York
Image courtesy Ed Yourdon

The Gong on the Hook and Ladder of 1905 (?) is another of Ives' experiments with a primary emphasis on rhythmic interaction, as well as revealing his innate sense of humor. In trying to depict a local small town parade - in this instance that of the volunteer fire department - it emulates their struggle with heavy equipment in the slow march through town. Although the amateur musicians' band depicted was barely able to keep an even beat (illustrated musically by the irregular rhythmic notation), nor was able to play in tune (simulated by Ives' carefully alternating pitch alignments), the up-and-down terrain would cause the firemen unintentionally to vary their pace, as the efforts to keep the engine gong ringing steadily often resulted in it being out of step with the music. In order to capture the humor of the situation, almost funnier as the company went downhill than uphill, Ives applied his newly evolving methods to build complex rhythms and harmonies into patterns that only came together every so often.

To do this required incorporating the displacement and combinations of rhythms to mimic natural phenomena, thinking on multiple levels and in different speeds, while exploring new melodic and harmonic structures as well as unlikely instrumental combinations. This demonstrates once again that Ives' ideas frequently stemmed from real life situations of his own experience, inspired by randomly or naturally created sounds, yet represented musically, sometimes aleatorically, by the most highly organized and controlled means outside commonly ordained musical practices of the time. In this case, the apparent wild, musical chaos has been artfully worked out, revealing Ives, the consummate craftsman and storyteller.

19th Century fire truck
{{PD-Art}}

Ives' famous little ragtime *Scherzo: Over the Pavements*, of 1909, scored for small chamber orchestral ensemble, is a further demonstration of the rapid development of multi-compartmented ideas; here he combined many rhythmic and harmonic entities in apparently uncoordinated patterns, though unsurprisingly, cyclical ratios play a formative role in both the partitioned elements and chord structures. In this instance, the piece was inspired by the random patter of horse and foot traffic on the street below. Remarkably, Ives also captured the sonic essence that we equate with Stravinsky's future works, from the ascending and descending close-note chords in the piano (*Petrouchka*, 1911), to the bright and clipped *neoclassical* rhythms (*L'Histoire du Soldat*, 1918). The rhythmic and harmonic complexity mind-boggling, the sound utterly appealing and effective, Ives might well have been conducting what was only an experiment, but the result is high art.

First Set for Chamber Orchestra

As Ives continued to immerse himself in more musical experiments - and though many were undertaken only to test his ideas - he came to recognize that a remarkable number of them stood up well as little works in their own right. Subsequently, later he would begin to group some of these pieces together according to features they had in common, such as in the *First Set for Chamber Orchestra* of 1907 – 1913. This is an assembly of six of these experiments; far from being merely exercises detached from any real world context, Ives had incorporated a wide range of what would have been contradictory, even raucously vernacular elements into them in which his friends could participate.

- *The See'r*, a lively scherzo, like many pieces later adapted into a song, opens the set in a dissonant ragtime idiom, with jazzy rhythms almost cast further within a neoclassical style. Here, certain cyclical components and augmented harmonies are built into a complex structure of intricately syncopated and opposing lines that compliment each other by their shared gravity towards a common rhythmic pulse.

- *A Lecture* is a highly amusing representation of a college memory. Multiple rhythmic elements, even actual chatter (!), combine to suggest a college classroom being called to order by the professor (a cornet). Thus, with the lecture proceeding, complex monotone rhythmic articulations in compounding sequences represent the students vigorously jotting down notes; in this case, the professor's disjoined melodic line combined with the students' independent linear rhythms are contrasted. (The wide leaps of the cornet line were the direct result of one of George Ives' piano lesson exercises: playing fast chromatic scales, each note in a different octave. Ives found the effect appealing as he grew accustomed to it, taking this idea into other works through to the *Universe Symphony.*) Adding other instruments into the fray, the lecture concludes with a summation of all the components and the victorious dismissal by the professor!

- *The Ruined River,* adapted much later (in 1921) from materials used in his experimental song, *The New River* of 1911, reveals Ives' political leanings; throwing in a brief reference to *Ta-ra-ra Boom-de-ay!,* the words from it and another version of the same song bemoan the dangers of machines, oppressive working conditions, and the age of entertainment. Aside from the chromatically descending burst in the upper lines at the outset, it is built largely out of whole step movements, the melodic line contrasting the vigorous, strongly figurative accompaniment (frequently an octave and a step apart), and some pivotal cyclical elements. Before the final rush to what resembles a car horn, a fanfare-like back-and-forth figure outlines the primary line, in the song version featuring the words, *"killed is the blare of the hunting horn."*

- Compositionally a late entrant into the set, *Like a Sick Eagle,* of 1913 is a graphic musical representation of

Keats' poem about a once majestic bird in its death throes. Believed triggered by Ives' sad recollections of Harmony's miscarriage in 1909, it features another harmonic experiment within a highly artistic context - that of quarter-tones amongst the sliding chromatic intervals in the violins - although Ives was not first to incorporate these into western music (such techniques having been occasionally explored by composers centuries before), Ives was likely the first composer to utilize quarter-tones in modern times. This movement also exists as a song; for more detailed analysis, see Chapter 8.

- *Calcium Light Night* c. 1907, often stands on its own, having started its life as a form of parody' that Ives listed amongst his 'Cartoons or Take-Offs.' Written again partly for the amusement of his friends, it gave Ives the opportunity to try out a large palindrome format. Programmatic in content, it was supposed to represent the sounds of students in a nighttime Yale parade. The piece features a large overall cycle of multiple elements: rhythmic, harmonic and melodic, superimposed on the drumming and tightly knit chords in the piano (four hands) according to other carefully determined sub-cycles. Manipulating variants of the fraternity tunes, *Psi Upsilon Marching Song*, against *A Band of Brothers in DKE*, and together with elements of *Few Days, Jolly Dogs, Marching through Georgia*, and *Tramp, Tramp, Tramp*, as the marchers approach and pass, the musical components reverse and drop out one by one in reverse order, making a 2-½ minute cycle in all. This little work was assembled by Henry Cowell in 1936 from disordered sketches and copious directions by Ives himself; Ives considered that the result fully represented his intentions.

- *When the Moon Is On the Wave,* (another celestial reference!) might date to as early as 1907, and is built on just two basic entities. First, a flowing arpeggiated piano part, (broken chordal lines in wave-like motion), is later joined by the flute in opposing motion. Second, in wave-like contours, a melody is initially divided between violins and cornet in staggered (canonic) entrances one step short of an octave apart. However, these lines bear little relation to the tonality of the accompaniment, the violin part being centered a half step lower. As the cornet takes the lead towards a peak, the motion ceases, all forces briefly come together, rhythmically and harmonically stepping up to the key of the piano accompaniment; with a shimmering chord hanging over the now-emboldened cornet, the violins join the final reflection of primary elements.

Paving the road to the stars

The successful results of this period would lead to the incorporation of many of them into more substantive, larger-scale works, such as the *Overture and March to 1776* (1903), and the *Country Band March* (1905). Both of these compositions would show up again later still, further developed together into the second movement *(Putnam's Camp)* of the important *First Orchestral Set*, better known as *Three Places in New England*. The set dates from around 1914 in its evolved form. In these, Ives freely mixed and matched compounded rhythmic elements to imitate the clash of different marching bands interacting acoustically, recalling a specific event in his and his father's past. It is worth briefly referencing the controversies long surrounding the dating of *Putnam's Camp,* substantively dealt with in Appendix 1 and effectively closing the matter. With the lineage clearly demonstrated to belong to earlier material, it becomes immediately apparent that *Putnam's Camp* was only the last stop along an extremely modern road already largely paved.

Thus, the experience Ives had gained of combining traditionally opposite multiple elements would become central to advanced compositions that featured parallel entities, this aspect having first been initiated, of course, by the enthusiastic fascination his father had shown in chance auditory phenomena. Together, within just a few years the combination of Ives' remarkable musical imagination and technical command, his ability to absorb his surroundings within musical contexts, together with the many other influences and philosophies central to his life, finally would provide the means, wide enough in scope and freedom to fulfill his destiny.

Because Ives merely utilized whatever technique suited the purpose in hand, no specific system dictated which ones we can expect to hear. Although his large-scale works continued to feature certain conventional elements - even at the far end of his output - they increasingly featured multiple newfound techniques coexisting in parallel. However, it is significant to note that many of the larger works composed during Ives' experimental period reveal the beginnings of the search for things that we do not find much in evidence before. As an increasing quest for meaning involved a type of spirituality that does not equate exactly with traditional religious expression, we can connect it partially to transcendental philosophies. Applying them to all that he would do in life, this search for personal meaning coincided, of course, with some truly remarkable music. If he had not yet cast off his bonds to Earth, at least he was looking skywards.

Two substantial works from this period have become standard repertoire. Originally Ives conceived them to be grouped with others, but eventually, recognizing certain features in common to both, only *The Unanswered Question (A Contemplation of a Serious Matter)* and *Central Park in the Dark (A Contemplation of Nothing Serious)* would be put together as *Two Contemplations.* However, whatever Ives' intentions, these two works are usually performed separately! An obvious experimental characteristic common to both was really an evolution of the antiphonal concept tried in many forms over musical history; another was the actual notation of multiple independent speeds, rather than simulating them in notation by complex divisions of a common meter.

Both works featured antiphonal writing, though far from new, it was rare in modern times. Centuries before, individual choirs of regal-sounding brass instruments were used by Giovani

Gabrielli (the Venetian composer of the reformation) on opposite sides of the grand and deeply religious setting of the Patriarchal Cathedral Basilica of Saint Mark in Venice. The wide-open sonorities in his music have long been considered amongst the most effective demonstrations in Western music of instrumental antiphonal writing. Placed in distinctly separated locations as intended, the 'spatial' effect is awe-inspiring. Handel tried the concept in some of his more festive works; the *Royal Fireworks Music* was reputed to have used widely separated forces across the River Thames. Ives would develop the idea further, creating not just separate, but entirely unrelated musical entities, as if they were suspended in different places in space and time. Mahler's work in this vein also is well known (see Chapter 1, *'Innovations and Nostalgia: Ives, Mahler, and the Origins of Modernism,'* by Leon Botstein), but the relationships between the separate forces remain linked from a musical standpoint; Ives' work linked them only emotionally. Their extreme contrast ensured the entities hardly could be more separate, being cast in different speeds, tonalities and character - indeed, in parallel realities.

The Unanswered Question (a Cosmic Landscape)

Of these two spatial compositions, *The Unanswered Question*, was perhaps Ives' first truly otherworldly spiritual work. Deceptively simple, it was contained within an experimental mode that projected the composer looking to a far away place across great expanse and distance, lost in deep contemplation about his place in eternity from the humble perspective of his own earthly surroundings and associations. If his experiments were beginning to allow him to glimpse his place amongst the stars, this piece probably marks the point that began to define it.

The experimental years

Image courtesy ESA/Hubble, R. Sahai and NASA

Significantly, for our knowledge of the timeline, it is known with certainty to have been composed between 1906 and 1908. As one of the best known of all of Ives' compositions, *The Unanswered Question* demonstrates his rapidly evolving creativity, and his newfound purpose in his music, being striking for its independent and parallel entities, expansive sonics, divergent musical components, partial cyclical elements, and strangely satisfying, yet bizarrely disembodied conceptual language. Perhaps, too, the earliest example of Ives' full transference of transcendental thought into musical sound, in one short work he produced something unique for the ages.

Listeners' guide

- An off-stage 'choir' of string instruments (sonically, all the more effective when played by larger chamber orchestra configurations to maximize the blend of pitch, unity of sound, and its otherworld, static character) plays an extremely slow and simple progression of diatonic chords, mostly in a descending and repetitive pattern. Commencing with a sustained G major chord, the 'choir' plays alone for the first minute, creating the impression of timelessness, acceptance, and a far distant horizon. Ives termed this *"The Silence of the Druids,"* in which the strings represent a serene state: *"Know, See and Hear Nothing."*

- A solo trumpet poses "the eternal question of existence" - in this case if the sheet music were to be turned on its side, the notation of this figure will appear curiously akin to a laterally inverted outline of an *actual* question mark. We have to assume this was the intent, although it could be argued that such a defining symbol might have been made to conform even more closely than it does. The figure occupies a vague key center that arguably could belong anywhere.
- The string choir begins to move at strategic moments relative to the trumpet figure; when it is active, the strings are passive, and vice versa.
- Answered quietly by four flutes (two of which may be substituted by oboe and clarinet), in a random atonal response of unknowing mumblings of a combined descending and ascending wedge of motion built from lines a half-step apart but spread over more than an octave.
- The trumpet question is posed another five times, each being answered by increasingly agitated and incoherent woodwind babble, it grows in intensity and shrillness with each huddled discussion, eventually taking the trumpet's notes in rapid, mocking derision of the question.
- In the final instance, after the final shrill screams of laughter from the flutes, we are left with the stillness of the strings holding a final G major chord, and one final plaintive, seemingly more reflective statement of the question; *unable to answer it*, we are left us hanging in space - indeed,

the great mysteries about life, death, and eternity, remain, as ever, irresolvable.
- Ives timed these competing entities to fall against each other at the most poignant emotional places against the string choir progressions in a manner nothing short of inspired - in spite of the fact that every performance will produce slight variations in the precise alignments. However, this results in *no change to the musical effect!* This loose coordination was something Ives allowed for in the proportions of the note values carefully assigned to the various parts.

Could it be that *The Unanswered Question* represents perhaps an emergence of Ives' own version of the 'Music of the Spheres?' This was Pythagoras' concept from the ancient world in which mathematical ratios between the eight known members of the greater solar system were thought to create a type of silent music in the Heavens that paralleled the eight notes of the scale as cosmic forces somehow reflected oneness with man.

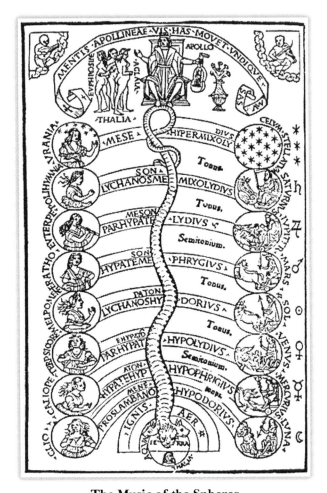

The Music of the Spheres
Italian Renaissance engraving showing the
planetary spheres and usical ratios
{{PD-Art}}

Thus, in the first decade of the new century, Ives had combined his harmonic and rhythmic experiments: using conventional harmony in the strings that stretched the perception of time to new limits, an *independently* moving solo trumpet, to be countered by further *independent* atonal flute responses in an accelerating tempo at each turn. With all three separate entities completely separate from each other in tonality and context, so was born the true 'parallel listening' concept that would feature increasingly in Ives' music. Consciously developed to new levels in the *Fourth Symphony,* and to its full incarnation in the *Universe Symphony,* Ives had taken a major step toward the stars in painting a cosmic landscape completely devoid of normal earthly references.

Although Ives would revise this work in the 1930's, its character was not fundamentally altered, even though the trumpet question alternates its last note back and forth (utilizing two different pitches) with each statement, and the flute parts become somewhat more shrill and complex. Thus it serves as a prime demonstration of the nature and extent of Ives' revisions, confirming that Ives conceived the major vision of any given work from the beginning, with later revisions seldom changing it in any substantive way. In this instance, the revised edition makes a smoother and slightly more colorful whole, although the original stands on its own feet in every way without need of apology - still the same piece. Thus, *one* question *did* get answered: how modern the original version of any work by Ives actually was.

The Unanswered Question has become almost institutional amongst Ives followers, and seems to be able to make a case as being one of the most iconic little masterpieces of the 20th Century. It is so early into the new century that it almost belonged to the one before.

Central Park in the Dark

At one time *Central Park in the Dark* was known by a longer title than now, *Central Park in the Dark in "The Good Old Summertime."* It owed the second part of the title to a popular 1902 Tin Pan Alley tune, setting the time of year, with the melody presumably having some special connotations in this composition. Ives referenced many sounds that could be heard from a park bench across the stillness of the night, from casinos, street singers, rowdy gadflies, people enjoying ragtime, a fire engine, street cars and the like, even to a runaway horse and buggy - all merging in and out of the still dark fabric of the warm night air in a scene still possible to experience today.

In this work, Ives would feature a number of quotes from the most vernacular of sources, primarily *Ben Bolt, The Campbells are Comin', Hello! Ma Baby,* and Sousa's *Washington Post March.* However, the identity of these fragments of tunes has been transformed in the classic Ives manner, especially to recognize within any normal context, so that none, with the exception of *Hello! Ma Baby,* are easy to detect; even that tune has undergone significant rhythmic and pitch transformation to give it a wilder and more recklessly jazzy character.

Image AC

Ives would incorporate concepts featured in *The Unanswered Question* to new extremes, developing the material of the independent string choir common to both. Here, it would feature the types of new experimental harmonic structures he had developed during the later 1890's up until around 1902 in experimental works, such as may be heard even in the first of the *Harvest Home Chorales*. The handling of the strings differs, too, from that of *The Unanswered Question* as the volume grows alongside the emerging cacophony elsewhere. Apparently, Ives also made certain revisions to the work as late as 1936, but this is not known with certainly. Overall, we can see quickly that *Central Park in the Dark* is anything but a spiritual expression, although its distantly mysterious spatial sonorities put it into a category of music that belongs to some other place and time; one does not need to have it pointed out that Ives' was already looking far outside his own physical limitations.

As a point of reference, it is worth commenting on a brief article about *Central Park in the Dark,* contained within a book, *The Philosophy of Music: Theme and Variations,*[7] by Aaron Ridley. Ridley presented a perspective and attitude typical of many that always have dogged Ives and his music. One can begin to surmise what it must have been like for Ives during his lifetime, having continually suffered at the hands of similarly ill-comprehending and closed-minded critics. With a type of empty commentary that we should not allow to color our objectivity, for it to have appeared anywhere near this day and age (2005) is more than surprising. Moreover, although published by a major university press, the lack of enlightened perspective and analysis is startling.

Although Ridley seemed well attuned to the intent of the music, even the significance of its priority, somehow the context, structure, or even the musical imagery of Ives' sound painting was beyond him. Dismissively mischaracterizing the deliberate inconsistencies of its musical components, Ridley appeared helpless in hearing what the music conveys in the absence of the kind of detailed, step-by-step program notes only a child would require. Its artistic value surely obvious to most reasonably sophisticated listeners today, however, Ridley quickly brushed that aside as well as substance of the music. If he remained blissfully unaware of the significance of Ives' unique transformations of fragments of simple tunes into new purposes and identities, perhaps most egregious of all was that he failed to perform, or was not able to do, even the most rudimentary of musicological analyses; such opinions are hard to take in the absence of a grasp of the subject at hand.

However, if we, instead, quickly ignore such vapid commentary, *Central Park in the Dark* stands as an iconic and futuristic soundscape, undiminished by the time of over a century, locked into a surreal and contemplative dalliance with the circumstances of its time of creation.

Listeners' guide

- The silence of the night is represented by the string section - as distinctive and effective a portrayal of an extra-musical concept as anything ever conceived. Its sound is curiously reminiscent of *Music for Strings, Percussion and Celeste* by Béla Bartók (1936). Harmonically, moving in parallel blocks in an endlessly drifting ostinato, Ives' 'night' chords are structured from unconventional intervals. (Such writing corresponds coincidentally, but more radically, to some even earlier works by Erik Satie). The level of dissonant harmonic tension fluctuates throughout, continuing independently in a repeating pattern, largely floating in parallel with a repeating sequence of rhythmic accumulation and relaxation, but avoiding any sense of perceptibly defined pace. Hauntingly, like a night owl, the clarinet twice gently hoots fragments of *Ben Bolt*, a popular song at the time.
- A good example of Ives' ability to transform whatever he was quoting - in order to infuse it with the character of another context entirely - is well demonstrated in these clarinet passages, its tonality and identity being utterly at odds with *Ben Bolt's* original context and spirit. Joined later by flute and oboe, even solo violin, in other fragmentary suggestions of tunes of long ago, the mood is interrupted by the rhythmic ragtime idiom ghosting *Hello! Ma Baby* in not more than a suggestion, but enough to identify it.

- The mood continues, followed by another reminder of *Ben Bolt* in the clarinet, and one more little reference to *Hello! Ma Baby*, before the music begins to pick up momentum at a rapid pace. Interestingly, the strings now maintain the original tempo while all other members of the ensemble move increasingly fast with each new segment.
- The music develops over a repeating 12-bar cycle built on *Hello! Ma Baby* in the piano; an earlier melodic fragment, set a half step and half beat apart in the flute and oboe, conjures up bawdy street musicians.
- The flute and oboe are joined by the E flat clarinet; in canonic response to the piano it stridently hoots a version of *Hello! Ma Baby* at a faster tempo still, the tune's curiously twisted identity now completely clear.
- An interruption from the trombone with rhythmic jabs in the second piano continues the musical buildup, while in the uppermost flute line appear short, discreet references to *The Campbells are Comin'* are placed so subtly into the part that one could be forgiven for missing them entirely. Later, the second piano enters with references to what appears to be *Freshmen in Park* in major key form, or perhaps it is derived from the ghoulish funeral melody of a minor key, *The Worms Crawl In*. In the major form it also suggests the nursery rhyme, *Boys and Girls Come Out to Play*, which certainly would not have been inappropriate in the context, so perhaps Ives had the latter tune in mind, too.
- Finally, *Hello! Ma Baby* bursts in with full force, the trumpet taking the lead, the E flat clarinet echoing it in canon, all while the second piano plays Sousa's *Washington Post March* off the beat, in the style of a street band; again, this may be hard to spot amidst the fracas.
- Compounding matters, *Freshmen in Park* shrieks high above the fray, ultimately assuming its own tempo, while the orchestra builds into the final frenzy that Ives described as a buggy's runaway horse crashing into a fence.

{{PD-Art}}

- The pandemonium, even what sounds like flapping bat wings, cuts off abruptly, leaving the string ostinato drifting into the stillness of the night, the clarinet once again intoning *Ben Bolt*, and a solitary flute and violin echoing the melody near the beginning.

Thus, with his newfound potential in sound, Ives would comfortably broach unknown musical dimensions. Freeing himself from larger mechanical constraints, this startling concoction is an unlikely blend of components that came about even before Schönberg made his move into *atonality* (the deliberate avoidance of key centers), or even his remarkably modernistic *Five Pieces for Orchestra* of 1909. At this stage of Ives' compositional life, it is fair to say that with *Central Park in the Dark* and *The Unanswered Question* there would be no turning back. Ives had embarked on a path that would take him far beyond known or accepted musical confines as he sought to express new dimensions of the human experience. He was building his road to the stars within a greater universe of sound.

REFERENCES

1. 'American experimental Music,' David Nicholls, *Cambridge University Press*, 1990, p. 33
2. 'Memos', Charles E, Ives, edited by John Kirkpatrick, p. 106, *W. W. Norton & Co.*, New York, 1972, p. 128
3. 'Charles Ives Reconsidered,' Gayle Sherwood Magee, *University of Illinois Press*, Chicago, Illinois, 2008, pp. 74–82
4. 'The Music of Charles Ives,' Philip Lambert, *Yale University Press*, New Haven and London, 1997
5. 'Charles Ives and His Music,' Henry and Sidney Cowell, *Oxford University Press*, 1969, p. 20
6. 'Charles Ives: "My Father's Song", a Psychoanalytic Biography, Stuart Feder, *Yale University Press*, New Haven, Connecticut, 1992, pp. 197-198
7. 'The Philosophy of Music: Theme and Variations,' Aaron Ridley, *Edinburgh University Press*, 2004

CHAPTER 7

Ives in Danbury

Ives' hometown of Danbury, Connecticut, was the focal point of his upbringing, and consequently his perceptions of America. Life in small towns during the 19th Century was rugged, simple and honest, their citizens' semi-isolated state of existence only reinforced by the difficulties of travel. Cultural traditions mattered. In Danbury, since most of its residents had direct links to the Civil War, its lingering spirit fostered mutual support of each other. Shared observance of patriotic holidays further bonded them, and the bond, in turn, was strengthened by communal worship in the practice of old-time revivalist religion.

Ives seemed to know that his Danbury horizons ultimately were too provincial, too limiting. More to the point, once he moved away, with his father having departed this life soon afterwards, it was as if the town also had gone with him, along with everything else he treasured most. Thus, in developing his own larger view of existence, Ives' brand of transcendentalism would propel him to new destinations far from the little town of his beginnings. However, with him spiritually until he found his place in eternity, to be reunited with all that he had lost. Surely it can be no coincidence that Ives never would return to his beloved Danbury to live, much less visit, apparently other than once. The decision must have been deliberate, because it was geographically fairly close to West Redding, where had built his country estate. We must assume that seeing Danbury would have been a painful reminder of the new Century that already had eclipsed all that he once knew, only to make him yearn all the more for what he had lost.

In witnessing an alarming invasion of all things alien to his philosophy, Ives saw hedonism, automation, mechanization, depersonalization, an increasingly superficial media and the slick and glossy world of entertainment that came with it advancing ever faster. Although the final blow would not take place until World War I and its aftermath, he tried still to hold out an unrealistic optimism for the future, in which an elevated, enlightened populace of the world might be free from oppression and the dictates of corrupt politicians. Thus, his gradual withdrawal into a near seclusion from society was as much a reflection of the discomfort with the outside world as it was dictated by his failing health and the inner peace that he had found, one it seems he was not unhappy occupying.

However, the Danbury in Ives' mind still could stay as it was, and be the compositional proving ground for the development of his earlier musical experiments. It could remain a place frozen forever in time, his sanctuary. The colorful memories sustained him, even as the citizens he had known faded from the scene, and with them the ways and traditions that had meant so much to him as an impressionable youngster. Thus, Ives' horizons would be untouched by the encroaching world; all that mattered to him did not have to be sacrificed on the alter of 'progress.' Ives could relive them as long as he wished. He only had to find the language with which to do it.

Ives would write many compositions that are centered on this colorful scene and nearby locales; they began with youthful little marches and organ pieces that evolved into larger soundscapes, such as the *Symphony of Holidays* (the subject of this chapter), *Three Places in New England*, the first three symphonies, some of the fourth, numerous assorted chamber works, not to mention smaller experimental works (many referenced in Chapter 6), such as the humorous *The Gong on the Hook and Ladder*. Although he expanded his horizons to include his experiences at Yale, (i.e. *Calcium Light Night)* then on to New York City (i.e. *Central Park in the Dark)*, the simple observations of life in Danbury provided his predominant musical subjects. If the basis of most of these works is not profound in itself, it is his personal connection to them that is a window into his extraordinary creativity.

Ives' experimental concepts, though not the complete basis in themselves for larger works, would be incorporated in them, amongst many other things. This included even the conservative musical language of Parker's training, as well as the characteristic quotations of religious and secular materials. If Ives did not consider that he owed much to Parker's influence - and certainly his later works have little in common stylistically to the writing evidenced in the *First* and *Second Symphonies* - many common technical and tonal elements remain present, nevertheless. Regardless, the unselfconscious blend of traditional entities with uncompromising, formerly experimental and systematic factors, seems to stand alone in all music.

The Symphony of Holidays

There is no more fitting representation of Ives' proving ground than we find in the *Symphony of Holidays*. Remaining safely within the sheltered confines of Danbury memory, here, he could build his bold revolutionary musical language; amongst it, four pieces for orchestra that reflected patriotic holidays. Collected together, Ives later would wrap the title 'symphony' around them. Immediately it is clear that originally Ives did not conceive the movements as a group, since the first three begin in a similar vein; thus we should not expect any type of formally considered contrasting plan for them as we would in a true symphony. Although all may be played separately, the four works share common festive themes that were the focus of the young Ives' cultural influence. They also picture the four different seasons, all of which are seen through the eyes of 'small town' New England, so they are sometimes loosely termed *Ives' Four Seasons*. Ives left fairly extensive remarks about the *Symphony of Holidays* in *Memos*, which serve to answer most questions. However, curiously, he always related his comments as if we are already familiar with the subject at hand, so not everything is addressed, despite the breadth of his discussion.[1]

As textbook examples of Ives' more mature evolved mid-style, the movements of the symphony reveal the modernist, yet one still immersed in days long gone. With the exception of *Thanksgiving*, Ives cast them through the perspective of his actual experiences (with his brother, cousins and friends?) growing up in that New England small town during the late 19th Century. Ives attempted to put the listener into the vivid scenes of these events as he knew them, but only some of the content is spelled out - the remainder being left to the listener's imagination. The last movement, *Thanksgiving*, differs from the others in being only to a degree programmatic, and is based more around community observance rather than his own.

Washington's Birthday

Far from being a composition steeped in reverence, Ives chose to paint a picture of the annual celebration in a work full of humor and near *irreverence*. Not that any disrespect was intended towards 'The Father of our Country,' but in Danbury the occasion marked a night of joyous winter revelry, rather than sedate observance. Starting, however, in a serious vein with imagery of winter snow scenes, the listener is led to expect an entirely different outcome as the music proceeds.

Ives in Danbury

{{PD-Art}}

Depicting a young person's celebration of the holiday, this little work features a romp across the snow to a celebration at the local barn dance. Finished around 1913 from preliminary sketches started in 1909, the movement features the smallest orchestra amongst the set, together with a Jew's harp (!), of all unlikely instruments to round out the ensemble. Thanks to modern amplification, only one such instrument is required, whereas Ives considered that up to a hundred might have been needed; in fact, many people at such a dance celebration would have had one with them, so such a number was far from a composer's unrealistic sonic pipe dream!

In 'barn dances' of the time, there might be as many as three or more actual separate dances taking place within the cavernous space; other players would improvise their own additions to all that was going on, while still more might fall out of line, probably due to the free-flowing libation! Ives tried to simulate the scene, one he had witnessed many times since childhood and that almost defied precise analysis. The naturally resulting multiple speeds, separate musical layers, unusual harmonic entities, and random events corresponded perfectly to Ives' natural instincts, as he tried to capture what he had seen and heard. As such, *Washington's Birthday* is highly instructive and revealing. By incorporating the fruits of earlier experiments into larger structures and concepts, Ives created the type of multi-faceted sonic imagery we find in many of his later compositions.

Regardless, the movement is closer to the music of *Thanksgiving and Forefathers' Day* in harmonic and rhythmic texture than the other two, which is surprising considering its relatively late date. It parts company with the earlier work in its more varied language and complexity, the multi-layered polyphony and polytonality belonging decidedly to a later time.

Listeners' guide

- *Washington's Birthday* opens softly as Ives paints the picture of a cold, snowy landscape. John Kirkpatrick considered that it is likely that the section contains quoted material derived from two tunes that feature home life. Certainly, what seem to be references to these can be heard in a musical dialog, as something resembling the beginning of *Home, Sweet Home* in the violins, and *Old Folks at Home* in

the horns. However, neither are blatant quotes (except, perhaps, the initial horn utterance), and one could be forgiven for not identifying them at all.
- The horn references over, the violins quote their material a couple more times in a hauntingly high register, leading into a scattered section with the flute; again there appears to be a tiny reference to *Old Folks at Home,* now in the violins.
- An extended section follows, apparently to paint the bleak winter horizons; it does not appear to feature any quoted material.
- Gently ringing bells join the ensemble in abstract writing, presumably to further paint the glistening scene (or was it sleigh-bells?).
- The horn joins with a serene melodic line, accompanied by fragmented strings.
- Suddenly we become aware that something is changing, as increasing motion emerges out of the stillness of the snow scene. Portraying the romp through the snow, the strings take over in up-and-down waves of strident chords representing the hills and dales, moving in parallel and built from unconventional intervals. The music grows increasingly energetic and pronounced.
- In the flute we hear a snippet of *Turkey in the Straw,* followed by an even smaller clip from *Sailor's Hornpipe,* thought by Kirkpatrick to represent possibly the distant sounds of music wafting across the snowy fields from the barn. However, because the music winds down, perhaps these only were the sounds of the musicians warming up before the partygoers arrived.
- With a burst of stridently happy string chords, the dance begins! For a time, it takes a largely traditional gait, with some humorous touches, until a fragment of the *Sailor's Hornpipe* in the flute tells us that some dancers have broken away on their own. Before long, another group has separated to strains of *Camptown Races.* Obviously, someone is singled out for a pat on the back because we hear

- a fragment of *For He's a Jolly Good Fellow* interrupting the flow of the music.
- The music clumsily lurches to a stop as someone takes out a Jew's harp out of his pocket to join the group, which has now started playing *The White Cockade*. The flute chimes in a fragment of *Turkey in the Straw,* followed by 'Down in de cornfield' in a low register *(From Massa's in de Cold Ground),* both more like half-hearted attempts to get something else going. The flute, now sounding lost, adds to the general feeling of humorous near-chaos that seems to be growing, with separate dances breaking out all over the barn!
- *Turkey in the Straw* now joins again more fully and confidently, eventually switching to piccolo, *The White Cockade* continues in the strings, with *The Campbells are Comin'* joining in the musical disarray.
- The horn morphs into *Garryowen,* which only further compounds matters when it switches to *St. Patrick's Day* as the piccolo tries to play *Fisher's Hornpipe.* By now, the musicians are becoming increasingly disorganized as near chaos takes over, the increasingly polytonal and cyclic texture vividly depicting Ives in his funniest vein.
- With the group coming to a screeching halt, all we are left with are the "sentimental songs" (in the strings, later joined by horn and bells), and a solitary violin still playing in a more lively vein, apparently reluctant to call it a night: a blend of *Pig Town Fling* and *Turkey in the Straw,* unsurprisingly in different keys, is a throwback to the *Second Symphony.* Soon, all we are left with is a final adieu, with *Goodnight Ladies* in the strings and flute, as the exhausted partygoers head for home with a weary and slow trudge through the snow in the middle of the night.

Washington's Birthday ranks with *The Fourth of July* as being amongst the most lighthearted compositions of all of Ives' larger scale works. One should approach it with this in mind and not try to intellectualize the music too greatly; intended to be taken in the spirit of the festivities they represented during Ives' adolescent years, these pieces are some in which we can all share in the fun.

Decoration Day

In America, Decoration Day was the 19th Century forerunner of Memorial Day, instigated as a national public holiday after the Civil War, in which brother fought brother and so many souls were lost. The holiday must have evoked strong emotions and memories for Ives, because his father not only was a survivor of the Civil War, but also led the band every year in the march back into town from the cemetery. Now he, too, had departed. In his book Stuart Feder stated his belief that Ives pictured his father as a central figure in this piece, which seems completely believable and resonating with the tenor of the music. However, Feder's further interpretation of what some of the underlying imagery represented seems self-consciously stretched beyond incredulity into the realm of the ludicrous.[2]

{{PD-Art}}

Dating of this work is a little tricky, because stylistically it appears to fall in line with the dates Ives provided (1912/1913), but what survives of some original sketch materials (a version for violin and piano) places it a couple of years later. Whether these came into being after the orchestral version, or the other way around has been questioned, but significantly, Ives noted many years later that the violin version was arranged from the orchestral score, which would seem to solve the riddle, although Kirkpatrick disagreed! Actually, parts of the work might date from far earlier (even to 1886), according to Ives' remarks in *Memos,* having apparently existed in other formats (now lost), including the 1887 *Adeste Fideles* section featured so prominently in the middle of the piece. This possibly was once part of Ives' teenage *Slow March* for brass band that he had referred to as the material he had reused for the portion.[3]

Decoration Day remains firmly planted in New England soil. With the heart of this work thoroughly tied to Ives' small town associations, not only is it decidedly late coming as it does in the timeline, but also is a less radical composition than we might have expected. Possibly the key is its somber spirituality and Ives' continuing ties to the memories of his father; perhaps, therefore it is a last solemn reflection of his roots and a deliberate, reverent suppression of his more experimental leanings. In any event, it is still decidedly in advance of the *Third Symphony*, but greatly distant from the *Fourth* or *Universe Symphonies*. As in the *Third Symphony,* Ives featured a part in true shadow counterpoint - here an extra violin plays a line throughout the major portion of the movement that shadows the primary material. Feder's speculation that the violin might represent his father certainly is possible, but in view of similar writing in other works this type of symbolism remains far from known - possibly just a standard *shadow* instrumentation - in fact, one often chosen for its ability to provide the right type of sonic wash.

From a technical standpoint, we can consider *Decoration Day* to belong to Ives' mid-point of stylistic development. Oddly, there are moments that seem to speak of the poetic works of Delius - the British composer whose music shortly predated him - with a similar type of impressionistic imagery, (i.e. *Brigg Fair* of 1907). Whether Ives had heard any of that composer's work is not known, although it seems unlikely. Overall, however, the writing speaks in a distinct harmonic language (and hence *sound),* the chord structures often being formed from notes a step or even only a half step apart, though placed in *different* octaves. The intervals between these notes have a ghostly angst about them, almost ethereally invoking the spirits of the dead. Ives thus had continued to expand and develop his range of harmony and expression to better suit his needs, not content to rest upon only his own earlier experiments.

Weaving in and out of different tonalities seamlessly, mixing both tonality and atonality freely much of the time, the music has an almost dreamlike quality. In another interesting development, common to some of Ives' other works of the time, many of the melodic lines feature increasingly wide leaps between notes. As previously noted, he would develop this technique fully in the *Universe Symphony*.

Listeners' guide

In Ives' description of this piece, the people of the town gather in the early morning to collect flowers to decorate the graves of those lost in the Civil War. He reflected upon the generally somber mood of the people as they assembled, partly reflective of old tensions going *into* the Civil War. After all, the lives of many close relatives and friends were lost in what they would have considered an avoidable conflict, and we hear overtones of near anger at times. As the flowers are readied in the town, the parade begins to assemble, consisting of horses, carriages, veterans, army members, the town band, even the fire engine company with its bells gently ringing. The townsfolk march slowly in procession to the cemetery, accompanied by the solemn sounds of *Adeste Fideles* and low drums. The graves are decorated. With the paying of *Taps* and the hymn *Nearer, My God to Thee*, the band strikes up a rousing march back to town, as the evening encroaches.

- In the quiet opening representing daybreak. Some have suggested that muted violins seem to suggest we hear combined fragments of *Taps* and *Nearer, My God to Thee*, hauntingly changed into a ghostly premonition of the decoration service; more likely it is *Adeste Fideles*.
- The English horn states the principal theme of the first part of the piece (based on *Dies Irae*), as the violin lines seems to float upwards, answering in response in a short dialog with the French horns and oboe.
- This is followed by various restatements and versions of this material, sometimes seeming more like short variations.
- An anxious rush and surge in the music would seem to be one of the moments that Ives described as representing

the tense mood amongst those looking back with some bitterness over actions that had led the country into war.
- With the music subsiding in wistful sighs, the *Dies Irae* theme resumes in the strings. With a glimpse of *Marching through Georgia* in the horn, followed by flute, oboe, and even a brief hint of *Massa's in de Cold Ground* in the bassoon (then the violins), lightly ringing high bells add the sounds of the fire engine company that joins them to signify the gathering of people together for the march to the cemetery.
- The music becomes more militaristic, rhythmic and strident, presumably indicative of resolve of the towns' people as they gather and organize.
- With deathly, even sickening sighs in the upper strings, along with shuddering in the lower strings and the eerie ringing of the fire engine company bells, the solemnity of the occasion becomes ever clearer.
- The slow march to the gravesite commences to a creatively modified *Adeste Fideles* (the *Slow March?*); the steady march can be heard in the 'walking' pizzicato (plucked) bass line, in one of the moments reminiscent of Delius.
- In a connecting passage, pulsing notes in the strings hint of the *Fate* motif, in a treatment similar to that in the third movement of the *Second Symphony,* even perhaps a fleeting glimpse of *Taps*, although here they lead to a quotation from *The Battle Cry of Freedom* in the first violins - written, of course, in an entirely unexpected setting, so typical as always in Ives' use of quotations. The strings round out the passage with an extension of the *Adeste Fideles* material amidst a further shuddering in the lower strings: the most solemn time of the day has come.
- In one of Ives' most magical and poignantly moving moments, a distant trumpet plays *Taps* (clearly taking his father's role in the proceedings!), while a choir of violins plays *Nearer, My God to Thee* in a quietly shimmering background, surprisingly matched in tonality if not precise harmony - a precursor of what would emerge

more prominently in successive compositions as a key feature along the road to the stars.
- We hear heavy footsteps; the band is coming to lead the people back into town; in a burst of exuberance, the *Second Regiment Connecticut National Guard March* (David Wallis Reeves), one of Ives' personal favorites, pierces the solemnity with all of the 19th Century frills, typical of actual practice at the time.
- A few extra wrinkles of polytonality might be lost on the casual listener, while underneath the bellowing marching band, a lone viola and gentle bells continue to play *Taps*, surely more out of symbolism than practicality. As the march continues, the upper woodwinds play something resembling *Reveille* (but not quite!) in another key, imparting the sound of the rough, country town musicians Ives knew so well.

Unfortunately, the exhilaration is so great that some of these details tend to become obscured unless the performers pay special attention to them. We know that Ives, far from oblivious to practical considerations of orchestration, as some have suggested, was keenly aware of balance problems and the need to separate and place instruments in performance; certainly, advances in technology have made things possible now in ways that Ives surely would have embraced. Indeed, many of the sounds that he had in mind, especially those that are spatial, could use much more care for their realization than in many readings we hear; perhaps most can be attained even without special means. So, rather than blaming Ives' orchestration, more heed should be paid to the unique requirements of each piece; for him, easy music making was no more desirable than easy listening. We cannot take hearing the intent of Ives' musical panoramas for granted.

- With a final victorious cadence, the procession has arrived back in the town and the somber mood of the day returns, the music reflective once more with the quiet sounds that began the day; it is now evening, and time for the town people to renew their sprits for a better future.

The greatness of Ives' music in *Decoration Day* initially might not be obvious; like so many of his works, trying to hear the landmarks first lures us in, and as we gradually awaken to the sonic representations and multiple layers emerging, the unique moods and imagery Ives painted finally speaks to us. It provides an ever-clearer picture of his search for real meaning and reinforcement of his values, as he struggled with all that was taking place in the real world and the loss of his past.

The Fourth of July

Conceived without need for elaborate justification or intellectual fanfare, *The Fourth of July* was supposed to invoke the preparations, build-up, celebrations and final firework display of Ives' childhood memory - a rip-roaring good time to be had by all! Indeed, Ives wrote the piece discarding most practical considerations - even by his standards - believing that it might not even be playable at all.

{{PD-Art}}

Ives used every trick in his book to achieve the result he had in mind, resulting in about six minutes of some of the most tangled orchestral writing ever put on a page of manuscript. We hear the multitudes of people, street musicians, parades, the town band marching down main street, an accidental explosion, gunfire, brawls, rowdy drunkards, even baseball (!), in short, the sheer pandemonium of a crowd's frenzy and celebration, with a fireworks display set against an array of associated tunes and fragments that punctuate the texture, culminating in the traditional last burst of the fireworks. We feel as if we are right there with the crowd on Main Street as the brilliant lights and trails of smoke light up the sky.

Written somewhere early in the second decade of the 20th Century, its precise date has been difficult to determine. However, it is not unreasonable to consider that the piece was laid out in some form prior to 1913; it is a large-scale realization of most of the complex textures of most of Ives' earlier experiments, including one from 1904 that depicted an explosion on the boat *General Slocum*.[4] To achieve the astonishing effects Ives had in mind required considerable thought and planning; he even wanted to imitate the excited, but terrible performance of the town band, all out of tune, wrong notes, and coming apart at the seems with regularity. Ives thus threw everything into this piece, intending to invoke his boyhood memories A vivid representation of general revelry, common then as it is today whenever there is an excuse to celebrate, rather than conceived as 'high art,' this was precisely Ives' intention.

This particular holiday, though the habitual favorite of the young, was quite a dangerous time in the 19th Century. With little supervision of any kind, and unreliable and unregulated fireworks, the injuries and accidents were often horrifying. Ives mentioned the Town Hall being set afire in his program notes, and also the implication of other things going wrong: the depiction of the accidental fireworks explosion is unmistakable. Ives did not shy away from realistically painting this not always universally happy scene. He must have witnessed it numerous times, his recollections utilized as his visual guide to the techniques he would design. The number of them used in such a short time frame is remarkable by any standards - a greater assemblage than in any prior piece; it seems few are missing! Specifically, however, if we isolate them we can observe the following:

- ***Melody and Harmony***

Ives was enamored of the tune, *Columbia, the Gem of the Ocean* for his entire life, and he placed elements of it throughout the texture. Surrounded and frequently accompanied by a multitude of other tunes, all of them are similarly fragmentary and in various guises. However, *Columbia* is predominant, *and* heard in its entirety near the high point of the piece - one of few melodies Ives would ever quote complete. Sharing that distinction with the *Second Symphony*, here, too, it implies *cumulative form.*

Ives built some of the harmonies from intervals outlined by the *Columbia* melody. For example, using pivotal notes at and within the melody's extremes spaced at intervals a fourth (2-½ steps) or fifth (3-½ steps) apart, (actually these really are just inversions of each other), and building the harmony from notes stacked at these same intervals, Ives created new chords. Furthermore, his systemized developments and progressions of these chords reveal the organizational influence of his earlier experiments. Additionally, Ives threw some tone clusters into the mix (notes piled upon one another without spaces in between), both *aleatorically* (leaving the choices of notes up to the performer), as well as notated.

- ***Tonality***

As in many of his earlier experimental works, we can find cyclic manipulations of 12-tone row sequences. Normally associated with Arnold Schönberg and his formal adoption nine years later of (dodecaphony), the twelve possible named pitches are arranged successively with no pitch repeated. Schönberg developed it according to an elaborate system. In his comments on the score of *Majority*, dating from about the same time as *The Fourth of July* (see Chapter 11), Ives dismissed such strictly contrived methods as a primary basis for composition.

- ***Rhythm***

The composition is also defined by the applications of many of Ives' earlier rhythmic experiments, including multiple mixed rhythmic divisions, multiple speeds, the use of seemingly unrelated complex rhythmic contours, and even separations of the alignments of bar lines. The latter involved mixed parallel meters (rhythmic groupings), by which the ensemble falls deliberately out of synchronization. Rhythmically cyclical concepts are utilized in various ways, including sliding *(glissando)* clusters in opposing motion in the string section at the climax of the piece. Rhythmically, the constantly changing, multiple and varied textures are as striking as is the visual nature of the sounds themselves, the intentions easy to grasp in this orchestral tour de force.

Listeners' guide

- Opening under the approaching dusk, a quiet tone cluster in the lower strings provides a muted backdrop to a fragment of *Columbia, the Gem of the Ocean* in the first violins (rendered almost unrecognizable in classic Ives fashion), soon joined by the second violins with a quiet 'bugle' call; things are already stirring.
- Declamatory statements in the basses - slightly ominous, yet eager in their anticipation - (again based on *Columbia, the Gem of the Ocean*) are followed by chords and nervous motion in the upper violins, together with a further hint of *Columbia* in the low trombone over punctuated, slow chords in the lower strings.
- A flurry of activity follows in the strings and woodwinds, striking in its use of contrary motion and atonal linearity; we hear a militaristic hint (of a bugle call?) in the piccolo.
- The entire string section (plus tuba) builds upon the anticipatory material that has been initiated by the basses, while flute and piccolo add more fragments of *Columbia*.
- With a skittering of notes in the strings, the woodwinds join the discourse, continuing to develop the earlier anticipatory figuration with the strings. The strings again take over with snippets of *Columbia* material spread between the woodwinds and horn.
- A tiny quote in the cellos from *The Battle Cry of Freedom* (perhaps hard to discern) anticipates a prominent *Columbia*-based passage in the flutes and piccolo amidst another

hint of a militaristic bugle call in the clarinet; before *The Battle Cry* material leaves off, we hear a stirring quotation form *Marching Through Georgia* in the trumpet, rhythmically set off the beat.
- The strings take over and build, interrupted by a ringing, echoing gunshot simulated across the orchestra, followed by stern string writing and militaristic references in dialog within the winds.
- Against conflicting jazzy rhythms in the woodwinds, aficionados of Ives' songs will recognize a brief reference *Old Home Day* in the violins (Ives quoting Ives!); there are also hornpipe quotes, in the oboe, flutes and piccolo, a prominent reference to *The Battle Hymn of the Republic* in the strings, and another fleeting reference to *Old Home Day;* (Ives officially dated this song at 1920, but clearly it was extant before *The Fourth of July* in order to be quoted here!)
- The horns burst in with a reference to *The Battle Cry of freedom,* developed into a strong rhythmic passage in the strings, joined by *Reveille* in the horns, then trumpet.
- The feeling of growing revelry continues, including a further *Columbia* reference, interrupted by a brief allusion to *Hail, Columbia* in the bassoons and clarinet.
- Marching down the street comes a corps of fifes and drums (in a different speed to the rest of the orchestra), which morphs into a quotation from *The girl I left behind,* while the strings develop the material from *Old Home Day.*
- A short reference to *London Bridge is falling down,* divided amongst the woodwinds anticipates an 'accidental' firework explosion across the orchestra, achieved with multiple complex rhythms, tone cluster scales (strings), and a large chord of closely placed notes that dissipates into a multitude of cascading descending rhythms and pitches, like light flashes in the sky.
- *Old Home Day* again emerges in the violins, seemingly undisturbed by the commotion, then *Garryowen* in the xylophone; generally disjoined writing adds to the sense that

crowds are gathering. Excited children are everywhere, musicians are practicing; many in the crowd have already 'partied' beyond remaining orderly. *Columbia* quotes are everywhere as the percussion section shifts in and out of synchronization. The xylophone takes *St. Patrick's Day in the Morning*; again we hear *Reveille* in the trumpet. Firecrackers are being let off randomly while the mob pours into the town square; the trombone can be heard practicing passages from *Columbia*. A wavelike tone cluster cycle in the strings (featuring contrary motion between upper and lower) gradually gains in momentum to provide the crowd's surge and nervous energy.

- This section was developed from the 1903 *Overture and March "1776"*. The town band arrives, erupting in *Columbia, the Gem of the Ocean*. Sounding all out of tune and out of step - everyone wants to play the tune! - and simulated by ingenious pitch, rhythm, even volume displacements, it is joined by another parade playing the *Battle Hymn of the Republic* (in the cornet and woodwinds, humorously mixing up verse, chorus and rhythm). Others play *Katy Darling* and *Dixie* (piccolo), *Hello! Ma Baby* (horns); *Yankee Doodle* (xylophone), ensuring that complete pandemonium ensues (the Town Hall is accidentally set ablaze!). Then, the big moment of the night: the grand finale of the firework display.
- Created within the space of just five bars, this is the most complex orchestral texture Ives had attempted at that date; indeed, it has scarcely been surpassed. An amazing array simulates the fireworks: figurations utilized in the first explosion, twelve-tone rows in the woodwinds built from opposing atonal three-note patterns (broken *trichords*) and multiple rhythmic divisions, astounding rhythmic fragmentation of other punctuating entities, while the strings' massive glissandos build to the frenzied climax of their wave cycle.
- Heralding the end of the festivities is the launching of the rocket over the church steeple. With a final surge and

hold in the orchestra, the rocket reaches its apex and falls away, petering out with sputtering sparks. Simulated by seven solo string players and one flute, a final pizzicato note (with timpani) signifies the last spark as it dies out and the scene fades to black.

Thanksgiving and Forefathers' Day

As the final and longest movement of the collection of holidays pieces, compositionally, one might have expected *Thanksgiving and Forefathers' Day* to be the most recent and advanced of the group, when in fact, the primary composition of this movement represents the *first* of them to take form, and is the most conservative from a technical standpoint. Interestingly, much of the material dates from Ives' Yale days, having started out in organ pieces for a church service *(Prelude and Postlude for a Thanksgiving Service,* 1897. Ives was organist at Center Church, New Haven during his Yale years, which provided a source of income.) These organ works, nevertheless, reveal that he was actively writing in experimental idioms right under Parker's nose, and evidence that he was not too reticent to inflict a certain amount of modernity on them, despite his protestations to the contrary! Either that, or it must have been a tolerant congregation.

More important in the *Thanksgiving* material, though, is the early date of some decidedly remarkable harmonic leanings that announce two keys together from the outset (C major and D minor), continuing and compounding their separate ways within the section. Thus, the work provided a substantial outlet for Ives' earlier harmonic experimental ideas within a larger fluid framework for even more experimentation, even including some from a rhythmic standpoint.

{{PD-Art}}

Ives dated the piece to 1904, which, based on surviving manuscript pages and his stylistic language of the time, seems entirely proper to within a year or so. Appearing only two years after the 'failure' of *The Celestial Country*, *Thanksgiving and Forefathers Day* appears to be the most significant work of the relatively barren years of large-scale works between 1902 and 1906. The full title *(Thanksgiving and Forefathers' Day)* reflects the historic associations of the pilgrims and Plymouth. The hymns at its core also reflect the context of the original work written for church services. Harmonically, it is clearly datable to pre-1902, with the mixing of conventional chords of different keys much in evidence, often between 'choirs' of lower and higher instruments. Within a few years, Ives progressed to entirely new chords built from intervals other than the conventional that often moved in parallel, although these, nor melodies built from unlikely note combinations are present in *Thanksgiving*. Instead, this entirely satisfying modernistic composition is differentiated from later works (that feature more rapidly varying soundscapes and colorations) by its melodious sustained textures and frequent near-conventional harmonies often mixed with the experimental, even the radical.

Ives made a push as late as 1932 to produce what we have today in a final reassembled edition because it had never been put into a finished score. So much for those who have stated that he was incapable of such intellectually grueling activity at this stage of life. Architecturally, it is built on an old traditional form - three-part (ternary) form - in which materials introduced in the first part of the piece, (A_1), reappear in the last, (A_2), with a middle contrasting section separating them, (B). However, the extraordinary development of this simple structure might leave the casual listener completely unaware of any such form, although the thematic structure unifying each 'side' of the work is clear.

Listeners' guide

- Most of the 'A' section is structured primarily around three hymns *(Federal Street* - so named for the composer, Henry K. Oliver, after the church he attended; *Duke Street* - so-named because composer John C. Hatton lived there), plus highly prominent fragments of *The Shining Shore*. Gentle fragments of other hymns *(Laban; Nettleton)* are introduced as counter-lines in places; not easily caught in casual listening, their role being more symbolic, or for harmonic coloration against the primary materials than for separate identification. More significant is the manner in which Ives treated the primary hymns - they are set in remarkable ways harmonically, rhythmically and melodically, evolved in ways that make them assume totally different musical colorations and impact.

- The piece commences with the strong, sturdy writing of the *Postlude* (one of the *Thanksgiving* organ pieces); Ives' early mentor, the organist John Cornelius Griggs compared this part to the almost stark values of the Puritans. Ives built this on a theme representing the harvest, the polytonality being fairly obvious to the ear. The primary thematic material includes fragments of *Federal Street* incorporated with its rhythmic figuration. As the music proceeds, keen ears will catch references to *The Shining Shore* in the low flutes, briefly echoed in the trombones immediately and loudly.
- A building 'stinger' chord announces more strident string writing, and another prominent reference to *The Shining Shore* in the trumpets, followed by another similar building chord in the brass (by chance, amazingly reminiscent of moments in John Williams' score to the 1977 movie *Star Wars!*) that introduces a premonition by the violins of a statement of *Federal Street* in the low strings. This is echoed shortly thereafter in the horns, and again in the violins.
- Amidst the complex harmonic language, *Federal Street* assumes a new identity, as the music gains power and momentum, moving towards a sequence of four strong detached descending chords in the orchestra, developed from *Duke Street*. This descending figure is further exploited (now smoothly articulated) as the music builds around an announcement of *Duke Street* in the low brass. Subtle references to *Federal Street* continue in league with those of *Duke Street* in the lower orchestra.
- With the music gaining speed and syncopated rhythmic energy in the strings, and the woodwinds further reinforcing these elements, the trumpets burst in with a development

of the middle of *Duke Street*; the music builds to an increasingly tangled and strident climax, amidst much syncopation and counter lines - this is the scything action that Ives had alluded to.[5]

- Squarely landing on a strong section built on the opening material, the music settles down into a quiet transitional portion that is highly reminiscent of *Central Park in the Dark*, (which would follow in just a couple of years). The section works its way downwards, ending with a brief build in the cellos and basses that also reminds us of something else: the opening of the *Fourth Symphony* many years later.
- From here, the music enters the *transition* to the 'B' section, drawing us in with a dreamlike setting and a prominently placed statement of *The Shining Shore* in dialog between the oboe and flute. The diametrically opposed harmonic presence of the accompaniment against the melody is haunting. The section reaches a pause as we become aware that it is superimposed on a faintly 'glowing' string chord in another tonality - seeming like something looming out of an evening mist - in one of the work's most striking moments.
- As the chord emerges, a full statement enters of *The Shining Shore* in the upper violins, (as we already know, such an occurrence is a rarity in Ives' music). It is a ravishing, but simple setting. Ives gave the 'B' section a distinction in its tonality: it is now in just one key. *The Shining Shore* comprises the essential makeup of the 'B' section, and also has links to the *Postlude*. The second part of the melody is played again in dialog between flute and oboe, while underneath, in the cellos, an alluring trace remains of Dudley Buck's influence, manifested in a descending and ascending chromatic (motion in half steps), closely voiced harmonic line.
- As the impetus quickly picks up, the hymn is miraculously transformed into a rhythmic and festive variant. Though clearly recognizable, essentially it reverses the order of the notes (retrograde) into a lively, almost jazzy setting, Ives' early rhythmic experimentation already evident. Suddenly, the 'classic' sound of the American 'hoedown' appears, more associated with another composer, Aaron

Copland - and especially in his composition *Appalachian Spring* of some *four decades later!* Frequently this has been wrongly identified as the harvesting section to which Ives had alluded.[5] Independent hymn-based lines buried in the oboe parts have been described erroneously as shadow lines; in fact, they are not 'spun off' the dominant lines at all as true 'shadow' entities.

- The 'B' section winds down with much of the material from earlier, and we sense, somehow, a nostalgic yearning for something lost, an element we have grown to anticipate increasingly in Ives' maturing music.
- The return to 'A' (A_2) material marks a decided change to its former identity, although the rhythmic figuration of the early Thanksgiving organ work is present, along with fragments of *Duke Street* building in the lower voices. Again, the polytonality we heard in the first 'A' section returns. Increasingly strident accented writing leads us through some massive pounding chords, surging into the *Coda*.
- The chorus and trumpets enter to the melody of *Duke Street*, set against *Federal Street* in the lower instruments. A bell choir clangs in celebration, with strings and woodwinds reinforcing the sound by mimicking the pealing of church bells. Characteristically, the hymns' identities are greatly affected by the uniqueness of Ives' setting.
- As the music recedes, elements of this accompaniment and the end of the melody remain, gradually falling away, clear polytonality, even more the avoidance of harmonic resolution becoming increasingly evident. The piece ends with an 'amen' cadence, but the last chord is never reached. Ives increasingly drew upon this technique for poignancy.

Thanksgiving represents a significant milestone during a time just before Ives' frenetic re-engagement with composition and the highly energized activity that would follow. A perfect representation of his evolving musical language early in its ascent, the scale and richness of this work makes it an ideal finale for the *Holidays Symphony*, but offers little hint that Ives' Danbury days soon would be left far behind.

REFERENCES

1. 'Memos', Charles E, Ives, edited by John Kirkpatrick, p. 106, *W. W. Norton & Co.*, New York, 1972, pp. 94-106
2. 'Charles Ives: "My Father's Song", a Psychoanalytic Biography,' Stuart Feder, *Yale University Press*, New Haven, Connecticut, 1992, pp. 240-242
3. 'Memos,' pp. 101-102
4. Ibid., pp. 104-106
5. Ibid., p. 39

CHAPTER 8

The Songs

Ives' songs offer us a further window into his musical and spiritual evolution, each one being a microcosm of his expanding universe. Most of his songs, as would be expected, are not lengthy works, by default; however, they provide another encyclopedic record of his creativity, extending from the beginning to the time he stopped composing. Typical of the composer, we will find many of these songs reflected in other compositions or portions of them; they might even be reworked into other pieces, or have been excerpted from a larger work after being downsized into a song.

In 1922, the composer, largely recovered from the most serious bout (in 1918) of his recurring health condition, determined to try to address his musical anonymity. Assembling and publishing a collection of 114 songs at his own expense, he distributed them as far and wide as he could. Although they were received mostly without comment, he would endure more than his share of callous rejection and sarcastic rebuke for his trouble. Nonetheless, having cast such a wide net, it was sure eventually to snag the attention of a few receptive individuals.

Clearly, Ives' push to place his music into the larger world reflected his brush with mortality, and his keen awareness that fate could come knocking at his door again at any time. If he made no effort to gain some attention to his compositions, and failed to organize, revise and complete many unfinished scores, his life's work in music might be forgotten before it ever was noticed. Certainly he was in a position financially to do something about it. The collection of songs was one way he could introduce a broad cross section of his music to a populace that by now had been slowly introduced to the 'modern' sounds and new techniques of the European radicals, such as Stravinsky and Schönberg. The practical aspect was that the songs usually only required two performers, singer and pianist.

As late as 1940, despite growing fame and notoriety, Ives was still paying for some of his music to be heard and published. The contract for the publication of two of his songs, (at right) is interesting historically, in that the publisher *(Arrow Music Press)* had been set up as a non-profit organization dedicated to the music of American composers. It had been established by several of them, including Aaron Copland. Ives paid the princely sum of $66.14 for the privilege of having two songs put in print. Both songs are distinctly personal. One was written for his adopted daughter, Edith, and her friend *(Two Little Flowers)*; the other (apparently noted here in Edith's or Harmony's hand) just happens to be this writer's personal favorite *(The Greatest Man)*. The former reveals in the most captivating and touching way the strong bonds between his adopted daughter, Edith, and himself; the latter seems symbolic of the lingering emotional bond Ives felt for *his* father. However, both songs came late in his output, and from a technical point of view do not tread new ground; indeed, they have reverted to much more familiar, even near-conventional territory of at least 20 years before. Ives' signature is replete with his characteristic 'snake tracks,' his deteriorating physical condition now readily apparent.

The Songs

Arrow Music Press Song Contract
From the author's collection

Although the new schools of writing in Europe gradually had conditioned American audiences to accept new sounds, and these had met with some success, anyone as 'provincial' as an American composer - even more a radical - still was unlikely to be regarded as having any merit at home. Ives would have run into further resistance because of his non-professional status, and being an unknown quantity in the musical community at almost 50 years of age cannot have helped. Even though Ives legitimately could make claim to have been first, or amongst the first, to pioneer most of the new techniques, who would listen? Thus his compositional efforts usually were received with disinterest, dismissiveness or outright condemnation. However, a ray of hope began to shine where none existed before. The American avant-garde movement was emerging; a new body of radical composers was coming of age, and presumably Ives was well aware of it. Despite his deeply held reservations about what lay behind the culture of many of its standard bearers (that 'bohemian' element), which did to a large degree reflect much of what Ives thought detrimental in society, he would finally know the embrace of kindred spirits. After many years of being left out in the cold he would at last experience acceptance from a new, more open-minded generation eager to open peoples' ears.

However, it would take most of the 1920's before it was clear that his outreach was bearing fruit, and a new chapter was being written in his life. It turned out that much of his future recognition stemmed from his efforts also to promote the *Concord Sonata* and the accompanying writing *Essays Before a Sonata,* (which we will discuss in Chapter 9), while the songs would, for the most part, wither on the vine, despite attracting the interest of a few key people. Finally in 1932, his compatriot, Aaron Copland, noticed the songs, and decided to feature some of them at the First Festival of Contemporary American Music at Yaddo, (an artists' community in Saratoga Springs, New York), which Copland largely had organized.

Although Ives' songs cover a similar cross-section of development as his other works, some of the primary differences between them and the latter can be summarized as follows:

The Songs

- Many of the songs are succinct works, often without traditional verse and chorus structures, sometimes taking the form of single complete thoughts or concepts.
- Because they feature only piano and voice (with one or two exceptions), there are limits to the prospects for polyphonic and polytonal language, as well as the complex rhythmic elements we hear in Ives' larger-scale works; these often require coordination by up to three conductors. Multiple part layering in different speeds and entities therefore is limited, simply because it was necessary to enable the performers to stay synchronized. However, the frequent use of unusual divisions of the beat in the songs, and the flexibility it offered leads us to a greater understanding of the larger scale works too; in effect, they simulate multiple elements of speed and texture.
- The piano also is limited, by default, in the range of sounds that is possible; similarly, the non-sustaining character of its sound restricts many of the techniques Ives was able to employ elsewhere.
- Because pianistic textures feature techniques of the type evolved over centuries,[1] notational characteristics specific to the piano do not necessarily translate to other instruments. Utilized historically by composers - especially those who were pianists, too - in ways that substitute for some of those instrumental characteristics the piano lacks, composers were able instead to take advantage of their knowledge of the uniquely positive strengths that the piano encompasses. In this way, Ives also benefitted from his background as a pianist; as in most respects of his writing he explored new directions without necessarily jettisoning the old, maintaining a large degree of the traditional approach in writing for the instrument.[1] (See also Chapter 3: *Links to other music.*)
- Many excerpts of other works were developed into songs, and vice versa, and were subject to revision and redevelopment; with the songs, Ives thus was able to play and sing much of his music. Again, it is clear he was not nearly

as lacking opportunity to hear it physically as some commentators have depicted.
- The songs illustrate clearly his thought and working processes, since he was not encumbered by the need to build large structural or extended forms in most of them. As distilled musical cameos, frequently they serve as direct insights into his larger developed compositions.

Because Ives' opportunities for hearing his music were confined mostly to playing the piano and singing during his busiest creative years, it is not surprising that we have such a treasure trove of songs left behind; it becomes clear that he must have worked out many of his greatest works while at the keyboard. It is interesting to note that in the first published collection *(114 Songs)* he included some early songs that he had grown to consider unworthy of attention, referring to them as examples of what *not* to write! It is hard to know if he was serious, and certainly he had a delightfully self-deprecating sense of humor; indeed those few songs in question are well beneath his artistic potential. Emanating for his earliest years as a composer, they are sentimental and largely predictable, to be sure, and likely written mostly 'for hire' at various social occasions, or even for his friends; it is inconceivable that Ives would have composed these as serious representations of his work. The question remains why he chose to include them anyway, having fundamentally disowned them!

Other songs from Ives' earlier years are interesting to hear, if not indicative in any way of what was lurking just over his musical horizon. In most commentaries, the better-known and lengthier ones have been reviewed to the exclusion of the lesser-known little gems from his output of approximately 200; we will concentrate mostly on the latter, although the timeline is the most important consideration. Those selected are sequenced according to their time of composition, from earlier to later.

The Songs

Selected Songs over the course of Ives' most productive years

When Stars are in the Quiet Skies

Image by Tim Sprinkle

When stars are in the quiet skies,
Then most I pine for thee; (Ives substituted the word *'long'* for *'pine'*)
Bend on me then thy tender eyes
As stars look on the sea. (Ives added *"down upon the peaceful"* after *"look"*)
For thoughts, like waves that glide by night,
Are stillest when they shine;
Mine earthly love lies hush'd in light (Ives would change *"mine earthly love"* to *"All my love"*)
Beneath the heaven of thine.

There is an hour when holy dreams
Through slumber fairest glide;
And in that mystic hour it seems
Thou should'st be by my side. (Ives substituted *"ever, ever"* for *by"*)
My thoughts of thee too sacred are
For daylight's common beam,
I can but know thee as my star,
My angel and my dream. (Ives changed this wording to *"my guiding star, my angel and my dream."*)
(Bulwer-Lytton)

    The seemingly fitting title of a poem begins the selection; this song apparently dates from Ives' Yale days, and was reworked at the turn of the century. As such, one would expect it to show some of Parker's influence, and indeed it does. Although a simple and utterly conventional song, there are independent melodic components (moving notes) that break up what otherwise soon would become monotonous had the predictable broken chord accompaniment we hear at the outset been maintained for long. In choosing the text, by omitting the third and last stanzas (out of six) Ives ended the song with the word *"dream;"* he provided an alternate ending that extends the vocal line to finish on the fifth note of the scale (key), providing a less final, more ethereal exit.

    However, beyond the fact that this is a simple setting of a song of religious devotion, we do not have to look far for potential hidden meaning in the choice of words. Though more likely to be found in later examples of Ives' work, the references to heavenly things, dreams and guiding stars here are striking reminders of future directions he would take. Regardless, the idiomatic language of late Victorian romanticism is on display here, as are the chromatic leanings from the influence of Dudley Buck in Ives' earlier life.

The Songs

From "Amphion"

Dating from a similar period (1895, but adapted into its present form in 1896), it has been proposed that this song was written for Parker's class - apparent compelling evidence that Ives was studying with Parker, at least in an informal sense before his junior year, something that some have attempted to disprove in order add weight to their case in discrediting his reputation (see Appendix 1). As such, again we should rightly expect it to conform to the genteel style of the language of his teacher; and again, it does. Ives selected just eight lines from Tennyson's poem by for his song.

> The mountain stirr'd its bushy crown,
> And, as tradition teaches,
> Young ashes pirouetted down
> Coquetting with young beeches; (Ives repeated *"Coquetting with young beeches."*)
> And shepherds from the mountain-eaves
> Look'd down, half-pleased, half-frighten'd,
> As dash'd about the drunken leaves (Ives inserted *"The sunshine lighten'd,"*)
> The random sunshine lighten'd.

Here, Ives had written a largely conventional late Victorian song, using the popular musical language of the day, but with a few wrinkles that suggest he had something more waiting in the wings. The song begins with an unusual flourish in the piano, followed by a simple introductory passage. When the voice enters, its chromatic descent, followed closely by harmonies in the piano, again remind us of the 'barbershop' quartet harmonic style associated with Buck. We know Parker would not have approved, although the song apparently survived.

Ives echoed the word *"coquetting,"* with a rooster-like figure in the piano that in another composer's work might seem strangely out of the song's character. The song continues, however, in the vein in which it began until near the end. Here, the piano (ascending) moves dramatically in the opposite direction to the voice, finishing the song with another flourish as it began, the last two repeating notes (the tonic, or fundamental pitch of the key) of the vocal part dividing the final word into corresponding syllables (*"light-en'd"*).

Tarrant Moss

Ives would pen this remarkable little song in 1902-1903, with the words taken from the first and last stanzas of the poem by Rudyard Kipling. At the time of the publication of *114 Songs* Ives did not yet have permission to use the poem (it was still protected by copyright), and so all he could do was quote the first few words! Seeming conventional enough, a closer examination reveals that melodically and harmonically it is decidedly experimental. Jumping through rhythmic figuration from one key center to another, ultimately mixing more than one, Ives still was not sure that vocalists could manage the challenge, so he all but doubled the line in the piano part.

The vocal line - strangely angular in contour - is accompanied by a jolly and rhythmically metrical piano part, frequently grounded in the opening key of C Major in the bass line. Despite the unlikely harmonic incongruities, the modern sound was achieved without making use of experimental chord structures overall, notwithstanding the final chord. Thus, a handful of 'foreign' notes give the song its altogether avant-garde ring, considering the early date of its composition.

> I closed and drew for my love's sake
> That now is false to me,
> And I slew the Reiver of Tarrant Moss
> And set Dumeny free.
> And ever they give me gold and praise
> And ever I mourn my loss–
> For I struck the blow for my false love's sake
> And not for the Men of the Moss!
> (Kipling)

The Songs

Kipling
{{PD-Art}}

Ives set the vocal line very much around the natural rhythm of the words, the staccato character of the last line of the poem finishing it off abruptly. He chose an accompaniment of chords, mostly spaced in open intervals, the final one being completely outside the key of the song (the exception being the lowest notes of the chord). Overall, musically it is somewhat startling, despite its deceptively simple appearance on the page. In its entirety, just how many 'foreign' notes are there? A mere seventeen.

Hymn

Ives arranged the music for this song from *A Set of Three Short Pieces,* a composition from 1904 for string quartet, bass and piano. Using words from the 18th Century hymn by Gerhardt Tersteegen, and a melodic quote from *More love to thee,* Ives took an expansive vein, with rich harmonic breadth built on unconventional intervals, and a few *rhythmically* irregular bars that build asymmetrically mid-song, and falling back to near symmetry and harmonic resolution towards the end. Characterized by flowing ascending broken chords, the piano part alternates between a yet to be clarified F tonality and F# Major. True to its title, *(Hymn)* it utilizes a limited number of chords, in this instance of an unconventional nature and non-determinate key; by subtly altering them, Ives suggested many diffuse tonalities, and with the exception of the final chord, never confirmed. The piano gradually introduces waves of up-and-down motion, alternating with the ascending figuration and some imitative gestures derived from it.

Thou hidden love of God,
Whose height, whose depth,
Unfathomed, no man knows,
I see from far
Thy beauteous light;
Inly I sigh for Thy repose.
My heart is pained,
Nor can it be at rest till it find rest in Thee.
(Gerhardt Tersteegen)

The Songs

NASA, ESA, and M. Livio and the Hubble 20th
Anniversary Team (STScI)

Reaching the word *"see,"* the piano briefly holds a chordal flourish, followed by the repeated words *"Thy beauteous light."* Broken ascending motion based on the opening chord suggests C# Major. The musical high point over, an increasing transparency with clearer tonality around F Major begins to emerge as the up-and-down waveform returns. With the word *"rest"* a further hold is reached, as the song winds down to the tonality that began it. But now, A# drops to A, the major third of F7 is finally confirmed. After repeated and ultimately overlapping waves, the final chord in the piano alone reveals the mystery tonic key of B flat Major. The chromaticism, still implying the influence of Dudley Buck, now takes on entirely new ground. Again Ives' choice of material - with its references to light and Heavenly thoughts - is significant. It is hardly surprising that Emerson considered the text of this hymn the ultimate in expression, and that Ives chose it; even as early as 1904 transcendentalism was central in his consciousness.

The Cage

Ives made a startling break with the past in this short, but remarkable song. Written in 1906, it falls precisely into the latter period of Ives' most radical experimentation. The words are few, hardly poetry (they were by Ives himself), and merely describe the animal's aimless pacing from meal to meal; a child observing posed the philosophical question whether this reflected life itself!

{{PD-Art}}

Ives simulated the monotonous, hopeless pacing of a caged leopard by both harmonic and rhythmic innovation. An evolving cycle of chords built from the unconventional interval of fourths (2-1/2 steps), in which the spaces between notes are further apart than in conventional chords (thirds: 1-1/2 or 2 steps), represents the circular pacing and aimlessness of the leopard's life. Musicologist Philip Lambert observed, in addition, that these cyclic chord progressions follow a *circular* pattern, amongst other apparent mathematically encoded links to the music.[2] Lambert termed the culminating chord of each sequence a 'meal' chord, when the leopard pauses for food; as such, it is differently structured, with no clear relationship to the others, evolving in greater tension with each cycle.

After repeating the primary harmonic cycle - in which the inertia pushes towards the meal chord - the singer enters with a monotonous line, each phrase built entirely of whole-step movements. The piano develops the harmonic cycle, but now as it approaches the meal chord the motion of the newly transposed cycle retards instead, inverting the notes in even wider intervals (fifths: 3-1/2 steps). Rhythmically, neither part has anything in common, but they are entirely complimentary, the vocal notes lying within the coincident chords. With endless cyclic harmony depicting the leopard's boring pattern of existence, the even-paced vocal writing its heavy footsteps around its barred cell, soft drum tones in the small orchestra version imply even its heartbeat.

Watchman

> Watchman, tell us of the night,
> What its signs of promise are.
> Traveler, o'er yon mountain's height,
> *See that glory beaming star.*
> Watchman, does its beauteous ray
> Aught of joy or hope foretell?
> Traveler, yes—it brings the day,
> Promised day of Israel.
> (John Bowring)

NASA, H.E. Bond and E. Nelan (Space Telescope Science Institute, Baltimore, Md.); M. Barstow and M. Burleigh (University of Leicester, U.K.); and J.B. Holberg (University of Arizona)

As in so much of Ives' music, this short song provides a link between two other works and further insights into Ives' experimental period, its origins dating to 1908 and before. It was reworked into his *First Violin Sonata* of 1914, then into this song (of 1913!), and apparently from that work into the *Prelude* of the *Fourth Symphony* (1910-1911)!! Despite the confusion of the retrograde dating revealed by this unlikely timeline, the fundamental musical material clearly existed nevertheless at the outset of *one* of the finished compositions! In the event that the movement of the symphony came before the song (as indicated by the dates), Ives claimed, nevertheless, that the song's origins were with the sonata. Adding further to the confusion, in his listings, Ives connected the song to the <u>Second</u> *Violin Sonata;* however, the numbered titles of violin sonatas have been updated in reference to an earlier work that shares some of the material and is now known as the *Pre-First Violin Sonata*.

The significance, however, of this song is that Ives would add the words of the hymn's first verse that were absent in the sonata, creating an aura that seems worlds apart. We see this in the symphony, too; this text (which Ives expanded slightly at the end) brings clearly to mind the otherworldly vision we finally grasp fully in the *Prelude* of his symphony - the course of evolution of this one element reflecting how Ives' thoughts grew with each step, and pointing to the sonata as indeed coming first.

Rhythmically and harmonically the song clearly belongs to the post-experimental period. It opens with a short piano introduction, taken directly from its context within the third movement of the violin sonata. A fast descending three-note figure morphs and slows into the accompanying upper line in contrary motion to the melody. The 'Watchman' melody itself emerges as something of a surprise, with the regular pacing of its accompaniment and near-conventional harmonies. However, we should not take this to mean that it is a conventional setting, since the harmonies are remarkable and unexpected, nevertheless. Because of the tonality of the melodic line, we expect the harmony to be in the relative implied major key (D, the key sharing the same pitches). However, Ives seems to tie us both to that *and* the 'relative' minor (B), which shares the same notes but is based a minor third (1-1/2 steps) lower. Despite thus a bass line one third below our expectation, we never escape the gravity of the 'relative,' higher major key, for two reasons:

- First, there is the natural key center of the melody itself.
- Placed higher in the harmony of Ives' song is the tonic (the first note of the expected major key, and also adjacent to the low 'B' in the bass), plus the seventh of the major key (C#, the 'leading tone' half a step below the tonic) that also instinctively leads us towards the major key (D).

Although there are obvious ways to explain the tonality (as a true minor harmony) and its relationship to the melody, it is the way Ives sets it up that causes our perceptions to be constantly kept off balance. On the page, the minor key harmony is easy to see; we just do not hear it that way. Thus Ives continued to 'toy' with our expectations and perceptions, even moving briefly to the relative major key as the song progresses, amidst some striking rhythmic, harmonic and pianistic effects. These carry the piano part far higher than the vocal line with colorful dissonance (the 'glory beaming star'). Only as the song concludes is the relative major finally confirmed, in a profoundly telling descending passage offset by the ascending vocal line; it is as if Ives is dreaming in space. Likely he was.

The Indians

Written in 1912 and further arranged in 1921 for inclusion in *114 Songs* as an elegy to a people left to despair, it was one of the seven originally selected by Copland to be performed at his festival at Yaddo in 1932, garnering the first real acclaim for Ives' song catalog after its long period of rejection.

The vocal part uses mostly the notes of a pentatonic scale (corresponding relatively to the black keys on a piano) to symbolize the music of Native American tribes. Though demonstrating a remarkable awareness of indigenous culture for that time, it is not surprising from someone so attuned to social issues. The piano part is built on a two-bar segment that expands and contracts with the text, the chords being *dominant*, harmonically, and thus with expected resolutions to new key centers. Instead, these chords move in parallel, each dominant chord answering itself within the chord with the tone of resolution in the top voice.

{{PD-Art}}

Alas for them! - their day is o'er,
Their fires are out from hill and shore;
No more for them the wild deer bounds;
The plough is on their hunting-grounds;
The pale man's axe rings through their woods;
The pale man's sail skims o'er their floods;
Their pleasant springs are dry;
Their children, look! by power oppressed,
Beyond the mountains of the west
Their children go to die!
(Charles Sprague)

Remarkable, too, mid-song is the use of parallel speeds between the piano and singer. Although the more complex works for large ensembles often require more than one conductor because of the need to maintain coordination between multiple instrumentalists, the possible relationships between just two performers are fewer and more likely possible to notate without resorting to writing in *actual* different speeds. Essentially, the effect was attained in this song by dividing successions of 'pulses' (simulated beats) by a common unit, in which 4 'pulses' in one line occupy the same time as 3 in the other. However, this is an oversimplification since Ives changed the *meter* (number of beats per bar) regularly, too, often by uneven numbers!

Regardless, both 'speeds' are easy to comprehend as the audible result of dividing an actual common speed: i.e. if, mentally, we divide one beat into equal subdivisions in groups of 4 and 3, and *accent* just the first note of each subdivided group, the total *subdivisions* common to both before the accented notes coincide again will be 24, effectively simulating 6 full (accented) beats in one speed and 8 in another; the subdivisions allow for coordination between performers. However, Ives complicated the situation yet further by maintaining even metric divisions of the beat in the vocalist's line, while irregularly grouping them one, two, or three notes at a time to create an utterly free, but tangled rhythmic texture. The independence of elements achieved it is more closely aligned with Ives' later symphonic essays than the relatively more limited medium of piano and voice.

Like a Sick Eagle

In one of the most definitive little works by Ives in existence, *Like a Sick Eagle* might first have emerged in 1909 as a piece of the same name. In any event, it seems that Ives set Keats' words into the song for voice and piano in 1913, although possibly it might date a little later. Regardless, it would appear in his published collection, *114 Songs*, ultimately to be incorporated as a movement into the *Set No. 1 for Chamber Orchestra* of 1915/16. On the sheet music in that version, Ives wrote Keats' words to the poem above the melodic notes. In, *114 Songs*, he did not mention

The Songs

the sliding, quarter-tone effect between pitches that is a feature in the orchestral scoring, made possible because it included writing for violin. However, in a later song edition *(Thirty-four Songs,* 1933), the distinction was made, and instructions were made for the voice to do so, too. The piano obviously cannot accommodate the slides between notes in this version. Because it doubles the moving (eighth-note) in its inner middle line, the effect is accomplished efficiently by the vocalist's 'ghosting' of that line.

The chromatic vocal writing, essentially moving by *half-step* increments, paints the heavy anguish of the eagle; the piano right hand (upper line) moves in parallel with the voice, but by *whole-steps* instead. This causes the lines alternately to separate or threaten to merge to a degree, as the music seems to flex like an accordion, with interesting harmonic consequences.

{{PD-Art}}

The spirit is too weak; mortality
Weighs heavily on me like unwilling sleep,
And each imagined pinnacle and steep
Of godlike hardship tells me I must die,
Like a sick eagle looking towards the sky.
(Keats)

During most of the song, Ives chose to keep moving eighth notes as a constant in both the vocal line and the accompaniment, and to remain essentially at a static low volume. In contrast with the metrically measured requirements needed for coordination in the instrumental version, independent rhythmic groupings in the lines are freely established in this un-barred setting from the outset. In the piano, the respective notes of the left and right hand have been grouped into individual phrasings, and are different in each. Additionally, the vocalist has further independent groupings of notes, though rhythmically they coincide note for note in their commonly shared constant metrical divisions and speed - in the manner outlined in the previous example, *The Indians* - effectively allowing continually evolving independence of the parts. An effort, thus, should be made to hear the song in separate linear, not vertical, components, in order to appreciate the 'inner' rhythmic subtleties that pervade its entire length; the constant variations of harmonic consequence caused by the shifting relationships between the vocal line and the accompaniment are no less compelling.

From the third line of the verse until the conclusion there is a slight increase in volume and tension, the piano writing becoming increasingly *syncopated* (rhythmically displaced from the beat), while it continues to develop in rhythmic motion. After the word *"God"* is highlighted with a startling broken chord in the piano and a wide leap in the vocal line, the song winds down as the eagle that can no longer fly looks *"towards the sky."* The music 'looks' up too, with a mildly ascending melodic line and perceptively grief-stricken accompanying chords.

So may it be! (The Rainbow)

{{PD-Art}}

My heart leaps up when I behold
A rainbow in the sky:
So was it when my life began;
So is it now I am a man;
So be it when I shall grow old,
Or let me die!
The Child is father of the Man;
I could wish my days to be
Bound each to each by natural piety.
(Wordsworth)

It is now (1914), and we are closer to the cosmic territory in which Ives formulated his pathway to the heavens; in some ways the journey had already started, because his piano compositions often were the first incarnations of materials that would continue to evolve in later, larger works. By now, what is striking about Ives' mature songs is the remarkable independence of both entities (voice and piano), yet they feature a unity of purpose and effect that dominates how we hear and perceive them. Without the possibilities of true independence with the multiple speeds and trains of thought we find within his orchestral writing, and especially its wide potential for coloration, Ives achieved many of the same outcomes, nevertheless. Producing extraordinary variety and creativity with each little masterwork, Ives proved it was not necessary to write in common keys, rhythms, or even within traditionally prerequisite balanced shapes.

Originally scored in 1914 for strings, flute, piano or harp, celeste and organ, Ives wrote *So may it be!* for his wife, Harmony, to celebrate her birthday in their new summer home in West Redding. That year Ives had reached 40 years of age, and his own father's untimely demise before turning 50 must have weighed heavily and often on his mind, especially with his own health history ever present and looming. Although dated 1914, Ives did not arrange it for voice and piano until putting his *114 Songs* together in 1921, at which point he had turned 47. With this in mind, his thoughts had become increasingly reflective, so it is easy to see why he chose this short poem by Wordsworth at that time.

The song is essentially divisible into two parts; opening with the piano rushing towards the singer's entrance; the optimistic words of youth, *"My heart leaps up"* is thus represented and anticipated with a vocal line initially built largely out of fourths, an interval Ives also used in the song to construct chords for emphatic words. With a flourish, and a wide arpeggiated chord that follows it, are the words, *"I behold a rainbow in the sky,"* set to an arching curve as if to outline it. Everything to this point being more of an introduction, the song continues with reflective words, more or less in whole-step motion, under two repeated segments consisting of two gentle broken chords leading to a static, higher chord. Suddenly landing strongly on the highest chord of the song, again structured from fourths, the word, *"man,"* at the mid-point in the song signifies the mid-point of life. Signaling an abrupt change in character, more reflective words about growing old are matched by gentle descending chords still built in fourths. With the word *"die!"* a further abrupt change takes place, set optimistically to a hopeful sounding high chord of mixed tonalities (E augmented and B minor) to herald the second part of the song.

A precipitously descending and fading vocal part is accompanied by a uniquely Ivesian setting based on the hymn *Serenity*, and a musical style colored by notes that belong outside the prevailing tonalities. The accompaniment features a slow upward arch every two bars, and musically it proceeds through D Major, E Major, and A flat Major, through neighboring chords to settle in conclusion in B minor, though arranged, as in *Watchman*, to imply D Major with an uncertain confirmation of the tonality. Rhythmically, both the piano and voice, which have seemed utterly independent until now, only loosely coinciding, finally 'walk' together effectively in unity. Interestingly, Ives chose this moment when referencing father and child - a connection again with his own feelings - as the song concludes at a state of peace he was looking for within himself.

September

This song from 1919, with text by the early Italian poet, Folgore da San Giminiano, brings us to territory surrounded on all sides by Ives' greatest works, the grandest being the *Fourth Symphony*, the *Concord Sonata*, and of course, the *Universe Symphony*. It should not be surprising that we find parallels to the type of musical language Ives employed in them within this song, too, and indeed we do. With piano writing strongly reminiscent of that of the *Concord Sonata*, by now Ives was thoroughly entrenched in the complex methodology he had been developing for years. Ives' use of mathematically ingenious techniques, often cyclically within others, was by now so endemic that having attained his goal of developing expressive yet formal structure gave him the flexibility to use only what he needed; systematic elements are present, regardless. Unfortunately, much of this will be hard for the average listener to discern as such.

{{PD-Art}}

And in September,
Falcons, astors, merlins, sparrow-hawks;
Decoy birds that lure game in flocks,;
And hounds with bells;
Crossbows shooting out of sight;
Arblasts and javelins;
All birds the best to fly;
And each to each of you shall be lavish still in gifts;
And robbery find no gainsaying;
And if you meet with your travelers going by,

> Their purses from your purse's flow shall fill;
> And avarice be the only outcast thing.
> (Folgore da San Giminiano)

The voice opens the song, briefly in scale-like segments built in whole tones (fairly common in Ives' melodic lines, and even a structural feature in his concurrent *Universe Symphony*[3]). It is followed by the piano accompaniment with rhapsodic broken chords (built largely from augmented intervals - the bottom of the chord descending in steps while the top ascends to form a widening chordal spread), and strongly suggestive of the flight of birds depicted. With the mention of *"crossbows shooting out of sight; arblasts and javelins"* the texture fragments into repeating figurations to imply the scattering of the flocks, their winged flight represented by the widest of all the rhapsodic broken chords. From now, the right hand of the piano shadows the melody, adding supportive harmony between the words:

"And each to each" - to - *"gainsaying,"*

while the pianist's left hand plays a repeating flourish based on the opening of the song. While the flourishes resume movement and expand as before, if the emphatic nature of this section implies the significance of the poet's benevolent wishes to mankind, the next implies that it is incumbent on all of us to give something back, wherein flourishes of a similar structure to those of the opening, though developing in descending cycles in the bass, might imply that we are supposed to give flight to our benevolence. With *"And avarice be the only outcast thing!,"* the piano part is emphatic and declamatory, rising to a dramatic peak after the vocal line has concluded, as if to insist that we heed the words!

Afterglow

Written also in 1919, using a short poem by James Fenimore Cooper, Jr. (grandson of the famous novelist), this song is mystical in its distant thoughts. Ives had just survived his most serious illness (1918), and in its aftermath must have spent considerable time reflecting on his own mortality - indeed, a terrible afterglow of that event itself. If his mind had been transported to distant places, he was already traveling to the stars. Indeed, a lack of normal reference points corresponding to his earlier music is quite clear, as this song seems to waft in and out of earthly bonds, the day-to-day human experience, or even consciousness.

{{PD-Art}}

 At the quiet close of day,
  Gently yet the willows sway;
   When the sunset light is low,
    Lingers still the afterglow;
     Beauty tarries loth to die,

The Songs

> Every lightest fantasy
> Lovelier grows in memory,
> Where the truer beauties lie.
> (James Fenimore Cooper, Jr.)

Ives instructed the pianist to play indistinctly, using both pedals to create the floating sound. Unfortunately the song is often marred by 'heroic' antics at the piano, completely destroying the otherworldly qualities that he was trying to convey. If one is fortunate enough to hear it played according to the composer's intent, its reflective remoteness becomes clear, for surely this is an expression of Ives' gazing into his inner thoughts - even to space itself - and a fitting commentary on his spiritual growth, commencing in earnest less than 20 years before. Interestingly, he would also specify a similar approach to the last movement *(Thoreau)* of his legendary *Concord Sonata*, the subject of the next chapter, and one that similarly suffers all too often from a heavy hand.

The song is entirely unbarred, allowing for considerable flexibility, in order that the performers can gauge the sounds appropriately. Opening with gently alternating broken chords, and light, even vague, melodic notes uppermost, a deep 'pedal' tone in the bass sounds from time to time over the ringing of the chords, the mood and quietly fading light of the evening reflected in the words introduced thereafter, and musically, with a fragment of *Erie*. The piano continues between further broken chords, until gaining movement and a flourish towards the word, *"light;"* gradually both voice and piano drop and fade into the word, *"afterglow"* and hushed high 'bell' tones, ascending as if skywards. With the final words accompanied by a repeating cycle of broken chords ringing into each of their own sonorous 'afterglows,' the words must also have reflected Ives' thoughts at the time. After, *"every lightest fantasy lovelier grows in memory,"* the piano climbs to the highest notes of the song, thereafter dropping with the voice (and a clear reference to *Erie*) to fade.

Although Ives could not have known about, let alone envisaged, the ultimate afterglow of the cosmos: the Cosmic Microwave

Background (the leftover radiation still remaining from the Big Bang some 13.7 billion years ago), such a reference somehow seems not far removed. It was only a matter of time before he would continue the flight he had already embarked upon in the Zen-like *Universe Symphony*.

The **Cosmic Microwave Background Radiation**
- Afterglow of the universe
NASA

REFERENCES

1. 'Ives's Concord Sonata and the Texture of Music,' David Michael Hertz, from 'Charles Ives and his World,' Edited by J. Peter Burkholder, *Princeton University Press*, Princeton, New Jersey, 1996, pp. 75-117
2. 'The Music of Charles Ives,' Philip Lambert, *Yale University Press*, New Haven and London, 1997, pp. 150-159
3. 'Memos', Charles E, Ives, edited by John Kirkpatrick, p. 106, *W. W. Norton & Co.*, New York, 1972, p. 107

CHAPTER 9

The Concord Sonata

Concord, Massachusetts at the turn of the 20th Century
{{PD-Art}}

There are many musicians and commentators who regard this work as Ives' single greatest masterpiece; it is impossible to deny that the monumental *Concord Sonata* certainly is *one* of his most momentous compositions, representing the very core of his life's work, seen through his experiences and surroundings in the search for new meaning in musical forms. Representing a plane of thought and creativity of his own making, the *Concord Sonata* did not rely on models from any foreign soil: this is true American music without nationalism, the quest for artistic relevance in the New World, and for a new world in music. Technically, it is a colossus, a tour de force for any pianist to master. Considered unplayable for many years - to everyone, that is, except Ives - it was John Kirkpatrick who assured us Ives could play everything he wrote.[1] It was fitting that in 1939 Kirkpatrick would be the first to perform the complete sonata in concert, and would go from there to becoming the leading Ives researcher and historian in the world, one whose commitment to the composer has bequeathed him a permanent place high atop the keepers of the greater Ives legacy.

Through the vehicle of the piano - Ives' instrument - his epic second piano sonata put him within reach of his final destination amongst the stars. It exists as one of a group of three large-scale works we can define as the most mature representations of his output, (the others being the *Fourth Symphony* and the *Universe Symphony*). They illustrate convincingly that Ives, in effect, had embarked on his spiritual journey, the result of endless experimentation, dreaming and soul searching that would take him where he needed to go. The *Universe Symphony* and the *Concord Sonata*, one way or the other, would remain present in Ives' mind from the moment of initially contemplating them until the end of his life. We know he was still working on the *Concord Sonata* as late as 1947 for the Second Edition, in which he made numerous additions and changes; even after that, he continued to tinker with it, adding his revisions to the printed page into his final days. To put an accurate date on it is hard to do; probably even Ives himself did not know. Actual formal notation of the first version possibly was not begun until about 1915, but was complete by 1919, and it seems certain that Ives already had built most of the material - albeit in other proposed works - from as early as 1904, having a fairly comprehensive concept of the sonata by 1911. Thus, during most of his adult life it represents a lengthy evolution and highly personal expression of all that mattered to him.

The Concord Sonata

How can we tell that the sonata was not in fact, the ultimate example of Ives' musical maturation? Was this work, in fact, the spiritual place at end of Ives' road to the stars? The fact that Ives was still working on the first movement of the *Concord Sonata*, *(Four Transcriptions from Emerson)* until the time he ceased writing music almost entirely in 1927, and also preparing the Second Edition in the 1940's illustrates well, nevertheless, the proximity of the sonata to his final destination. However, the early dates of its raw materials (prior to subsequent revisions, of course) and completion put it well before Ives' farthest musical development. Both the *Fourth* and *Universe Symphonies* reveal advancement beyond even the vastly wide confines of the *Concord Sonata*. There are other, more telling clues, too. In the sonata, Ives still was quoting hymns and vernacular melodies, as well as two distinguished references to Beethoven, not to mention allusions to some near light-hearted earthly things. Admittedly, the Beethoven references were near spiritual to Ives, but nevertheless, a gradual evolution away from secular melodic quotations through his maturation is evident over the years. From there, a movement towards religious material is quite clear, although it by no means follows an even curve. Ultimately, even the whittling down of religious melodies becomes increasingly noticeable, leaving little melodic residual in their wake. Thus, the groundbreaking finale of the *Fourth Symphony* is significant in this regard; few hymns are quoted, and significantly, limited mostly to *Nearer, My God to Thee*, *Missionary Chant* and *Dorrnance*. At the end of the journey in the *Universe Symphony*, we find virtually nothing so 'earthly' as a melodic quote, save for a few diffuse references, again, *pivotally* from our perspective, to *Nearer, My God to Thee,* as well as to *In the Sweet Bye and Bye,* and curiously *Massa's in de Cold Ground*. Some have noted an apparent absence of *Nearer, My God* in the sonata. In theory, this separates this work from the last two surrounding symphonies. However, it *is* there, as will become clear.

The *Concord Sonata* is both tonal and atonal, but frequently consists of a highly diffused polytonal mix, crossed with freely conceived atonality. Its remarkably improvisatory feel presents listeners with a dilemma in deciding exactly where to place it amongst Ives' other musical structures; the degree to which he forged it through a deliberate and careful evolution of the materials into his adopted 'cumulative form' - versus utilizing a freer, improvisatory approach, weaving thematic components into the fabric at the keyboard almost incidentally - remains the question. Perhaps this even does not matter. If we must find an answer, then the problem is always limited by the lack of Ives' documentation of his working methods; he never discussed them. However, the ongoing incorporation and evolution of multiple earlier experiments is evident; his more traditional European based music, of course, shows a keenly developed sense of form, so clearly valid structure was of paramount importance to him. Although Ives would share his inner thoughts about his mature creative aims and thought processes (in *Essays Before a Sonata*,[2] published concurrently with the *Concord Sonata* itself), he still did not divulge anything about his composing methods, or the system(s) by which he had arrived at his results. It was as if discussing them in mechanical terms would destroy the magic of their creation.

To what degree did the Second Edition change the sonata? For the most part, Ives restored material into the *Concord Sonata*'s first movement from sketches originally conceived for a large work for piano and orchestra - what was to be the *Emerson Concerto* (sometimes called the *Emerson Overture*). This eventually evolved into the sonata. It contained a lot of additional material in the orchestral parts that was missing in the First Edition of the sonata. Ives grew to miss those musical elements, and did his best to build them into the definitive version of the work he would leave behind: the Second Edition of 1947, clearly a very late date indeed along the timeline. Kirkpatrick, however, having lived with the work for a long time, was slow to warm to the changes in the new version, ultimately settling on a blend of the two. Clearly, however, Ives could hardly bear to put this sonata to rest, even expressing that he wished he could leave it unfinished so it might always continue to evolve. Since something along these lines also was said (reputedly, but not necessarily by Ives!) about the *Universe Symphony*, it is worth bearing in

The Concord Sonata

mind that the *Concord Sonata*, however, had been put into two *complete* performable forms, one from 1919, putting it squarely at an earlier date than the symphony. However, regardless of any version of the sonata we hear, it remains still the same piece.

For musician and non-musician alike, the sonata is daunting. Its technical complexities are nothing short of orchestral, its meaning profound and personal; musically, the demands on the performer - even the listener - are beyond intimidating. It holds such an enormous reservoir of one man's imagination that it can consume performer and listener alike for years, and even then, no one will ever know what lay within it as did the composer. It is clear from the outset that Ives created the impression of multiple speeds, layers and textures by free flowing, unmeasured or unevenly balanced events and sub-structures. In fact, there are few bar lines at all; Ives' own recordings amply demonstrate the flexibility that he intended. Unfortunately, the immense scale and complexity of the sonata, coupled with the textural uniformity of the physical sound of the piano itself - despite the huge range that Ives was able to extract from it - makes following normal descriptive references problematic for the listener. It is not possible, therefore, to provide the same type of analysis for the *Concord Sonata* as has been done previously with other works; the approach will take a broader perspective.

Listeners' guide

The *Concord Sonata* was written in four movements (one for each of the most influential Concord transcendentalists in Ives' life). This is one movement more than found in most standard sonatas, but it is hardly a rarity in such literature either. However, the sonata differs further from most in that it features several significant thematic elements throughout all of the movements that are used freely in multiple guises, seldom appearing in their complete form. Being built around an evolved type of *cumulative form*, Ives conceived the structure into something even grander, that would evolve further over the course of *multiple* movements rather than during any one, individually - something confirmed and revealed by the conclusions of each: form within form. Regardless, the essential concept of the structure was retained within each movement, and each movement still is accorded a greater degree of freedom in this respect than we find probably in any other work, even by Ives.

Ives was captivated, even haunted over his entire compositional career by the four famous declamatory notes (the so-called *Fate* motif) that open Beethoven's *Fifth Symphony*; he heard them as man's fate knocking at the door, presumably having heard them knocking at his own more than a few times. These four notes, along with what has been generally accepted as another quote - from Beethoven's *Hammerklavier Sonata* - often follows them in the sonata, and represent two of the principle external references. The *Hammerklavier* quote is not clear-cut, however. At least in the similarities and differences it offers with the *Fate* motif, the case has been made for its origins - not quite the same thing as conclusive, nevertheless.

Hearing the opening of the *Hammerklavier Sonata* itself makes clear that if Ives indeed had this work in mind, rather than quote it verbatim he assembled a curious amalgam of *both* Beethoven entities. By retaining the essential rhythm of the *Fate* motif within the outline of the *Hammerklavier*, and imposing the repetitive rhythm of the former on the slow-fast-fast rhythmic pattern and chords of the latter, the melodic variances above and below those notes provide a means to extend the *Fate* motif, which always precedes it.

These two quotes are sometimes stated in blocks of closely voiced *chords;* hymns are normally associated with such writing. In choosing two hymns to escort the Beethoven fragments within the greater work - *Missionary Chant* and *Martyn* - Ives was well aware of some shared common *melodic* traits. This allowed him to use the materials interchangeably, together and separately, both supported by chords, or only as a single line, giving him the freedom to build and weave his ideas. A further theme termed the *Human Faith Melody* weaves the fundamentals of all four external musical sources in many ways; if the

Beethoven fragments are clear in their melodic contours, the influence of the hymns can be felt in the *Human Faith Melody* when it exists in chordal settings.

To hear the *Human Faith Melody* in its entirety, however, we will have to wait until the end of the third movement *(The Alcotts)*, in which it is revealed in its fullest form. Thus Ives built his greater cumulative structure over no less than three movements, in addition to within the movements themselves. It is only here that we finally hear the Beethoven quotes, the hymns, and the *Human Faith Melody* clearly bonded, stated, and all together. One cannot miss this focal point here; it concludes the movement, and arrives clad in grand hymn-like chords. Perhaps the best starting point for the new listener to the sonata, therefore, should be this part of *The Alcotts,* and also to allow several hearings. For further references, we can glimpse *Missionary Chant,* too, in the opening bars of *The Alcotts* and how it intrudes on the melodic line. Meanwhile, suggestions of the first parts of *Martyn* can be heard in the middle of *Hawthorne,* simply harmonized between outbursts of frenzy, again not easily missed. Identifying these elements early on will be an advantage in recognizing them wherever they appear throughout the sonata, especially when they are well disguised or infused with other material.

We should not expect the *Concord Sonata* to sound conventional in any way, of course. Even the quotations are rendered entirely new with each twist and turn, and do not necessarily sound tonal - even though, in themselves, they are. Ives frequently used multiple key centers at a time, and freely mixed atonal sounds with tonal; the blended effect typically is decidedly atonal in *sound.* However, knowing that there are key centers that indeed can be located amongst the textures might give a little encouragement to those perplexed or stunned by their first hearing(s) of Ives' towering piano masterpiece.

- **Emerson**

It was hardly surprising Ives would choose Emerson as his inspiration for the first and most substantial movement of the sonata. Emerson, to Ives, for his revelations about eternity and the cosmic depth of the human spirit perhaps was greater than any other American. Ives saw him as being almost limitless in his larger vision, standing alone in his endlessly renewing thought processes and modes of expression.

In this movement, there can be no doubt of the magnitude of what we are hearing; the music is as vast in scope, expanse, and free from any predetermined modes of construction as anything Ives ever would write. If it seems overwhelming upon first encounter, so it should; Ives had not intended his music to be easy on the ears or the mind. The challenge for the listener is to look beyond familiar confines. With repeated listening and openness, we become increasingly aware of places far beyond normal sonic horizons; indeed, most of the time the music seems to have no boundaries at all. In *Emerson*, Ives endeavored to forge a musical representation of all that Ralph Waldo Emerson stood for. As such it is as close to Ives' final destination as we will find in his music, save the last movement of the *Fourth Symphony*, and the colossal revelations of the *Universe Symphony*.

Apart from the materials originally conceived for the *Emerson Concerto*, a segment from his 1912-1913 piano study *The Anti-Abolitionist Riots* was incorporated into the movement as well. In preparation for the Second Edition, Ives can be heard playing the *Four Transcriptions from Emerson* in private recordings he made over the years from 1933 – 1943,[3] so we can quickly gain insights into how he envisaged the nature of the music, as well as the freedom with which he expected performers to interpret it.

In *Essays Before a Sonata*, Ives remarked upon Emerson's writing methods; any restrictive protocol, such as carefully balanced phrases, structured or constrained progressions of thought, indeed anything else that might limit his horizons would not invade his thought processes; he took an entirely different tack. Rather than have one part of a structure lead to the next in normal sequence, Emerson looked at things from all sides, building a composite image from what we might term 'circular thought.' If we can accept this concept as being capable of revealing greater truths, in Emerson's writing one must look beyond two seemingly unrelated consecutive paragraphs, consecutive

The Concord Sonata

phrases, thoughts or the like. Instead, these elements are tied to the next and beyond by common gravity (rather than the conventionally expected connections), and thus it is possible to understand how one should try to grasp the far larger realities he was trying to convey.

This approach is exactly what we can expect to find within the movement, too, as Ives indeed created a sonic representation of Emerson's approach. Thus the movement's extravagant and wildly free design makes increasing sense in the large picture, as we begin to resolve fragmented detail into connected thought across its entire length, *having looked at it from all sides*. However, certain specific aural guideposts that we can listen for will enable our recognition of the larger considerations of the design. First we need to discern them, then anticipate them, and finally build our composite 'three dimensional' image of the abstract, but philosophical musical imagery Ives painted.

Aside from the four distinct thematic components that can be found throughout the sonata, others are specific only to this movement. One that seems to be a representation of Emerson himself: a marked, rhythmically angular 5-note motif that suggests a person of striking and stoic character. Appearing near the beginning, at the top of the second 'rush to the top' the piano part leaps quickly from the bottom to the upper register to announce the motif in the first of many later, but identifiable guises. The other motif has been termed the *quasi-pentatonic melody*, due to being comprised of notes that resemble the five 'black' keys on the piano - an immediately familiar sound - and the same five-note scale structure that Ives had used in the song, *The Indians* (see again Chapter 8). A segment of this material appears early in the bass just a couple of notes after the *Emerson motif*. Although harder to catch (especially if one is not able to read and follow the music), a keen ear will pick out elements of this idea throughout *Emerson,* and as always in Ives' works, deceptively couched in varying character and application. However, it shares another, far more significant connection to the pivotal hymn, *Nearer, My God to Thee;* see *Thoreau,* later.

We have thus the basic thematic information that was incorporated into the movement. Amongst them, never have quoted works sounded so different! However, the limited number of quotations and themes is indicative of the fact Ives was moving away from using them, as well as towards balancing his music by an almost impossibly intricate weaving of musical textures. In any case, Ives surely would have preferred that we do not overanalyze the music, his intention being for the musical components slowly to work their way into our consciousness. The most important consideration is to let the music unfold its grand design with each hearing, as we 'look at it from all sides' in the true Emersonian tradition.

- *Emerson* opens with dramatic flourishes and bold writing, in which all the musical elements are laid out. Because they are brief and often buried deeply within the whole, some of them might be difficult to identify, though the Beethoven motifs seem obvious enough, as well as that of Emerson himself, always characterized by its rhythmically marked ('dotted' rhythm) and slightly angular contour. The *quasi-pentatonic* material is introduced in the bass. Continuing with other material derived from both the *Human Faith Melody* and the Beethoven *Fate* motif, the *Emerson motif* periodically intrudes to announce his presence. Ives identified this 'exposition' section with a small subtitle, ***prose***.
- As the music unfolds, Beethoven's *Fate* motif reinvents itself constantly in the sonata; it is transformed into slower bass figures under ascending motion in the upper lines built on the first notes of the *Human Faith Melody*. The *Emerson motif* appears regularly, too, as the music becomes increasingly restless.
- A new section of a different, gentler character follows, built around a new lyrical motif. Ives subtitled it, ***verse***, at first it appears softly and slower. We might realize it is comprised of *quasi-pentatonic* material by the character and motivic references of this section. The music

grows increasingly turbulent as we hear fragments of the Beethoven motifs, too.
- David Michael Hertz pointed out the direct tie to the standard blues progression in a second *verse* segment.[4] Broken chord-like movement accompanies line of the extended *quasi-pentatonic melody,* while the blues progression may be distinguished easily in the bass line. Grounded to the root of the tonality, it is punctuated by the characteristic alternating chords one fourth higher (2-1/2 steps), and in this instance at the end of each musical paragraph. Hertz did not remark upon the harmonic language here that features the characteristic lowered seventh of the scale in both chords, just as found in the 'blues,' or that it shares pentatonic elements, too; the link to the *quasi-pentatonic melody* in this movement thus is logical.
- The segment soon develops into swirling writing in the bass line, with the *quasi-pentatonic melody* appearing in massive broken chords, (somewhat reminiscent of the music of Maurice Ravel), evolving through a section built out of pentatonic and whole-tone elements, even a snatch of the *Fate* motif, to a further statement and development of the earlier 'blues' treatment as it winds down.
- As if in recapitulation, a new section, prose, clearly identifies this later part of the movement with the opening material; now it is reflective, featuring gentle reminders of the *Emerson* and *Fate* motifs, evolving into a further extended development of the primary *Emerson* material, and further maintained by an extended section based on fugal treatment of a theme from Wagner's *Prelude* to *Tristan und Isolde.*
- Another *verse* section follows, built as before on the lyrical motif, alongside reminders of other key motifs, especially *quasi-pentatonic* material; Emerson's motif is never far away, as it and the Beethoven motifs slowly become dominant, now in ever more reposeful settings.
- The movement winds down as the Emersonian revelation now becomes clear - Ives had clearly built a cumulative

structure in which order would emerge out of chaos - in much the same way he regarded Emerson's thought processes. We have looked at all sides of the material, and now see the heart of it in its purest state, devoid of clutter and disorder: both Beethoven motifs and Emerson's stand on their own. A final, slow-paced *Fate* motif statement appears in the bass as the movement concludes.

• Hawthorne

If one's impression of this movement were to be based solely on some of the commentary written about it, all too likely one would conclude that the second movement of the *Fourth Symphony* is merely an orchestral transcription of this sonata movement. Although indeed one movement is an outgrowth of the other, and contains materials in common, nothing could be further from the truth. Though many passages of *Hawthorne* were reworked into the symphony, the casual listener would only be aware of several readily identifiable parallel places. Mostly, the symphonic movement will seem completely new. That is not to say, however, that we should not look to both for direct comparisons, because there are many. Familiarity with the related movement in the *Fourth Symphony* (the subject of the next chapter) will make this even clearer.

Ives was inspired by the fantastic and otherworldly visions of Nathaniel Hawthorne's writings, which often projected colorful visions of strange, mystical sights and weird contradictions around every corner. He decided to set Hawthorne's imagination and creative vein to music, rather than the deeper themes of his thought - those being the dark side of man's conscience and the consequences of guilt. Ives' music in both the sonata and the symphony is intended thus as something of an adventure, free, chaotic, reckless, extravagant, even hair-raising. In a similar vein to the evolution of *Emerson,* much of this movement was based on another of Ives' earlier prospective works for piano and orchestra. In this instance, it was the *Hawthorne Concerto* (c. 1910?), the major materials for which were lost. In addition, other materials conceived for piano comprised some of the movement, all of them suitably fantastic and similarly wildly imaginative. Most notably amongst them are a preliminary version of *The Celestial Railroad*, the lost *Demons' Dance around the Pipe*, and also *The Slaves Shuffle*. If Hawthorne's origins are as early as Ives dated them (1911), this is truly a remarkable flight of the imagination, coming as it would some two years prior to Stravinsky's *The Rite of Spring*.

Both in the sonata and corresponding symphonic movement, we will hear fragments galore of a number of vernacular tunes, indeed the last vestiges of Ives' lost world on Main Street, Danbury; however, here the *Concord Sonata's* central themes are never far away. Other than those, specifically, amongst the melodies stepping in and out of the fabric we may catch: *Columbia, the Gem of the Ocean, Martyn, The Battle Cry of Freedom, In the Sweet Bye and Bye,* Debussy's *Golliwog's Cake-Walk* - even Ives' own music - *Country Band March, He Is There!, Majority* (it is hard to know which work came first), and *Take-Off No. 3: Rube Trying to Walk 2 to 3!!*. Although clearly revealing some fragmentary elements of these as the music progresses, the movement serves more as an evolution towards the revelations of the *next* movement, *The Alcotts,* than it does a model of typical *cumulative form,* per se. Regardless, the larger 'cumulative' thought process is there.

Hawthorne is a romp, and not supposed to plumb the very depths of profundity that we find in *Emerson*. However, it is exceedingly dense and tangled in texture - as great a phantasmagoric display as Ives could muster, conjuring up in every way visions as supernatural in scope as the best of Hawthorne's imagination. Ives considered it as a 'scherzo' (as well as its counterpart in the *Fourth Symphony*), a comedy or joke of sorts, although it is nothing like lightly scored scherzos of traditional works. Nor are either of these virtuoso tours de force especially funny!

- The movement opens with flurries of activity; keen listeners will be able to hear the fast sixteenth note references to *The Celestial Railroad* common to the solo piano part in the *scherzo* of the *Fourth Symphony*. Early on, we hear a fragment of *Columbia, the Gem of the Ocean,* identifiable by its 'dotted' rhythm; shortly thereafter, the first three notes of the *Human Faith Melody* (in a high register), just to remind us that it is still there.

- After some dashing flourishes from bottom to top, a new section emerges that again quotes the first three notes of the *Human Faith Melody* in various guises. This leads into a quiet passage that required the use of a 14-¾ inch board to play gentle clusters of 'black' keys that accompany other material! At the time of the work's first performance, many mocked such techniques and derisively dismissed the entire sonata because of them - akin to throwing out the baby with the bath water. Significantly, this section resembles in many ways part of Ives' song, *Majority,* in which similar clusters of black keys are utilized to much the same effect and style, including what it accompanies, although in that instance it is utilized very forcefully.

- Leaving the section with one further reference to the *Human Faith Melody,* the music picks up speed and urgency, when all of a sudden a clear quotation of *In the Sweet Bye and Bye* appears out of thin air in the bass - another connection to the movement's counterpart in the *Fourth Symphony.* A repeating 3-note sequence (the *first* three notes) again from the *Human Faith Melody* is intertwined, alternating back-and-forth, as the gusto and incessant swirling continues.

- The *Fate* motif, and its adjoining *Hammerklavier* variant twice interject, winding down to a brief moment of repose built on the hymn, *Martyn*. This is directly comparable to similar moments in the second movement of the *Fourth Symphony,* although here Ives quoted a different melody *(In the Sweet Bye and Bye).* It is in the way it is approached in this context that clearly tells us that it was supposed to imply it had always been present, existing underneath at an independent level and speed (again, just as in the *Fourth Symphony*). With a passage of

brilliant flourishes, *Martyn* intones again, this time more complete, but altered from its former state in the original hymn.
- Out of the blue, the music lurches into material from the rip-roaring 1903 *Country Band March* (also used in *Putnam's Camp* of *Three Places In New England*), and one of the few places that sounds exactly like the corresponding spot in the *Fourth Symphony*.
- As the *Country Band March* works its way out, an extended section evolves recognizably built on Debussy's *Golliwogs' Cakewalk*, curiously present here since Debussy was amongst Ives least favored composers!
- After a frenzied build-up, the music pauses, gently lowering us into a section built on *Columbia, the Gem of the Ocean*, again, much along the lines that we hear also in the scherzo of the *Fourth Symphony*. The entire section concludes with a passing reference to *The Battle Cry of Freedom*, and Ives' *He is there!*, the song written in 1914 in anticipation of America's involvement in World War I. (*The Battle Cry of Freedom* appears in the song as well.)
- From here, the music assumes an increasingly fantastic display, with one last reference to the *Human Faith Melody*, while both Beethoven motifs appear forcefully, as if to underline their importance. A last high registered fragment of *Columbia, the Gem of the Ocean* (listen again for its characteristic 'dotted' rhythms), and a tiny reference to *Martyn* conclude the movement in a final mad dash to the end.

- ## The Alcotts

Amos Bronson Alcott and Abby Amy Alcott, parents of famed novelist, Louisa May Alcott *(Little Women)*, occupy an important place in Ives' transcendental outlook. Louisa May Alcott's father, Amos Bronson Alcott, in many ways the least successful among the mighty figures (that include notably Emerson himself, who had drawn Ives to the philosophy), nevertheless is assured of his place in the pantheon of transcendental thinkers. Choosing a near-Spartan lifestyle, his inability to find success in the workplace often necessitated his family's surviving on loans and the help of others. His writings had mixed success, many being deemed unfathomable, even incoherent, but his evolution of transcendental philosophies into education and teaching methods in general have been recognized as truly significant. His remarkable and predictive philosophies were a testament to his influence amongst the transcendental community, many of them speaking to modern social rethinking, far across the distances of time.

Despite Ives' stated reservations about the elder Alcott's accomplishments and practicality, it seems he was especially drawn to his simple virtues and the lack of materialism that he and his wife instilled in their family. The movement celebrates more the quiet, happy tranquility reflected in their homestead than it does any specific attainment, one in which inner strength and resolve was as good an example of transcendentalism as any. As Ives grew older, the Spartan lifestyle of the Alcotts was echoed in many ways in his own. And in spite of his substantial means, Ives lived simply, without even a radio, wearing the same simple clothes and hat year in, year out, an old Ford Model 'T' remaining his most conspicuous private transportation. Carl Ruggles remarked that he hardly ate anything![5] Simplicity and contentment, then, is the central theme of the movement. In some of the most touching music Ives would ever write, he would reference the Beethoven motifs extensively, as well as the *Human Faith Melody*. We can also hear clear elements of the hymn, *Missionary Chant* woven into it. Ives saved the full expressive evolutions of all these elements for this movement, finally revealing them in their most extended and complete forms at the conclusion.

Almost as if viewing the first three movements as one continuous thought, Ives also saved the fullest state of cumulative development of the sonata's common materials for his depiction of Alcott. Structurally, it is built on the earliest materials found in the sonata (1902 - 1904), the themes being from the lost *Orchard*

House Overture, perhaps one and the same as the *Alcotts Overture,* and thus the date of the movement itself (1914) is fairly late for its style - a *relatively* conventional sounding and technically less challenging piece compared to the complex sprawls of the two prior movements.

- The movement starts softly with the *Fate* motif, set in such a contemplative, reflective mode that it is easy to miss its musical identity entirely. Perceptive listeners will notice now that Ives infused the motif with key elements of the *Missionary Hymn,* choosing not to let the line progress immediately into the *Hammerklavier* motif. The music moves to an extended section built on of the *Human Faith Melody,* to lead back to more forceful restatements of *Missionary Chant, Hammerklavier* and *Fate* motifs conjoined, gaining in energy and speed while increasing the divergences from simpler tonalities. Loud statements of the *Fate* motif lead to a brief reference to the *Emerson motif,* just to remind us of his strong influence upon Bronson Alcott, followed by further quiet snatches of the *Hammerklavier* and *Fate* motifs, before finally settling down into a contrasting section.
- A gentle ragtime influence pervades a two bar fragment (possibly original to Ives) that sounds more than a little like *Bringing in the Sheaves,* (of a similar though more reflective vein to the second movement of the *Second Orchestral Set)* followed by a remarkably placed (and easily missed) reference to the end of the verse of the traditional Scottish song *Lock Lomond,* placed there because the Alcotts' home was often filled with Scottish airs (or as Ives mistakenly called them "Scotch" songs). Reuse of such fragments of material in ways that render them hard to recognize at first typify all too well the philosophies of the transcendentalists: taking something that already exists to cast it in new light and meaning.
- It is followed by a softly gentle cadence - an easily identifiable short fragment of the *Wedding March* by Wagner,

(signifying the wedded bliss of the Alcotts), and an extended section built on a quotation of the minstrel song *Stop that Knocking at My Door* continues the segment. Perhaps Ives was trying to deny fate the opportunity to take him, especially in regard to his thoughts about the *Fate* motif! The entire segment repeats to build into the final moments. In Ives' own recorded performance, his fleet fingers show the fluid, unmeasured way he conceived the music.[3]

- At last, the full, grand and massive statement of the entire *Human Faith Melody* - with its Beethoven references, chordal and hymn-like - appears in this summation of the three movements that preceded it; fittingly, the movement concludes with a low and reposeful C major chord, quietly ringing out as much to reflect Ives' own inner peace with the world and eternity as it does Alcott's.

• Thoreau

Ives decided rather than trying to depict what was specific to Henry David Thoreau's thoughts, philosophies or writings, he would paint a picture of a summer's day of contemplation around Walden Pond near Concord. Its thoughtful setting was the subject, of course, of Thoreau's great writing, *Walden; or, Life in the Woods,* that stemmed from the two years he spent there living in a simple cabin next to the lake on Emerson's property. A truly impressionistic piece of music, one can trace links to other contemporary artistic movements of the day, especially to some of the liquid floating sounds we find, too, in many of Debussy's textures. Largely reflective, this movement seems to be one last glance back to Concord and all that it represented, the place that had inspired Ives towards the ultimate musical journey upon which now he was departing.

The Concord Sonata

Walden Pond, Concord, Mass.
Image by John Phelan

Ives instructed the pianist to play the movement at a lower dynamic level than the rest of the sonata, and to make continual use of both pedals. This results in a fluid quality to the sound as much as it does to the style of the writing itself - the pond being clearly depicted from the start as ripples seem to radiate outwards from the use of spreading contours of sustained notes. Incorrectly often considered the only movement conceived from the start specifically for the sonata, in fact, it was built largely from another lost youthful work, *Walden Sounds,* (no exact date known), for piano, strings and woodwinds. Ives recreated this material into the movement we have today, although apparently he considered that the original version had been a superior setting of the material, presumably due to the more varied instrumental coloration. In 1915 Ives took the music from this movement into a song of the same name, taking the following text from *Walden; or, Life in the Woods:*

> *He grew in those seasons like corn in the night, rapt in revery, on the Walden shore, amidst the sumach, pines and hickories, in undisturbed solitude.*

In linking these words to the music, just as he had done in quoting *Loch Lomond* in *The Alcotts* to suggest "Scotch" songs, Ives again took the chorus from *Massa's in de Cold Ground* ('Down in de cornfield') to represent the corn patch by Thoreau's lakeside shack. Geoffrey Block, in his book on the sonata, referenced the possible 'discovery' of a 'musical pun,' amongst other connected motifs between this fragment and the otherwise curiously absent, *Nearer, My God to Thee* - the hymn so significant in many of Ives' late works, and the last quotation along his road to the stars. *Far more striking, however, is the far stronger connection of the hymn to the so-called* quasi-pentatonic melody, *the first strain of which shares the same notes <u>and</u> sequence, the second, further yet implying its high point!*

- The movement opens with the gentle imagery of the sun sparkling on expanding ripples moving across the water. The music is free and flexible, proceeding in a highly extemporized manner that feels more like a cadenza; indeed, in this summation of the sonata, such loose washes of sound seem fitting and right amongst more subtle motivic elements.
- The fleet-footed virtuosity calming, we hear the first appearance of 'Down in de cornfield,' discreetly placed; soon it reappears, and yet again high in the upper register, the notes subtly changed but still identifiable; it continues to pervade the expanding music, rhythmically and flexibly characterizing the liquidity of its waters.
- As the music continues, mixing rhythms and groupings with remarkable freedom, (as described in the songs), it simulates to as great a degree as we will find anywhere the multiple speeds and independent 'choirs' of sound that so typify many of Ives' orchestral works. We hear a reference to the *Fate* motif - just the first three notes - but enough to let us know that it never was far from his mind. Similarly, a reference to the *Hammerklavier Sonata* - just an

outline of the first four notes (and one 'pick-up' note) - leads to another 'Down in de cornfield' quote in a high register to conclude the section. 'Dotted' rhythm references seem to imply the presence of the *'Emerson'* motif, and thus the master transcendentalist over all others, by default.

- Mixed and varying rhythmic groupings, followed by a progression of chords in contrary motion between both hands, take us out of this wildly improvisatory-sounding section. The structure of the chords is conventional; their existence in two keys at any point is not. Pausing for a moment, tranquility returns; another 'Down in de cornfield' quote quietly informs the listener that the sonata is reaching its final stages. Even the *quasi-pentatonic melody* of the first movement makes a return in a different guise as the music drifts along.

- Out of the blue, a distant flute enters with the *Human Faith Melody*, (although the sonata may be played without it), across shimmering liquid sounds in the piano, albeit, sounding nothing like the grand form in which we heard it in *The Alcotts*. Used in this instance, it is a further example of Ives' spatial writing, and perhaps we might be reminded of the flute solo in an eerily reminiscent passage of the early (1906) experimental piece, *The Pond*. Repeating the sequence, with gentler piano writing, we finally hear the melody once again in its full and most recognizable form. Extemporizing a little further, 'Down in de cornfield' makes two final appearances, with elements of the *Human Faith Melody*. With one last pebble thrown in the water, ripples once more spread out, *Fate* weighs in as the music retreats, echoing across the waters into the stillness of the air and final silence.

Stuart Feder theorized that the surprising entrance of the solo flute to join the piano towards the close was a representation of his father, George Ives, and his efforts to learn the flute.[7] It would indeed be a fitting tribute to his father's memory, even if the movement was supposed to be about Thoreau! It might thus tie into George Ives' "echo" experiments, as did *The Pond;* the choice of instrument seems eerily linked. However, Feder's charge that Ives' chapter about this movement in *Essays Before a Sonata* was "angry" does seem off the mark. Passionate? Yes. Ives was writing about an ideal world, likely never attainable, it is hard to conceive that he would not have been completely comfortable living under the new societal rules he proposed. Indeed, he lived that way already. And perhaps, just perhaps, George Ives really was present.

REFERENCES

1. 'Charles Ives Remembered, an Oral History,' Vivian Perlis, *University of Illinois Press,* Urbana and Chicago, 1974, p. 224; CD: 'Ives Plays Ives,' Charles Ives, CD recording, *Composers Recordings, Inc,* New York, 1999
2. 'Essays Before a Sonata,' Charles Ives, *Knickerbocker Press,* New York, 1920
3. CD: 'Ives plays Ives,' track 42
4. 'Ives's Concord Sonata and the Texture of Music,' David Michael Hertz, from 'Charles Ives and his World,' Edited by J. Peter Burkholder, *Princeton University Press,* Princeton, New Jersey, 1996, p. 114
5. Perlis, p. 173
6. 'Ives Concord Sonata,' Geoffrey Block, *Cambridge University Press,* 1996, p. 35, & p. 55
7. 'Charles Ives: "My Father's Song," a Psychoanalytic Biography,' Stuart Feder, *Yale University Press,* New Haven, Connecticut, 1992, p. 271-272

CHAPTER 10

The Fourth Symphony

{{PD-Art}}

Ives' star-spangled *Fourth Symphony* occupies a unique place in the pantheon of great masterpieces of the 20th Century, and until the realization in 1995 of a complete version of the *Universe Symphony*, (the successor to the *Fourth*) it seemed Ives was represented by no higher musical aspiration or accomplishment. Culminating in the miraculous forward-looking last movement, Ives' *Fourth* does indeed leave us far along the road to the stars, and looks into the depths of spirituality, time, space and the unknown as the composer contemplated his place within it. A monumentally transcendental work, the clues are everywhere; a correspondingly vast array of performers features no less than three pianos, three conductors, even a chorus to put flight to Ives' imagination, from the page into sound it lifts us up on a wave of victory and absolution.

The relationship between the two late symphonies becomes clearest, however, by the time we reach the last movement of the *Fourth*. Interestingly, no less an auspicious figure than Bernard Herrmann,[1] a devoted Ives disciple (who would ultimately secure his greatest legacy in Hollywood with such legendary scores as Hitchcock's *Psycho),* would remark that the fourth movement of this symphony "belonged to some far distant future." Remarkably, he had the special skills to judge it at a time when the music existed only in written form, never having been performed.[2] Commenting that the universal qualities of this music occupied a truly *cosmic realm,* it seems Herrmann already was aware of Ives' destination.

Leaving off where the *Universe Symphony* begins, the *finale* of the *Fourth Symphony* has major features in common, not the least of which are its otherworldly sounds and spatial imagery. Neither sounds like Danbury any more. There would be no turning back; *spiritually,* too, Ives seized many of the same tenets that would be central to the *Universe Symphony*. In emphasizing that the primary aesthetic for the *Fourth* was the search for the larger questions of existence, if he did not find all the answers here, he would find them in the symphony's successor.

The *Fourth Symphony* embraces multiple idioms, so the movements are anything but uniformly bound together in style, but entirely consistent with Emerson's writings. Utterly logical and balanced in their progression, nevertheless, they illustrate transcendentalism irrespective of any technical philosophy. The symphony represents the summation of Ives' preparation for his ultimate spiritual journey, as well as the refinements gained from a lifetime in the proving ground of musical discovery.

Though not conceived initially in the form that would finally evolve, (does such a work by Ives exist?), the *Fourth Symphony* gradually assumed its identity over a period of years. Ives considered it to have been composed between 1910 and 1916, but

The Fourth Symphony

it is thought likely he was still refining it until 1919. The sketch materials, dates, copied and partial scores are numerous and confusing. Revisions to the first and second movements date from a later period, generally thought to have been between 1921 and 1925. Unlike any of Ives' symphonies that preceded it, in totality the work no longer bears any relationship at all to traditional symphonic form; thus, now Ives had fully abandoned European symphonic *structural* traditions, although he still retained the name and large-scale concept for multi-movement orchestral works, as he had done also with the *Symphony of Holidays*. Thus:

I. The *First Movement,* the shortest of the four is cast in the form of a prelude. Serving as an introduction to all that follows, its function is dissimilar to most symphonic first movements, which usually are the longest and weightiest.

II. The *Second Movement:* Ives originally decided to use his earlier *Hawthorne Concerto for Piano and Orchestra* in its entirely as this *scherzo* (literally, a joke), something that existed fully in sketches. However, in 1916, he had a change of heart and completely recomposed much of the *Hawthorn* material into its new identity within the second movement of the *Concord Sonata*, as well as this movement. Conspicuously, though these works can be heard to share musical material in common, as previously discussed, the two subsequent derivative works are far from carbon copies. In 1927 Eugene Goossens and some members from the New York Philharmonic Orchestra undertook the considerable challenge of playing the first and second movements in a special performance. Out of everything he wrote, the second movement was the largest-scale work that Ives would ever hear in person; after years of existing only in his mind, it must have been an auspicious occasion for him. Elliot Carter recalled that Ives invited some of the percussionists to his New York residence to help them with the tangled rhythms by pounding them out on the dining table.[3]

III. The *Third Movement,* a double organ fugue dating to Ives' days with Parker, would find its way into his *First String*

Quartet, only to be adapted many years later for use in the symphony. Surprisingly, this most immediately accessible of all of the four movements had to wait another six years before it, too, would see the light of day. First performed in New York City in 1933 by the New Chamber Orchestra, it was under the direction of none other than Bernard Herrmann, who had been so tireless in his early support and recognition of the unknown composer. Originally intended as the second movement, the first performance of the *prelude* and *scherzo* caused Ives to switch its position with the *scherzo*. This was a fortuitous decision indeed, since the fugue movement clears the air following the boisterous romp of what became the second movement, and most importantly accomplishes this before the extraordinary musical and spiritual journey of the finale.

IV. The *Fourth Movement* had been copied into full score in 1923, but it was decades later before all aspects of the final score were set in stone out of the vast pool of sketch materials. The symphony had to wait until 1965 for its first complete performance, under the direction of Leopold Stokowski and the newly formed American Symphony Orchestra, (assisted by conductors David Katz and José Serebrier), the multiple conductors speaking to its independent speeds and complexity. Thus the last movement was finally played for the first time almost 50 years after its completion, and so Ives did not live to hear the supernatural sonics and true real beginning of his voyage to the stars. However, he was aware of its significance at the time, considering it the best thing he had written; indeed it was.

Parallel thoughts

Ives wrote some 'conductor's notes' following the first performance of the scherzo, one which was not completely satisfactory due to the players' unfamiliarity with it and its unprecedented complexity. This included a small essay on some of the philosophical ideas behind it, but significantly, Ives also added some of the most detailed markings and indications that we will find in any of his scores, revealing a lot about the way he perceived aspects of balance in his music. Even more importantly, in the 'conductor's notes,' Ives' outlined something we will encounter again - remarkably, the very same concept he would feature and describe as his vision for the *Universe Symphony!* Here, however, he had raised it for the scherzo of the *Fourth Symphony*, almost to a word. Because he wrote his commentary long after writing both works, it is conceivable that he related the concept only in hindsight for the *Fourth*, the element he considered common to both works being scarcely recognizable in the same sense.

Scenery in the Adirondacks again had been the catalyst to both of these symphonies' germinations, and directly related to Ives' stays in the area (see Chapter 11). Specifically, Ives compared the effect of viewing the skies and clouds above while being aware of the landscape below to *"parallel listening,"* in which multiple musical levels can be appreciated together, though differently. While selectively shifting one's attention to either of them, awareness of the other is reduced but not eliminated. However, it is well known by now that the same 'real world' scene and representation in music may be found in Ives' descriptions of Section A of the *Universe Symphony*.[4] More surprising, however, is that he did not relate this concept to the *last* movement of the *Fourth Symphony*, because here the idea really is closely aligned with that of its successor.

So if not these, what was the parallel element Ives was referring to? Much of the content and imagery of the *Fourth Symphony's* scherzo (the second movement) recalls local scenes once again, the traditions of small town America, and bustling life in the big city. In relation to this movement, it hardly compares with the panoramic vistas he enshrined in his *Universe Symphony*. Aside from some short episodes that feature a soft quarter-tone group continuing independently of loud interruptions, true parallel entities are not the predominant feature of the movement.

Even in those instances in which true 'parallel' elements occur, usually they consist of measured rhythmic groupings of notes - sometimes as patterns - that coincide with others by their common denominators, only to repeat the cycle over again. In this sense, they were never designed as the separate panoramic components of Ives' grand descriptions and references.

Since the other complexities cannot be considered in the same light, perhaps Ives was referring to the sonic depiction of Hawthorne's *The Celestial Railroad* within the movement, (also featured prominently in the *Concord Sonata*). Here, he envisaged a truly cosmic scene that does have simultaneous parallel elements, although still not in the sense that was to be projected in the *Universe Symphony*. The *Celestial Railroad* in the *Fourth Symphony*, instead, is a cacophony of wildly disparate elements, including multiple fragments of near countless vernacular melodies, so it hardly offers the listener a chance to settle on separate levels of the same vein as conceptualizing the skies above and the earth below!

Perhaps, though, Ives had decided to broach his concept of parallel listening relative to a work that actually *had* been completed and performed, lest it never be raised at all. We must remember that by 1929, the date of these comments any prospects of completing the *Universe Symphony* largely had faded from view. Regardless, long before this time, of course, Ives already had featured parallel listening concepts in many other prior works in different guises and contexts, of course, dating back to *The Unanswered Question*, and even before. Although these hardly can be compared to the grand scenic vistas he later would have in mind, the germ of the concept was far from new to him. However, perhaps the most significant aspect is that Ives himself now had umbilically tied the *Fourth Symphony* to his ultimate musical destination, the *Universe Symphony*.

Thus, as we encounter so often in Ives, many ideas and materials emanate from before, albeit in different guises, showing a mind that was flooded continually with his *entire* creative output - right up until the point at which he found himself at the time. Just as he demonstrated with his tendency to continually revise his music, we can begin to understand how his composing processes took place. He could always see new potential for existing ideas, and seldom saw them as fully explored; once again, clearly reflected in the transcendental philosophy of continual renewal.

It is in the *finale* that we are confronted by even more complexity, on grander scale, yet completely different to anything we have encountered before. Ives' masterpiece as a whole was criticized by some for being beyond the ear's capacity to resolve - that his orchestration was fundamentally at fault. However, since Ives knew his orchestration, we can put that criticism aside. Extending the discussion beyond what was raised in Chapter 3, Ives also was aware of the laws of physics in which dominant sounds cancel out lesser ones,[5] but rejected that the ear was unable to hear what did not correspond to a theoretical "graph." Writing about the proper placement of instruments to help combat such issues, it seems that Ives more was aware than his critics of the ear's ability to catch glimpses of things within the larger texture, and the effects of coloration that every part played in the whole. The *finale* had broken new ground in instrumental textures.

However, it seems clear that Ives heard things concurrently in a linear fashion, too, essentially extending the parallel concept. As with Bach's music, this challenges us to hear horizontally, instead of merely vertically - the latter being the easiest of listening skills. Few people indeed can claim *honestly* that they can resolve all the parts individually in Bach's contrapuntally complex music. However, everyone hears them *in combination*, which is certainly part of the desired effect, if not all of it. Even if not comprehended at quite the same level that these composers intended, everyone still is experiencing the music in full. And no one can deny that just the combined *vertical* effect of Ives' (or Bach's!) horizontal linearity is an awesome noise indeed.

Perhaps, though, most striking in the *Fourth Symphony* are the various celestial and spiritual references. Ives was looking towards the heavens, his thoughts perhaps now moving rapidly towards *another* celestial journey; with his father's early death, Ives might have thought his own ascendency out of the physical realm also could follow soon.

Movement 1 - Prelude

Conspicuously, the most significant quotes in this movement are from hymns. The music also gains its powerfully moody effect from the unique and telling blend of diametrically opposite tonalities, rhythms, and simple traditional elements. In its otherworld quality, it is clear that Ives had already left Danbury and New England, this movement seeming to have more in common with the last movement than it does with the next - almost as if written out of sequence. Perhaps, indeed it was - if not *in deed,* in thought.

The movement has an interesting history, with a portion (a setting of John Bowring's poem, *Watchman, tell us of the night*) having started out in a simpler vein in the *First Violin Sonata,* indicating again that Ives seemed long to have had harbored visions of the cosmos. However, at this point the music was represented in its basic form only - without the words. This is more significant than it sounds; in his 1913 song, *Watchman* - when the words were added in the adaptation of this portion of the sonata - suddenly certain visions jump out at us (see Chapter 8) with all that follows in Ives' settings.

We already know that the timeline presents a confusing picture - Ives claimed he had sketched out this movement between 1910 and 1911. Since the song version of *Watchman* apparently dates later (1913), it appears to complicate our knowledge of just when this version came about. We might never know exactly how thus the movement evolved, but it seems hard to question that it must have been the *last* incarnation of the material.

The Fourth Symphony

Image courtesy ESA/NASA & R. Sahai; nasaimages.org

"Traveler, o'er Yon Mountain's Height, See that Glory Beaming Star!"

Listeners' guide

- With a stormy bluster announcing great things to come, the symphony begins. As an introductory prelude rather than a traditional first movement, we are instinctively aware that the main substance of the symphony lies beyond it. The violent short opening figure in the low instruments is immediately echoed upside down (inverted), in the high violins. We might recognize this inverted figure, since it found its way here from Ives' *First Piano*

Sonata. (Heard again early in the last movement of the symphony, it bears some links to the opening notes of *Nearer, My God to Thee.*)

- Immediately we hear a distant 'choir' of harp and two violins playing independently of the larger group - again with celestial things in mind (and a reference to the 'glory beaming star'). Playing a disguised version of the opening three notes of *Nearer, My God to Thee (Bethany)* in E Major, the sound of this little group seems to be suspended in space. Such writing is a direct descendent of the spatial music we encountered earlier in *The Unanswered Question,* and *Central Park in the Dark;* it continues for most of the movement, seemingly unaffected by what surrounds it, far removed and further indicative of Ives' evolving cosmic musical horizons.

- Another variant of the opening motif leads into the main part of the movement. The violin and harp choir continue, as a plaintive solo cello plays *In the Sweet Bye and Bye,* (a melody that not significantly shares certain melodic traits with *Nearer, My God to Thee),* but here is set in an entirely different key: A Major. This is the key that would normally be the result of a harmonic progression from the E Major tonality (of the violin 'choir'). Instead, we hear both the 'before' and 'after' keys sounding together simultaneously. The combination reveals these melodies in ways they have never sounded before, a throwback to Ives' early years of harmonic experimentation. With yet another different harmonic ingredient, the piano is set in an even less likely tonality, joined by the flute playing the first three notes of the (Beethoven) *Fate* motif, while the celeste plays another variant on the notes of *Nearer, My God.*

- The cello gives way to a chorus of actual voices, singing *Watchman, tell us of the night* and building orchestral textures, while the flute continues and is joined by the strings. Listen carefully: it is possible even to make out the unexpected, but familiar sounds of the *Westminster Chimes* (symbolizing time?[6]) in the celeste! Curiously, Ives

indicated that he would prefer this section of the movement to be performed *without* voices, their melodic line being covered within the orchestra. This is not how it is usually heard, however, although the strong celestial underpinnings of the words, *"See that glory beaming star!"* make actual voices seem inevitable; indeed, it is written thus towards the end of the movement.
- The high point of the melody is the crux of the movement. Similar to the setting of the song *Watchman*, be sure to listen for the extraordinary low line in the cellos, which seems to plumb the very depths by being one and a half steps lower than the expected, dominant D Major/B minor tonality. After quoting *Something for Thee*, and *Proprior Deo* (significantly, often an alternate setting of *Nearer, my God to Thee*), towards the end of the section the flute and strings take a fragment from the ending cadence of *Bringing in the Sheaves* (or possibly, *I Hear Thy Welcome Voice*), to conclude with one more quote from *Nearer, my God to Thee*. This kind of seamless interweaving of otherwise well-trodden melodies demonstrates again material not only re-energized, but sounding completely new.
- A brief interlude separates a yet fuller and noble concluding statement of *Watchman;* the music thins out, fragments and trails off into the distance.
- The celestial 'choir' of violins and harp, which had briefly fallen silent, returns to conclude to remind us of that 'glory beaming star' hanging brightly in the still night sky.

Movement 2 - Scherzo

Image courtesy NASA, ESA and A. Schaller
(for STScI); nasaimages.org

There's a land that is fairer than day,	To our bountiful Father above,
And by faith we can see it afar;	We will offer our tribute of praise
For the Father waits over the way	For the glorious gift of His love
To prepare us a dwelling place there.	And the blessings that hallow our days.
	Refrain:
We shall sing on that beautiful shore	*In the sweet bye and bye,*
The melodious songs of the blessed;	*We shall meet on that beautiful shore;*
And our spirits shall sorrow no more,	*In the sweet by and by,*
Not a sigh for the blessing of rest.	*We shall meet on that beautiful shore.*

This is an extraordinary concoction; perhaps only in Ives' *Fourth of July* do we hear such a raucous cacophony on this scale. However, that it precisely the point in both; they are sonic representations of the fantastic. Though modeled closely on parts of the second movement of his epic *Concord Sonata* for piano, especially Hawthorne's fantastic but ultimately horrific visions in his own *The Celestial Railroad,* if the subject matter has barely changed, the content and scope is drastically more all encompassing. Here Ives included many aspects of local flavor, and recalling for one final time his youth in Danbury, piled them all on top of one another in an amazing cacophony of orchestral showmanship and reckless abandon. Fittingly, the *coda* of the movement erupts in what might just be another vision of the Fourth of July holiday. If it is fireworks exploding amid the sounds of celebration that we hear, this time, though, it is on a grander scale than anything we might have seen in a small country town (Concord, according to Bellamann's 1927 notes); fireworks over the Statue of Liberty, perhaps?

It is no coincidence that the hymn melody, *In the Sweet Bye and Bye,* features so prominently in this movement as well as the first. Though not a prime component of *Hawthorne,* the second movement of the *Concord Sonata,* in fact it was introduced discreetly in it, and therefore was clearly present in his thoughts throughout the process of forming both works. Once aware of the words, it is not surprising to find this melody appearing in so many guises in this ultimately spiritual *Fourth Symphony,* even more since Ives incorporated the Pilgrims in the setting, too. In the highly reflective circumstances of Ives' life at this time, the words are completely fitting. Perhaps meeting his father on that beautiful shore was in his mind.

If the subject of the second movement was considered by Ives to be a 'comedy' in the manner of a romp through life (and in this case his memories), more particularly it is an excursion into the realm of the supernatural. Despite having the same musical genesis as the *Hawthorne* movement of the *Concord Sonata* it is very different music, and only gradually do we become aware of its many ties and similarities. Ives again would incorporate his musical vision of Hawthorn's work into a late solo piano piece based on the same material, *The Celestial Railroad* (1925). The cosmic component is revealing, too, since 'celestial' thoughts again link this work to the otherworldly concepts we will find in the *Universe Symphony.* True to Ives' music in general, one work serves only as a basis upon which the next proceeds to go further, in this movement Ives seems to have had his gaze fixed ever more closely on the stars, amidst the earthly chaos seemingly struggling to delay his departure.

A celestial railroad
The Milky Way imaged in Death Valley, California. Image courtesy NASA/National Park Service

Gayle Sherwood Magee claimed that the movement - even more, Ives' carefully prepared score for its 1927 premiere - somehow, represented a more radical departure from anything Ives had attempted prior to 1918.[7] The implication was that it could have been 'updated' to garner ready acceptance from the avant-garde of the 1920's. However, this does not add up on several counts. In fact, the movement does not represent any particular departure from Ives' evolved language of the time, although it certainly was one of his most massively complex orchestral textures to date. Furthermore, near-fully scored portions of the *Universe Symphony* from around 1916 reveal that this scherzo certainly was *not* the most radical concept Ives had contemplated before 1918. If Ives were trying to impress the avant-garde, would he not have chosen and prepared something from one of his most advanced efforts? It would have been no harder to prepare the almost ready first section of the *Universe Symphony* than this movement.

However, there is a larger point to be made. Even within the *Fourth Symphony*, the *finale* is far more advanced in compositional design than the second movement, indeed representing a near-culminating example of Ives' furthest developed art, and appears to date, at least in some form, to before 1916. The first complete edition of the movement, prepared by a copyist, was made from Ives' manuscripts in 1923, *four years before* the preparation and first performance of the scherzo movement. Although a Second Edition of the *finale* was made in 1944, Ives did not revise his manuscripts beyond the time of the first edition, a date at which he was still unknown to the musical avant-garde. So if Magee is correct, why would he select and update a less advanced movement in 1927 instead of the latter, which was already complete, fully revised, and known to have been of great satisfaction to him?

Returning to the scherzo, to better understand it we need only look to Ives' life, since many friends and acquaintances had remarked that the composer appeared to live and work in complete disarray, though knew where everything was, be it in his office, studio, or most importantly, his mind. Again, he was the living personification of order rising out of chaos. In the second movement, as he rode his own railroad in the sky, Ives revealed multiple trains of thought and the remarkable ability mentally to compartmentalize all of them. The huge and complex tour de force was the closest he would ever come to creating *musical* order out of chaos, and within its approximately 12 minutes we will experience a blend of all manner of 20th Century techniques in league with popular melodies, civil war tunes, hymns, ragtime, barn dances, and more. Ives was not concerned that we necessarily separate all of these components. Some were meant to color the sound with complex interactions of tonalities and rhythms, others were not necessarily intended to draw explicit attention to themselves, but rather to be perceived jumping out of the texture at times, while still more are meant to be heard together to support the dominant, readily resolvable elements. It is an amalgam of virtually all of Ives' experiments over the years - seen through the parameters of his life expressed in music.

However, despite Ives' description of this movement as a comedy or romp, there are religiously spiritual differences, too, between it and *Hawthorne* in the *Concord Sonata*. Not only due to the repeated references to *In the Sweet Bye and Bye*, but also the steady backdrop and reminders of the pioneering Pilgrims, he does not let us escape the more religious overtones saved for his two mightiest symphonic excursions. In their own journeys in life and "through the swamp," we often hear the Pilgrims in quiet hymn-based episodes punctuating the mighty bustle. Ives thus presented all manner of imagery, never letting us forget the struggles of the past and the quiet fortitude of his ancestors. It ought to be said, though, that the sheer power of Ives' orchestral excursion is so great that any expectation of finding Ives' 'religious fervor' or soul-searching spirituality in this movement is likely to be misplaced.

Stuart Feder made some very perceptive observations about the relationship of the second movement to Hawthorn's *Celestial Railroad* text,[8] quoting a portion of the text as a comment on its substance:

> *"We heard an exulting strain, as if a thousand instruments of music, with height, with depth, and sweetness in their tones, at once tender and triumphant, were struck in unison, to greet the approach of some illustrious hero, who had fought a good fight, and won a glorious victory, and was come to lay down his battered arms forever."*

However, in illustrating perfectly what lay behind Ives' *scherzo,* it seems Feder mistakenly applied this to the entire symphony, whereas only the second movement reflected such heroic visions. He also proposed that Ives had essentially given up composition after the *Fourth Symphony* as a "sacrifice" to his father, who had done the same in music at the same stage of life in order to try to better support his family. The fact that Ives did not makes such commentary puzzling. Contradicting himself later, Feder proposed *another* similarly unsupportable theory to explain why Ives stopped composing in the 1920's, (see Chapter 11).

In the second movement, the number of quoted tunes and melodies is overwhelming; listing each and every fragment buried in the score would hardly be practical or helpful. Musically, it is full of patriotic calls to arms, secularism, even religiosity between outbreaks of bombast; in this sense it can be considered philosophically different to the rest of the symphony, which has stronger spiritual implications. Here in the scherzo, however, we cannot doubt that Danbury still is predominantly on Ives' mind. Perhaps its massive scale and gigantic indulgence in the memories of his past is evidence of a struggle to hold on to it just a little longer, while grasping the stairway to his own celestial road. If he failed to make terms with a changing world and the threatening clouds of war meant that he never would return to Danbury, physically (other than that one brief, disillusioning visit), or philosophically, the tie still was strong.

Amongst the melodies referenced in the movement, present in one form or another, many are listed below; if some are easily missed, it is not because they were always placed as brightly lit signposts:

The Beautiful River; Beulah Land; Camptown Races; Columbia, the Gem of the Ocean; God be with you; Hail Columbia; Happy Land; Home Sweet Home; Hello! Ma Baby; In the Sweet Bye and Bye; Irish Washerwoman; Long, Long Ago; Marching Through Georgia; Martyn; Massa's in de Cold Ground; Nettleton; Old Black Joe; On the Banks of the Wabash; Pig Town Fling; Reveille; St. Patrick's Day; Street Beat; Tramp, Tramp, Tramp, The Boys are Marching; Turkey in the Straw; Washington Post March (Sousa); *Westminster Chimes; Yankee Doodle.*

The melody, *In the Sweet Bye and Bye,* appears in countless guises at many more points than listed in the guide; we find it often coincidental to more prominent lines. By its uniquely Ivesian context, most of the time it might not be readily recognizable to most listeners. The hymn must have been extremely popular around the time of the First World War, not only because it is so prevalent in this movement, but it was the same melody sung by the entire crowd gathered at Hanover Square on the day of the sinking of the *Lusitania* in 1915. This event would inspire the writing of the last movement of the *Second Orchestral Set,* a work apparently that preceded this movement. As with everything in Ives, his music was a collage of memories amid new horizons;

certainly, the events at Hanover Square stayed with him for a long time.

Listeners' guide

- Kirkpatrick thought the rumbling sounds that open the movement represented the sounds of "an awakening city," which does seem an apt description; New York had become a large part of Ives' life at this stage.
- Immediately following, a chorale section of quarter-tone writing (very obvious) in the violins (representing the Pilgrims), might require an open mind for the uninitiated. It takes part of its identity from *Home, Sweet Home*, and sets the tone for things to come. Quoting a fragment of *God Be with You*, a flute and solo violin lead us into a mighty section modeled on Hawthorne's *The Celestial Railroad*. Continuing alongside the incoming sonic onslaught, it is one instance that does align with the parallel listening concept Ives had discussed, even though it becomes deliberately buried into inaudibility beneath the interrupting pandemonium of Ives' celestial train.
- This is immediately recognizable by its locomotive-like sounds, and most notably by its whistle (piccolo, flutes and clarinets) blowing loudly at times. We will hear fragments, albeit characteristically transformed almost beyond recognition, of the Civil War song, *Tramp, Tramp, Tramp* in the trombones, bursting in with declaratory fashion.
- After the first *Celestial Railroad* outburst, another quarter-tone section follows in the violins, as if oblivious, built on *In the Sweet Bye and Bye* and *Bethany*, but still symbolic of the Pilgrims' stoic journeying.
- A 'full steam ahead' part of the train ride ensues - an amazing noise - while the quiet pilgrim journey continues underneath, once more drowned out by the mighty locomotive.

The Fourth Symphony

- The railroad briefly out of earshot, the pilgrims can be heard once again persevering, until the locomotive bursts in - again! Listen carefully after *Tramp, Tramp, Tramp* reappears, because in the high violins can just be heard another melodic twist: *Turkey in the Straw*.
- A section featuring a jazzy and jumpy clarinet line (based on *Camptown Races*) sounds as if we are now on that train ride, complete with the clicking of the rail joints. Near the end of the section the flute intones a slow suggestion of 'Down in de cornfield,' from *Massa's in de Cold Ground*.
- The orchestra crashes in again with *Hail Columbia*, written in a rhythm that seems at odds with all that surrounds it - it is! - followed by a further elaboration of *Camptown Races*; then:
- Metrically tangled strains of *In the Sweet Bye and Bye* (violins, clarinets, trumpet and trombone), *Camptown Races* (flutes), and *Nettleton* (low pizzicato strings).
- As loud derivations of *Columbia, the Gem of the Ocean* (common to the *Hawthorne* movement in the *Concord Sonata*) interrupt, and the music assumes a militaristic character, did Ives have in mind the Civil War, or was it the storm clouds of World War 1?
- Trailing out with a snatch of *Columbia, the Gem of the Ocean* by trombone and cellos, the ending to this section is in a deliberately labored manner.
- A short, tongue in cheek moment is reached as the violins play a little 'salon' styled interlude, meant here as a reflection of what Ives found in poor taste. This was the kind of music so embraced by the 'lily pads,' those whom with Ives could never get along politely. Such music, 'schmaltz,' (a Yiddish term for chicken fat!) typified what Ives described as "allowing the ears to sit back in an easy chair."
- From here, the music wafts through a haze of distant memories, with *In the Sweet Bye and Bye* heard in a solo ('extra') viola; the piano dominates the moment in a wildly different musical context.

- A section based on some ragtime-inspired writing in *Hawthorn* appears in the solo trumpet, under a soft quotation, again from *In the Sweet Bye and Bye* in the flutes; the ragtime is continued in the woodwinds and trombone, until the flutes and piano take the lead, with passagework based on an apparent fragment of *Nearer, My God to Thee*. Underneath, in the low strings and pianos, is a fragment of the *Human Faith Melody* from the *Concord Sonata* (in staggered entries), which then morphs into *In the Sweet Bye and Bye*.
- A musical haze (of building steam?) is punctuated by a tolling clock and *Westminster Chimes* in the high bells. The trumpets (and the piano set a beat behind) join loudly with a rhythmic triplet figure built on a fragment of *Long, Long Ago*, until the high violins take over with a striking variation of *Hello! Ma Baby* set against a stream of sonorities that have an almost 'Schönbergian' sound to them.
- The theme is subsequently taken by the trumpets, again influenced by ragtime, leading to a brief respite of sorts, then marked by a strong dotted triplet rhythmic figure in the violins; the second trumpet and piano reference the *Human Faith Melody*, while the flutes play the refrain, 'Down in de cornfield,' from *Massa's in de Cold Ground*. Some of these other elements under the violins might be hard for the unpracticed ear to separate.
- A brief section follows, when the violins and piano lead a jaunty ragtime moment with another derivation of *Hello! Ma Baby;* the rhythmic complexity mounts.
- With an interruption of more ragtime figure in the trombones, the trumpets take the lead. We might be able to glimpse the Beethoven *Fate* motif referenced in the clarinets, then the trumpets, and superimposed under the cornets as they play the refrain, 'Down in de cornfield.' Further superimposed over *Beulah Land* in the trombones is *In the Sweet Bye and Bye* in the piano - this is only a fraction of what is going on across the orchestra!

- This is followed by a very brief return to the Pilgrims with the hymn tune *Martyn* in the piano (well disguised by the alien tonalities surrounding it), only to be interrupted by a huge explosion in the orchestra. Although the lower trumpets and trombones dominate with *Beulah Land,* the score is littered with references to *In the Sweet Bye and Bye* across multiple parts. The section suddenly culminates in another statement of 'Down in de cornfield' - this time much more boldly, the tumult culminating in a vibrant shimmering chord in the strings and piano while "everybody holds," (a term Ives used in the score of *The Majority!)*
- This melts into a sweet violin solo of *Beulah Land,* against which is set a tangled quarter-tone (!) piano part, and other seemingly unrelated rhythmic textures, again with the hymn *Martyn* in the (conventionally-tuned) piano.
- The music from here owes its origin much more obviously to *Hawthorne,* which, as it continues, in turn owes its origins to his much earlier *Country Band March* (1905?), with *Turkey in the Straw* in the violins, viola and bassoon parts, and other quotations superimposed. Amongst the more prominent of these is yet one more reference to *Long, Long Ago* in the cornet, with *Yankee Doodle* in the upper woodwinds. The latter quote provides a premonition of the final statement of that tune that will eventually resonate across the entire orchestra to bring us out of the movement. In some ways reminiscent of *The Fourth of July,* the movement concludes as the ensemble falls apart and trails off like a falling stack of pick-up sticks; it is also Ives' farewell to Danbury, its people, band music, festivals and his father's place in it.

By the time the *scherzo* resolves into the peace of the upcoming third movement - a reversion to a simpler spirituality of long ago - Ives had reached the end of the line with the locally centered musical language he had refined over many years. He needed to take one more step to go further, and the next movement would serve as his bridge to it.

Movement 3 - Andante moderato

For this movement, Ives chose to rework an old *fugue* - actually a *double fugue* that uses two primary hymns as themes - and one in which fugal form is easy to follow. (As structures based on imitation, fugues pass the melodic elements from one to another and develop the materials according to an ancient formal design.) Because it was written in an entirely different musical style to all that surrounds it, the movement raises an interesting specter, because its incorporation occurred well after Ives had rejected Parker's predominant European musical structures. However, in truth, many elements of that tradition always remained within the fabric of all of Ives' music, and shows again that Ives was not engaged on a campaign to eliminate this part of his life from his music. However, the fugue does not sound as if it could have possibly come from across the Atlantic, due to the unique handling of the materials and Ives' 'Yankee' vision of an old baroque form.

Mountains of Greenland
Image courtesy Jensbn

Regardless, the fugue must have had some special meaning for Ives, because having started out just as an exercise it would become an organ piece, now lost, only to reappear as the first movement of his *First String Quartet,* to which Ives assigned the dates 1897-1900. After more than a decide of lying dormant Ives resurrected and rescored it to become the orchestral movement that we know today. If initially it seems at odds with the tenor and language of the symphony, the glowing tranquility of Ives' 19th Century Yale relic - written under Parker's tutelage - serves as the perfect moment of repose, clearing the air between what has just occurred and the profound implications of the next movement.

Constructed around familiar hymns of his youth, the sound is ultimately rapturous, and reflects a time of optimism and happiness. In addition, Ives possibly paid oblique homage to Bach by borrowing a syncopated (displaced) descending figure offset against an ascending figure (on the beat) from the *Toccata and Fugue in D minor* (BWV 538). It appears in many guises throughout, sharing common ground also with a fragment of *All Hail the Power of Jesus' Name* that forms the secondary theme. Such dual purpose with linking classical thematic materials and vernacular elements was a technique we have seen before, of course, and is typical of Ives' methodology for structural development and formal integrity.

Listeners' guide

Overall, as a relatively straightforward piece of music, Ives' fugue should not prove troublesome for the listener to follow, although it is worth outlining some key points in its progress that might easily be missed:

- As the primary musical basis that establishes the character of the movement, the cellos open the fugue with a fragment of *From Greenland's Icy Mountains,* followed by multiple statements and responses across the much-reduced symphonic ensemble. This ensemble consists of just the string section, with a small woodwind group, solo trombone (or horn), organ and timpani.

- Because this is a double fugue, Ives used two primary themes - in this case the second theme is the third section of the verse from *All Hail the Power of Jesus' Name*. Announced by the trombone, and set against the former melody *(Greenland)* in the violins, soon it is traded off to upper violins *(All Hail)* and cellos *(Greenland)*, and so forth in other combinations as the fugue unfolds. Descending syncopated beats (in thirds: i.e. 1-1/2 or 2 steps) that appear in the violin line are based on that thematic material, and also provide the link to the Bach quotation; it is a prominent accompanimental feature throughout the movement.
- With a mighty return of *Greenland* we reach a grand pause, followed by developed fragments of *All Hail*, soon to include *Greenland* fragments.
- Eventually a grand 'pedal point,' consisting of a massive bottom 'C,' supports continued development of *All Hail*, while the music assumes a glowing aura as it continues to climb. The flute seems to play something very similar to what we commonly encounter as part of the *bass* line in *Battle Hymn of the Republic!* There follows a brief deflation of the dramatic tension.
- The impetus resumes, this time leading through strident writing and massive chords to a truly ecstatic cadence and further pause.
- The *Stretto* occurs, announcing that the conclusion of the fugue is near (where theme entrances are rapidly compounded upon each other). It is built on *Greenland*, and reaches a high point before:
- *Greenland* returns in augmented form (stretched rhythmically into longer notes) into a majestic, stately summation of all that has taken place.
- The *Coda* (end section) features a surprising, new thematic entrance in the trombone, and leads to the conclusion. It is built on the middle part of the melody, *Joy to the World*, but played here at half the normal speed. As an addition to the original string quartet version, the

placement here of this particular melodic fragment surely was symbolic of Ives' state of mind at the time, one that was still optimistic for a better world.

Contrary to the assertions of some commentators, Ives must have felt true joy in his life at the time he scored the movement for the symphony, especially since he believed his political passions and ideals had a chance of becoming reality. However, perhaps reflecting on his father's untimely departure into eternity, the third movement captures an ecstatic state of hope, as if in preparation for cutting his own cords to the past for a future at peace with the outside world.

Movement 4 - Finale

It is at this point that we know Ives really had embarked on his ultimate journey, because the *Universe Symphony* surely follows where the *finale* (Movement 4) of the *Fourth Symphony* leaves off. Both have many traits in common. The crowning glory of the entire work, the finale is perhaps one of the most extraordinarily spiritual, powerful and overwhelming pieces of music conceived during the 20th Century. Unsurprisingly for Ives, it has some of its roots lying in part of an earlier work, the *Memorial Slow March* of 1901, which was lost. The hymn upon which that was based, *(Nearer, My God to Thee)*, is the most prominently quoted melody of this movement, too, dominating its fabric from beginning to end.

The *finale* finally was put in a definitive version as late as 1944, but Ives' failing eyesight was presumed responsible for the version never gaining his final approval. However, so much trouble was taken in its assembly that it is hard to imagine that this edition is not one he would have ordained; he had already approved the version from 1923, of which this contained refinements and resolutions to some details (birdcalls!) previously considered indecipherable.

Image courtesy NASA, ESA and the Hubble Heritage Team
STScI/AURA)-ESA/Hubble Collaboration

However, it is here that the same *parallel listening* elements used later in the *Universe Symphony* really would appear in earnest, along with some similar sonorities to those of the latter work, albeit within a more tonal context. Remarkably, just as in the *Universe Symphony*, a battery of percussion plays in its own independent speed and context throughout the movement, although here, it is joined by occasional tuned instrumental lines (in the piano, oboe, clarinet) at a few points during the movement. Thus Ives' words about the second movement would have been more apt and telling here.

Ives would continue to reference melodies of his youth, but now they were virtually all religious in nature. Constructed of ethereal and subtler language, the finale seems to reach for another place; indeed, it is. The conclusion leaves us in hanging in space as it wafts far into the distance, Ives' journey to the stars well under way, his remarkable creativity and original thinking never more profound or revealed. With the question of the "reality of existence" being much on his mind as he wrote it,[9] Ives described the movement in religious terms. The particular hymn-based content is strongly indicative of Ives' state of being at this point of his life.

Since the movement had grown out of a distant memory in which the singing of *Nearer, My God To Thee* had stayed with him, Ives' attempt to recreate it at this emotional high point was as much to do with recalling the sound itself as it was the profound impact it had on him. Remembering vividly the sound as well as the slow march that accompanied it, it remained with him over the years and became the backbone of the movement. Although *Nearer, My God* pervades its entire length in one form or another, the degree that he presented the material in metamorphic states is considerable. Generally, he chose to quote just the middle portion of the melody - its high point. It is also significant that the hymn had become so important to Ives in this transcendental work late in his output that it would be the *only* melody (with the exception of two other less significant quotations) that he would carry with him into the *Universe Symphony*, his ultimate destination.

In this movement, it is particularly noticeable that the quoted melodic components generally are less clearly outlined than those found in the other movements. Being woven more subtly into the texture than in most of Ives' prior music, it is clear that Ives' creative needs were rapidly outgrowing the use of *any* type of vernacular material. Interestingly, although the inner part writing is exceedingly complex to a degree even Ives seldom devised, the *type* of line comprising these lines is utterly different to anything we find in the second *scherzo* movement, or virtually any other prior major work. However, it is much closer to that found in the *Universe Symphony*, this kind of counterpoint resulting in vaguer, but more highly colored effects, new sounds that are less demanding of precise alignments between the other supportive parts. The effect is a colossus of powerfully tangled washes of ethereal color and stark bass lines, with splashes of ill-defined textures and sounds throughout the orchestral range superimposed upon the more massive foundations of its original religious inspiration.

Listeners' guide

- With the percussion 'battery' starting the movement in a gentle fashion and its own speed - truly a harbinger of things to come in the next symphony - the tone of contemplating the unstoppable march of time has been set. Referencing a processional 'street beat' with pulse-like rhythm in the snare drum, the percussion group continues throughout the entire movement, just as does the vast percussion orchestra in the *Universe Symphony*. (See Chapters 12 & 13.)
- A quotation from *Nearer, My God To Thee* (from the middle portion of the melody) soon follows in the basses, mutating into the opening notes from the *Prelude* (first movement), but here it is dark and mysterious instead of dramatic.
- This leads into a brief reflection in the full string section of material also based on *Nearer, My God to Thee*, easily lost behind the ascending trumpet and horn parts. Immediately tying into a recognizable 'glory beaming star' moment, this time it is played by five distant violins, a distant choir and harp; significantly it still outlines *Nearer My God to Thee*.
- The basses again lead, building on the inverted opening notes of the *Prelude* (again reinforcing the *Nearer, My God to Thee* connection); the orchestra takes it further.
- The 'glory-beaming star' material now follows much enlarged in sound, trailing off into a remote sounding invocation of *Dorrnance;* the music sounds literally as if it is floating Heavenward. The section develops substantially.

The Fourth Symphony

- A strongly figurative viola line tends to obscure a low variant of *Nearer, My God To Thee* in the first violins, followed much more audibly in solo trumpet.
- Amongst the most ethereal sounds Ives would ever write, there follows another (well-disguised) setting of *Nearer, My God*, (flute, oboe), as well as a hint of *Martyn* (in the second violins). These melodic components are effectively buried in the texture, but provide the harmonic and sonic basis.
- Suddenly we become aware of an energized, urgent awakening, as the orchestra takes on nervously divergent rhythmic lines, again built on a fragment of *Dorrnance* (three notes of the concluding bars) The extraordinary power of the jagged lower descending lines, set against the tangled and rhythmically marked upper lines is exhilarating and a uniquely original musical treatment.
- An interlude follows, the flute and piccolo taking the lead (birdcalls), tying into another 'glory-beaming star' fragment (very brief), accompanied by the strings intruding with moments in quarter-tones amidst another variant and fragment of *Nearer, My God.*
- Another extraordinary passage of truly otherworldly music follows, with a chromatically meandering upper violin part superimposed on a remnant of the *Missionary Chant*, then we reach the section presumed to have been modeled on the lost *Memorial Slow March.*
- The *Memorial March,* built collectively on *Nearer, My God* woven with *Missionary Chant* and *Dorrnance* begins prominently in the trumpet and horn. Even the four notes of the *Fate* motif were worked into the primary thematic component, and can be caught by an astute ear. The bass lines begin an evolving cycle that persists in various guises until the end of the movement, consisting of a descending scale; as the music builds, the range from an octave shrinks, cycle by cycle, until spanning only a major third (2 steps).

- With a musical crescendo, into the triumphant high point of the movement, still developed from the same three hymns, the bass line now once again occupies a full octave, its rapid evolution and periodic faster stepwise movement breaking the cycle form.
- Mighty Wagnerian chords lead to the dramatic and powerful climax; from Ives' words on the sketch of the *Second String Quartet* about a comparable passage it is clear he had cosmic visions in mind. The descending scale is now chromatic and spans only a minor third (1-1/2 steps).
- With a short connecting section emerging out of the sustained chord that completes the section is a dialog between flute and oboe (birdcalls again), reflectively with the 'glory-beaming star' shimmering in the distance.
- A glowing segment of peace and harmony is a telling indicator that Ives was glimpsing his place in the cosmos. The bass cycle having resumed gently a step higher assumes its original identity; within this section also are floating fragments of *Missionary Chant, St. Hilda, Martyn,* and *Dorrnance.* Their purpose here was more for the coloration they provide together than for their individual discernment.
- Drifting towards eternity, we feel near to it as the chorus enters with a wordless variant of *Nearer, My God to Thee* in multiple parts. This assumes increasing significance as the orchestra thins out and recedes, only to be followed by the chorus itself; the bass cycle shrinks to hover over a major third, the remnants of the 'glory-beaming star,' seeming to imply time and the pendulum of a ticking clock, fall away, to leave just the percussion battery trailing off into nothing and the depths of space.

This movement is amongst the most extraordinary accomplishments of Ives' entire output; with its unique originality, powerful conception, awesome sound, and telling spirituality, the magic of his orchestration and otherworld instrumental coloration never more evolved or striking, it is at once readily apparent why at the time he sensed he had done something remarkable. Subconsciously or otherwise, he knew he set his course for the stars. There was nothing left to do but write the *Universe Symphony*.

REFERENCES

1. 'Charles Ives Remembered, an Oral History,' Vivian Perlis, *University of Illinois Press,* Urbana and Chicago, 1974, pp. 155 - 162
2. 'Four Symphonies of Charles Ives,' Bernard Herrmann, Modern Music 22 (May-June 1945): 215-222 (reprinted in 'Charles Ives and his World,' Edited by J. Peter Burkholder, *Princeton University Press,* Princeton, New Jersey, 1996, p. 394 – 402)
3. Perlis, p. 142
4. 'A Conductor's Note,' Charles Ives, *New Music,* San Francisco, January, 1929
5. 'Memos', Charles E, Ives, edited by John Kirkpatrick, p. 106, *W. W. Norton & Co.,* New York, 1972, p. 67
6. 'The Music of Charles Ives,' Philip Lambert, *Yale University Press,* New Haven and London, 1997, pp. 149, 227
7. 'Charles Ives Reconsidered,' Gayle Sherwood Magee, *University of Illinois Press,* Chicago, Illinois, 2008, p. 157
8. 'Charles Ives: "My Father's Song", a Psychoanalytic Biography, Stuart Feder, *Yale University Press,* New Haven, Connecticut, 1992, p. 277 - 280
9. 'Memos', p. 66

CHAPTER 11

The Universe Symphony

George Ives once told his son that he would not get much of a ride to paradise if he relied on pretty music for his transportation.[1]

NASA/courtesy of nasaimages.org

And so to the final destination: the *Universe Symphony*, a place it seems even Ives himself did not realize was to be his resting place. This, his ultimate masterpiece, is a work that reaches us without revisions, because it was never fully organized, or laid out in any complete form; that would have to wait until decades after his death. What we hear is the work as it was left in his initial sketches, unless we should include, to paraphrase Cowell, "a note or two added occasionally up until the time he died." Realizations of the materials only became possible over time through the skills, patience - and diligence of others. The 'profusion of confusion' of materials that Ives left in his wake would require heroic efforts and interpretations to produce concert-ready music. However, only one of these attempts would succeed in finding a logical roadmap for the totality of the symphony that Ives had envisioned. Utilizing all of the sketch materials, it would result in - as officially designated - a 'realization' of the *complete* work. The others remain only partial versions at best, and re-compositions at worst.

The first encounter with any of these might leave one bewildered and likely to put the *Universe Symphony* aside; it is an astoundingly avant-garde composition by any standards. However, the music possesses a strangely captivating lure that reels the listener back for 'just one more' hearing. This cannot be said necessarily about most unfamiliar avant-garde compositions; if these seem equally inaccessible at first blush, more likely the listener will never return to them. In the *Universe Symphony*, however, Ives would challenge our perceptions, awareness and sensory boundaries. Its cosmic scope required him to carry his visions literally to his limit; the resulting epic, venturing far into space, was to be his magnum opus. In design, it would represent in sound a view of the cosmos, as seen and experienced from his perspective, looking up into the skies above, through the past and future - even more, the rise of humanity, spirituality and ultimately, eternity; the symphony was a transcendental vision of man's place within it. It also would clear the way to Ives' destination amongst the stars; though formally unfinished, the symphony existed clearly in his mind.

Ives dreamed up many of his most profound musical visions when away from the hustle of New York, at a number of magnificent and serene locations within the Adirondacks (in upstate New York). These places were within relatively easy reach (a day's travel) of the big city. Many of his favorite haunts within the region, such as Saranac Lake, Elk Lakes and Keene Valley would trigger the initial conceptions of his most inspired masterworks. Mark Tucker,[2] documented that whilst in the Adirondacks Ives would hatch his creative ideas for the *Three Page Sonata*, the *Concord Sonata*, the *Robert Browning Overture*, parts of the *Third and Fourth Symphonies* and *Second Orchestral Set*, various songs and chamber works, and most significantly of all, the concept for the otherworldly *Universe Symphony*.

Thus, his visit to the Adirondacks during the fall of 1915 gave Ives the idea for the symphony, although possibly what he envisaged might have been an expansion of an initial concept that dated from as early as 1911. The awe-inspiring view of the landscape and skies high on the Keene Valley plateau inspired him to write its equivalent in music: a colossal work as cosmic in scale as it was in scope. The symphony finally materialized into concrete form with many detailed - and less detailed - sketch materials, as well as descriptive instructions and prose written all over them. However, by 1916, Ives only had sketched the first section (Section A), apparently adding to it (and refining it?) around 1919 - 1920. What he left from this period is substantially complete in itself, and for a time this was the extent of the materials.

Image AC

Noted Ives scholar, the late David Porter, theorized that Ives might have been re-inspired to pick up the dormant symphony again following Hubble's announcement in 1923 that the universe was comprised of multiple island universes just like the Milky Way. Indeed, the later materials seem more closely aligned with the modern universe than many of the earlier sketches. Prior to this time, the universe, though still seeming overwhelmingly large in the early 20th Century, was thought nevertheless to exist wholly within the boundaries of our own galaxy, the Milky Way. In 1915/1916, Hubble had not yet separated the universe into other galaxies. In 1922-23 he would do so, when those mysterious nebulae turned out to be comprised of billions of separate stars, proving they were island universes - *other* Milky Ways - in their own right! Nobody from earlier times had the slightest notion of the true and terrifying, even indefinable, vastness of the universe we know today, one consisting of *billions* of galaxies!

Not insignificantly perhaps, 1923 also corresponds to Ives' 49th year, that of his father's death, and perhaps a final trigger for the symphony's reawakening. The new material from 1923 was substantial, if less fully sketched and ordered, and included a plan for three main sections with a prelude to each. Thus the symphony expanded from a one-movement work into a far-reaching three-section monument. If it seemed more akin to the universe of Hubble than the classical astronomers who had preceded him, its perspectives might have been steeped largely in the 19th Century, but were expressed in an idiom aligned with the 20th. Remarkably, Ives seemed to have his feet firmly planted in *both* centuries! If in Ives' universe the Earth remained firmly at its center, musically it crossed the cosmos.

In his descriptions of the symphony, Ives broached the crystallization of a compositional technique he had been developing for years. Interestingly, as referenced in the previous chapter, other commentators seem not to have noticed that we encounter virtually the identical use of words in Ives' descriptions of the second movement in his prior *Fourth Symphony*. Here, he had already commented on the multiple levels of the music and the need to be aware of different levels while focusing on just one at

The Universe Symphony

a time. Comparing it to various aural scenarios, but significantly looking at the skies while remaining conscious of the landscape below, or vice versa, it required an awareness of the listener, one that he termed *parallel listening*.[3] Now, in their ultimate context, finally we find these words taking on real descriptive meaning.

Ives thus would challenge us to follow him through a complex maze of competing and separate musical entities. Additionally, he would superimpose one further musical level - the representation of the energy of the universe - with a mighty percussion orchestra intoning a kind of cosmic heartbeat as a backdrop, featuring constantly changing variables in cyclic waves within definable divisions of time.

The challenge for the listener

Unfortunately for the casual listener, this monumental work also is a profoundly far-reaching piece. It is not easily grasped even after *several* hearings - that is, unless it is known *how* to listen to it, what to look for and what it represents. Structurally, the symphony is also difficult to fathom, because virtually all of the familiar or expected landmarks the listener might be accustomed to leaning upon have been replaced with others. Neither is the music melodic in the normal sense of the word, nor written with any of the expected textures and protocols of orchestral music of the day. Ives thus had set course in uncharted space that makes normal musical comparisons and reference points largely absent. In leaving Danbury behind, its memories and the tiny, limited sphere of his upbringing, Ives' transcendentalism would now be transported to its natural place in the cosmos.

Significantly, as Michael Berest had noted in his 2005 article,[4] musical quotes are largely absent, although he missed a few oblique, but significant, references to the hymn, *Nearer, my God to Thee*, early, middle and late in the symphony - a hugely appropriate reference for this work, again, tying the symphony to the finale of the *Fourth Symphony*, plus some references to *In the Sweet Bye and Bye* - hugely appropriate in the spiritual context of Ives' later music. There is also one small reference to *Massa's in de Cold Ground*, too, in Section A, which seems odd in this context, especially since Ives finally had escaped Earth's musical gravity. However, its otherwise odd context is instructive in that part of that song was prominent in the final movement of the *Concord Sonata*.*

---

* Of those quotes, in Section A perhaps the listener might catch most readily the first of a couple of little snatches from the middle part of the melody *Nearer, my God to Thee* looming out of the texture in the solo trumpet and clarinet lines. Another quote from the same part of the melody can be found in the flute parts in the *Coda* of Section B, and again in the *Coda* of Section C. Furthermore, there are fragments of it in the upper woodwind and string parts leading into the *Coda* of Section C, and remarkably still more allusions to it near the beginning of the section - encapsulated within the specific relationships of the predominant pitches rather than in melodic context. Thus, there can be no doubt that this particular hymn represented Ives' ultimate musical, spiritual and cosmic connection, and is a unifying thread in the symphony, as well as the connection with the finale of the *Fourth Symphony*. We do not find such similarities anywhere else in his output; even the primary use of *the middle portion* of the melody in both works speaks to the strong ties between them. The small snatch of *Massa's in de Cold Ground* in Section A and *In The Sweet Bye and Bye* in Section C might be harder to catch; repeated hearings make them more noticeable. See Chapter 13 and Appendix 2 for more discussion of these fragments.

Regardless, it seems that almost all of the familiar signposts we are accustomed to hearing simply are not there. By Ives' own description, this symphony was not conceived as music in the conventional sense. Because he described it as being more akin to a representation of the universe in "tones," this indicates that extended linear sonorities, spatial sounds and far-reaching textures were primary ingredients, rather than melody, or even more especially the incredibly dense language and tangled web of the second movement of the *Fourth Symphony*. That is not to say that the music is not exceedingly complex; however, Ives undoubtedly was exploring new sonic concepts necessary for the larger universe of his imagination.

There is no doubt that this music would have seemed beyond all comprehension at the time it was written. In fact, it is not easy to fathom even now, virtually a century after Ives dreamed up

The Universe Symphony

the original concept. Fortunately for the modern listener, in the years since its composition we have become increasingly accustomed to various types 'assaults' on our ears - good and bad - so that we might at be least open to the possibility of experiencing something new. However, in the *Universe Symphony* we still need to know where to look, and what to look for! Because it poses so many aural demands, the absence of knowing what those elements are makes it impossible to grasp more than a fraction of them, even assuming the most open of minds. This makes early and easy comprehension remote, but offers instead continuing revelations, even after the work has become as familiar and comfortable as an old shoe.

Although Ives never thought twice about mixing and matching anything that suited his purpose, as witnessed in the *Fourth Symphony*, the *Universe Symphony* seems quite consistent in style and idiom. Despite this, it does reveal a kind of musical evolution as it unfolds into something in which everything comes together in the Emersonian sense. As far as symphonic form was concerned, Ives applied the term 'symphony' increasingly loosely, and as a work it arrives at a place that has far less in common with its European counterparts than does even the *Fourth Symphony* - that is, except the overall shared concept of a large-scale work of symphonic forces, in a large, united but contrasting musical structure.

Ives' *Universe* initially may sound completely atonal (that is, without a clear sense of key center, such as we identify in a traditional melody), but actually, this is not the case. Unlike Arnold Schönberg, Ives did not set out deliberately to avoid tonality. The sketches frequently reference standard chords, albeit highly expanded or differently constructed. In this respect, we can trace a direct link to his early experiments with harmonic language. Gravitationally, eventually the listener anticipates the strong pulls of different key centers throughout the work and within the motivic material itself; established tonalities lead to the next in an expected and logical sequence, although other less forceful key centers might be in play simultaneously.

Stuart Feder referenced that Ives had dabbled in the 12-tone system within the *Universe Symphony*, comparing it against the later developments of Schönberg.[5] We can locate other instances of 12-tone rows in Ives' music, too, such as those in *The Fourth of July*. Feder considered that this and other such uses of disparate and unrelated intervals indicated that a formulaic methodology had replaced true creativity, claiming that Ives had used such a device as a 'fallback.' However, such irregular notation was hardly new to Ives, although in sketching the *Universe Symphony* he remarked specifically upon a deliberate effort to seek multiple technical avenues that even he had not fully explored.[6] Many earlier works also feature some of these, if not quite with such a deliberation to push the musical envelope to the new aural extremes that we find here.

The *Universe Symphony* does indeed contain some examples of 12-tone and near 12-tone rows; however, it also contains many other types of device, such as whole-tone scales and quarter-tones. However, none was used as an end unto itself, weaving in and out of the texture for the very specific purpose of creating new sonic blends and aural references. Thus, it is entirely improper that Feder would claim that Ives relied upon a degree of 'formulae' in the composition of this work, especially considering the astounding level of creativity found in the *Universe Symphony* materials, and the fact that 12-tone components are not primary to it.

Even more particularly, we do not find anything as predictable as the formulaic manipulations of 12-tone rows in the *Universe Symphony*, or in any other work by Ives for that matter. Rossiter,[7] discussed Ives' approach towards 12-tone writing, correctly pointing out that Ives saw no value in imposing mathematical patterned successions of notes within music, other than for limited atonal effect. The sometimes near and not-so-near sequences of notes we find in Ives' music are, however, *not even remotely* along the lines of Schönberg's 12-tone system, a strict method that imposed mathematical order and succession of the 12 possible pitches for a composition *throughout its entire length*. Would Feder have proposed that Franz Lizst was guilty of the same thing, having used what was probably the first 12-tone row in history for the opening of his *Faust Symphony* in 1857?

Furthermore, in a footnote on a rejected page of the orchestrated version of his song *The Masses* (also known as *Majority*), Ives himself would use Feder's term "formulaic" to denounce the mechanical usage of the 12-tone concepts that would be developed in dodecaphonic musical composition. Ives considered that although formulaic methods had their place in totality, they were "a weak substitute for inspiration." Conspicuously, there is no technique exclusive to any new school of musical thought in Ives' music. Utilizing whatever would serve him best, artistic constraints, or anything that resulted in predetermined successions of notes were alien to him. And *tonal* backbones seem always buried deep within Ives' music, diametrically opposite philosophically to that of Schönberg.

On the same page of *The Masses,* there is a curious choice of words that might just be another clue to Ives' mindset. After he directed that the players adopt an aleatoric (random) succession of the twelve named semitones of an octave - indeed, it is a 12-tone 'row' - he then specified that each player hold the last one, describing this as finding his 'star.' With Ives' remarks about Emerson "on the lookout for the trail of his star," (see Preface, page xx), and the many celestial references throughout his music (even that 'glory beaming star'), this hint provides a further glimpse into Ives' perspective, such references to the universe - in these instances, stars - seeming to imply that it is no idle speculation that he might have seen his philosophy, indeed his music, in cosmic terms.

Out of all of Ives' catalog, it seems only the *Universe Symphony* has cast such pronounced and lengthy shadows, or raised the protective ire of so many who still stand insistent that it be allowed to remain an incomplete and unfinished monument. For these people, Ives' final masterpiece *must* always remain "unfinishable": the great "what if" symphony. This scenario is strangely reminiscent of the discovery (1985) on the ocean floor of the liner, *RMS Titanic,* another haunting relic from the same era. At the time of its final location deep in the Atlantic, its discoverer, as well as many others, expressed the wish that it remain hidden into perpetuity from all future prying eyes. In proposing that the site where the ship rests should somehow remain a sanctuary, forever a shrine to all those who perished on board that fateful night - despite that fact that the passengers' remains had long since departed the scene, and the ship and its contents were gradually decaying into oblivion - these presumably well-meaning individuals overlooked the fact that virtually all other sites of tragedy throughout history somehow have been fair game for archeological investigation!

Why Ives did not finish the symphony, and the 'Ives Legend'

After his return to the *Universe Symphony* in 1923, Ives found himself increasingly unable to organize or assemble the collective new and old materials into a work ready for performance, despite his best efforts. And even though he did try his hand at a few retrospective compositions later, he ran aground, finding he could go no further. We will look at the possible reasons behind this, but one way or the other he had reached the end of the road. Ives seemed to regret to his dying day that he was unable to muster the energy or stamina to complete his epic symphony. His typist (until 1951) remarked on his continuing fascination with it, and that he was heard occasionally muttering "if only" sentiments, but by then it was far too late.[8]

Contributing to Ives' inability to complete the symphony, there are several clearly discernible factors. Ives was suffering from accelerating and compounding health issues: a type of heart disease, diabetes, cataracts, theorized bipolar episodes, as well as Addison's disease, which induced sporadic shaking in his hands and made writing especially difficult. Furthermore, we already know that he was decidedly less optimistic about the world following the trauma of World War I and the defeat of his political ideals and champions. Ives simply had run out of steam following his even more serious health issues in 1918, (presumably due largely to having burned two sizable candles at both ends: business *and* music), the physical capabilities to complete such a giant project as the *Universe Symphony* being largely spent.

The Universe Symphony

However, he did look forward to regaining the strength to do it, so defeat was not amongst his sentiments.

Indeed, Ives left us with the impression that the fundamentals of the *Universe Symphony* were basically in place. In his comments in 1931 about it in *Memos*,[9] and pivotal to the discussion, he made reference to taking the time to *finish* the score during the upcoming summer of 1932. Even though he commented that the work had not yet been completed, the inference of his words implied that the symphony existed in large degree. He did not mention the additions made to his sketches as late as 1923, or even any beyond, only referencing Section A from 1916. However, parts of the last (Section C) were laid out in near complete detail; to a lesser degree significant amounts of Section B were almost 'ready to go'; the remainder never were left in a structurally finished state, despite a wealth of information being supplied for their completion, and the large amount of materials left behind.

Further key anecdotal evidence for Ives' general physical condition can be found in his own words.[10] Ives made it quite clear that after his serious 1918 illness it was all he could do just to handle the pressure of his office work, something that sapped the energy for the creative work he once did late during the evening and on into the night.[11] This condition also is recounted in the words of others, especially those documented by Vivian Perlis.[12] An arduous task such as anything on the scale of this symphony, especially one requiring intense creative decisions, would be indeed overwhelming to anyone in Ives' condition. Indeed, his output already had been more than most composers could hope to attain over an entire lifetime.

Another clue to Ives' failure to put his symphony into finished form is his father's early demise, which probably caused him to see himself in a race against time during his most productive years up until 1923; it must be factored into understanding his ultimate exhausted state of being. We know that Ives' time at the office was far reduced during the 1920's. By the time he fully retired from business in 1930, even the little remaining strength available to him was largely gone. Instead, after his serious illness, his creative efforts centered on organizing fully scored existing materials, adapting, sketching and revising others, and composing some songs. Such activities spelled out more feasible prospects for someone in his condition than would the undertaking of a large musical project. That his precarious health factors contributed to his failure to leave the *Universe Symphony* as a completed work cannot be doubted, and even if these were the main reasons he never made a final fully-scored version, it is not likely primarily why he stopped composing, nor can it be the reason that he never went beyond the symphony in scope.

It seems unfortunate that ultimately the *Universe Symphony* was allowed - even encouraged - to reach the mythical status, largely unchallenged, that it never had been *meant* to be finished, this being a byproduct of what has become known as the 'Ives Legend.' (See Appendix 2.) The longer the symphony stood incomplete, the larger the myth grew. No doubt due to having discounted the real possibility that Ives wished to finish it, this part of the legend was not laid to rest by most of those in a position to dispel it. Outside officially sanctioned circles, it seemed there was little enthusiasm to grant official blessing for a posthumous collaborator to complete it. Thus, the mythical work was supposed to languish and retain its unattainable status into eternity, deeply buried under the well-established aura of being something that existed only in the composer's mind.

We can understand the timeline of the growing myth. Once Ives himself realized that his health and creative strength would not allow him to put his great symphony into a finished score, from here on out, the public 'plan' for the work would expand like the universe itself, with ever-grander projections becoming its new identity. Better that it should expand forever into dimensions grander than any human being could deliver - the "unattainable masterwork" - than for the composer to admit that completion now was beyond him! However, in the 1940's, Ives asked composer and champion of his music, Henry Cowell, to help him finish it, which does not sound like someone convinced that it was beyond completion. (Cowell meticulously had assembled some of his other music from sketches.) Daunted by the task, Cowell declined, and thus ultimately and unfortunately, the myth became the stuff of folklore, regrettably finding support amongst the most reliable of authorities. Sadly, Cowell was a willing participant, even the creator, in the new projections of the symphony.

Thus, Ives' extravagant descriptions of multiple orchestras (as many as 15), and even a chorus of 2,500 scattered around numerous mountaintops and valleys date from the period of association with Henry Cowell. It is no secret that the delusional grand statements of intent and concept of the *Universe Symphony* belonged to the composer's later years, increasingly appearing with each advancing year of his decline. And so the story continued to grow about a work so monumental in concept, so unfathomable in design, so vast in scope, that no one person, perhaps not even any group of persons could possibly hope to see it through to fruition. The preposterous descriptions of gargantuan choirs and orchestras sprouted like new shoots in springtime. No one ought to be unaware of this timeline. However, the myth persists in spite of itself.

Significantly, clear indications on his more detailed sketches *detail* an orchestral force *far* from the inflated concepts we have read about - such were not at all in evidence in his sketches; in fact, the *precise instrumentation* is listed and specified on Ives' sketch score (Neg. = q3027). These forces are surprisingly modest, in light of all that we had heard - and in some ways (for example, the string section) decidedly less formidable than we find in the *Fourth Symphony* that preceded it. Thus, it seems that the original concept of the *Universe* orchestra amounted to fewer than 75 players at most, although this included no less than nine flutes and a minimum of thirteen percussionists! Ives' sonic concept for forces used in this symphony was unique, even to him.

Certainly the Cowell-inspired projection of the symphony played well into the hands of the ailing Ives, who had already retreated into a mindset prone to remember details incorrectly and possibly exaggerate the glories of his life. As Ives' compositional activities receded, they were replaced by his legend (the 'Ives Legend'), with ever more bold, unattainable ideas.

Increasingly he would idealize the less than remarkable musical career of George Ives, his nurturing, kind, albeit remarkably musically curious father and teacher, as he dwelled upon whom really *had* inspired him. By the time of Ives' involvement with Henry Cowell, he had already deteriorated into the condition whereby completion of the masterwork had become totally unrealistic. The final nail in the coffin already had taken place long before; in 1927 tearfully he informed Harmony, his wife, that he was unable to compose anymore - somehow he could not keep things going.[13]

Remarkably - even at this late period of time - in her 2008 book,[14] Gayle Sherwood Magee once again recycled the myth of the symphony's unfinishability, having dissected and negated the 'Ives Legend' into oblivion. Although able to see through it at every level, it was only *here* that she bought into it, hook, line and sinker. Magee also incorrectly asserted that most of the surviving materials date to after 1923[14]; this is far from accurate, as most of the very detailed sketches for the longest part (Section A) appear to date clearly from 1915 or 1916, as well as other sketches for use in the symphony. If, as she proposed, becoming an accepted newcomer to the avant-garde scene in New York was behind Ives' revisiting his masterwork in 1923, so be it, although the Hubble connection seems more likely. The fact remains, however, that the primary concept of the symphony predates this time, and is clearly linked to his stays in the Adirondacks.

The sketches from 1923, or perhaps just a little beyond, mark the end of the line of Ives' creative vision; anything from here on out was a rather tired regression to earlier musical language. If the symphony was to go no further relates to his failing health and energies, more plausibly it was to an awareness that he had indeed managed put his thoughts down with sufficient clarity to return to the symphony later when 'he felt better,' allusions to his hopes for an improved state of health indeed cropping up in his writings.

Could it be, therefore, that he might have considered the symphony largely done? Could it be that he would not

The Universe Symphony

yet count it as such for his catalog in the absence of a reasonably organized sketch? These suppositions seem eminently reasonable.

Of course, the state of renewed vigor Ives had hoped for never materialized. The rest of the *Universe Symphony* myth seems to be a fiction born out of Cowell's wishful thinking. Magee asserted that Ives might have been influenced by the scope of Scriabin's *Mysterium;* Ives was familiar with his piano music, so this is possible. However, *Mysterium* was never finished and would have been little known in America even in the 1920's. More likely Ives' vision for his symphony was conceived independently. There are other factors in play as well, however. Returning to Stuart Feder's book,[15] in it Feder would read other meanings into the carefully descriptive words Ives had written directly on his *Universe Symphony* sketches. In trying to tie some kind of *mental* decline and the incomplete *Universe Symphony* together,[16] he described the sketches as relying more on words than actual musical notation.[17] This is anything but true; there is musical notation in spades. In fact, Ives had always peppered his sketches and scores with liberal quantities of words, humor and sarcasm.

Worse, having decried the Cowell-Ives Legend, Feder, again like Magee, further propagated its greatest misstatement - that it was Ives' intention never to complete it! We should remind ourselves that most of the *Universe Symphony* materials date from a period when Ives' powers were at their height. Although Cowell indicated that Ives continued to tinker with his enigmatic masterpiece even as late as 1951, we can be sure that the bulk of everything handed down to us represents the work of earlier times, when Ives' compositional activities and capabilities were still riding high.

Portrait of Charles Ives, 1947
Photo by Frank Gerratana

Certainly until perhaps near the very end of his life, and especially in light of his considerable pianistic virtuosity (dynamically on display in recordings made as late as 1943,[18]) even the descriptions of his work in preparing the 1947 Second Edition of the *Concord Sonata*,[19] there is no trace of mental disorder. We can look, too, at the many depictions of those having firsthand contact with him who described Ives' vigorous and engaging mind well into late in life. From his own words in *Memos*, to an abundance of anecdotal evidence, we find nothing to suggest it.

Indeed, Brewster Ives' commentary regarding the elder Ives makes it quite clear that his uncle retained a vital mind well into his late years, also as reported by many others, including John Kirkpatrick, Monique Schmitz Leduc, Lou Harrison and Luemily Ryder.[20] Howard Taubman visited him in 1949; in his account,[21] there is nothing that indicates anything other than a figure fully engaged, energetic in character, and spirited in persona; in short, the Ives we know seems still to have been largely intact even at *that* late date. Thus Feder's theory is perilously flawed, matching not even his own research.

Since the 1920's Ives had embarked on a vigorous frenzy to complete previously unfinished works, revise others, generally to sort through a maze of disorganized material, as well as photocopy it; he had also made a major effort to put printed copies of his music into the public arena, and financially to enable performances of it to take place. Thus we can see that Ives still was engaged, undiminished inside, even if physically worn out. Though disillusioned not only by the directions of so much he had hoped for, and also by the widespread and callous rejection of his music, still he had not given up.

If Ives was guilty of retreating into 'rants,' in this writer's view the only words truly fitting that description, and revealing any degree of real angst, occurred during the later section of *Memos*, entitled *Memories*.[22] Typical words of a loner, and from one who was sick at that, we can read far too much into them. As pent-up feelings that had festered for years, they really ought to be seen for what they are. At least we have Ives' direct utterances, unfiltered and refined by normal boundaries (as would have been the case had he maintained a busy social life) - we have just his thoughts, exaggerated and unleashed. Having had some of his highest-held hopes dashed by those entrusted with the public good, they surely signify no dark or mysterious meanings about his psyche.

Considering the things that had been said about his music at the time - even about him - by those too insular, provincial and egotistical to consider that perhaps there was a giant creative force in their midst, in the circumstances, his outbursts were remarkably restrained for the most part. Beyond these pages, we gain more comfortable glimpses into the man, his sentiments revealed as philosophical, even funny at times, especially regarding his passionately held social/political views, and those about the state of music in his day.

However, Feder attempted to support his case with summations of Ives' abilities as a writer in *Essays before a Sonata,* and surprisingly, *Memos.* Ives' words cannot possibly be held to the same standards as those used to judge his music, although this also does Ives grave injustice! His ability to 'speak' directly from the heart is remarkable, and he does so more effectively than Feder was prepared to grant. Ives' writings *are* remarkable in many ways, revealing insights into his personal outlook and values, as well as the true creative spark that set him apart. It is not too bold to claim that Ives' own words are more interesting, revealing and readable than anything anyone else has written about him, (this book included). Indeed, Ives had written extensively within the insurance business, not as an author of books, but rather in countless printed guidelines, articles, speeches for others, business concepts and correspondence; in this capacity he was widely known in the life insurance industry, even legendary. *Essays* is, in every respect, the work of a practiced communicator, in many ways remarkable and a lot better as literature, too, than Feder allowed. In fact, it is pretty good! Thus it was highly inaccurate to imply that the use of words was something new in the mix, and hardly surprising that Ives would have wished to leave behind some of his own thoughts about music and life.

Furthermore, *Essays* dates from the time of Ives' greatest creativity, so it is even harder to make a case that it represents a time of decline. *Memos,* on the other hand, was not conceived as a literary work as such, but as a simple recounting of his memories concerning all things connected to his music - it reads far more like answers to questions than a work of prose. Furthermore, the collection of reminiscences was the result of dictations, not literary writings. In fact, most telling in *Memos,* however, are Ives' accounts of things important to him, related with a totally engaged mental acuity, humor and energy; and this was in 1931 and beyond. Regardless, *Memos* is a commentary covering his lifetime of music, people and events as he recalled them to a secretary 'off the cuff.'

The real purpose behind the words

In general, Ives' use of verbal notations in his sketches would serve as signposts for those times when he would return to a dormant composition; as Ives' ultimate musical vision, the *Universe Symphony* demanded detailed notes. It seems yet, however, that the real key to the extensive verbal details provided in the later sketches lies elsewhere. More than for Ives' purposes, they provided something tangible for *others* to comprehend, so they would know what he had in mind - in the event he was unable to complete the work himself. This is, of course, exactly what he referenced in *Memos*.[23] Because this work was so important to him, as well as the fact that he harbored increasing doubts about his capabilities to complete it, he took the trouble, at least, to leave a paper trail about the more complete sketches - a recipe of sorts, and the clear indication that this was the purpose of his annotations.

The journey over

Looking further, perhaps it is *now* reasonable to deduce that the overriding factor behind Ives' inability to continue to compose, aside from his flagging health and energies to undertake large-scale projects, was that:

> **He no longer had anything left to say.**
> **Ives had reached the stars,**
> **his ultimate destination.**

Returning to his 2005 article,[4] Michael Berest was perhaps the first to proffer this speculation, and it seems he just might have hit the nail on the head. The *Universe Symphony* does indeed seem to go to the limit - even by today's standards. So despite increasing physical factors, there are more likely creative ones, too, to account for the rapid onset of Ives' period of compositional decline. This possibly might be compared to the depression experienced by some astronauts who went to the moon; what else was left to do? There is only so much that any mind is capable of creating; even Einstein could not come up with anything much beyond the *Theory of Relativity*. This was something that he formulated early in his career - and no one ever suggested that *he* suffered from mental decline!

Ultimately, it seems Ives just might have completed the essential materials for the symphony, providing just enough for a later collaborator to carry out what Ives was physically unable to do. Perhaps, too, Ives feared its completion, because he knew it represented the end of the line - the terminus at the end of his own celestial railroad. Perhaps this is why he largely put it aside for seven years, until briefly inspired to pick it up again in 1923, at which time it was presumably too late to summon the strength to see it through. The evidence for being able to go no further may be seen precisely in Ives' late attempts at composition in the 1920's. They reveal a retrograde step to a language at once more familiar; it is easy to imagine a situation whereby the composer was unable to think in such cosmic terms again, finding subsequent compositional efforts to be more a chore than an excursion and exploration into something stimulating. Because finished new works in this decade were mostly small scale, and tended to be more conservative, revisions, completions, or reworked compositions, Ives' large-scale efforts at composition were left incomplete or otherwise abandoned. Regardless, virtually everything failed to break new ground. Interestingly, Magee referenced for this period, *On the Antipodes,* and *Psalm 90,*[24] as examples of his remaining modernity. However, it appears that the harmonic basis of this former, at least, was derived from Section B and a prelude of the *Universe Symphony!*

On a smaller scale, some of his songs from the period, such as, *The One Way* (poking fun at traditional song formulae), and *Two Little Flowers* (a touching tribute to his daughter and her playmate), are as delightful as could possibly be, but they are far from a forward step or revolutionary technically, being conventional and tonal. Magee considered that Ives deliberately returned to earlier styles in the 1920's, his modernistic status assured.[25] This does not seem plausible either, especially since some of those reversions to earlier styles during this period came about in highly personal ways, such as the little song for his daughter; this was meant for her, not the world. The other example *(The One Way)* was an example of what *not* to do in song writing, so Ives would not have written negatively about something he was now embracing.

Ives also made some attempts at larger scale composition shortly before the later period of working on the *Universe Symphony*, and even beyond. Although such works were left largely incomplete, there have been efforts made to assemble some of those materials. Ives researcher and noted musicologist, the late David G. Porter was no stranger to completing unfinished Ives works. Amongst them are the first two movements of the *Third Orchestral Set* of 1921-1926. The first movement, for which Ives had left a very comprehensive sketch, leaves an impression of total authenticity, and is strongly imbued with Ives' unique sound in a darkly moody tone, despite its somewhat awkward transitions between sections. It is highly expressive and dreamlike, though *saying nothing very new* (sounding not unlike the *Second Orchestral Set*), and certainly it is an evolutionary step *backwards* towards more familiar turf.

However, by the time Ives arrived at the second movement, his inspiration seems largely detached, rambling, far less satisfying, and less even in quality. Incompletely sketched, it sounds like something Ives felt he *should* have been doing, but lacked the passion to pursue. Composing was becoming a chore. Perhaps the clearest evidence, however, of the waning of Ives' previously unflagging need to write may be seen in the barely sketched *third* movement. Ives was spent, creatively and physically. The *Universe Symphony* encompassed everything; other than this, not only had he nothing left to say, he had no reason to say it. It was not as if anyone was commissioning works from his pen. Rather, few people showed any interest in his music at all. It should not be hard to understand the compounding of factors behind his cessation of all composition by 1927. Ives had already arrived at the celestial terminus some time before. Now he knew it.

Interestingly, Porter also produced a piano and orchestra realization of the abandoned and uncompleted earlier forerunner to the *Concord Sonata,* titled unsurprisingly, the *Emerson Overture (or Concerto)* of 1910-14. In rebuilding and realizing a work as envisaged by Ives, it appears to be well researched, and a very effective, convincingly authentic Ivesian statement, having been assembled largely but fastidiously from the composer's notoriously chaotic surviving sketches. We can probably assume it to be a completely authentic recreation of the original. Porter himself assembled a version of the *Universe Symphony* from the masses of sketch materials that Ives left behind, from all that he regarded possible to complete. (See Chapter 12.) However, he produced a far shorter work than intended by Ives, and from a fraction of the materials, believing to his dying day that a complete version was impossible to produce.

Another musician saw things differently, having evaluated the sketch materials for himself. Venturing his belief that Ives had, in fact, essentially completed the symphony, albeit in disjointed and loosely laid out sketches, Johnny Reinhard saw a pathway through the materials and set about realizing the <u>entire</u> *Universe Symphony*. The next chapter details his and others' remarkable efforts to free the symphony from its tomb.

REFERENCES

1. 'Memos,' Charles E, Ives, edited by John Kirkpatrick, p. 106, *W. W. Norton & Co.*, New York, 1972, p. 132
2. 'Of Men and Mountains: Ives in the Adirondacks,' Mark Tucker, from 'Charles Ives and his World,' edited by Peter J. Burkholder, *Princeton University Press,* New Jersey, 1996, p. 160
3. 'Memos,' p. 106
4. 'Charles Ives Universe Symphony "Nothing More to Say," Michael Berest, 2005, www.afmm.org/uindex.htm

5. 'Charles Ives: "My Father's Song", a Psychoanalytic Biography,' Stuart Feder, *Yale University Press*, New Haven, Connecticut, 1992, p. 298
6. 'Memos,' p. 107
7. 'Charles Ives & His America,' Frank R. Rossiter, *Liveright*, New York, 1975, pp. 137-138
8. Feder, p. 349
9. 'Memos,' p. 106
10. Ibid., p. 112
11. Ibid., pp. 112-113
12. 'Charles Ives Remembered, an Oral History,' Vivian Perlis, *University of Illinois Press*, Urbana and Chicago, 1974, *for example:* pp. 103, 153
13. Ibid., p. 224
14. 'Charles Ives Reconsidered,' Gayle Sherwood Magee, *University of Illinois Press*, Chicago, Illinois, 2008, pp. 157 – 158
15. Feder, pp. 292-297
16. Feder, pp. 292-297
17. Ibid., p. 296
18. 'Ives Plays Ives,' Charles Ives, CD recording, *Composers Recordings, Inc*, New York, 1999
19. 'A Descriptive Catalogue of The Music of Charles Ives,' James Sinclair, *Yale University Press*, New Haven, CT, 1999; see 'Comment,' Concord Sonata, http://webtext.library.yale.edu/xml2html/music.ives-sinclair.nav.html
20. Perlis, pp. 77-80; 98-99; 128-129; 205; 219-220
21. 'Posterity Catches Up with Charles Ives,' Howard Taubman, from 'Charles Ives and his World,' edited by Peter J. Burkholder, *Princeton University Press*, New Jersey, 1996, pp. 423 - 429
22. 'Memos,' (1932), pp.133 -136; 'Essays before a Sonata,' *The Knickerbocker Press*, New York, (1920)
23. 'Memos' p. 108
24. Magee, p. 151
25. Ibid., p. 161

CHAPTER 12

Resurrecting the symphony

The sketch materials

Contrary to the commonly held perception, a surprisingly large quantity of sketch materials exists for the *Universe Symphony*. With much of it being sufficiently comprehensive to justify the efforts of some later composers to try their hand at assembling at least parts of the masterwork, in fact, this was precisely what Ives had proposed, once he began to realize that completing it probably would remain beyond his capability. The file of sketch materials is pure, raw Ives, for the most part without revisions or afterthoughts, and certainly with no chance of different versions emerging over the years following any initial completion. As such, it provides a unique insight into the workings of Ives' creative processes. More significantly, it tells us once and for all that Ives' music was truly innovative at the time of its initial conception; the *Universe Symphony* sounds as avant-garde even as anything written today.

Regardless, mischaracterizations of 'missing sketches' *still* continue unabated in some circles, and continue to show up unabashedly now and then. David G. Porter (whose credentials were impeccable) railed against such characterizations, since they are oddly out of step with what became clear during the 1990's from research carried out on the materials Ives left behind. Porter became totally exasperated by the continued propagation of the myth. If anything was missing, he argued, it was because it never existed! Whether what we have represents *all* of Ives' intent for the symphony, and this remains a matter of some discussion, attempts to produce a concert work are well supported by the scope of what exists. However, only the realization by Johnny Reinhard resulted in a work coinciding with Ives' plan that also sounds complete. It is also not insignificant that sufficient material existed to occupy the duration of all ten prescribed percussion cycles (that continue throughout the entire work), something that supports Reinhard's contention that all of the necessary musical content indeed was present in the collective sketches.

Conceived ultimately in three 'sections,' A, B and C, the majority of the materials of Section A: *Wide Valleys and Clouds*, are highly detailed and date mostly from around 1915-1916; some formerly (and famously) 'missing' bars were identified by Reinhard as belonging to Section A, (though the level of detail provided for them is considerably less; see Appendix 2). In utilizing this previously unassigned sketch material to complete the section, Reinhard found that logically it also fitted the plan and matched the existing tonal references for the subsequent realignment with the *remainder* of the sketch materials, as well as the upcoming percussion cycle (#6). Aside from some possible additions Ives made up to 1919, as well as composing other materials for the expansion of the work, for a time this collective material comprised the extent of the symphony, and as such, Section A was left largely complete.

As late as 1923 a larger general plan was laid down for a work built in three sections, labeled A, B and C, with *preludes* for each, as well as something resembling a second prelude for Section A. Many less fully worked out sketches originate from this date, right at the cusp of the most precipitous decline of Ives' compositional activity. Of these, some are clearly labeled 'Section B,' so there is no dispute regarding their placement; that of the less than clearly labeled *coda* to that section was straightforward to deduce because of the completeness and specific naming of the other two. Other sketches are clearly related to the designated Section C materials, so their placement there can be confidently deduced, even when not specified. Yet further substantial and highly detailed labeled portions of Section C appear to date also from around 1923.[1]

Ives himself alluded to all of the above in *Memos,* where it is quite clear that Section A was conceived initially; later, the larger symphony was to incorporate it within the grand plan, along with the prelude to each section.[2] Although the preludes date from 1923, that belonging to Section C has remained shrouded in controversy, with most authorities considering it lost or never written. Significantly, some other sketch materials are dated 1915, and were labeled specifically for inclusion later in the symphony, showing that Ives had thoughts about a larger design all along beyond Section A.

The following is the final plan as it had evolved for the *Universe Symphony* by 1923, together with what has been traditionally considered the status of each part:

I: Fragment; *Earth Alone* (existing fragment in sketch)
II: Prelude #1; *The Pulse Of The Cosmos* (plan described and partly sketched by Ives)
III: Section A; *Wide Valleys And Clouds* (fully sketched, with 3 orchestral units believed missing)
IV: Prelude #2; *Birth Of The Oceans* (believed incomplete)
V: Section B; *Earth And The Firmament* (believed incomplete)
VI: Prelude #3; *And Lo, Now It Is Night* (believed lost)
VII: Section C; *Earth Is Of The Heavens* (believed incomplete, except for the coda)

The opening fragment was taken from the *coda* of Section A, in accordance with Ives' suggestion. *Prelude #1: The Pulse Of The Cosmos,* the first three of ten cycles of the remarkable battery of percussion, was intended to be heard alone, the remaining cycles continuing in various guises throughout the symphony's length. Well described by Ives, nevertheless he had not worked out the specific mechanics for coordinating all ten cycles prescribed with the orchestral materials, let alone the symphony's eventual assembly, although the percussion prelude and its continuing undercurrent throughout was conceived from the start.

Even though Section A was left in virtually complete full sketch score, the sketches for the remaining Sections (B and C), together with the preludes, have been the subjects of much controversy all along. Even in *Memos,* Ives did not claim much for the entire symphony. The fact that this remaining material is less well laid out than that of Section A may be the explanation that even in his own 1931-1950 catalog Ives listed only Section A. Thus, apparently he did not consider what he had put down to be sufficiently detailed for him to declare it "sketched." However, quantities of these materials certainly exist, and are fairly comprehensive at that! Despite being less fully worked out than the sketches for Section A, the lack of acknowledgement of them by the composer, nevertheless, is a confounding and perplexing aberration of the record.

A plan for the overall assembly of the symphony had long remained a challenge to determine. Quite aside from the lack of agreement about the completeness of the sketches, the fact that many of the materials for the two last sections are much less fully detailed than those of Section A - indeed, some are downright obscure, their precise sequence or purpose is not always clear. Their assembly require good powers of deduction, and perhaps even greater patience in order to organize and extract any valid realized version. Such 'decoding' demands considerable expertise and knowledge of the composer's work, in addition to his written and implied clues. Naturally this comes with all the inevitable questions about the correctness of any reconstruction or realization.

Although the symphony is built around three main sections, they should not be considered *movements* as would be encountered in a conventional symphonic model. Each came with its specific challenges for realization into a performable edition. The question naturally arises whether there was enough material to assemble an entire symphony, let alone whether there was the necessary information to organize it with a reasonable certainty of its correctness. Reinhard not only argued that this was the case, but also having succeeded in assembling the only fully realized version of the *Universe Symphony*, Ives' grandest and lengthiest structure finally stands revealed. Unlike anything before or since, it is indeed Ives' magnum opus. As a musical manifestation of his life's contemplations, it is why Ives' hopes for its eventual completion into a performable state had remained so important to him. Fortuitously, as it happened, Reinhard believed there existed just enough of an evidentiary trail finally to provide the keys to free the symphony from one man's mind into the cosmos.

Paving the road for the listener

In *Memos*, Ives mentioned his piano studies and 'cycle rhythms;' these are directly related to the concept behind *The Pulse of the Cosmos*.[3] Clearly, the idea for this came from rhythmic experiments Ives had carried out soon after the turn of the century; (see Chapter 6). In Chapter 6 it was revealed that *From the Steeples and the Mountains* features cyclical rhythmic divisions not unlike the expansions and contractions of the *Pulse* cycles. Another composition, *Rondo Rapid Transit*,[4] (otherwise known as *Tone Roads No. 3* - Ives considered it a joke more than an exercise) features a substantial *harmonic* cycle of expansion and contraction, again not unlike the *Pulse* cycles.

We can see direct comparisons and significant clues to his train of thought in the finale of the *Fourth Symphony*, in which Ives put the concept of an independent battery of percussion instruments into practice in advance of developing the concept for his *Universe Symphony*. The primary difference, though, is that the percussion line in the *Fourth Symphony* is developmentally static, neither evolving within itself, nor within the progress of the movement, although it continues throughout its length. However, immediately we can see where Ives was going; the *Universe Symphony* took the idea to the next level, once it was hatched. This ought to eliminate all further discussion about the appropriateness of the percussion entity continuing underneath the music in the *Universe Symphony*; Ives had already demonstrated the idea in a work linked to it.

Ives' rationale to impose on the listener a lengthy unconventional section of non-tuned and tuned percussion at the outset (almost 30 minutes) must have been threefold. First, it would convey and establish the timeless 'heartbeat' of the cosmos itself, while second, serving to bind the whole work together through enhanced awareness of it; third, it would also illustrate and emphasize the 'inner' symmetries that could be built by such seemingly disparate rhythmic entities, mimicking nature at every level in the cosmos.

We know that the concept of 'parallel listening,' was not entirely new to Ives - since much of his earlier music involves multiple lines of musical thought - but the strong visual connotations of the *Universe Symphony* presented the idea more prominently than before. Although the basic reference tempo (speed) for the entire orchestral forces is extremely slow, it allows internal movement through multiple divisions and related parallel tempi, while avoiding the dictates of a tempo that is obvious or dominant. Thus, encompassing one level of separate independent percussion cycles, plus another two levels that are primarily melodic and harmonic, the actual tempo (speed) of any given part is not the main consideration. Indeed, the conductors' beats (yes, Reinhard's realization requires at least two conductors) act only reference points for coordination, and as such, the tempo governing any part will be hard to discern, precisely as was intended. However, there is a distinct independence of movement of the three primary levels that becomes clearer upon repeated hearings, again exactly what Ives had in mind.

Melodically, in works such as *The Fourth of July* and *The Masses,* Ives also tested some of the wide leaping intervals found in many individual lines in the *Universe Symphony*. All this says nothing of his experiments in microtonal tunings directly referenced in *Memos*. Thus in the *Universe Symphony* we will encounter tunings in both tempered and natural scales, and structures built from scales of overtones, intervals of less than a half-step, whole tones and more,[5] as well as the combined benefits of multiple experiments and even new ones.

From these qualities alone, it should already be clear why the *Universe Symphony* cannot present itself as an immediately accessible work, even upon *successive* hearings if encountered in a vacuum. Thus, we should not expect this music to jump off the page as an obvious work of art in the absence of a degree of effort towards it by us. Thus, in the absence of quotations in the *Universe Symphony* (well, near absence!), we need to approach it knowing that it is supposed to sound as if it belongs to another place. Musically, the *Universe Symphony* is profoundly uniform in concept, a monumental vision of someone possibly aware of his own mortality, but most certainly looking far into the cosmos and the eyes of his creator. Normal worldly references, other than those relating to Earth's place in the cosmic order, cannot be expected to occupy a significant part, and thus, being a final fulfillment of Ives' cosmic vision, we should not *expect* the music to sound as it did before. Therefore, to anyone still unfamiliar with Ives' *less* radical compositions it is likely to seem all the more inaccessible!

Ives at one time thought this lengthy work might be performed twice in succession to allow audiences to experience and grasp it fully from all perspectives! Actually, this was a reasonable, if totally impractical wish at the time in the absence of alternative ways to allow listeners to familiarize themselves with the different levels of music. If a double performance was not possible, Ives also suggested that strongly identifying fragments of the three parallel entities be allowed to stand on their own - at the outset of the entire piece and elsewhere. He hoped in this way that the listener, unaccustomed to what might at first appear to be an unfathomable tangle, would better see a way through the sonic maze, and be more able to separate the components aurally in the ways he had intended. Regardless, he must have known that this would only partially solve the potential problems for all but the most sophisticated listener, but at the time there was no viable alternative. Such is the advantage of modern recordings, with high-resolution sound and separation - things Ives did not have available to him. With this in mind, familiarizing oneself with just a portion of the symphony at a time ought not to be frowned upon; perhaps, too, the listener will find later sections are more readily approached than earlier ones.

The soundscapes consist of countless expansive, evolving musical colors, effects built from unusual instrumental and note combinations within multiple complex lines of thought, like broad irregular washes of paint on three-dimensional *moving* canvases. If traditional melodies have been replaced by 'thematic motifs' - usually more fragmentary than extended, however diffuse or irregular many may seem - Ives had written music of another kind (Music of the Spheres, again?), certainly not likely to be considered 'music' as such at the time of its composition. For those unable to relate to its wildly futuristic sounds, while bemoaning the absence of familiar melodic ingredients of Americana, more is the pity, since here we have one of the most magnificent musical flights of the imagination ever conceived. Thus, the plea to give this symphony *time*.

To put the scope of this visionary work into perspective, 1915 is the date that Holst composed *The Planets,* also amongst the first true examples of space-inspired music as we know it. With nothing but the greatest respect towards Holst's magnificent composition, the 'night and day' disparity between their respective 'languages' shows just how advanced Ives' *musical* and *conceptual* scope was in its day. Remarkably, this still is the case, and the *Universe Symphony* would not sound out of place today in a program featuring the most far-reaching avant-garde, even electronically oriented compositions. We should remind ourselves, too, that Ives' otherworld sonic landscape was attained with no high-tech means at all. The astute listener might be aware already of the electronic sounding textures that Ives had created earlier in the finale of the *Fourth Symphony.*

Remarkably, even in the *Universe Symphony,* ultimately one can find certain ties to more familiar music, and for those with a little musical background, tonal centers and logical harmonic progressions become increasingly discernible after a few hearings. Isolating individual instrumental motifs and lines, too, wherever possible will reveal thematic connections that tie together and identify the material of each section. Because the entire lengthy symphony is played with no breaks between 'movements' (Sections), this results in a continuous stream of uninterrupted consciousness.

The Three Orchestras

Reflecting the typical view of the time that put Earth at the center of attention in the universe (at least in the sense of its importance!), we can see this reflected in the plan of the symphony. Ives conceived a separate orchestra for each primary component. Although the dominant forces of the **Universe** are represented from the opening of the piece (manifested in the percussion orchestra as *The Pulse of the Cosmos*) and are present throughout the symphony, a separate orchestra representing **Earth** and its varied landscapes, and another for the skies above (the **Heavens**) dominate the orchestral portion of Section A. The oceans (still part of Earth) begin the middle section, (B), one in which Earth remains centered in the foreground; however, the cosmos, viewed more from an external standpoint makes its 'entrance.' Nevertheless, it is only when we reach the final grand designs of Section C that are we freed - even propelled - into the cosmos fully on its own terms, and Earth is finally seen in the perspective of being only a small part of it. It is as though Ives finally saw the cosmos through Hubble's eyes, because the sheer sound is utterly amazing and dumbfounding, seeming to speak to a new musical order! Each of the three independent instrumental 'orchestras,' or groupings, thus has its own identity and independent purpose. More specifically:

- The **Earth Orchestra** features a lower aural component (the ground below our feet) and a specific group of instruments to represent it. With two primary functions, the first orchestral sub-group was to represent features such as mountains, rocks, outcroppings, trees, rivers, fields, forests, and so forth, ranging from close-up to far in the distance,[2] Principally harmonic in nature, the *Earth Chord* - a complex structure, assumes central significance in the section, its underlying code at its foundation; other 'chords' are made up largely from whole steps or unconventional intervals. The *Earth Orchestra* also features free polyphonic elements that represent the actively forming world; reaching up to symbolize them - jagged intervals and rhythms. Although the *Earth Orchestra* is dominated by low to mid-range sounds, often the trumpet, clarinet and oboe soar skywards as might features during creation.

The *Earth Orchestra* features striking lines for trumpet; Ives' choice of this prominent instrumentation remained a characteristic throughout most of his instrumental and orchestral output, and especially in those in which American quotations were featured. From *The Unanswered Question* to *The Fourth of July*, we find this sound, altogether reminiscent of the dominant instrument of the local town band, and hence by default, Ives' father, George Ives. Certainly this sound must have been ingrained on Ives' consciousness from earliest times. Transformed here, however, it is still a strong reminder of that paternal presence: was it perhaps an indication that Ives felt he was glimpsing the place where they would be reunited?

- The **Heavens Orchestra** is altogether gentler, more smoothly linear and chordal in nature, to project the floating sounds of clouds spanning the skies. Outgrowths of earlier experiments, grouped chordal blocks move together against others in opposing directions and rhythms.
- Consisting of no less than nine flutes, clarinet, violins, violas, glockenspiel and celeste, and being rhythmically and harmonically divided further into sub-groups, Ives was trying to paint moving, interacting cloud formations. Unsurprisingly, its overall register and character is significantly higher in pitch than that of the *Earth Orchestra.*
- Much of the time in Section A, the *Heavens Orchestra* also exists within its own tempo (its own universe, indeed),

at those times moving at a speed 150% that of the *Earth Orchestra*. This imparts an even greater floating quality to it, once the ear has resolved and identified the group with its unique sonic characterizations and motions. For the rest of the symphony it exists within the same time frame as the Earth group, sometimes not being so strongly differentiated in character; indeed, often the two orchestras co-exist entirely as a unified ensemble - that is, when Earth and sky are not being painted as separate entities.

The **Pulse of the Cosmos** orchestra is another matter, however. This 100% percussion ensemble plays on its own as the lengthy prelude, to reinvent itself through the ten cycles as it continues totally independently throughout the *entire symphony*.

- The 'Pulse' moves in its own integral tempo, exactly half that of the *Earth Orchestra*. (We have already referenced that for the conductor this means pacing each beat at 2-second intervals - incredibly slow and not easy to do.) Because the 'Pulse' forms the foundation of the work, the slow reference speed upon which everything else depends has caused some misconceptions, with some critics of the symphony mischaracterizing it as being slow music. Perhaps they were listening with their eyes, not their ears, (watching the conductor instead?). Indeed the music is neither fast nor slow; the speed is indeterminate. The 'Pulse' cycles are built by *adding* instruments in various divisions or compounds of the basic beat until the peak of the cycle is reached, then *subtracting* the instruments in reverse order to which they entered. Depending of factors dictated by material of the *Heavens* or *Earth Orchestras*, in certain respects these cycles are coordinated with these other musical entities.
- Each cycle is developed from combinations of multiple divided 16-second units (termed the *Basic Unit*), the instruments maintaining equal divisions of time within the unit. The tones of the percussion instruments feature

a wide range of sub-divisions of the Basic Unit striking together once every 16 seconds; instruments are added or subtracted at the outset of each Basic Unit. The effect of the full compliment of prescribed percussion instruments playing together at the height of a cycle is reminiscent of many clocks ticking in one room. Curiously, we begin to anticipate a point every 16 seconds where the tones all seem to *wait* before coinciding.

- Durations of tones within this 2-second beat range from the very long to the very short. Superficially, it might sound as if the players are playing *irregular* rhythmic divisions, but this is only due to the mathematical misalignments of each separate instrument as they divide one basic unit to the next.
- Regardless, the 10 separate percussion cycles of *Pulse of the Cosmos* require at least 13 players, continuing in an uninterrupted flow from the beginning of the symphony to the end, (the one exception being the third cycle, which includes tuned percussion instruments with *piccolo*). The length and total number of divisions of each cycle are partially dependent on the lengths of each of the three major sections to which they are tied (A, B and C), their high and low points, and the associated preludes to each. One other variation of the concept concerns the last cycle (10th) differing in one aspect from the others. As the only cycle to commence at its peak with a sudden explosion of sound, each instrument drops out one by one, leaving just the low bell tone that began the first cycle standing all alone after everything else in the concert hall has fallen silent.

All components together

In those portions of Section A that require three independent speeds, we can comprehend the relationships between them by the following simple formula - that of the relative tempi (speeds) of each three orchestral units:

- 24 beats of Heavens Orchestra
  = 16 beats of Earth Orchestra *(One Orchestral Unit)*
  = 8 beats Percussion 'Pulse' Orchestra
  = 16 seconds
  = BU *(One Basic Unit)*

In itself, this is straightforward arithmetic, though made infinitely more complex due to the vast array of rhythmic sub-divisions within each orchestral group. Clearly more than one conductor is needed, and to date it has been performed with only two. A good case could be made for three, all of whom would be required to stay in close coordination. However, the *regular* divisions of the beat in the percussion group (with the exception of Cycle 3, and the short ad lib percussion portion of Section B) impart an entirely unique quality to it.

Realizations of the Universe Symphony

Because all of Ives' music and sketches still falls under copyright, one is not at liberty to rework or utilize the material in any way one chooses, certainly with any public presentation in mind. *The Charles Ives Society* also jealously guards the composer's legacy, and unauthorized claimants of complete realizations will not likely meet with their blessing; fair enough. However, although fulfilling a noble purpose, such effective controls could also stifle legitimate work undertaken by individuals not necessarily recognized by the society, or approved by the publisher. Further, it could be argued that if a member of the Society or publishing entity had an interest in realizing unfinished Ives works, that person could also be involved in sanctioning or denying similar efforts by others, regardless of the ethics or good intentions of the official body. Thus, we should weigh the intrinsic value of such musical archeology relative to the circumstances of any realization.

In that not everyone interested in the *Universe Symphony* was prepared to accept the traditionally and commonly ordained sentiment that it was beyond completion, or had been intended to be left incomplete, it seems hard to imagine that any composer - in this case, Ives – would wish for this sorry state of affairs for anything that had taken such a prominent place in his imagination. Fortunately, three composers have sought to bring Ives' vision to life, *and* met with the approval from all concerned to proceed. However, because only one of them (Johnny Reinhard) fully incorporated everything that Ives left behind to produce a coherent whole to result in the requisite amount of music to occupy all ten percussion cycles - he alone produced a work that filled Ives' allotted span.

First out of the gate was Larry Austin, long an avid Ives follower. Austin spent almost 20 years sorting through the available sketch materials in an effort to assemble what he intended to be perceived as a total 'Ives experience.' The author, while a member of the same university faculty during the 1970's, actually played some low 'Earth tones' from the sketches for one of Austin's early, recorded *Universe Symphony* experiments. (Could we collectively justify some kind of first performance claim?!) However, Austin's version, completed in 1993, did not incorporate all of the sketch material, and Austin has been accused of taking Ives' invitation to work up the idea well beyond his indications.

The result of this effort is a very different piece to the other realizations, even though we do hear the more complete *Earth* and *Heaven Orchestras* material from Section A essentially preserved amidst the sonorities. This cannot be expressed without a caveat here because here it is played exactly twice as fast as the tempo that Ives had indicated! (Austin could not accept that Ives' tempo specification was accurate; see discussion in Chapter 13). This speed causes the material to be garbled, as Ives' carefully crafted lines become almost unrecognizably blurred, and otherwise subverted by the continuing frenetic ad libitum percussion outside the prescribed format. Further, the tempo of the *Pulse of the Cosmos* causes Ives' low tolling bell at the beginning of each Basic Unit to occur so frequently, (and in the first recording being placed in a register so high), that it draws further undue attention to itself, ultimately becoming an irritant.

Austin wished his efforts to be experienced as something close to the symphony that Ives had envisaged. We can be sure that this was his intent, but it is harder to argue that it achieves this result, much less to know if the sonic effect of the resulting musical conflagration was anticipated ahead of its first performance. Many critics have argued that the material suffers from Austin's additions to it; although it is clear that we are hearing not only what Ives himself had indicated but also Austin's contributions, we must also allow that Ives did openly invite other composers to build upon his foundations if they so desired. Austin, thus, took Ives at his word, whether or not everyone is in agreement that it represents what Ives really intended.

Austin's *Universe Symphony* also is not helped by its adherence to the more limited plan of Ives' original concept, instead of the *final* plan of three clearly defined preludes with three similarly defined main sections. Although Austin was within his rights to make his own interpretation of what was the best approach to take, there can be no question that his realization comes across as a compressed shadow of the monument that Ives had in mind. However, we must acknowledge the sincere attempt to extract a performable work from the sketches. It was indeed the first completed effort to bring the symphony to life and to take up the composer's plea for a collaborator to do so. Kudos to that.

Much closer to the original concept, in as far as it goes, is the version of the symphony by David G. Porter. Consisting of excerpts taken mostly from the first section (Section A) and partly from the last, it was performed for the first time at the Aldeburgh Festival in England recently, but as of this date, (2012), however, it has not as yet been released as a commercial recording. Apparently, Porter was unable to trace the clues of assembly for the many remaining sketches, choosing to exclude them from his realization. Although well set in his feelings about other attempts to realize the score, Porter, nevertheless, was a noted Ives Scholar, and at one time historian to the Charles Ives Society. Notwithstanding the opinion of many that he made the incorrect assessment that the percussion part was not to be played concurrently with the other orchestral sections, we would be right to presume that he followed closely Ives' instructions and sketches, at least in what he presented. However, Porter also had different ideas about the shape of Ives' ten specified percussion cycles that interfere with their overall shape, due to an alternate interpretation of the waveform that Ives specified.

Careful examination of the sketches appears to support, however, Ives' plan for the percussion cycles to continue throughout, because on the opening sketch page Ives clearly indicated that the entire symphony was to consist of "one movement," and that the percussion was to continue "through the whole movement." This makes even more sense when one takes into account the sheer duration necessary to fill out anything close to Ives's implications regarding specifications for the cycles. They could not possibly be heard isolated in full while still expecting the audience to be present at the end! Further, at the outset of the Section B sketches is an indication by Ives that the *Pulse* should continue, and the number of players given is 12, which is closely in line with Reinhard's realization and theory about the scale of the symphony. The continuous nature of the *Pulse* also has seemed completely clear to others, too, amongst them Austin, Reinhard and Feder, who also pointed to the comments by Ives.[6]

Johnny Reinhard recalled that this first sketch page was split and that the top part continued as the lower half of the page began. He also observed that musical clues to the assembly were in evidence through Ives' instrumentation, as revealed by the subtleties that the cross rhythms of the crescendos/decrescendos indicated. Thus he contended that Porter misinterpreted the signposts. As a consequence, the differences in the percussion tracks between Porter's and Reinhard's realizations, quite aside from the incompleteness of Porter's version, set them apart. Regardless, in Porter's own realization, one can criticize his conclusions or even his method, but one cannot fault his sincere convictions and credentials in trying to correctly interpret Ives' intent.

Soon after Austin's version of the symphony had debuted, Johnny Reinhard's complete realization appeared on the scene. Reinhard's position that the sketches were largely complete seems reasonable considering his extensive research into the materials, Ives' own remarks, and the sheer quantity of surviving sketches themselves. Having run into several roadblocks before taking on the project, Reinhard fitted perfectly into the mold of an outsider claiming to see what insiders could not, receiving his share of criticism for his troubles. *The Charles Ives Society*, as well as the owners of the publishing rights (Peer Music), ultimately, though, gave Reinhard the green light for his realization and first performance. Remarkably, despite the concurrence of that position by David Porter (as the society musicologist), Porter would later become a staunch critic of attempts other than his own to realize the work! Possibly related to the commitment he had dug in towards the differences between his and Reinhard's versions, and notwithstanding his insistence that the 'Pulse' should be a separate movement, he had staked considerable resource and reputation upon constructing what Reinhard termed "beautiful diagrams" of the percussion cycles. Reinhard seems lucky to have been allowed to proceed.

However, Reinhard made the case convincingly that he had indeed been able to tread where Ives had gone before. In producing a full, balanced work, *without adding any additional material*, he believed that all sections of the symphony were, in fact, *sufficiently* represented by the sketches. Despite scrupulous efforts to utilize *only* those notes Ives had written himself, and having been completely open regarding his methods, it was ruled, nevertheless, that it should be known as *'Ives' Universe Symphony, as realized by Johnny Reinhard,'* if for no other reason that it is impossible to be 100% sure about Ives' final intentions. After all, Ives did not provide this finished score! Furthermore, the materials, if judged against many of Ives' large scale works, might easily lead one to fall into the trap of believing that the music needs 'filling out' with added substance, as Austin had done. It does not. For those who argue that the usage and placement of every single sketch cannot be claimed with certainty, we can at least be sure of Reinhard's effortless musicality and logic in deducing and assembling all of Ives' extant *Universe Symphony* material; had Ives completed the symphony himself, would it have emerged an *entirely* different work? Reinhard's is a version that finally we can listen to it without wondering how much of what we are hearing is by Ives himself. It is *all* by him.

Microtones

As Director of the American Festival of Microtonal Music (AFMM, New York), originally Reinhard was lured towards the *Universe Symphony* by its extensive specifications of microtones. Such terminology refers to divisions between the normally recognized smallest intervals of pitch in Western music. As the sketches proceed into the later phases of the symphony, the specific notations of quarter-tones become increasingly evident. Quarter-tones are half the amount of what is commonly recognizable as the smallest division of pitch. Contrary to impressions gained from a poorly researched review of the first performance by Richard Whitehouse of Porter's version in June 2012 in England,[7] Reinhard only included in his score those microtones that Ives himself had written in his sketches and throughout his compositions. Even the Charles Ives Society has recognized this. However, this did not stop Whitehouse from criticizing the wide use of microtones in Reinhard's version. It needs to be understood that it is only because the composer's microtonal indications increasingly characterize the music of the symphony as it approaches its concluding destination, Porter's version, by default, largely excluded the relevant sketch materials from his realization.

Additionally, Reinhard was able to trace a strong connection to further unconventional tuning through some of Ives' other music. In the *Universe Symphony*, Reinhard made a very convincing case that Ives, in fact, was writing with *Pythagorean* tuning in mind - even more since Ives made direct and distinct references to alternative tuning concepts for this work during his recollections about the formation of symphony.[8] Indeed, such notational 'spellings' may be found in the sketches. As such, Reinhard incorporated this system into his realization.[9]

Although the Pythagorean tuning is fairly complex to grasp, and might be a subtle distinction to many ears, a special flavor is imparted to the overall sound by its usage; it seems completely at home in the *Universe Symphony*. In creating new blends of sound, too, in the chordal structures Ives set up perhaps these pitches ought not be considered microtones, per se, but rather another tuning protocol governed by the relationships of the compounding spiral of mathematically pure *perfect fifths*.

It might be instructive to spend a little more time to understand why, in conventional Western music settings, notes of the same name are necessarily *different* from key to key. Such instinctive tuning involves the seventh and third notes in major scales (and ascending sevenths in melodic minor) - which are pitched slightly higher - and respectively the third in minor scales, which appear slightly lower. The conditioned ear has become accustomed to these shadings, and though necessary in solo lines, they are problematic in conventional chords; hence the piano, with non-sustaining tones, non-adjustable tuning, and chordal attributes, is an ideal candidate for utilizing 'equal temperament' tuning. To play effectively within ensembles requires constant adjustment by musicians, in which all concerned normally tune to the *average* pitch center - just as in piano tuning. Thus, equal temperament is just another tuning protocol, and again not interchangeable with the concept of microtones, which by some definitions, divides the octave mathematically; the difference is not great, but to a practiced ear, it is audible. Ives often wrote what would be normally considered 'enharmonic' notes within the same chords; he 'heard' tunings outside those normally dictated by the commonly ordained tuning protocols for each key center. These would have developed in his inner ear as he became increasingly adept in writing polytonal music, in which these shaded tunings would apply to *each parallel key center*. In this way, it is easier to appreciate the subtle distinctions he made. Thus, with Pythagorean tuning, it seems that Ives was seeking something more in line with the natural laws of the universe - better here than anywhere!

The story behind Reinhard's realization

Reinhard's documentation of the realization and assembly of the sketches, 'The Ives Universe – a Symphonic Odyssey'[10] reviews the process he followed. In this book-length account, he duplicated the major source material while providing a description of how he had 'connected the dots.' Of those finer details that are not spelled out, they may be deduced by analyzing the sketches reproduced within the text, or the full score.[11] *The Charles Ives Society* worked closely with Reinhard during his realization and concurred that his claims of having used only Ives' materials, while adding nothing of his own, were totally accurate.

In asking Reinhard for information on certain specifics that were not always clear, (see Appendix 2), his openness was testament to his passion for Ives's masterwork. Fortunately, too, a remarkable recording of the symphony is available of his realization, in which he conducted the AFMM Orchestra. Painstakingly undertaken in a unique layering process that ensured authenticity and precision, as such, it remains the sole recording of the only realization of the *entire* symphony. The result is a highly successful first recording of an unfamiliar work.[12]

Even after we move further into the work and Ives' sketches become less consistent or immediately clear, Reinhard's case for the essential completeness of the materials remains compelling. Whether Ives would have continued his work beyond the existing sketches for the Sections B and C is impossible to know, but as they stand, there was no shortage of material for a complete symphony. What was included to build the hitherto 'incomplete' Section C was either clearly indicated to belong to it, or deduced by its cues, style, and references, even by its obvious unsuitability for inclusion elsewhere. With each fragment meticulously placed, the final outcome is a mighty testament to Ives' creativity, but also a mighty testament to the skills, patience, dedication and perseverance of its eventual 'realizer.'

The Ives sound

Some have commented that this symphony does not sound like Ives. If one's expertise to identify the composer's work is limited by a dependence on hearing familiar musical quotations, certainly this would be so. However, the presence of other traits common to much of Ives' output makes the landmarks clear and evident. In fact, the *Universe Symphony* sounds exactly like Ives.

For those who argue that Ives would have added even more in texture had he completed the score himself, this does not seem in accord with his stated purpose, as well as his descriptions of the music itself. Nor does it jibe with the results of what we have in fairly complete sketches, which are nevertheless exceedingly complex. It would have been difficult to pile more upon what is already in evidence and preserve the stated concept and the unique sound desired - one that almost fully displaces traditional methodologies. Thus, it seems reasonable to believe what we are hearing is close to what Ives had in mind, in much the same way as his sketches of other works often have led to their finished counterparts. Indeed, from a sonic perspective alone, the finished texture, even if existing within a far vaguer tonality, is strikingly reminiscent of the finale of the *Fourth Symphony*, in that the inner lines of both works are more ethereal and less defined.

The difficulties of realization

Realizations of composers' unfinished or sketched works are tricky undertakings, to be sure. Hollywood film score orchestrators have developed an almost uncanny ability to do just this with the widest possible range of materials provided them imaginable - from the extremely carefully detailed sketches by some of the most accomplished figures, to the efforts of a few who bring to the table little or no background, or even composing skills! Although Ives was often extremely detailed in his directives and intentions, his sketches are a profusion of muddle and disorder, his scrawled notations frequently jammed onto every available scrap of manuscript paper sometimes in no semblance of apparent sequence, whatsoever. It takes a special kind of person to decipher and bring functionality to them.

Meanwhile, it is worth recalling that certain details of the finale to the *Fourth Symphony* were long considered indecipherable. Regardless, no one ever raises the specter of validity in regard to this work, the efforts of Theodore A. Seder in the 1940's to put the movement into a finished state not being seen as controversial. This cannot be claimed always in the case of the *Universe Symphony!*

REFERENCES

1. 'A Descriptive Catalogue of The Music of Charles Ives,' James Sinclair, *Yale University Press,* New Haven, CT, 1999; http://webtext.library.yale.edu/xml2html/music.ives-sinclair.nav.html
2. 'Memos,' Charles E, Ives, edited by John Kirkpatrick, p. 106, *W. W. Norton & Co.*, New York, 1972, p. 106-108
3. Ibid., p. 101
4. Ibid., p. 64
5. Ibid., p. 107
6. Ibid., p. 108
7. 'Aldeburgh Festival 2012 - Charles Ives's Universe Symphony,' Richard Whitehouse, *www.classicalsource.com,* June 24, 2012
8. 'Memos,' p. 107
9. 'The Ives Universe - a Symphonic Odyssey', Johnny Reinhard, available from www.*afmm.org,* 2004, p. 99-117
10. Ibid.
11. 'The Universe Symphony', realized by Johnny Reinhard, AFMM, New York, p. 37-46, 2004
12. 'Charles Ives UNIVERSE SYMPHONY realized by Johnny Reinhard,' AFMM Orchestra, CD recording, *The Stereo Society,* 625 Greenwich St. New York, NY 10014, 2005

CHAPTER 13

A listeners' guide to the Universe Symphony

The Sombrero Galaxy in infrared light; NASA/courtesy of nasaimages.org

Any incarnation of the *Universe Symphony* will not jump out and grab the listener in the conventional sense. Its aural demands are such that reaching out and hitching oneself to it is a necessity. Because this music seems already so far outside ourselves, on first impression it might be compared to walls of incoherent sound. Some critics have remarked on a relentless similarity throughout its duration; such comments, however, could only emanate from those who are not sufficiently familiar with the music to appreciate it on its own terms. In fact, Ives' ultimate masterpiece might be likened to the eyesight of a newborn child, to whom the world appears to be a formless jumble of colors and light; learning how to make sense of everything takes a while. Similarly, we should not expect the *Universe Symphony* to reveal itself with just casual listening. However, there has hardly ever been anything written more worth the struggle to understand. Perhaps we should not consider it such; it is more of an adventure.

I: Fragment: Earth Alone (also later: *Heavens music fragment*)

In Reinhard's realization, we have an opportunity to hear the *Earth Orchestra* and its key motifs in isolation at the outset of the symphony before the *Percussion Orchestra* begins, just as Ives had suggested. In a similar fashion, Reinhard chose to work Ives' recommended separate hearing of the *Heavens Orchestra* and its motifs into the end the second *Pulse of the Cosmos* percussion cycle (one of the lengthiest such cycles in the piece) and the beginning of the next. This seemed the most appropriate position for it, since Ives had encouraged the freedom to locate these elements (in performance) at any place that best introduced the material to the listener.

It is interesting that previously Ives never had similar concerns for any of the rest of his music. The importance he placed in identifying the sonic landscape of this anything-but-familiar essay thus is clear, its independent components pivotal in his conception. Even more is the tacet implication that the performers be attuned to the strategic motifs and sonic representations, knowing they will be *immersed alongside other competing materials within the symphony.*

A listeners' guide to the Universe Symphony

Image by Chris Pearson

The fragment of 'Earth' material was borrowed from the *coda* of Section A, because it features many near-isolated primary motifs. Reinhard judged that the use of this particular fragment at the outset would best serve the composer's intent.

Most listeners will require numerous hearings in order to fully grasp the 'Earth' material, though it provides a starkly stated introduction to set the scene for the incoming *Pulse of the Cosmos;* unmistakable cues contained within the material can be identified readily within the larger main Section. The fragment begins with an ominous deep assemblage of low tones (the 'Earth Chord'), followed by jagged melodic fragments and figures, quite believably symbolic of rocks, outcroppings and jagged cliffs - order rising out of primordial chaos (just as Ives wrote at the end of the excerpt, "Earth formed").

So identified, we will catch continual references of this very material throughout Section A, and hopefully be more likely to differentiate 'Earth' from 'Heavens' material. Bear in mind, however, that these motifs do not appear necessarily in identical guises along the way; it is their variants that feature similar rhythmic and melodic relationships from note to note that impart the specific character, sound and presence of Ives' writing.

II: Prelude #1; Pulse Of The Cosmos

Using a massive battery of tuned and non-tuned percussion instruments, the 'Pulse' was intended to represent endless time and limitless space. A kind of 'heartbeat of the universe,' it seems to parallel Einstein's *space-time* continuum, and also Pythagoras' ancient view of a mathematically balanced order. The similarities are striking, regardless of Ives' awareness of the parallels. Regardless, the 'Pulse' ties together seemingly disparate elements into a circular chain of inevitability, its significance at the very core of the symphony seeming to speak of cosmic forces throughout all of the universe. As such, initially, we should listen to at least *some* of the extremely long first prelude (a half hour), all but scored for percussion alone, to occupy a full 3 of the 10 total cycles.[1] (The author is not alone in commenting upon that curious sense of waiting at the end of each basic unit - 16 seconds - just prior to the alignment of all of the instruments again at the beginning of the *next* basic unit.)

Galaxy Messier 81
NASA/courtesy of nasaimages.org

Even if Ives considered hearing the 'Pulse' orchestra alone for the full three cycles to be an important step in preparing the ear and mind for all that is to follow, quite frankly, to appreciate *all* of it comes only as an acquired benefit after one has become familiar with the symphony, overall. Indeed, it is probably too much to expect anyone new to the piece to tolerate such a lengthy immersion *and* appreciate its special power and pacing. Only after the total proportions of the symphony have been fully comprehended, (curiously, it seems to contract with repeated hearings), does the true value of the complete percussion prelude begin to resonate.

- Cycle 1 features non-tuned percussion only, and a large succession of added divisions, before reversing by subtraction out of the cycle.
- Cycle 2 is shorter, based only on primary divisions; by now, the ear and mind have absorbed the concept of the inevitable 'pulse.'
- At the tail end of Cycle 2 and 3 Reinhard introduced the 'Heavens' music, as suggested by Ives. He specified that any of the appropriate material could be introduced at fitting moments during this portion of the symphony, but did not define any particular place, since many possibilities could be equally valid.
- Cycle 3 differs in that tuned percussion, piano and piccolo add to the regular non-tuned divisions a series of cyclical and irregular pitches (not quite 12-tone rows!).
- Cycle 4 coincides with the beginning of Section A, below.

III: Section A; Wide Valleys And Clouds

This long, dense and complex segment is the first extended orchestral segment, and utilizes the most detailed and extensive sketches of the entire work. It also poses perhaps the greatest aural challenge of the symphony, since primordial chaos is represented, but its extraordinary coloration might prove just sufficient to inspire the listener to keep looking for aural handrails, to return again for just one more glimpse of the scenes increasingly revealed behind its hypnotic lure.

- The section - beginning in a manner more like a second prelude to Section A - opens in quiet mystery with the low *Earth Chord,* (specifically mentioned by Ives), gradually interrupted by compounding counterpoint of low 'Earth' material built around the thematic devices introduced in the opening fragment, while swelling chordal sonorities brood in the higher strings.
- This moody opening gradually builds with more detailed motivic development, while adding elements of the *Heavens Orchestra.* These appear in lockstep 'cloud' chord groups, divided between flutes and violins, already moving independently of the *Earth Orchestra,* though not yet turned loose in an actual different speed - the purpose being as much musical as it has been functional, in order for the listener to gain more familiarity with the elements and separate orchestral entities. The music leads up to a grand pause and point of tension.
- Following the grand pause and build, (Ives labeled this moment, *"Earth Created")* the 'clouds' of the *Heavens Orchestra* take off, moving precipitously faster, further dividing into several independent 'cloud' systems, (but within one overall *Heavens Orchestra* speed) while the music continues to evolve. As it proceeds, we hear the fullest manifestation of the parallel listening concept that Ives described so vividly.

A listeners' guide to the Universe Symphony

Image AC

Through extended portions of much of the movement, the lower orchestral group (the *Earth Orchestra*) counterbalances the sky and clouds group above it (the *Heavens Orchestra*), both in register and pacing. Although we might not be aware of the specific tempo, per se, of each group, there can be no doubt that the orchestra of the skies seems to float along at a faster pace, reminiscent of the wafting movement of transient clouds over a static landscape. Listen carefully; Ives allows us first to grasp these upper constituents as they establish their independent range, speed and character, one that is smooth and floats above the fray, well clear of other factors in play in the *Earth Orchestra*. The entire musical texture evolves and grows ever more complex.

Wishing to draw attention to the *Earth* and *Heavens*, much of the time Ives strategically separated the register of pitches between the two groups by as much half an octave (between B below middle C, and E above). However, even he allowed that this necessarily could not be maintained precisely throughout the section, as his ear and imagination dictated less rigid formulae. Should it be problematic to focus on all levels simultaneously, Ives asked only that we remain aware of the other levels while focusing on *one*. We already know the idea for parallel listening concepts were not entirely new to Ives, since he had variously incorporated them in his music from early days. In the *Universe Symphony* we were never supposed to hear everything in detail, *all* of the time. We are free to shift our attention frequently from one to the next as long as we do not lose an awareness of the other levels. Thus, the music will reveal different aspects with each listening, and we might become aware of different melodic features or figures variously jumping out of the texture.

- The 'Earth' texture soon expands into higher territory, most obviously in the jagged or ascending trumpet and clarinet lines, and then expands further into the low brass - all of which can be identified having a totally different idiom and speed to the 'Heavens' music. We may become aware of various technical features, especially the scales of different intervals (such as whole tones) that Ives referenced in his descriptions of the mechanical fabric for the *Universe Symphony*.[2]
- In character, much of the *Earth Orchestra* counterpoint is angular, with various parts opposing others and supposed to represent Earth in its formation: the "outcroppings" Ives referenced, mountain peaks, ravines, canyons, etc. - everything comprising the random chaos of nature at work. It is not hard to visualize the panoramas Ives was trying to portray (from his position high on the plateau), and his successful representation.

The challenge is to listen through the actively moving musical lines, which might otherwise be interpreted only as activity and motion. Although the representation of cloud movement with that of the *Heavens Orchestra* is entirely appropriate, the 'Earth' material is a little more problematic. Because music is built around time, rhythms, and low to high pitches, any intrinsic musical motion might easily be interpreted as *actual* physical motion. Thus, since jagged and rapid movements comprise much of the *Earth Orchestra* material, we might visualize bustling streets and car horns, for example - exactly the opposite intention! Furthermore, the conflict between the gentler fabric of the *Heavens Orchestra* and the angularity of the *Earth Orchestra* might easily be perceived as just a conglomerated stirring unless we make the conscious effort to separate them. To know Ives' intent is to understand his music.

There is also a natural tendency, however, for the higher trumpet and clarinet lines to dominate the 'Earth' group, and so ideally one should set one's listening equipment to bring maximum emphasis to the mid-low range. These lower lines are no less significant than anything else within the whole; once aware of them the music is transformed. We should not overlook that beyond this, of course, the *Pulse of the Cosmos* continues to weave in and out of the texture, depending on which part of any given cycle is occurring. Being also independent, the result is a lot for the ear to take in.

- After an extended segment of Earth and sky soundscapes, including two direct references to *Nearer, My God to Thee* (first in the trumpet and clarinet lines, then clarinet alone a fifth higher), the *Earth Orchestra* moves together into a massive high point (the thrusting up of a mountain peak, perhaps?), as the jagged 'landscape' gradually begins to recede. Perhaps it was Ives' attempt to emphasize increasingly what just might have been the Keene Valley plateau itself with somewhat calmer skies above. Smoother contoured *Earth Orchestra* lines emerge, as do gentler cloud depictions.

* The matter of the correct tempo *

In regard to the references to *Nearer, My God to Thee* that Kirkpatrick discussed, when they do leap out of the surrounding maze of sound, in Reinhard's realization *they appear in the normally expected tempo*, which should end any further discussion about the correct speed of Section A. It is significant that Ives never quoted materials, especially religious, at speeds *other* than in their original context, except in *rare* instances when the transformation resulted in another equally dignified incarnation, (i.e. in what is often incorrectly termed the 'harvest scene' of

Thanksgiving and Forefathers Day, Ives miraculously transformed the hymn *The Shining Shore* into a lively segment, just as dignified, but utterly symbolic of the festive spirit of the holiday he was trying to convey). It is also clear that the references are not merely the chance placement of tones, because they are distinct entities *unlike* the material that precedes, follows, or surrounds them. Thus in Austin's realization, the hymn's references are not recognizable as quoted derivations, sounding flippant, even comically cartoon-like, and further disproving his position that Ives' tempo indication should have been placed at one second per beat and not two - assuming one can make the fragments out underneath Austin's frenetic percussion.

- Immediately preceding the slow calming of the texture is a brief reference to *Massa's in de Cold Ground* in the trumpets, taken from the end of the bridge that returns the mid-portion of the melody to the beginning. Here again, in the context of the tempo rendering this fragment recognizable, is further confirmation that Reinhard's adherence to Ives' tempo indication was correct.
- Following this extended segment comes a differently textured middle section; easily identified by the prominence of the piano, it provides contrast after the preceding sonorities. This is the portion that was considered lost or missing prior to Reinhard's deductions and realization (see Appendix 2). After a repeated segment at each side of it (listen both times for the high trumpets playing a line with high dissonant long tones just a half step apart), a lush contrasting middle part intercedes with a vaguely impressionistic sound and deep, spacious chords. (In this middle part a more rapid, thinner cloud movement in the flutes and oboes briefly still can be heard.) Although Ives did not indicate what this whole segment represented - we can only speculate thus - it sets the stage well for balance and proportion leading to a brief

- return of the earlier sonorities, and the conclusion of the larger section.
- Briefly, the former musical character and momentum now resumes, along with the familiar cloud movement, in conjunction with the *Earth Orchestra* texture; however, it does not linger for long. Some truly otherworldly sounds begin to emanate from the *Heavens Orchestra* as the *Earth Orchestra* backs away, largely to dissipate - perhaps suggesting the landscape at night with clearing skies. It is hard to imagine anyone other than Ives who could have envisaged such remarkable sounds in his day - 'electronic' in character and years ahead of the time in which the symphony was conceived. As the horns and trombones again take the leading role the *Earth Orchestra* builds to another block, presumably another large rock formation.
- Suddenly, everything stops towards the conclusion of Section A, and we hear the *"Earth formed"* segment again that begins Reinhard's realization, placed precisely according to Ives' connecting icons at the conclusion of the section. Since the verbal terminology Ives utilized represents a subtle difference from a term used earlier, ("Earth *created*") we should rightly presume the conclusion to Section A represents the difference between creation and the state that Earth ultimately attained ("formed").

Section A, perhaps more than Sections B and C, will not fully reveal itself without numerous hearings and a serious effort to separate the components, because of its complexity and scale. Without normal cross-referenced lines, it creates an illusion of very free form; these independent lines complement each other to create unique colors and shapes, but one needs to permit the sonic representations of programmatic entities to form and establish themselves in the mind.

IV: Prelude #2; Birth Of The Oceans

Image AC

Much of the sketch materials are vague, although Reinhard was able to find the clues for assembly; he made the not unreasonable assumption that the same relative tempos between the percussion and orchestral units was retained:

- Seeming to depict Earth's basins slowly filling with water - long, building tones compound upon one another in chordal entities containing structural codes, and more 'Earth formation' chords. Inner movement derived from the harmonic foundation creates anticipation.
- Some chords of the Heavens Orchestra group connect the prelude harmonically with Section A, while the second half seems to allude to the *"Earth formed"* passage (also of Section A) before larger sonorities envelop it in apparent representations of the ocean masses themselves.
- A trombone solo, and what can only *be* described as a moving, ascending cluster between the trumpets, horns and harp, are followed by two isolated chords found on a single sketch page, designated as belonging to *"Prelude #2,"* lead to Section B.

V: Section B; Earth And The Firmament

Here, Ives began to turn his attention into the vast expanses of space; this is where the *Universe Symphony* finally escapes the perspective of the cosmos from earthly confines to cause us to look up.

- *Earth Chords* return to symbolize completion, amongst new 'Earth' material and an increasing usage of quarter-tones; a trombone stands for *"Free Evolution & Humanity;"* a *"just intonation machine"* (in Ptolemaic untempered tuning) and marble slab (!) improvise; new and preserved harmonic entities from Section A represent *"Heaven, Planetary skies and clouds."*
- A sudden buildup and subsequent explosion of ultra-modern sonorities inform us in no uncertain terms of that we are looking out to space; thematic and harmonic structures are closely tied. The fire and fury announces the only portion of the work in which the percussion also breaks its bond to the cosmic heartbeat within a bombastic and free cadenza (Cycle VII), according to Ives' instructions. Again, referencing *"Earth formed"* material in sustained string and organ writing, the sketch page is crowded with details and instructions.
- The middle of this sonic conflagration is what Ives designated as the *coda*; in the flute writing is another reference to *Nearer, My God to Thee* through to the end of the most dramatic part - highly significant, though problematic to identify easily, due to the surrounding complexities; there is a growing use of microtones.
- Towards the end of this astonishing, awesome spectacle, the percussion once again yields to the rule of the cosmic pulse before ending the cycle abruptly at its height.
- The music settles down more reflectively, as a new percussion cycle commences suddenly with the low bell taking the largest (16-second) division alone, the music of the *Heavens* and *Earth Orchestras* gaining in colorful and fragmentary figurations and chords.

- Subsiding further, the mysterious tones seem to indicate that Ives was again looking at the universe from the confines of Earth, and the section concludes with the chord that contained the clue to Pythagorean tuning.
- Interestingly, Philip Lambert considered the note 'spelling' of that now famous final chord likely a mistake![3]

Image courtesy NASA (Apollo 8)

VI: Prelude #3; And Lo, Now It Is Night

This prelude remains shrouded in mystery; it is not clear whether the major sketches utilized were, (a) intended for inclusion as part of the prelude at all, (b) a graphic representation of still unclear intentions for Section C, or (c) just a working diagram of the structural makeup. However, there is a clear distinction made between this material and that which Reinhard deduced to be the true beginning of Section C. Although all these prelude materials are specified for this section, the words written on what appear to be the actual start of Section C: a main title - ***"The Earth***

& the Heavens," "III," and a collective subtitle for the entire assemblage of prelude and section in two distinct parts: *"And lo - now it is night, & " Earth is of the Heavens"* - confirms that this particular sketch was intended as the *actual* start of Section C itself.

Despite the paucity of materials for the prelude, enough was present for Reinhard to produce something workable, regardless of whether it resembled anything along the lines of what Ives had envisaged; indeed what Reinhard produced involved the only creative decisions he made in the entire symphony.

Image courtesy NASA, ESA, and L. Bedin (STScI); nasaimages.org

- Starting with some loose, isolated tones at extreme registers, the prelude moves onto a succession of structurally systemized chords (24) with microtones. Critically, these were designated by Ives as the harmonic/thematic foundation of Section C, providing further clues for Reinhard's simultaneous combinations of some fragmentary materials that had been only minimally sketched. Reinhard superimposed the radical crescendos and decrescendos heard near the beginning of Section A, along with accumulating rhythmic energy and values, common to some of Ives' earlier experimental works. These, he offered were his greatest contributions to the work; we can only presume they would have pleased Ives in the absence of clear directives of his own!

- A final sketch, joined by symbol to the prelude, leads to a grand 'fall-off' of descending chromaticism across the orchestra, along with an accumulation of chordal elements as it does so. As it turned out, there was just enough material to build a prelude. With this we are led into what may seem like a musical abyss. In fact, we are staring at the heavens above. The effect Reinhard unearthed is stunning.

We are now approaching the destination of Ives' lifetime of musical evolution, the end of his road to the stars. The ultimate transcendental revelation, the listener need only to allow him/herself to be immersed in the sonic totality to experience Ives' astonishing vision of the very depths of space, eternity, and absolution at his spiritual destination. This is where he has brought us; indeed, it is easy to see why he could go no further. It seems we can sense with a degree of certainty now that Ives, indeed, had nothing left to say.

VII: Section C; Earth Is Of The Heavens

Commencing around screaming sonorities following the eerie downward spiraling of the outgoing Prelude, Section C explodes upon us as if the skies have opened up. Indeed they have; Ives notated here that it is night. We are gazing into the vast expanses of space as if surrounded by the spectacle; it gradually settles and leaves us in stunned awe. Ives referred to a perspective of ravines and jagged formations pointing up to the heavens, with the vast vault above them representing eternity.

A listeners' guide to the Universe Symphony

NASA/courtesy of nasaimages.org

- Percussion 'Pulse' Cycle 9 commences at the outset of Section C, initially with just the low bell tone, carefully leaving the increasingly strident-sounding percussion divisions of the Basic Unit until later.
- As the music descends and calms, we hear fragmentary dialog emerging from the texture, and also a discreet reference to the 'Earth' material between flute and clarinet - which makes sense since Section C represents "*Earth is Of The Heavens.*"
- The music comes to a brief halt, heralding two short pick-up notes (also suggesting the upcoming trumpet motif) into a vast sonic panorama that signals Ives is going much further in opening up the cosmic landscape to something as big as the universe itself. Such was the vault above as Ives now saw it, lending further credence that Hubble's discovery and announcement indeed was behind the rebirth of the symphony. It includes quotes from *In the Sweet Bye and Bye* (flutes), and one from *Nearer, My God to Thee,* (see Appendix 2).
- At this point, we might also become aware of the *Heavens Orchestra* once again appearing as a clearly separate entity,

independently moving above the fray in rhythmically moving chords as we look out into space, in spite of being locked to a shared single speed. Could they now represent *galactic* nebulae? This microtonal chasm of sound feels like a flight through the heart of a galaxy.
- It is followed by a short fanfare-like statement by solo trumpet, consisting of cascading descending intervals and upward leaps, announced in short notes comprised of thirds - i.e. 1-1/2 or 2 steps apart - sometimes with a repeated note at the lowest extremity.

Listen for this trumpet figure, seeming to resonate with the heavens and the energy of the moment. Once again, a dominant theme is centered on the trumpet (or cornet), this constant reminder of his father long being one of Ives' calling cards.[4] Was this now perhaps a hint that his father was calling from the depths of space to join him? Somehow, it solidifies the material that binds together much of what we are hearing. Fragments and references to this motif are central to Section C and throughout the first part of it. It is probably no coincidence that the trumpet should define the figure and herald similar and related motivic material glimpsed throughout this portion of the section. We even hear a hint of the motif introduced by the trombone earlier during the transition between Prelude #2 and Section B. Even earlier in the symphony, a short declamatory 'Earth' motif fragment in the high solo bassoon seems to allude to it, too.

- Later, immediately following the trumpet statement itself, the figure appears again placed high in the violins and as an inverted variant. This was also an overlapping connecting point of the patches in the assembly of the movement.
- Variations of the motif are immediately touched upon in the violas below, then the cellos, as well as in the succeeding dramatic violin writing.
- As Cycle 9 reaches its high point, growing, powerful orchestral chords reach a climax at a place that Ives labeled in his sketch "*SEA,*" a fitting point for the massive percussion activity.

A listeners' guide to the Universe Symphony

- Immediately following is a strong statement in the violins that further references the trumpet figure. The violin part here, again, not only seems to carry the trumpet motif, but incorporates within it intervallic fragments of 'Earth' motifs! This portion further evolves into a turbulent sequence accompanied by a strongly prominent descending pizzicato line in the cellos. (For those who question the correctness, idiomatically, of this kind of pizzicato line in Ives, refer to the *Adeste Fideles* section of *Decoration Day* where there is a near identical usage of lower pizzicato writing.) The strategic placement of these fragments illustrates Reinhard's logic in organizing the materials in the symphony; they are intrinsically linked in ways related only to Section C.
- The segment resolves as the percussion cycle winds down (seeming like a calming of the waters), with some material in the cello, appropriately scored for its register, and also to provide continuity to the larger segment shortly to follow, being musically related to it and the former 'Earth' material. Reinhard included two short connected fragments (*Sky* and *Rainbow*). It seems fair to have used them in Section C through lack of opportunity to place them elsewhere:
- "*3rd Sky Theme*", and another ascending figure, labeled "*Sky,*" (originally appearing in Section A *Heavens Orchestra*); here, Reinhard chose to orchestrate this now familiar Section A 'cloud' material differently.
- "*Rainbow*" in texture is briefly reminiscent of some of Ives' late songs, and features a brief dialog between flute and clarinet at the outset.

Although what is represented by these two short fragments might not be immediately obvious, they will become at least identifiable by their harmonies and the brief ascending figure in the oboe, prior to a more extended bridging dialog between the cello and winds that begins the inexorable push to the finish.

- Ives titled the next segment, dated 1915, *Theme from the Universe Symphony*. Reinhard scored the primary melodic line for cello, in keeping with the thinly scored sketch materials, comprised of what amounts almost to two 12-tone rows (minus a note or two), a characteristic of Ives from long before. The cello line, nearly identical to the *"Free Evolution & Humanity"* trombone line in Section B, was incorporated as a relatively reposeful point here, especially as the percussion recedes. Musically leading to what follows, even a logical outgrowth of original 'Earth' material, this serves to build the tension before ever-greater cosmic expanses open up.

- An amazing opening of the Heavens (pure color!) and the gradual introduction microtones propels us towards Ives' final destination, also effectively tying us to its conclusion. Joining into additional sketch material dated 1915, we feel the pull of growing anticipation. Cycle 10 also announces this anticipatory passage, commencing at full force from its maximum (the only cycle to do so) with all the percussion instruments and divisions for the cycle in play from the start. Thus, it differs from the otherwise 'fade in, fade out' structure found throughout the rest of the cycles. The instruments thus participate in what effectively is a *half* cycle, dropping out one by one through the end of the work, something never more appropriate than it is here. Ives' indications do seem to allow for such a dramatic variation at this juncture, fitting the scope and shape of the movement perfectly.
- As we proceed, the *Heavens* group again references the skies, but now it seems we are looking *through* the clouds floating high above! They are still rhythmically tied to the rest of the larger group, however, instead taking their own independent speed to continue into the final *coda*. Indeed, musically this element also ties these sketch materials together thematically, fully justifying their placement precisely here, quite aside from their shared tonalities. In modern symphonic literature the powerful impetus and sense of anticipation through to the end of the colossal *coda* are hard to match, as we sense that the symphony is

'wrapping up.' If we pay close attention, a brief restatement of the opening 'Earth' motif may be heard one more time, superimposed midway during the growing buildup. (Listen for this; it is easy to miss it entirely through being swept up by the musical momentum.) Beyond it are well-disguised and discreet hints of *Nearer, My God to Thee* in the flutes and violins; the implication of the hymn, as outlined by the note relationships, seems clear, despite the absence of the actual melody.

- As we burst upon the final *coda*, a final section, marked clearly by Ives as *"end of Section C, Universe Symphony,"* it feels as if the very fabric of the cosmos has been torn asunder, cutting loose an incredible sonic conflagration like a million fireworks in the sky. If it seems akin to a musical version of the 'Big Bang' - here it is, long before anyone thought of such a concept! Invoking such an event is appropriate, since so many musical components are set in diametric opposition and motion. The high point is not unlike that of the climax of the *Fourth Symphony*, which remains our best preparation for this entire work. Here, though, the music seems even more awe inspiring, the sketch materials being virtually complete in detail.

- Finally - in the most telling quote of all from *Nearer, My God to Thee* - a substantial portion of the melody (the high-point from the middle) is referenced in the flutes at the outset of the celestial explosion, descending as the bass line ascends; never was it more appropriate than here to lead to the conclusion of Ives' journey to the stars. Since clear references to the hymn were made in the same manner as in the materials leading up to the *coda*, this should end any remaining doubts that the link from those sketches to this one is correct. However, one might be so overawed by the sonic spectacle that identifying the hymn amidst everything else that it happening could be a challenge! Rest assured; it is there.

- Gradually the massive sonics are shed, a 'wind shear' remaining of all that has passed leaving one in a near trance. This is punctuated by leaping solo bassoon intervals in shaded microtones, finally tinged by a strange superimposed fading organ chord seeming to come from some distant horizon, (similar to those that have characterized moments in the work, such as toward the conclusion of Section B). Although seemingly at odds with its surroundings, magically, the chord somehow is in total peace with them, an utterly universal expression that leads to a silent backdrop for one last deep bell tone that rings into eternity.

If no person ever has imagined a mightier scene painted in sound, or achieved it with such a systematic and orderly technical means, for Ives it was the culmination of a lifetime of building his own means of expression. Arriving at his destination with deliberate resolution, we are left to share some of the awe he felt as he pondered the great unknown from his mountain lookout long ago. If one allows the music to penetrate any residual bias, it is possible to recognize Ives' greatest creative moment, his representation of the final ordering of primordial chaos, and man's spiritual place in the larger realm of the cosmos. As the sonic manifestation of his destiny, he finally had reached the goals set in motion early in his life. That he had been so driven, and had dared not rest - or die - until he had done so suddenly has meaning.

Is Reinhard's realization the Symphony of Ives' imagination?

We know that what we are hearing in Reinhard's realization of the *Universe Symphony* is all by Ives, unembellished, 'unimproved,' and unadorned. The grandeur of the work that he imagined seems undiminished by his failure to complete it - at least in as much as producing a formally completed score. For those who say that we cannot know what might be missing or was never sketched, we only have to hark back to Ives' own words from 1931. Certainly no evidence, other than the later grandiose words of its ailing creator and his still unclear written instructions for Section C, indicates that he had further ideas in mind for the work than may be found in the existing tangible materials. In addition to Reinhard's own documentation, the reader, however, is strongly encouraged to read Appendix 2, which contains further information about the materials and the approach taken in the assembly of the symphony. These additional insights cannot be found in any other available source.

Inasmuch as Reinhard included *all* of the sketches, and determined the sequence best to present them in the later portions of the symphony, he assembled a coherent and musically viable chain that readily states its case. We can argue that the musical connections between the sketches from many technical standpoints strongly confirm their placement and usage, although some have continued to question the nature of Ives' written intent, and whether, in fact, Reinhard did match the elaborate yet convoluted written directives. Regardless, the realization is a complete, satisfyingly structured work, convincingly laid out and resembling the model of Ives' originally stated inspiration and plan. And impressive it is, to be sure. It is so imposing and profound that it deserves pride of place alongside the *Fourth Symphony* - the *Universe Symphony*, however, seeming almost to make an even grander, more stylistically consistent statement. And the final reference to *Nearer My God to Thee* (having appeared in each section) seems further to affirm that Ives indeed had reached his spiritual destiny, having won his race against time to find the place his father inherited, and from which he long had beckoned. And it is ever clearer that at the end of this road there was no compelling reason for Ives to write anything more.

REFERENCES

1. 'Charles Ives UNIVERSE SYMPHONY realized by Johnny Reinhard,' AFMM Orchestra, CD recording, *The Stereo Society*, 625 Greenwich St. New York, NY 10014, 2005
2. 'Memos,' Charles E, Ives, edited by John Kirkpatrick, p. 106, *W. W. Norton & Co.*, New York, 1972, pp. 107-108
3. 'The Music of Charles Ives,' Philip Lambert, *Yale University Press*, New Haven and London, 1997, pp. 197-199
4. 'Charles Ives Remembered, an Oral History,' Vivian Perlis, *University of Illinois Press*, Urbana and Chicago, 1974, p. 88, & 225; & 'Charles Ives: "My Father's Song", a Psychoanalytic Biography, Stuart Feder, *Yale University Press*, New Haven, Connecticut, 1992

APPENDIX 1

Revising Ives

In the 1980's a period of re-evaluating the composer briefly tarnished Ives' image of ascendancy. Many of the negative assessments did not deserve the traction they gained in the first place, but certainly it was fair that some of the questions were raised. In 1975, following a less than completely head-over-heals portrait by Frank Rossiter,[1] the revisionist period for Ives began in earnest, with the publication of what is considered now in some circles an infamous paper by Maynard Solomon.[2] Overnight, it garnered international attention, prompting many eager critics to seize upon any opportunity to dismiss America's new favorite musical son as some kind of fraud, at least in as much as his claim to priority in 20th Century music was concerned. The main period of debunking lasted for at least a decade and a half; even now it has not completely vanished, as it appears not everyone in America wants to be convinced of the significance of their own great native musical icon.

Some who had been stunned to read Solomon's paper immediately went of the offensive, choosing to label him an 'Ives hater.' If one reads the paper carefully, though, it can be seen that really he did not fit that model; Solomon actually admired the composer's music greatly, though certainly he had questioned Ives' character and methods. Regardless, the true 'Ives haters' came out of the woodwork, now armed with 'scholarly' ammunition to discredit his music, although it seems this had not been Solomon's intention at all. These individuals failed to recognize that he had taken pains in his paper to pay Ives due homage, and certainly was not trying to diminish the quality or artistic value of his work.

In the 1930's, long before Rossiter's book came on the scene, Elliot Carter, the prominent American composer, though thoroughly European-trained (under Nadia Boulanger), asserted that he had witnessed Ives adding dissonances to Putnam's Camp, *(the second movement of* Three Places in New England), *during a visit with him in 1929.*[3] *Carter wondered just how original Ives really had been at the time he was composing his supposedly pioneering music. With this kind of 'evidence' in hand, Solomon would add to it, subsequently charging Ives with possible 'falsification' involving a supposed pre-dating of his manuscripts, questioning his motives and even psychiatric makeup. We can only wonder if this was what triggered Feder's psychobiography, even if he did not agree with Solomon's assessment.*[4]

To admirers of Ives, one of the worst aspects of the whole episode was that Americans were devouring their own, having for so long sought such a champion in their midst. Ives was declared guilty in the public courts without a trial. Most, if not all of the revisionism had come from American critics and not from overseas. During Ives' day, critics routinely would accept experimental avenues in music when it emanated from European composers, but not when it came from a domestic figure. In the same light, Ives' music initially was found more acceptable and interesting in Europe than at home, so that in a very real sense, the recent period of negative assessments in America revealed that nothing much had changed. All of this might have been fine if all composers were treated with the same degree of, dare we say, suspicion.

Charles Ives in 1913, shortly after the first complete draft of
Three Places in New England
{{PD-Art}}

The Americanism in Ives' music that became emphasized in his image also has become distorted, since he did not seek to write nationalistic music; his music represented an immersion in a place and time. Involving scenes and events near and dear to him, the intent was personal and philosophical, not nationalistic. In fact, at the height of his creativity, Ives was decidedly <u>anti</u>-nationalistic in temperament; his transcendentalism ensured that. Ives certainly loved his country, but his patriotism was *aligned with the spirit of freedom and democracy as exemplified in the US Constitution; he wanted the same for all mankind across the world.*

The 'Ives Legend'

The negative portrait of Ives came about largely in reaction to the unrealistic picture painted of him in the 1930's, principally through the efforts of the avant-garde American composer Henry Cowell, a fine composer himself and a young leader of new music in America. Needing a strong paternal figure for American music, and especially its priority during the period of innovation in the new century, Cowell found the figure he had been searching for in Ives. Although Cowell's enthusiasm was highly instrumental in bringing Ives' music to the foreground, he became a little carried away with his narrative in rescuing the little-known composer and his cause from obscurity. In hindsight, he might have embraced the full picture a little more carefully than his enthusiasm fostered.

The aura surrounding the life and music of Charles Ives has been termed the 'Ives Legend.' We can trace its evolution to the 1930's, when Cowell established a near mythical persona surrounding the newly 'discovered' first great American composer. Cowell's need for an iconic figure to stand at the top of the American avant-garde community was to bring attention to the cause of new music in America. Ives could be seen as an authentic American original, the first true voice in American music, and a figure to champion. As the supreme promoter of Ives' music, Cowell, with his wife, Sidney, would write one of the most definitive volumes on the composer and his life.[5] However, through his efforts was born the larger Ives legacy, where exaggerated claims grew about the composer, although there was indeed more than a grain of truth in these claims: Ives' early experimental works from before and immediately after the turn of the 20th Century really do predate those of most others, and his father really had been the most significant musical influence in his life.

In brief, the Ives Legend promoted the image of lone composer, neglected and scorned by society, totally unaffected by, even unaware of any of the musical developments in the outside world, with a musical education almost exclusively due to his prophetic father, at odds with his Teacher at Yale, Horatio Parker, (almost to the degree that he graduated in spite of him), and who, purely to keep his artistic integrity intact dutifully made the choice to pursue a business career, and infused his music with a deliberate American voice. Although the story had been 'embroidered' with gilded thread, the worst image that revisionists could paint had been given the wherewithal for it to fester and grow. Thus, some exaggerations in which Cowell had indulged blurred the authentic picture of the composer and man, and for a while the brutally opposite stance taken by many revisionists did Ives' reputation great harm.

Regardless, Ives also was a sitting duck for other negative agendas, and the upshot of Solomon's paper was surely as unkind as it was declarative. Flying in the face of everything previously believed about the composer and man, effectively it reduced him to the status of some kind of con artist - even mentally disturbed individual (yes!) - at least in the eyes of some. Quickly, his followers rallied around their hero, even though at the time they did not have the means to mount a proper defense. The damage was compounded for a few years; even now some revisionists continue to project the most questionable image of a noble and remarkable individual, along with increasingly controversial justifications for new interpretations of the dates of his compositions. However, thanks to diligent research, and the fairer perspectives of many other noted scholars and interested parties, a more careful examination of all the facts surrounding the composer continues to cast new light, and with it a much more balanced portrait. Today, Ives does not look much the worse for wear, the shabby treatment he received seeming increasingly ill placed and pejorative.

Questions of Veracity

Providing the real grist for the revisionists' mill, however, we return to Solomon's assertions that Ives might just have 'cooked the books' regarding the dating of his compositions. Why would this be important? Significantly, some of the 'Ives Legend' mystique centered on the claims of those promoting his music that uncannily, he was working in most 20^{tth} Century techniques, if not necessarily philosophically tied to them, long ahead of all others. Ives' usage of these techniques themselves was not in question, but the claim of his priority was.

However, one only has to examine Ives' known experimental work at the turn of the century (and even before) to realize what he had accomplished. Because Cowell had emphasized it as a 'reason for being' in itself, it was as if Ives, somehow, had been focused primarily on being a pioneer rather than merely searching for ways to express himself; the experimental works had been the means to isolate and develop new ideas. The fact that many of them are worthy as substantial musical works in themselves, and that their fruits would be incorporated over a period of many years within larger musical soundscapes, was lost on the critics. The simple fact remains that Ives indeed did come up with many, if not all, of these revolutionary techniques well in advance of others.

The dates and other irregularities

Solomon had outlined his case by displaying the 'evidence.' This consisted of multiple sketches, revisions, re-workings, combinations of more than one original work or thought, incorporations of multiple portions of them with further re-worked parts, turning fragments of other pieces into new ones - often in totally different contexts - along with the general disorder we find throughout Ives' working process, as referenced in Chapter 2, pages 35/36. Solomon alleged - through listing the profusion of dates and disordered pages that included addresses, personal contacts, phone numbers, comments, reused manuscript paper, multiple pens and pencils, revisions (and only some in the same place!), instructions to see some annotations in other places entirely, cutting the margins off pages (consequently eliminating dating and other information) - that the composer was guilty of falsification!

The controversy exploded. Any attempt to form an objective picture of the composer was buried in the aftermath. The court of public opinion was already rendering a guilty verdict based on the accusation. Only a negative interpretation of the evidence had taken hold. However, considering the breadth of research materials available, even at the time of the paper, and Solomon's learned background, many felt these assertions to be highly subjective, judgmental and ill founded, his claims immediately being questioned or dismissed outright by many other Ives scholars. Indeed, it appears not to have been discussed that sometimes Ives' dated works to <u>later</u> times than those of their creation! *We find examples of this quite frequently, especially amongst songs in the 1922 book,* 114 Songs. *Even more fittingly in the context of this book, Ives dated his initial* Universe Symphony *sketches to 1915, but an address on the manuscript was for a former residence that he left in 1914! Unfortunately, only what served the argument had been used against him.*

Complicating the task of analysis, often even the original sources were lost (frequently organ, or organ and choir works from his church organist days) - although recorded somewhere in Ives' notes by dating or referencing them in some way. Those notes were dependent upon which part appeared first and in what piece, such sources thus remaining problematic. Some would argue that this allowed for deliberate obfuscation and pre-dating of the original source. These same critics were unlikely to acknowledge it is known that Ives left many such works on the shelves at the Central Presbyterian Church; further, that these works were discarded at the time of the church's relocation to Park Avenue in 1915. Often, too, Ives left the original dates of the first draft of a composition intact as it developed, or assigned the dates of later works to those essentially spawned by earlier ones, while his jumbled manuscripts and working methods seemed as inexplicable as his extraordinary musical visions. Numerous finished copies (by copyists) of works no longer exist in manuscript; countless other works were assembled from multiple sources and different batches of sketches and other materials. It stands to reason that there might have been some confusion!

As a notoriously messy practitioner of script, Ives had no reason to try to work otherwise, since public performance, let alone acclaim and examination, were far from his mind. Jokingly, he is known to have forwarded to composer John Cage a blank sheet of manuscript paper - a diametrically opposite comment on his working methods! 'Completed' did not necessarily imply completed scores - what Ives considered so might have been just as likely a full score as the sketches necessary for a later one. As such, it is entirely conceivable that he would have considered that his works dated from their first incarnation. Thus the all-too controversial dates should be seen for what they are, especially since copyists made many of the first finished scores. And as far as Ives was concerned, further cleanups, revisions, refinements or even enhancements were no reason to change the date. He probably never thought about it; indeed, probably we have all been 'guilty' of this in organizing many things. Regardless, one can see how 'conveniently' this could be tied into what has been termed the debunking of the 'Ives Legend.'

The vast number of compositions Ives had under construction at any given time also illustrates the difficulties of the task of organizing a timeline of his work, even for the composer himself, which explains the many contradictions in his own materials. Although some critics were swift to pounce on such quirks in relation to his pioneering techniques, and claimed they represented some kind of duplicitous subterfuge, a little careful research, however, reveals that perhaps all of the works in question actually had started out in a pretty advanced state to begin with!

In her 2008 book, Gayle Sherwood Magee speculated that since Cowell had himself altered some dates of his own compositions in the 1950's and 60's that this might share a common approach with the composer.[6] *However, the confusion surrounding Ives' manuscripts far predates Cowell, as can be readily demonstrated by the physical evidence, and has been a primary case against Solomon's assertions. Ives would have had no reason to engage in such activities during his most productive period, when Cowell was nowhere in the picture; adding and altering dates significantly to the degree that we find later would have been all too easy to trace. Had Cowell himself taken such actions based on the confusion he had observed, it was entirely his own doing. Regardless, Magee considered it problematic to propose that Ives would have gone to systematic falsification through such tangled means. However, she, too, raised the specter of Ives' dating a given work to its <u>initial</u> composition, in which revisions and additions had been undertaken later.*

Magee would, however, proceed to come up with a 'new chronology' of dating for Ives' catalog, one that others readily adopted in their own positions and texts. Most notably, perhaps, Peter J. Burkholder adopted it in his **All Made of Tunes**, *referenced in Chapter 3. It should be noted, however, that other leading Ives scholars, Jan Swafford and Carol Baron amongst them, would wholeheartedly reject these new dates, contending that they were formed without accurate basis or merit. These scholars have maintained steadfastly that the entire episode raised by Solomon was ill judged and incorrectly surmised; as Baron contended in her paper of 2000, published in the* **Journal of the American Musicological Society 53/2 (Summer 2000): 437-444,** *Magee's 'new chronology,' as* *well as Solomon's hypothesis ultimately would be repudiated. The musical 'drama' presently is unfolding and promises to offer more 'acts' in the foreseeable future.*

Meanwhile, with a better understanding of the man and his approach to everything that he did, other explanations for many of the inconsistencies began to emerge, more likely representing a kind of unique evolution in which many works were under construction, one way or another at any given time. The revisionism that Solomon referenced thus was a function of Ives' approach to all of his music, not an effort to obfuscate the provenance. In truth, Ives probably never saw anything as completely 'finished.' The extensive reworkings, and his own recorded, somewhat improvisational readings of the four **Emerson Transcriptions** *(for the Second Edition of the* **Concord Sonata**) *stands in testament to this; Ives wanted to keep the music alive and growing to his dying day, actually even expressing the wish that the first movement,* **Emerson,** *in the monumental sonata would never be finished.*[7] *Unlike the* **Universe Symphony,** *actually it would be.*

Certainly nothing we know about Ives would have allowed him to have any part of the dishonesty others have ventured; his life philosophy was strongly opposite to such behavior, especially from one with Ives' resolute values, and his lofty aspirations for mankind. Further, to imagine that Harmony, his wife, would have been unaware of it, or similarly dishonest to the point of actively being involved, again stretches the boundaries of rationality. Anything on the scale of what Solomon proposed seems absurd, even less plausible had it occurred during the years that he inferred, when Ives had difficulty mustering the effort to write anything at all, and never even had accomplished the organization of all of his works and sketches. Feder, too, recognized and acknowledged that such actions would have been totally at odds with Ives' character and the way he had led his life, his inherent honesty, outlook on life, the resolute admiration in which he held man and the original transcendentalists that would have prevented any such actions, let alone thoughts.

Ives' creativity was a classic example of order rising out of chaos. Indeed this is the hallmark of his music, and his work in business (his studio, as well as his office in New York were prime examples of it). His multiple efforts also to provide reliable catalogs, after the fact, do nothing to affirm any hypothesis other than further illustrating that very chaos, because the dates he assigned in his various catalogs, again, were frequently at odds with each other. Ives never took the time or trouble in earlier years to establish a legacy trail; they were not important to him, nor presumably were they contemplated. Only as he became increasingly aware of the importance of establishing provenance did he try to do so, but clearly, years later, it was too late and certainly his memory played its fair share of tricks.

Ives did not help himself, however, by his strong critiques and rejections of the work of most of his contemporaries, as well as his idealistic (and probably unrealistic) claims about the training he had received from his father, George Ives. In connection with the 'Ives Legend,' whether this latter claim really reflected the influence of Cowell we can never be sure, but it does seem clear regardless, however, that his father really <u>had been</u> his foremost influence, at least, in all that mattered to Ives. In respect to Feder's scenario regarding the strong father-son relationship, it was completely likely, even an accurate portrayal, although this surely is hardly a rare scenario in society. Parker's influence was in providing the development and refinement of the skills that enabled Ives to write proficiently in the manner that he chose; his fine training is quite clear in the extraordinary quality of his early works, including the first two symphonies. However, the strongly European-based language of these two works, unto themselves, was not natural to him; following roads long paved by others was alien to his temperament and growing philosophies. But as a backdrop, his father's music <u>was</u> natural to him, notwithstanding that a large amount of it had emerged from earlier European origins!

Magee seemed caustically judgmental about George Ives' role in his son's training, although it was not unreasonable to examine the actual degree of its sophistication.8 In any event, George Ives' open-minded approach of according validity to all available expressive means remains the key to Ives' high regard for his influence, and something that many still do not recognize. Thus, it becomes clearer what lay behind his seeming paradoxical positions praising Parker at times, yet just as often rejecting his influence - while overly attributing his own musical skills and development to the teachings of his father. And as raised earlier, Ives most likely would have gained the tools to compose effectively anyway, just as had many of the greatest composers in history. Genius is genius.

Solomon also appeared to take Ives to task for his habit of revising so much of his music. At the time Ives was actively engaged in most of these changes, he and his music were still flying low under the radar screen. For all he knew, this might have been the way things would always be. Many of his more advanced compositions frequently reached us in their final form many years after the date of their initial creation, Ives having tinkered with the details over the years, and sometimes only when a finished performance edition was finally needed. This was part and parcel of Ives' unspoken attitude about his music; <u>it had to grow</u>. Certainly, at this time Ives could have had no inkling of providing some kind of ingenious paper trail for hoards of later musicologists and 'gotcha' detectives. More to the point, Solomon did not seem to acknowledge that Ives' more daring compositions did not suddenly become so by way of any revision.

Some commentators still seem further perplexed that Ives might have regarded his music as <u>his</u>, to do with it what he wished! The implication was that he had no such right, revealing a remarkable sense of their own entitlement to someone else's property, if ever there were one. Ives' work reveals a highly creative spirit, always vital, never satisfied, just looking for something a little better. He was not a conventional figure by any standards. We should not treat him this way.

Regardless, Solomon's position was sure to light fires. What was most striking, however, as others also have pointed out, was that he never questioned Carter's motivation or psychiatric makeup when he had made <u>his</u> assertions. The young Carter had been to some degree a protégé of Ives before further pursuing his musical training in Europe. We already know that the dominance of European music in the America of Ives' day was anathema to Ives, like waving a red flag in front of a bull. Thus, Carter had succumbed to it (presumably in Ives' view), and had set up pronounced differences, as he, himself sought to establish his own reputation. Carter, however, went further, in a review he later regretted.[9] *Certainly his comments in that review in* **Modern Music** *in 1939 were bitterly critical, almost contemptuous, surprising, even disappointing, especially in light of the fact that Ives had initially taken the young Carter under his wing.*[10] *Regardless, the* **Associated Press** *obituary after Carter's passing (November 6, 2012), made no mention of his apprenticeship with Ives, merely that Ives had encouraged him; it seems Carter indeed had successfully disowned the record.*

Rossiter was amongst those who had raised the perspective of the potential, or even likely, double standards in 1975,[11] *and seemed remarkably attuned to the perceptions of others. If we look to Ives himself, we might find some answers, too. If he had lashed out at Parker because of his contempt for all he (Ives) held dear, and then at the next moment remember him with fondness, even elevating him - just as Carter presumably had done - Ives separated himself from those former stylistic influences he did not embrace once his compositions developed within their own individualistic language. Could it have been that Carter, in addition to having parted with Ives' music for a different compositional model, might have been trying merely to establish his own identity and illustrate differences between them - and most especially at a time when Ives' meteoric rise to prominence was in the spotlight? Regardless, it illustrates that we must proceed with extreme caution when trying to determine what might be on display.*

Meanwhile, other evidence refuting some of Solomon's assertions began to emerge out of the fog. Little riddles slowly were solved. Kirkpatrick solved the issue that had been raised about the cutting down of manuscript pages, recalling part of Ives' later efforts to organize his music by putting photocopies into files that were a little too small to accommodate them. This was just the start of reevaluating the reevaluation.

Putnam's Camp

As prime evidence for his case, we return again to the startling and foretelling **Putnam's Camp** (*from* **Three Places in New England**), *in which Solomon had challenged that Ives had tampered not only with the score, but the dates of its composition as well. In her book,* **Charles Ives Reconsidered**, *Gayle Sherwood Magee revealed how Ives had only redistributed dissonances, previously diluted throughout the entire ensemble in the chamber orchestra version that has survived, (as adapted by Ives for the first performance), merely restoring those dissonant intervals back to the piano part of his original version.*[12] *Although no score of that particular version is known, the 1929 version was clearly Ives' best effort to reconstruct it from the reduced version. Additionally, it is easy to show that much of the musical materials in this piece existed years earlier,* *within other works! (See also Chapter 6, sub-heading: 'Paving the road to the stars.') Thus, Carter had misjudged what was actually taking place. It is unfortunate that this incident became central to the argument and had caused so much harm.*

Similarly, Stuart Feder, in his book,[13] also referenced detailed work undertaken by noted Ives Scholar Carol K. Baron,[14] who, having analyzed the manuscript and handwriting of a number of Ives' compositions, and notably an early score also of 'Putnam's Camp' *amongst others, was able to demonstrate that Ives' mixed up dating was incidental to his use of both pen and pencil – a practice that had led to incorrect assumptions and conclusions. In fact, it could be shown clearly under careful analysis that the notation written in pen and pencil dated from the <u>same</u> time. Proving her point, tellingly, Baron was able to show that Ives' writing of clefs (i.e. treble, tenor or bass) varied in a consistently observable manner over the years, providing a significant tracer in analyzing his handwriting. Baron believed that it appeared virtually conclusive that Ives had not undertaken any revisions <u>at all</u> to this early version, and further that Ives was not guilty of any indiscretion - even less since there had been occasions in which Ives himself had discussed correcting the date on a manuscript (i.e.* Washington's Birthday). *Baron also referenced Rossiter's questioning of this point,[15] in which Solomon had been happy to accept Carter's version, de facto, without considering a possible alternate explanation.*

Feder also broached the subject head-on from another standpoint,[16] hitting the issue at the source quite squarely. In his detailed history of Ives' life and work, Feder considered that despite the possibility of temptation to do so, such a determined and complex series of actions as Solomon proposed would have been beyond the <u>mental</u> capabilities in the ailing composer! However, Feder's theory about Ives' failing capabilities at the point of time under discussion is completely at odds with the volumes of anecdotal and other evidence, and thus it seems hard to give it any credence at all. (see Chapter 11.) However, he did reject the larger hypothesis.

Common sense

There is something else that we should consider. Many critics have not accepted that Ives could have been oblivious to all outside musical influences at the time, and thus consider him not as original as had been claimed. Thus, we must turn first to Ives himself, and then simply again use our own common sense in making a reasonable judgment. In Memos, *he discussed this very issue; quite frankly, it ought to settle the argument on its own.*[17] *If one considers how much time in his life was occupied by his business, compounded by writing such a huge volume of music over an extremely short creative period, any free time left for attending concerts - or, in fact, anything! - would have been seriously limited, by default.*

Notwithstanding that for a time Ives did indeed go to concerts, and would have heard a number of modern works, a finite upper limit on his time nevertheless would have existed if he were to have had the time to accomplish anything at all of his own. And to the extent that the state of music in America early in the 20th Century would not have encouraged the widespread premieres of numerous radical works of any kind, coupled with the well-documented limited expertise of performers in playing the newly evolving styles, it is hardly likely Ives could have been exposed to more than a small amount of new music, if indeed, even that. We must consider, too, how many new works would have been performed routinely at regular season concerts of the day.

It we count further the residual effect that Ives described - after attending musical events unintentionally recalling new music in his ears while trying to formulate his own - it is hardly surprising that he chose eventually to stay away from musical performances as much as possible. One only has to ask any composer how hard it is to keep one's mind clear and focused, let alone live and work in Ives' circumstances.

Issues of mortality

The 1920's were a period of increasing physical challenges for Ives, and being mindful as ever about his father's early demise, he must have seen himself in a race against time to organize his life's work. This involved completing many compositions that existed only in short score, sketch, or disjoined rough materials, assembling them into some kind of orderly sequence - just in case he was unable to produce final versions himself, or might otherwise have left other materials too jumbled and scattered for others to decipher. He also sought to photocopy as many of his finished scores and sketches as possible, a much larger undertaking than it is today. Some of the questions about his integrity concern this very time, consistently failing to take into account the reasoning behind his actions. Additionally, Ives now was in a position to promote some of his music, and publish his collection of 114 songs, having assembled the Concord Sonata into a finished edition and write Essays Before a Sonata to accompany it, even to pay for performances and help in promoting other unknown composers.

Cultivating the new avant-garde in America

Magee cited those few forward-looking compositions from the 1920's as evidence Ives was cultivating the avant-garde in America, although in style, most of them predate this period by more than a few years. It seems incongruous to try to connect these works to her theory, or to the organizing, revising and finishing work in which he was engaged. His later pieces were the simple product of existing ideas, most of them far from new. However, not much time passed following completion of the journey symbolized by the Universe Symphony *before even Ives himself realized that he was spent - that work remaining far in advance of any other he would ever contemplate. Because Ives effectively had reached his compositional boundary, it is thus not at all surprising that those few new works that he undertook during the century's third decade would not approach it in any way, falling far short of the outer limits of his greatest musical vision.*

Fortunately, the Universe Symphony *provides some of the answers to numerous questions, including those posed by Solomon. Perhaps the most telling refutation of his arguments is provided by this work's sketch materials - largely unfiltered and fresh from 1915-1919 and 1923. Far from being the breaking straw, as it turned out, the* Universe Symphony *conspicuously gave weight to Ives' authentic and extraordinary modernity. This is clearly demonstrated in his most definitively modern work of all - <u>just as it was left in its initial incarnation</u>. The music is radical enough to have been written today - or even tomorrow.*

A question of deceit

We cannot leave the line of investigation without some other related, but telling comment. On the last page of narrative in her book, Magee used the term 'deceitful' about Ives - admittedly amongst a number of other more positive terms. Unfortunately, 'deceitful' is an unflattering and rather dubious sounding characteristic that the historic record makes clear was opposite to Ives' character. To further support her position, however, on the pages leading up to those final words in the epilogue, Magee raised the issue of the famous last chord of the Second Symphony. *The dissonant 'blat' that has become a hallmark of the work resulted from a last minute change made only in 1950 for the premiere of the symphony. Thus, it had taken another 50 years following the symphony's initial completed score to settle on an ending, the dissatisfaction with its original version clearly having twisted and turned in Ives' mind during the interim. Indeed, he had changed the ending more than once before.*

Charles Ives in 1889, at around the time of his little composition that would later find its way into the end of the Second Symphony

{{PD-Art}}

Magee postulated that the idea for the new chord was likely Henry Cowell's,[18] and that it was an effort, presumably urged by Cowell, to confirm Ives' avant-garde image. But why would Ives seek to tag a work that he is known to have held dear, even more the otherwise conventional sounding symphony's chances of being taken seriously in the future? Fortunately there is another explanation that Magee appeared neither to know, or chose not to reveal. What was explained in an article published in The Music Quarterly *in 1951, following the symphony's first performance, was written by none other than Henry Cowell.[19] In it Cowell stated that Ives had told him common practice in his father's ('Pa's') Danbury Band was for the musicians to play any note they chose on cue, to signify the end of the last Saturday night dance - a 'blat!' Thus Ives was paying a final late light-hearted tribute to his dad, invoking one last memory for the symphony's first outing. And yes, it does work, especially following what may be another tribute at the end in recalling the "shorter piece" he had written in 1889, which his father's band had played. Later, that very piece would be reworked into the* American Woods Overture *before being incorporated into the* Second Symphony *to become the part of the symphony that led up to the final chord.[20]*

However, perhaps even more the crux of the argument speaks for itself. Surely it must cause us to ask ourselves, would anyone seriously believe that throwing in a dissonant joke to end a thoroughly conventional work could make its composer appear avant-garde? Or modern? It is hard to take Magee at her word. More to the point, even if we wish to believe that Cowell was so dishonest as to invent the whole story, what possible gain could he have had in mind by immediately following up the performance with something <u>other</u> than a type of cooked-up explanation for an avant-garde shenanigan any detractor might have expected? Instead, Cowell explained the chord away without any pretense of it being anything more, and thus, without being under any pressure at the time to do so, it seems that now we know what really was behind the ending. So, contrary to Magee's assertion, it seems what Ives was really doing was nothing more than memorializing 'Pa's' humorous custom.

Perhaps the most troubling aspect about Magee's approach, though, while not being overall a negative appraisal of the composer, is an attitude of accusatory condescension towards Ives, as if he were somehow under some kind of prosecutorial examination in which he had a lot to answer. For instance, in one reconstructed event of her imagination between Ives and Parker, she portrayed Ives in a light in which he could only lose.[21] Needless to say, it is safe for any person to venture scenarios in which neither party is around to discuss them, after the fact. As with some of the other musicological studies we have raised, the picture painted is of one who seems strangely at odds with the person we can readily discover for ourselves. Magee, wrongly or rightly, appears to treat a man who had accomplished much and stood for even more with an apparent lack of respect due him. Despite the accolades that Magee does indeed accord Ives, her approach is yet another that seems to damn the subject with faint praise.

Psychobiographies

It is important to realize that not everyone has accepted as a valid science what New York Times communist Donal Henahan, referred to as "the controversial craft of psychobiography," in his 1990 article about Solomon's paper.[22] After all, these are attempts to prove a point in which the subject of the study is under examination in absentia, not unlike the scenario by Magee just raised here. Beyond that, even if had Ives been present and agreed to psychoanalysis, there is no guarantee that what motivated his decisions, or even more specifically his creativity, could have been determined with any greater degree of accuracy. Genius and originality cannot be explained away with any type of analysis. Feder's large work, Charles Ives: "My Father's Song," a Psychobiography, is, of course an elaborate example of the type of literature raised in Henahan's critique.

Four years of study with Parker: a controversy settled

One additional controversy raised with regard to Ives' studies with Parker warrants comment. Despite Ives' obvious failure to recollect his precise timeline of events decades later, Solomon again used another irregularity from some supposed correspondence with his father (who was deceased!) to support his case of deliberate and fraudulent datings - that of Ives' *claim to studying with Parker for four years.*[23] *This was a curiously odd perspective to take from an insignificant statistic that proves nothing about Solomon's primary theory. Magee cited a curious lack of any reference to such studies in his correspondence to his father, but, we must again remind ourselves that not much time had elapsed from the time Ives entered Yale before his father died.*[24] *Upon doing so as a freshman, Ives made just one oblique reference to Parker in his only known letter from Yale to his father. It is probably inconsequential. Ives' father would pass away from a stroke shortly after that letter was written, and not long after Ives had begun his studies. A lack of more frequent correspondence likely would be no more out of character for Ives than it would for any young adult just installed in an exciting new environment.*

The answer......
John Kirkpatrick had already provided a plausible explanation for Ives' claim of having had four years of study with Parker.[25] *If Ives had sought any kind of private instruction, it seems quite possible that an insecure young freshman might take a little time to pluck up enough courage to approach the seemingly lofty professor for such tuition at this early stage in his freshman year; he did not even meet Parker until October 10, 1894. But Magee went further. She cited real evidence for Ives having audited Parker's courses in harmony and music history by referring to a book on Parker, so it appears that the issue has been laid to rest.*[26] *Finally. Excellent work after years of needless nitpicking, indeed.*

Summing up

Significantly, Solomon's paper ultimately would lead to a clearer picture of Ives, bringing more objectivity and information about exactly what he did accomplish. Ives' position ended up on more solid ground than his detractors might have liked. Despite the disagreements from many Ives scholars with Solomon's conclusions - Philip Lambert's was blunt to say the least, and very much to the point[27] *- as well as what motivated the eccentric composer, the upshot was less controversy and greater transparency than had existed before. The Cowell-inspired 'Ives Legend' finally had been replaced by something far more tangible and realistic,* *even if it no longer seemed conspiratorial. And everybody acknowledged that no person could have built* everything *Ives did in a total vacuum - as if starting from scratch. In any event, that could not have been further from the transcendental ideal that Ives was chasing, or more completely demonstrating failure to understand it.*

If the objective had been to find possible links to other outside musical influences, however, many had stepped into the same gray morass that Feder had done, by attempting to look too deeply into what they imagined was Ives' psyche; it projected a tangled and dark version of the man. To others, they simply missed the obvious. Thus, should one wish to believe the worst of Charles Ives, so be it. However, in an ideal world, if this is to be the approach, other composers just might be accorded a similar degree of scrutiny and even distrust. Regardless, Ives' music is the greatest testimony to his time on Earth, and it really does not matter what anyone thinks. Ives did not care one whit either; he had found his *road to the stars. Have they found* theirs*? It seems to this writer, at least, that Ives has emerged from purgatory with his head held high.*

REFERENCES

1. 'Charles Ives & His America,' Frank R. Rossiter, *Liveright*, New York, 1975
2. 'Charles Ives: Some Questions of Veracity,' Maynard Solomon, *Journal of the American Musicological Society*, Vol. 40 #3, Fall 1987
3. 'Charles Ives: "My Father's Song", a Psychoanalytic Biography, Stuart Feder, *Yale University Press*, New Haven, Connecticut, 1992, p. 138
4. Ibid., p. 138
5. 'Charles Ives And His Music,' Henry & Sidney Cowell, Oxford University Press, UK, 1969
6. Magee, p. 158
7. 'Ives Plays Ives,' 1933-1943; CD: CRI 810, *Composers Recordings, Inc*, New York, (1999), Tracks 3-6, 11-16
8. 'Charles Ives Reconsidered,' Gayle Sherwood Magee, *University of Illinois Press*, Chicago, Illinois, 2008, p. 20

9. 'The Case of Mr. Ives,' Elliott Carter, *Modern Music* 16, March-April, 1936, from 'Charles Ives and his World,' edited by Peter J. Burkholder, *Princeton University Press*, New Jersey, 1996, pp. 333-337
10. 'Charles Ives Remembered, an Oral History,' Vivian Perlis, *University of Illinois Press*, Urbana and Chicago, 1974, p. 139 - 142
11. Rossiter, p. 285 -287
12. 'Charles Ives Reconsidered,' Gayle Sherwood Magee, *University of Illinois Press*, Chicago, Illinois, 2008, p. 158
13. 'My Father's Song,' Feder, p. 355
14. 'Dating Charles Ives's Music: Facts and Fictions,' Carol. K. Baron, of *Perspectives of New Music*, Winter issue, 1990
15. Rossiter, p. 285-287
16. Feder, p. 355
17. 'Memos,' pp. 136-140
18. Magee, p. 175 - 180
19. Excerpt from *Current Chronicle*, Henry Cowell, in *The Musical Quarterly* 37, p. 399-402
20. 'Memos,' p. 52
21. Magee, pp.38-39
22. 'The Polysided Views of Ives's Personality,' Donal Henahan, Music View: *The New York Times*, June 10, 1990
23. 'Memos,' p. 116
24. Magee, p. 188, Notes: #18
25. 'Memos,' Appendix 6, p. 183
26. Magee, pp. 188-189[19] (re: Horatio Parker (1863–1919): His Life, Music, and Ideas, William K. Kearns, *The Scarecrow Press*, Metuchen, N.J. 1990)
27. 'The Music of Charles Ives,' Philip Lambert, *Yale University Press*, New Haven and London, 1997, p. 207 (Appendix A)

APPENDIX 2

The Universe Symphony Sketches

Readers who are able to read music and are interested in gaining a deeper understanding of the symphony, as well as the methodology Johnny Reinhard utilized for his realization, might do well to spend some time his book, *'The Ives Universe - a Symphonic Odyssey'*, available from www.*afmm.org*, 2004. Below are some additional observations. Reinhard was extremely helpful in addressing the author's questions about some of the sketches; his insights are provided wherever indicated, and are highly revealing.

General notes

Ives did not always provide smooth joining sketches, even when the materials were presented in clear chronological sequence. In cases of the most complete examples this does not apply, since he carefully considered all aspects in preparation for the final score. As the materials became less formally sketched, we find more examples of perplexing ties and other extensions across the end of some of them that:

- *Appear to lead nowhere*
- *Come to an abrupt stop without indication of what is to follow*

- *Place pick-up material ahead of the outset of the sketch with nothing to indicate how to incorporate it with what preceded it*
- *Omit instructions concerning aspects of assembly*
- *Are largely complete but lack precise details about rhythms and relative placements of notes, requiring fine skills to decipher and preserve Ives' intent*
- *Exist in fragmentary form with little reference, if any, to context*
- *Appear in various meters without instructing how they relate to other materials*

Much of the time the sequence is clear, the rhythms implied, and the linkage straightforward to plot. In other instances, such as in the above examples, for his realization Reinhard deduced convincing linkages of the less clearly defined sketch materials, handling the process logically, smoothly and stylistically to produce a virtually seamless result. He went to great lengths to place these 'patches' according to every possible clue - of which there were many. Only rarely did Ives leave sketch materials in a total vacuum. Reinhard has remained firmly convinced that Ives did, in fact, complete the symphony - at least overall, and especially in as much as he believes the extant sketch materials represent the entire component parts, despite details of their working often being left vague. The challenge was to correctly interpret these materials to complete a symphony whose full form and structure existed for decades only in Ives' mind.

According to the late John Kirkpatrick (legendary Ives researcher, documenter, curator of the Ives archive at Yale University, and promoter/performer of Ives piano music), most of the surviving sketch material for the Preludes, as well as that of Section B and Section C date from 1923, or possibly a year or two later. The basic timeline does seem beyond a doubt, with the exception being, however, of that pivotal material Reinhard properly assigned to Section C, which dates from 1915, according to the sketches. Ives' references to the total years of the symphony's composition extend this even further to between 1911 and 1928, although Henry Cowell commented that Ives tinkered occasionally with the symphony right into his final years; beyond adding a note or two, however, it is inconceivable that that what we have could encompass a total time frame significantly beyond 1923.

The Universe Symphony Sketches

Interestingly, Kirkpatrick noted that Ives incorporated elements from the symphony into a couple of later minor works, which also provided telling clues about the dates that Ives worked on the symphony. These are the songs, On the Antipodes *and* Eighteen, *along with some chords found in the earlier* Tone Roads No. 1 *appear to share a common origin with the earliest sketches. Both songs are from 1922-1923;* Tone Roads *dates to 1915 - both sets of dates clearly linked to the symphony, but not beyond, indicating further at the likelihood that the total encompassing years of its composition do not extend beyond that timeframe.*

Section A

After the fragment of Earth *material that Reinhard selected to open the work (according to Ives' urging), followed by the 'official' prelude to this section (the first three percussion cycles, interspersed with a fragment of the* Heavens *material, also as prescribed by Ives), there follows an introductory portion to the main body of Section A that more resembles a* second *prelude. This portion is amongst those materials dated later than the 1916 date assigned to Section A, and dates to no earlier than 1923. However, the main body of Section A itself clearly belongs to 1916, but the styles of the two parts are well matched.*

Regardless, the added introduction sets the stage for what is to follow, acting as a bridge between the lengthy percussion 'Pulse' prelude and the visionary music to follow. Allowing the hypnotic pacing of the percussion to remain in one's consciousness, the essential sonorities of the Earth *and* Heavens Orchestras *are gradually introduced. Even then, Ives only brings us to the full evolution of all musical elements together gradually and carefully, taking care to allow the ear to settle on each level before moving ahead. From here, the orderly layout from page to page proceeds, with various icons or directions connecting one sketch to the next.*

Much has been discussed and speculated regarding the extent of possible missing material in this symphony, and none more so than the middle of this Section (A). That some was missing was assumed historically to be true, but the amount was only put at 3 orchestral units - or 3 measures of the Earth Orchestra *material! However, Reinhard could not accept easily the official position concerning the "missing pages."*

JR: "The conclusion previously reached by Peer Music under Todd Vunderink, with support (on some level) from David Porter and the Charles Ives Society, is that page 8 was lost by Ives."

Reinhard argued that not only are the sketches largely complete, but the material previously believed missing does, in fact, exist, representing everything that Ives had intended to complete the section. The case for this may be demonstrated fairly readily, even beyond Reinhard's own documentation of the realization. One should always bear in mind that Ives' page numbering is highly confusing, and does not necessarily lead to correct conclusions; his disordered sketching on any available piece of manuscript (even adjacent to those of other works) is notorious. Ives was known even to <u>reuse</u> previous manuscript pages.

In fact, there is other material as well, apparently unrecognized by other researchers, and is in addition to the 3 supposed missing measures. It proved pivotal in filling out the necessary span of time for the percussion cycles in order for them to properly align where Ives had indicated. Thus, the sketch page Reinhard utilized provided the necessary missing material, having previously been misidentified. This one page, noted as Page 19, is clearly related musically to Section A, and appears to hold the keys to solving the puzzle, together with <u>further</u> sketch material found on Ives' Page 3 that previously had been left unassigned by researchers. Page 19 contains various pieces of information, including the missing measures at the bottom.

Thus we can deduce that a number of pages before 19 never existed, or at very least were discarded, because Ives specified that the music continue from page <u>8 to 9</u>, from which the music proceeds through to a defined coda and conclusion; since Section B continues at page <u>10, and then 11</u>, the inference is clear. Furthermore, Ives provided descriptive words that continue on page 19 from page 8, along with definitive indications that the material belongs to Section A. (Ives referred again to these same page numbers in the sketches for Section C, so we can see evidence of his habit of routinely using the same manuscript for other music!) In this instance, however, Ives had neglected to mention that the missing measures could be found in the material on page 19, and this had lead to all the confusion.

In tying it all together, what finally allowed Reinhard to precisely locate and align the measures and materials of Page 3 and Page 19 is a symbol appearing in both - a rectangle with a dot in the middle. Adjacent to that symbol is the beginning of a progression of some spelled out chords. However, the pivotal key is the explicit instruction next to the progression on page 3 <u>to go to page 19</u>. On the newly discovered Page 19, the same symbol appears, together with the full progression of spelled out chords, beginning with the <u>same ones</u> named in the page 3 sketch, further confirming the connection. This, then, is what ties pages 19 and 3 together definitively, solving and essentially laying to rest the riddle of the so-called 'missing' pages of Section A; there never were any.

The additional sketch material from Page 3 is marked 'TRIO' by Ives, implying a three-part structure (ABA). By repeating the first four orchestral units following the second four (that coincide with the spelled out chords), a 'trio' structure is thus produced. In fact, the math did add up relative to the high ending point of the prevailing percussion cycle (V), according to Ives' indication for the next incoming sketches. More telling yet is that the relative position of the succeeding sketch material matches up from a musical standpoint, also putting to rest any question that the material had been only intended for Section A, <u>and</u> in this location.

Section B

Ives wrote fairly comprehensive sketches to the prelude to this section (B), one way or the other spelling out the notes in a kind of musical shorthand that provided the necessary information. Here we can deduce Ives' intentions by the relative placements of the notes; ultimately they do not leave much to the imagination. Instrumentation is also fairly clearly implied by the layering in the sketches, which follows standard practices used in full score, a factor that assisted Reinhard's realization of much of the symphony.

In response to the writer's further inquiries on the methodology utilized to assemble certain sequences of patches in the Sections B and C, Reinhard kindly supplied some further information. They are reproduced below for reference.

AC: "For the Prelude to Section B, can you tell me anything about your methods in organizing the material from Patch 32 through 34?"

JR: "Patch 32 starts with a tuba pedal point that performs a glissando. String writing continues from the previous patch, thickening the tableau. Patch 32B brings in some Universe harmony terrain to support the melodic qualities of the other patches in combination. Patch 33 starts with a distinctive pickup, but quickly dissembles, making the opening needed for a close to this juggling of chaos."

We can see, by the connecting icons between Sections A and B, further clear evidence that this prelude was conceived later than those principal Sections, as previously referenced. Thus, the beginning of Section B itself can be determined with certainty. Within the prelude, the deciphering of Patches 32A & 32B (q3038) does seem to be the correct interpretation of Ives' directions. Amounting to a superimposition of the loosely sketched notation to make a whole, the downward arrow points to the succeeding material on the page. Although Ives was less than exact in assigning rhythms and instruments in some of his sketch materials, this is an extreme example. The majority are far clearer; Reinhard's interpretation seems logical and proper.

For the remainder of the prelude, the sketches are remarkably complete, albeit in shorthand. However, one final scrap, (Patch 35) consists of just two chords specifically titled for use in this prelude. They provide the musical link to Section B.

Section B itself is laid out more clearly than the prelude and essentially fully notated, if rather informally, and clearly marked Page 10. *It seems clear that all the intended material for Section B is present, the* Coda *being designated "from* Page 11,*" a number precisely in line with the page numbering of Ives' long score pages. The musical connections in the sequence of sketches further seem to support this, and the concluding sketch materials can be shown to be those intended for the* Coda *of Section B, rather than any other, by default, too, because of the clear labeling of the codas for Sections A & C. Significantly, this coda contains another reference to* Nearer, My God to Thee *in the flute parts, repeating the notes from the middle portion of the melody through the loudest and most active first part of the* Coda.

The thinning textures approaching the final chord of Section B seem to lead inevitably towards the Prelude to Section C. However, that closing chord provided further evidence of Ives' intentions for using tuning - other than according to equal temperament - for his Universe Symphony. *The chord was spelled out in apparent Pythagorean terms, a feature that Reinhard noted and others apparently had missed. Ives had made much of such notation in other works, clearly specifying that substituting enharmonic notation for <u>his</u> was not appropriate for the purpose. This provided a simple demonstration that Ives indeed had extended his tuning concepts into the* Universe Symphony *sketches.*

The 'lost' prelude & the mysterious Section C

The Prelude for Section C was considered lost or nonexistent; however, Reinhard found just enough material, separate to the main section that appeared sufficient to put something workable together. He concluded that some of the material labeled 'C1,' *and* 'Universe Sym. 3rd Section' *(designations appearing on the respective pages), along with some other materials - namely an opening sequence of tones, and a grand descending chromatic sequence with building chords leading into Section C - did in fact belong properly to the hitherto-believed missing prelude. Even more certainly was it not part of the main Section (C). The sketch, specifically labeled* 'Universe Sym. 3rd Section' *(as opposed to Section C), featured a series of 24 chord systems along with some fairly detailed instructions that further separated it from the main section. Regardless of their intended application, unfortunately, these instructions are not very specific, but it is possible to conclude that the main Section C sketches do, in fact, feature elements of these 24 'chordal scales' that Ives so designated; they were surely useful to Reinhard as he decided combinations of some of the more thinly sketched materials of Section C, some of which clearly represented only* part *of the sonic texture. Significantly, they also provided the material to complete the prelude.*

Both Reinhard and Austin (in his version) preserved these chord progressions and set them to stand independently as part of the symphony itself. In utilizing them in the prelude to Section C, Reinhard believed that Ives would have wished them to be identified by the listener ahead of the main section in which they were designed to be the harmonic backbone. Overall, despite the lack of formal identification of the materials as belonging to the prelude, per se, Reinhard felt that the case for their assembly as such was justified because they appear distinctly separate to the main section itself, and that it required the greatest creative contribution he made to the entire work - mostly namely assigning rhythms, instrumentation and dynamics to the notes of the 24 "chordal scales." It is still unclear exactly what further treatment Ives might have had in mind for these, other than further possible incorporations of them into his sketches for the main parts of Section C.

In his original plan for the symphony, Ives titled this section, 'Earth Is Of The Heavens.' Since the remaining material is labeled specifically 'The Earth & the Heavens' and 'III' it seems to confirm further that Section C itself was intended to start at <u>this</u> point, not with the previously titled sketches that comprise what we have of the prelude. An increasing usage of quarter-tones in the materials both for Section C and the Prelude serves to add further weight to the case made for their respective connection.

JR: "It is a good point I think to bring up that this Section C is NOT movement #3. At its start in measure 183, we have a deceptive sound for the start of a movement."

Reinhard also was able to show that other previously <u>unassigned</u> material that he used in Section C was not intended for some undetermined placement elsewhere in the symphony, nor were the 1915 sketches merely isolated materials for possible inclusion anywhere else within it. Regardless of the timeline of these materials relative to those from 1923, there can be no doubt that musically, Section C was built around them. Consistent with the identified Section C materials, some additional short and sporadic sketches (amounting to about two minutes of the section's eleven minutes total length) were not discarded, but were found unsuitable for use elsewhere in the symphony, again supporting Reinhard's conclusion that they were intended for the final section.

Section C (most of it previously considered lost and certainly not appearing in Ives' own listings) is a most powerful and impressive portion of the symphony in this realization. Clearly, thus demonstrated to exist, much of its surviving material dates from 1923 or even fractionally later, a time when some have considered Ives' well was starting to run dry.

However, it certainly does not present itself as the work of someone losing touch, especially in the way Stuart Feder suggested, see Ch. 10; Reinhard makes its case convincingly.

This writer is prepared to go 'out on a limb' regarding Section C and its assembly. The perfect continuity of tonalities between the progressions of patches, the strikingly fluid connections of their musicality, even the balanced tension and resolution, again lead us to question whether such a satisfying whole could possibly have been achieved <u>purely by the good fortune</u> of all of the materials happening to align satisfactorily. Indeed, aside from the referenced two-minute portion, the remainder is clearly linked by many common factors, more substantially sketched, and features lengthier statements. Overall, innate musical sense thus dictates something else likely was in play for the section as a whole - that is, many of these patches might well be located and utilized <u>precisely</u> as had been intended. Nothing else seems more supportive of Reinhard's view that Ives had largely completed the symphony, albeit only in rough sketch form. And certainly the sections seem balanced with each other, and in their respective lengths.

Reinhard provided additional clarifications and insights on the section's assembly, below:

AC: "How did you determine the connection from the opening sections to Patch 47? (Unlocated/Copyflow = 1849)"

JR: "When I began the project Todd Vunderink sent me a photocopy of the sketches in John Mauceri's transcription. They were sent in a particular order, and they accounted for all the known sketches of the Universe Symphony (divided among different folders at Yale because Ives would mix different pieces on large manuscript pages."

"Following the manuscript page labeled Section C, we find Patch 47 at the top of its manuscript page. Ives' words on the manuscript page of Patch 46 make the necessary elision possible. The simultaneous instruction on the same page to hold each note into silence leads us to a written word on Patch 46: '*ZERO*.' Two sixteenth note pick-ups in the clarinet and piano anticipate the change of mood in Patch 47. From Prelude #3 through this patch we find a finesse of quarter-tones in different perspectives."

"This patch had to be used as it was clearly Universe material, based on its microtones, its majesty, and the weight of Kirkpatrick's opinion. Its dynamism demanded the most ideal set up, which it gets in my realization."

Simple logic and deduction tells us that most, if not all the miscellaneous patches belong to Section C. However, there is more to this than meets the eye. Early in the section, the upper brass parts are related to Nearer, My God to Thee; *this is discernible because the notations of the instruments subscribe the notes of the middle portion of the melody - not in sequence, but as a succession of the requisite pitches defining the boundaries of the line. Once one is familiar with the music, this reference stands out quite clearly, and also represents a continuing reference to Ives' larger overall concept of cumulative form, in that material from early in the symphony is developed throughout the work - as in the large format of the* Concord Sonata.

Listen, too, for the fanfare-like trumpet motif at the end of Patch 48 (from the same sketch page, and clearly intended to follow Patch 47), appearing in various guises by other instruments throughout the segment from Patch 44, earlier, *and also* later, *through Patch 51B. Its characteristic sound, as described in greater detail earlier in the main text, is a pivotal unifying force during the first portion.*

In regard to the issue of the placement of Patches 47 & 48, Kirkpatrick only had designated them as part of the Universe Symphony. *Were they to be placed elsewhere, even in another main section, where would they go? Sections A & B are already well accounted for, with no obvious insertion points, and the mood and content of these patches are altogether wrong for this material. In the Section C patches, other common threads can be found, from descending bass lines, 'cloud' movements, as well as the general tenor of the writing. In this part of the section, elements of that trumpet fanfare motif appear so frequently and variously that they act as final confirmation. If Ives had not specified how he wished the material to be used, Reinhard teased out the clues, deducing a musical flow and sequence to the material where it had not been indicated, to*

The Universe Symphony Sketches

find solutions that supported continuity. Bringing in these patches after Ives wrote, "ZERO" is entirely consistent with the break in the music, the tonality and the context.

AC: "Going on (from Patch 48) to 49A & B - figuring out that it belongs there - how did you deduce the meaning of Ives' written indications and intent at this place?"

JR: "Patch 49A says on it, *"later part Sec. C Universe Sym,"* and here I was at a later part of Section C. However, it lacked a harmonic identity, which was provided by combining it with patch 49B. Patch 49B gains while 49A dissipates. Patch 49B has the most profound discussion of the piece by the composer of any sketch page."

Significantly, in as far as the tonality is concerned, (the connection to Patches 49A & B) this continues at the junction/overlap, lending additional support to its placement. Harmonically, the combination of patches was deduced and completed within Ives' system of 24 'chordal scales.' Musically, the high violin line does seem to echo and continue the solo trumpet motif just announced. Any remaining doubts that the simultaneous sounding, but minimal, fragment of Patch 49B belongs to Section C further can be dissipated by observing identical chordal syncopations (displacements of the beat) in Patches 57–59. Also, both of these patches are barred in small meters, metrically, something we do not find elsewhere.

Within Section C, Reinhard's reasoning for some overlappings, versus direct cuts and dove-tailings from patch to patch, can be best understood when examining the sketches themselves:

- *In many cases Ives laid out various sequences of patches quite clearly on the page.*
- *At other times he sketched in different meters, of unequal durations, and with no location indicated.*
- *Alternately, overlapping connections may readily be surmised by the way Ives set up the sketches themselves.*

- *Ives sometimes directed (in notation and/or writing) certain lines and moving figures that he wanted continued beyond the confines of the patch into the next.*

With this in mind, Patches 48 through 50 feature considerable overlapping, although it is difficult to be definitive about the Ives' exact intentions, despite the obvious relationships; Reinhard's solutions seem plausible and musical. We can see within Section C that not only was there a need to accommodate all of the existing material into one meter (for practicality), but also Ives' mathematical plan for the 'Pulse,' as well. These must have been amongst the headaches Ives faced in attempting to complete the symphony himself, and always had been stumbling blocks for others. With this in mind, Reinhard was careful within this segment not to superimpose conflicting major thematic, harmonic, or motivic elements upon another. Harmonically, the sum of the parts fits together in a complementary fashion, and seems supported harmonically.

If it cannot be shown that this sequence of events is <u>exactly</u> what Ives would have done, Reinhard's projections cannot have fallen far from the tree. In producing a logical and satisfying flow and form to the available material, while avoiding tonal or textural confrontations, not a single note of Ives' material was changed or expanded, while Reinhard steadfastly resisted the temptation even of simple part doubling.

AC: "I was very struck by the placing of q3257 *before* q3256 (Patch 50 followed by Patches 51A & 51B) - no doubt at all that it sounds correct, but how did you know to reverse them?"

JR: "Measure 203 (q3257) is marked the 'SEA.' The powerful waves of the percussion orchestra returns here at 19BU until its calming, the result of connecting to the end of the piece. The complexity and volume of the Pulse of the Cosmos percussion lends itself well to using patch 51A with its long sustained notes. I combined it with patch 51B, which I found independently from an examination of the original sketches. Its string pizzicatos fit well with the sustained sounds of patch 51A, and the climb of percussion to 23 divisions of the BU. I followed guide posts by CEI wherever I could find the right 'worm hole.'"

The dynamic character of the string parts makes musical sense when placed in this order, and that the numbering system is not necessarily indicative of Ives' intentions for the sequence of events. Additionally, as we listen, we will become increasingly aware of the growing power of the percussion cycle (#9). Reinhard's approach ensured that its maximum strength coincided with the part of the music that Ives had entitled "SEA," each succeeding BU (Basic Unit) resembling a large series of waves. Reinhard made every effort to ensure that the highest points did not compete with the important and complex orchestral moments, allowing the percussion to compliment less complex rhythmic or musical passages.

AC: "On Patch 51B underneath Ives' notation 'IMPORTANT,' there appears to be the directive that references: "to bar 25." In fact, that's about where it is in your realization. Was this a clue to placing it where you did? And is possibly the decision to combine it with Patch 51A also based on other directives that you traced as well?"

JR: "Patch 51A is explained above. And yes to your surmise above. In addition to idiosyncratic guideposts for making connections between patches, the counterpoint works here, lines are connecting in the strings."

AC: "Then 'Sky' and 'Rainbow,' and their positions and usage; Ives references page 4, so I assume this is a key."

JR: "Sky is necessary *before* having a rainbow. Sky is labeled the third theme, and it follows the SEA theme, and the un-named simultaneous patches of 51A and 51B. These were all inserts."

This section of joined 'inserts' again is complex in its interweaving, but is a highly effective usage of what might otherwise have been discarded by less savvy individuals; besides, their placement fits the description of the music of this section. Despite inconsistent meters in the various sketches, the numbered bar location in the sketch (25) of Patch 51B is about dead on, almost to the bar. And once again we can catch shreds of the material used for the trumpet motif (in the violins) announced in Patch 48.

With the possible exception of the 'Sky' insert (which incorporates Section A thematic material from the long score of Ives' page 4, and that Reinhard chose to orchestrate differently here), there can be little doubt that most of this particular material - formerly considered 'inserts' of no known location - was intended for incorporation into Section C. Logically, there can be no other possible place for them in the symphony. Beyond this, even if we cannot determine whether Ives necessarily would have developed any or all of this material further, the mere fact of its existence surely means it was intended for incorporation somewhere within the work.

The motivic form of the 'Sky' and 'Rainbow' fragments is comparable to the upcoming and more expanded, angular but melodic solo cello statements in Patch 54. This instrumentation was assigned by Reinhard to make it compatible with similar instrumental scorings indicated by Ives, and continues within a dialog of similar musical material in the flutes, oboes and clarinets. The cello line re-uses material from the trombones in Section B, labeled, 'Free Evolution & Humanity.'

Additional notes regarding the succeeding Patches 51 - 54:

Section C benefits in structure from having a less bombastic midsection than the material at the outset and conclusion. The progression through it (leading to Patch 55) is smooth and logical, serving as an outgrowth of the music as it progresses. However, the connecting icon -

- appearing at the end of Patch 51A, a circle with a dot in it, with accompanying words - "etc. to ⊙; see back P14" - raises some questions. It appears that, harmonically, the combination of this the next selected patch (51B) is the correct one, although the connecting icon (the symbol ⊙ within a circle) is not identical. However, we should also remember that Ives' page numberings and references also are often inconsistent and frequently misleading.

The Universe Symphony Sketches

AC: "And the connection from patch 54 to 55. What were the clues that led you to it?"

JR: "Patch 54 expands into patch 55, through counterpoint and the gradually increasing number of musical forces."

This musical material is closely related, and Patch 55 logically can be construed to be an expansion of Patch 54. Motivic similarities also may be seen with regard to the rhythmic and intervallic structure of Patches 54, 55 and 56. Musically and technically, the patches also are closely tied to the final coda - look at the angular thematic material, as well as the ascending and descending arpeggiated passagework of Patches 55 and 56. Hence, collectively, we have musical ties to all that surrounds these patches, with no other destination obvious, or actually even possible, especially since quarter-tones are introduced precipitously during this sequence.

Beyond this, significantly throughout the segment, percussion Cycle 9 continues to retrograde from its height, as the music builds through Patch 56. Linear musical intensity gradually takes the dominant role from this cycle as it wanes.

AC: "Another connecting point is patch 56 to 57; how you were able to determine that those next patches tied into the concluding section?"

JR: "Patch 56 is another dynamic, extroverted patch with lots of quarter-tone relationships. Patch 56 features two opposing orchestras a quarter-tone apart, following a third bass drum played behind the audience. This is really 'banging the can' in that this Ligeti-like idea is in itself historic. It is a most amazing surprise sound that brings a single musician to the audience covertly. (Almost gave my friend Pete a heart attack.) This is the surest evidence to me that this was planned by Ives for a concert stage (and not any valley between mountains)."

"Patch 56 enlarges dramatically until in Patch 57 a quarter-tone orchestra is established, which cleans the palette, like eating ginger between differing fish tastes of a sushi meal. It restates cleanly in a noble manner the core of the musical material, but in a way that obscures how "movements" would be constructed. The power of the piece is enhanced by its positioning, both before and after."

Patches 55 and 56 represent the beginning of the final segment, having musical content in common with the coda (Patches 60-62). In turn, this has material in common to Patches 57-59! We can see the resemblance of common elements such as the descending bass line (in Patch 56), and jumping syncopated figures (common to Patch 56 and to 60 – 62); we have already explored these ties to earlier material. Again, the meaning of Ives' multiple usage of the icon (on Patch 56):

⊙ *was not obvious. More especially there are:*

Ives' words at the end of Patch 55 ("to back P6", *with another reference* "back of P16"), and -
At the end of Patch 56, the same icon with remarks "see 5 back," as well as a triangular icon and "see back P.8," along with -
Other spurious placings of the same circular icon, numbers and indications!

However, the instructions and clues pertaining to filling out parts were clearer to Reinhard, having seen the original sketches for himself.
Dating from the earliest conception of the work, ultimately the next segment (Patches 57 - 59) seems <u>clearly</u> intended, beyond a doubt, for its placement here, since the thematic materials dating from circa 1915 are shared with the coda. Had Ives meant to further develop it, he did not need to, for it serves the purpose here perfectly, building in anticipation of the coda. Listen to the melodic high wind and violin parts (Heavens Orchestra clouds again) in these patches; they appear to have been derived from Nearer, My God to Thee.
If, as Kirkpatrick theorized, the Section C Coda dates from earlier times and originally had been intended for Section A, its designation confirms that Ives later changed his mind. In seeing it as something befitting the work's conclusion, and thus ultimately designating the sequence

of patches, "End of Section C," shares material only in common with Section C, and not Section A - and further, the surviving 1915 sketches make more sense in this context. This dramatic portion in the flutes features the lengthiest quote in the symphony from **Nearer My God to Thee,** *in keeping with the larger concept of cumulative form, and certainly significant in its musical intent at this precise point in the music; indeed, the flutes maintain elements of this melody almost to the end of the movement, drifting away only when it has fallen away beyond the extent of the quotation. Thus it can be seen that Ives developed the material from the 1915 sketches into the final coda.*

With the inertia created by Patch 57 leading to the conclusion of the symphony, it seems the sudden explosive beginning to Cycle 10 in Ives' plan is entirely appropriate, and helps to drive the music forward to the **Coda** *with a renewed and irresistible energy. Thereafter the* **Coda** *is allowed to assume its own gravitational pull, seemingly growing as this last 'Pulse' cycle recedes.*

The connections of all of these patches from 57 to Patch 62 works as the logical outgrowth of the original and other developed material, which reigns in full force towards the symphony's mighty conclusion. From a standpoint of connecting tonality, this too, is completely consistent from sketch to sketch, again lending credence that the succession of these final sketches is that which Ives had intended for the conclusion of his symphony. It is a stunning conclusion to a monumental work, as well as to a monumental triumph of realization.

INDEX

A

A Lecture, 116;
    wide leaps in, 116
A Band of Brothers, 117
Academic record at Yale, xxviii
Adeste Fideles, 144-145
Adirondacks, xxxii-xxxiii, 217, 246-247
Addison's Disease, 8, 254
Adler, Murray, xiv
Afterglow, 188-190
AFFM Orchestra, 288
Alcott, Abby Amy, 205
Alcott, Amos Bronson, xxxviii, 205;
    writings, 206
Alcott, Louisa May, 205
Alcotts, The (see *The Alcotts*)
Alcotts Overture, 206
Aleatoric effects, 114, 150, 252,253
    All Made of Tunes
    (Burkholder), 48-49, 322
All Hail the Power of Jesus' Name, 235-236
Amendment to the Constitution, 20th, 10,11
American Festival of Microtonal Music, 286;
    Orchestra, 288
American Symphony Orchestra, xiii, 216
Americanism, of Ives' music, 317-318
    of *Third Symphony,* 92
America the Beautiful, 83
American Woods Overture, see The *American Woods Overture*
Amphion, from, 169-170
An Election, 12, 37
And Now, Lo it is Night, 325
Appalachian Spring, (Copland), 158
Arrow Music Press, 162
Associated Press, The, Elliot Carter obituary, 327
A Set of Three Short Pieces, 172
Attention Deficit Disorder (ADD), xxviii
Atonality, 53, 122, 124, 130, 143, 150, 185, 193, 197, 251
Austin, Larry, 282-283, 343
Avant-Garde, in America, 164
Azmon,
    similarities to *The Shining Shore,* 96; in *Third Symphony,* 99-101, 102

355

B

Bach, J. S., 1, 13, 24;
  Three Part Sinfonia, 75,
    *Toccata and Fugue in D
    minor* (BWV 538), 235;
    his counterpoint, 219
Barn dance, 137,139
Baron, Carol K.,
  on Magee's new catalog
    chronology, 322; on
    Ives' character as a
    philanthropist and
    humanitarian, xliii; on
    Putnam's Camp dates
    and handwriting, 327;
    on Rossiter's questions
    of Carter, 327; on
    Solomon's conclusions,
    327
Bártok, Béla,
  *Music for Strings, Percussion
  and Celeste*, 128;
    regarding folk music
    quotations, 49
Battle Hymn of the Republic, 236
Bellemann, Henry, 19
Ben Bolt, 126, 128-130
Berest, Michael, 249, 263
Bernstein, Leonard, 49, 85,
  87
Beethoven, Ludwig van, 13;
  parallels to, 39; quotes
    from *Fifth Symphony*, 50,
    84, 196, 200, 208, 232;
    Hammerklavier Sonata,
      See under separate
      heading
Bethany, xxiv, 50; see also
  Nearer, My God to Thee
Beulah Land, 70, 83, 233
Birth of the Oceans, 302
Blues, 201
Borodin, *Second Symphony*,
  quote from 75, 83
Botstein, Leon, 8, 41, 120
Bowring, John, 175, 220
Boys and Girls Come Out to Play,
  129
Brigg Fair, (Delius), 143
Brahms, Johannes, xxx, 13, 24;
  comparison with his *Fourth
  Symphony*, 85; idiom,
    51; European musical
    tradition as defined by,
    106; orchestration, 57;
    place in time, 76; quote
    from *First Symphony*, 80,
    83, 85-88; quote from
    Third Symphony, 82
Bringing in the Sheaves, 81, 207,
  223
Broyles, Michael, 11
Buck, Dudley, 61-62, chro-
  matic harmonies, 61,
    158, 169, 173
Burkholder, Peter J., liii, 48,
  58-59, 322;
    analysis of *Second Symphony*,
    73, 75, 80; adopting
    Magee's chronology,

INDEX

322-323; *All Made of Tunes,* (see separate listing); on cumulative form, 97

C

Cage, John, l, 321
Cakewalk, 26
Camp meetings, xxiv-xxv, 25, 50, 60, 77, 91, 103, 239
Camptown Races, 86, 139, 229
Calcium Light Night, 117
Canon (canonic), 102, 118
Carter, Elliot,
    on percussion rehearsal for Fourth Symphony, 215; on (Ives) altering score, 316; on marginalizing Ives' importance, 325-326; on use of quotations, 43; obituary, 325
'Cartoons or Take-Offs,' 117
Central Park in the Dark, 119, 125-131, 158, 222
Charles Ives Society, The, 281, 283-285, 288, 340
Charles Ives: A Life With Music, (Swafford), 5
Charles Ives & His America (Rossiter), 4, 325
Charles Ives: My Father's Song (Feder), 4
Charles Ives Reconsidered (Magee), liii, 5

Charles Ives: Some Questions of Veracity (Solomon), 315-326
Children's Day, or *'Young Folks Meeting' (Third Symphony),* 101
Chromaticism, 61, 158, 168, 173
Church music, 60-62
Civil War, xxii, xxv-xxvi, 133, 141, 143;
    tunes, 25, 59-60; in *Second Symphony,* 77
Coda, 68
Codetta, 68
Columbia, the Gem of the Ocean, 79-81, 85-87; 112, 149-153;
    in *Hawthorne,* 203-205; in *Fourth Symphony,* 229, 231
Communion (Third Symphony), 102
Composing methods, 194
Compositional decline, 264
Concord, Massachusetts, xx, xxxiv, xxxix, 191
Concord Sonata, 12, 164, 191-212, 267, 323;
    Second Edition, 192, 194, 260, 323; timeline, 194; conception in Adirondacks, 247; *Massa* reference, 250;

357

Conductors, in *Universe Symphony*, 274
Cooper Jr., James Fenimore, 188
Copland, Aaron, 1, 14, 162, 178
Cosmic heartbeat, 249
Cosmic Microwave Background, 190
Counterpoint (see also polyphony),
Ives' 56-58; in *Fourth Symphony*, 219; Bach's 219; Brahms' 57-58,
Country Band March, 118, 203, 205, 233
Cowell, Henry, 19-20;
as a realizer, 117; on Universe Symphony, 256-259; Ives Legend, 256-259, 318-319; dating scores, 322; on last chord in *Second Symphony*, 328-332
Cowell, Sidney, 318
Cumulative Form, 97-98;
over multiple movements (*in Concord Sonata*), 195-197
Cycles, 111-117, 151, 185, 273;
multiple elements, 117; in *Fourth Symphony*, 241-242; in *The Cage*, 174-175; in *From the Steeples and the Mountains*, 111-112; in *Scherzo: All the Way Around and Back*, 112; in *The Gong on the Hook and Ladder*, 113-114; in *The See'r*, 116; in *Calcium Light Night*, 117; in *Universe Symphony*, 273, 279-280, 285, 294-295, 270-271

D

Damrosch, Walter, 5
Danbury, Connecticut, xx, xxiii-xxiv, xxvii, 15-16, 23-25, 133-135, 217, 331;
clashing bands, 56; in *Fourth Symphony*, 225, 234; musical influences, 58-63; social order, 17-18
Dating of manuscripts, 320-324;
counter arguments, 323
Debussy, Claude, 53;
textures, 208, *Golliwogs' Cakewalk*, 205
Decoration Day, 141-147
Delius, Frederick, 143-145
Demons' Dance around the Pipe, 203
Development, 68
Die Meistersinger von Nürnberg, (Wagner), quote from, 82
Dodecaphony, 53, 150
Dorrnance, 240-242
Down East Overture, 79

INDEX

'Down in de cornfield', 80, 84, 85, 86, 140, 210-211, 232
Duke Street, 156-159
Dvořák, Antonin, 17, 29; idiom, 51, 75; answer to *New World Symphony*, 79; resemblance to *New World Symphony*, 75, 83; European musical tradition as defined by, 106

E

Earth Orchestra, 277-278, 292-294, 296-301, 339
Earth and the Firmament, 303
Earth is of the Heavens, 306-312
Eighteen, 339
Einstein, Albert, 248, 264, 294
Emerson Overture (Emerson Concerto), 194-204, 266
Emerson motif, 200-201, 207, 211
Emerson, Ralph Waldo, xxxiv; ideals 11, 13, 23; on *Hymn*, 174; in *Concord Sonata*, 197-204; writing methods, 198-199; on 'finding his star,' xx, 253
Enharmonic notation, 55-56
Essays Before a Sonata, xx, 44, 57, 164, 194, 210; Ives' anger in, 210
Europe/European, perceived cultural superiority, 23, 76-77, 164; esteem held in by Ives, 75-76; Ives' resentment of, xli, 29, 73; forms & traditions, 67, 71, 75, 107; origins of American tunes, 31; tradition of rubato, 38
European model, xliv, 23, 61-62, 67-69, 76; in *Second Symphony*, 77; symphonic model, 67-69
Experiments, 107-131; amalgam of all experiments in *Fourth Symphony*, 227; of C.E.I, 63-65, 105-131; harmonic, 106-107; rhythmic, 108-108; of George Ives, 31; role in large works, 135
Exposition, 68; in *Second Symphony*, 82
Expressionism, 54, 77

F

Falsification of dates, 319-328; 'counter-evidence,' 321
Farberman, Harold, xiii
'Fate' motif, 50, 85, 86, 144, 196, 200, 202, 204, 207, 211, 222, 232, 241
Feder, Stuart, 4, 7, 10, 16-17, 316; on assertion of mental decline, 259-262; on 19th Century attitudes

towards musicians, 17; *Charles Ives: My Father's Song* (see separate heading); on Ives' alleged crankiness, 27-28; on *Essays Before a Sonata & Memos*, 262; on 'falsifications' of dates, 327; on Ives' use of descriptive words, 259-263; on Ives' honesty and character, 323; observation about second movement *of Fourth Symphony*, 228; on *The Pond,* 113; psychiatric conclusions, 7; psychobiography, 332; reason for ceasing composing, 228; ref., to Geo. Ives in *Thoreau?*, 210-212; on timing of political ideals, 10; on 12-tone system in *Universe Symphony,* 251-253
Federal Street, 156-159
Few Days, 117
First Festival of Contemporary American Music at Yaddo, 164, 178
First Orchestral Set, 118, 134
First Piano Sonata, 221
First String Quartet, 44, 215-216
First Symphony, see *Symphony No. 1*
First Symphony, Brahms (see Brahms)
First Symphony, Mahler (see Mahler)
First Subject, 68
First World War, (see World War 1)
First Violin Sonata, 220
First Set for Chamber Orchestra, 115-118
Fisher's Hornpipe, 140
Five Pieces for Orchestra (Schönberg), 130
Folgore da San Giminiano, 185, 187
Folk tunes, 59,
  in *Second Symphony,* 76
Foote, Arthur, 17
Four Transcriptions from Emerson, 193, 198, 323
Fourth Symphony, Brahms (see Brahms)
Fourth Symphony, see *Symphony No. 4*
Freshmen in Park, 129
From Greenland's Icy Mountains, 234-236
From the Steeples and the Mountains, 111-112
Foster, Stephen, 77
For He's a Jolly Good Fellow, 140
Frequency,
  pitch, 42; rhythm, 42
Furness, Clifton, 19
Fugue in Four Keys on "The Shining Shore," 95-97; similarities to *Third Symphony,* 95-97; polytonality in, 107

INDEX

G
Gabrielli, Giovani, antiphonal writing, 119-120
Garryowen, 152, 229
General William Booth enters into Heaven, liii, 107
German tradition, 62, 73
'Glory-beaming star', 175, 221-223, 241
God be with you, 229
Goethe, xlii
Golliwog's Cakewalk, (Debussy), 203, 205
Goodnight Ladies, 140
Goossens, Eugene, 215
Grainger, Percy, folk material, 49
Griggs, John Cornelius, 157

H
Hail, Columbia, 229, 231
Hammerklavier Sonata, (Beethoven), 196, 204, 207, 210, 211
Handel, George F., *Joy To The World*, 75, 236
Hanover Square, 230
Happy Land, (Far, far away), in *Third Symphony*, 101-102; in *Fourth Symphony*, 229
Harding, Warren G., 11, 37
Harmony, in fourths and fifths, 150, 175; compounded keys, 177; augmented chords, 187

Harrison, Lou, 261
Harvard University, xxxvi
Hawthorne, 27, 197, 202-205; relationship with *Fourth Symphony*, 202, 225; description as a 'comedy', 227
Hawthorne, Nathaniel, xxxvii
Hawthorne Concerto for Piano and Orchestra, 202, 215; relationship with *Fourth Symphony*, 215, 231
Harvest Home Chorales, 127
Haydn, Josef Franz, on quotations, 49
He is There!, 10, 203, 205
Health issues, 109-111, 254-255
Heavens Orchestra, 278-279, 292-294, 296-301, 339
Henahan, Donal, on psychobiographies, 332
Hello! Ma Baby, 126, 129, 153
Herrmann, Bernard, 7-8; aural skills of, 214; cond. New Chamber Orchestra, 216 on quotations, 49, 81;
Hertz, David Michael, 201
Holiday Quickstep, 74
Holidays Symphony, 135-136, 215
Holst, Gustav, 276
Home, Sweet Home, 138, 229, 230
Honesty, 327

Hopkins Grammar School, New Haven, Conn., 27
Hora Novissima, (Parker), xxx, 27
Hubble, Edwin, 248, 277
Human Faith Melody, 81, 196-197, 200-201, 206-208, 211-212, 232
Humor, 261
Hymn (Tersteegan), 172-174
Hymns, 25, 30, 43, 50, 60-62; in *Second Symphony*, 70; in *Third Symphony*, 92, 95, 96, in the *Concord Sonata*,193, 196; in the *Fourth Symphony*, 220, 227, 235; in *Thanksgiving*, 156-159

I
I Hear Thy Welcome Voice, 223
Illness, recurring mystery, xxxiii, 109-110
Impracticalities, of instrumentation, 57-59
Impressionism, 53, 77
Independent entities, 124-125
Innovations and Nostalgia: Ives, Mahler, and the Origins of Modernism, (Botstein), 120
Insurance industry, 18; agencies with J. Myrick, 110; career in, xxx-xxxii; crisis in, xlii, 109; reason for entering industry, 17-19
In the Sweet Bye and Bye, 50, 203; in *Fourth Symphony*, 222, 232, 233; important quote in *Hawthorne*, 204, 225
In These United States, 81
Irish Washerwoman, 229
Isolation, 54-55, 328
Ives and the Four Musical Traditions (Burkholder), 58-65
Ives, Brewster, 261
Ives, Charles, xx: accelerated development, 2; actuarial tables, xxxii; alleged crankiness, 27-28; as avant-garde composer, 39-40; counterpoint, 56-58; blending multiple elements, 48; career choice, xlv, 18, 27-29; on cessation of composing, 329; college camaraderie, 71; comparisons with Grandma Moses, 49; compositional ideals, 63; cycles, use of, 111-117; on credence lent to dates of other compositions, 329; eccentricities, xliii; on European formal constrictions, 44;

experiments, 63-65, 106-131; eyesight problems, 237; harmonic experiments, 107-108; health, xxxiii, 64, 109-110, 113, 161, 254-255, 256-257, 259; homestead in West Redding, Conn., xxxiii, 184; humor, 52; idiomatic foundations, 58-65; insurance company with Julian Myrick, 110; on laws of physics and sound, 219; musical roots, 43; nationalism, 44-45; Parker's guidance with *First Symphony*, 69; on quoting from European compositions, 47-48; regard for European music, 76; relationship with Parker, 63; resentment of Dvořák's remarks on *New World Symphony*, 75; resentment of Parker, 29; rhythmic experiments, 108, 111-115; shyness, 33; simple lifestyle, 212; skills acquired from Parker, 29, 32-34; pianistic abilities, 12, 15, 32, 192; pioneering of 20th Century techniques, 34; 20th Amendment to the Constitution, 10; 'snake tracks', 162-163

Ives & Co., 110

Ives, Edith, 162

Ives' Four Seasons, 136

Ives, George, xxi-xxiii, 14-16, 24-26;
effect of early death on C.E.I, 255-256; experimental approach & attitudes, 32-33, 63; father-son relationship, 324; idealizing of, 258, 318, 325, 210; influence in Charles, 31-32; on playing the flute, 211; on last chord in *Second Symphony*, 330-332; teaching, 30

Ives, Harmony (Twitchell), xxxii, 93, 258; influence, 93, 323

Ives Legend, 5, 256-263, 318-319, 333

Ives, Mollie, 8

Ives, Moss, xli

Ives & Myrick, 110

J

Jew's harp, 137-138

Jolly Dogs, 74, 117

Joy To The World, (Handel), quote in *Second Symphony*, 75; in *Fourth Symphony*, 87, 236

Just intonation machine, 302

K
Katy Darling, 153
Katz, David, 216
Keats, John, 180
Keene Valley, 247
Kipling, Rudyard, 171
Knussen, Oliver, xiii, xvi
Kirkpatrick, John, 20;
  on Ives cutting down manuscript pages, 326; on dating the *Second Symphony*, 74; on *Decoration Day*, 142; first performance of Concord Sonata, 192; on Ives hearing in his mind, 20; on Ives' pianistic abilities, 192; on Ives' (performance) directions, 55; on mental acuity, 261; on second movement of *Fourth Symphony*, 230; on *Washington's Birthday*, 138-139; on study with Parker, 333; on *Universe Symphony* materials, 338

L
Laban, 155
Lambert, Philip, 111, 175, 303, 333;
  The Music of Charles Ives, 111; on Solomon's assertions, 333
Leduc, Monique Schmitz, 261

Lieberson, Goddard, 14;
  on Ives' musical language, 35, 57; on orchestration, 57-59
L'Histoire du Soldat, (Stravinsky), 115
Like a Sick Eagle, 116-117, 180-182
Ligeti, György, *Requiem*, 37
Lily pads, the, xlvi, 39, 231
Lincoln, the Great Commoner, 10, 36-37
Listening skills, 57
Lizst, Franz, *Faust Symphony*, 252-253
Lock Lomond, 207, 210
London Bridge is falling down, 152
Long, long ago, 86, 87
Love's Old Sweet Song, 87
Lost manuscripts, 321
Lusitania, RMS, 229

M
Magee, Gayle Sherwood, liii, 5-6, 28;
  on altering scores, 326-327; *Charles Ives Reconsidered*, (see under separate heading); health issues, 110; on last chord in *Second Symphony*, 330-332; on modernity, 226-227, 267; re-dated catalog, 93; on dating scores, 322; personal criticisms of Ives, 6,

INDEX

330-332; on study with Parker, 333-334; on training with Parker, 33; on works from 1920's, 264-265; on *Universe Symphony* myth, 258; on inspiration for *Universe Symphony*, 259

Mahler, Gustav, 8, 18, 19, 120; quote from *First Symphony*, 81, 83, 86

Majority, (see *The Majority*)

Manhein, Frank T., 1

Manuscripts, disorder, 35-36

March No. 3, with My Old Kentucky Home, 74

Marching Through Georgia, 74, 117, 145, 152

Martyn, 196, 203, 204-205, 229, 233, 242, 243

Massa's in de Cold Ground, 80, 84, 140, 144, 210-211, 229, 231, 232, 249-250; in *Universe Symphony*, 250, 300

Marble slab, 303

Mathematical techniques, 195

Mauceri, John, 345

Melodies, linked, 81; wide leaps in, 116, 144, 274

Memorial Slow March, 237, 241

Memos, 2; 'cycle rhythms', 272; microtones, 274; reactions to prominent musicians, 38; recollections in, 29; rants, 261; religious music, 94; on *Universe Symphony*, 255, 263, 271, 273

Memories, 261

Microtones, 274, 286-287

Mental decline, (see Feder)

Minstrel music, 26

Missionary Chant, 84, 197-198, 207, 208, 241-242

Modernism, 20th Century, 41

Mortality, awareness, 328-329

Moses, Grandma, 49

Multiple keys, 29

Multiple speeds, 64, 109, 114, 119, 122, 129, 150, 165, 180, 195, 239, 281

Mutual Insurance, 110

Munch, Edvard, 54

Mutual Insurance, 28, 110

Music Quarterly, 331

Music of the Spheres, Pythagoras', 123-124

Music for Strings, Percussion and Celeste, (Bartók), 128

Myrick, Julian, 110

Mysterium, (Scriabin), 259

N

Nationalism, 44-45

Nearer, My God to Thee (Bethany), xxiv, 50, 143-145, 193; in *Fourth Symphony*, 193, 222-223, 239, 240-243, 250; based on *Memorial Slow March*, 238; in

365

Universe Symphony, 193, 240-243, 249-250, 274, 299-300, 303, 308, 311-312, 342-343, 346, 353
Neoclassicism, 53, 115
Nettleton, 84, 156
New Chamber Orchestra, 216
New England, 16, 23, 31;
    Culture and tradition, xxvii; music of 19th Century, 60, 135-136
New York, xxx-xxxii, 26
New York Life Building, xxxi
New York Philharmonic Orchestra,
    under Mahler, 81, 1927 performance of *Fourth Symphony*, 215
New York Times, review, 27
New World Symphony, Dvořák, 71, 72-73;
    answering by Ives with *Second Symphony*, 79; spiritual quotes, 72-73
Nicholls, David, 8

O

Old Black Joe, 229
Old Folks at Home, 138-139
Old Folks Gatherin' (Third Symphony), 99
Old Home Day, 152
On the Antipodes, 264, 339
On the Banks of the Wabash, 229
One Hundred and Fourteen Songs (114 Songs), 161, 166, 170, 178, 180, 184

Oral History American Music Project (Yale), 2
Orchestration, balance issues, 57, 146;
    in *Fourth Symphony*, 219
Originality, 41-43
Orchard House Overture, 206-207
Overture and March to 1776, 118, 153

P

Painters, French, 77
Parker, Horatio, xxviii-xxx;
    approach to composition, 29-30, 107; attitudes towards vernacular music, 29, 31; on connection with Walter Damrosch, 5; on "hogging the keys" 62; *Hora Novissima*, xxx, 27; marginalizing (by Ives'), 324; on Ives' *First Symphony*, 70; reputation/career, xxx; 5-6, 18; study with, 169, 318, 332-333; tolerance, 69;
Parallel listening,
    in *Fourth Symph.* common to *Universe Symphony*, 217, 238, 248-249, 274
Pathetique Symphony, (Tchaikowski), 71
Peer Music, 340
Pentatonic scale, 178, 199
Percussion,

battery in *Fourth Symphony*, 239, 273; in *Universe Symphony*, 271, 273, 279-280
Perlis, Vivian, 2-3, 255
Petrouchka, (Stravinsky), 115
Philharmonia Orchestra, xiii
Pianistic writing characteristics, 165
Picasso, Pablo, 53-54
Pig Town Fling, 81, 85, 87, 140, 229
Pilgrims, 228, 232
Pine Mountain, Conn., xli
Pitch, 42
Political views, xxxix, xliii, 10, 36-37, 237, 254, 261
Polyphony, 56-57, 138, 165
Polyrhythms, 64
Polymeters, 64
Polytonality, 32, 64, 95-96, 106
Popular melodies, 59;
  in *Second Symphony*, 76-77
Porter, David G., 248;
  Emerson Concerto, 266; *Third Orchestral Set*, 50, 265; on *Universe Symphony* 'missing' sketches, 269-270; *Universe Symphony* realization, 266, 283-284
Poverty Flat, xxx, 109
Pre-First Violin Sonata, 177
Prelude,
  Fourth Symphony, 220-223, 240; in *Universe Symphony*, 270-271

Prelude and Postlude for a Thanksgiving Service, 154
Primitivism, 50, 53
Prokofiev, Sergei, comparisons with, 80
Proprior Deo, 223
Psalm 67,
  polytonality in, 107
Psalm 90, 264
Psycho (Hitchcock), 214
Psychobiographies, 332
Psi Upsilon Marching Song, 117
Pulse of the Cosmos, The, 111, 240, 271, 273, 279-280, 294-297;
  correct tempo, 299-300
Putnam's Camp, 118, 205, 318, 326-327
Pythagorean tuning, 286-288

Q

Quarter-tones, 117, 241, 252, 286, 345, 352
Quasi-pentatonic melody, 199, 200-201, 210
Quotations, 43-50;
  authentic use of, 76; connections with transcendentalism, 44

R

Ragtime, 26
Rants, 261
Ravel, Maurice, 201
Raymond Agency, 109
Realizations,

of *Universe Symphony*, see
Universe Symphony, & *Johnny Reinhard*
Recapitulation,
68; in *Second Symphony*, 87
Reeves, David Wallace, 74
Reinhard, Johnny, 266;
on authenticity of his realization of *Universe Symphony*, 288, 338; Dir. AFMM, 288; on instrumentation of realization, 341-343; microtones, 286; *The Ives Universe: a Symphonic Odyssey*, 337; realization of *Universe Symphony*, 266, 282, 284-286, 288, 292-314, 339-355; on tuning in *Universe Symphony*, 286-287;
Relative major, 177
Relative minor, 177
Religious music,
for services, 94, 155; in *Third Symphony*, 94-95
Reuben and Rachel, 74
Reveille, 88, 146, 152, 153, 229
Revisions, 55, 125, 127, 192, 215, 246, 264, 269, 322-324, 329
Rhythm, 42;
experiments, 108; techniques, 149-150
Riding down from Bangor, 74
Ridley, Aaron, 127-128

RMS Titanic, 253-254
Robert Browning Overture, 9, 247
Rollo, ix, xiii
Rondo Rapid Transit, 273
Root, George, 46
Royal Fireworks Music, (Handel), 120
Rossiter, Frank R., 4, 28, 316;
on 19th Century attitudes towards musicians, 17; on questioning Solomon's of Carter's account of *Putnam's Camp* revision, 327
Ruggles, Carl, 9, 206
Russian 'Five', 53
Ryder, Luemily, 261

S

Sailor's Hornpipe, 139
Satie, Erik, 53
Scherzo: All the Way Around and Back, 112
Scherzo: Over the Pavements,
neoclassical sounds, 51, 115, 273
Schmitz, Robert, 19
Schönberg, Arnold, 1, 53, 130, 150, 162, 252-253
Scriabin, Alexander,
Mysterium, 259
Second Orchestral Set, 10, 207, 229-230
Second Regiment Connecticut National Guard March, (Reeves), 74, 146

INDEX

Second Symphony, see *Symphony No. 2*
Second Symphony, (Borodin), 75, 83
Second Violin Sonata, 177
Second Subject, 68
Seclusion, 134
Seder, Theodore A., 290
September, 185-187
Serebrier, José, 216
Serialism, 53
Set of Three Short Pieces, A, 172
Set No. 1 for Chamber Orchestra, 180
Shadow counterpoint, 58, 97-98
Silent Night, in *Third Symphony,* 103
Sketches, 35
Slonimsky, Nicolas, 7, 19
Slow March, 142
Social views, 261-262
Society for American Music, 8
Solomon, Maynard, 316-317, 319-326; 'evidence' of falsification, 320, 323, 332-334
So may it be! (The Rainbow), 183-185
Something for Thee, 223
Sonata Form, 68-69
Sonata for Organ, 79
Sonata-Rondo, 69
Sousa, John Philip, 126
Spatial writing, 112, 120

Spiritual relationships with music, 123
Sprague, Charles, 179
Stop that Knocking at My Door, 208
Stokowski, Leopold, xiii, 216
St. Patrick's Day in the Morning, 140, 153, 229
Star Wars (John Williams), 157
Starburst galaxies, 1
Stravinsky, Igor, xiv, li; neoclassicm, 51, 53, 115, 162; on Ives, 63
Street Beat, 229
Swafford, Jan, 5, 322
Symphony of Holidays, (see *Holiday Symphony*)
Symphony No. 1, 30, 62, 69-71, 83
Symphony No. 2, 69, 71-88; dates, 73-74; return to roots, 73; third movement origins, 75-76, 83; contrasted with *Third Symphony,* 98; throwback from *Washington's Birthday,* 140; final chord, 330-331
Symphony No. 3, 91-104, 247; 'American' character, 99; date, 92-93; harmony in, 94-96; rhythmic characteristics, 102; in relation to *Decoration Day,* 143

Symphony, No. 4, 35, 193, 213-242, 248-9;
  its advancement beyond *Concord Sonata*, 193; anticipation in *Thanksgiving*, 158; ceasing composing as sacrifice to father (Feder), 228; *finale*, 219; performance edition of *finale*, 227; *first movement (Prelude)*, 176-177, 220-223; first performance, 38; *fourth movement*, 237-243; *fourth movt.* link to *Universe Symphony*, 237; history, 234-235; many idioms, 214; in relation to *Decoration Day*, 143; relationship with *Hawthorne*, 202-204; *second movement*, 224-233; shared visions with *Universe Symphony*, 214; significance, 192-193; spirituality, 214; *third movement*, 234-237

T

Take-Off No. 3: Rube Trying to Walk 2 to 3!!, (Ives), 203
Taps, 111-113, 143-145
Ta-ra-ra Boom-de-ay!, 116
Tarrant Moss, 170-172
Taubman, Howard, 261
Tchaikowski, Peter, I., li; idiom, 51; *1812 Overture*, l; *Pathetique Symphony*, 71
Tennyson, Alfred Lord, 169
Ternary Form, 156
Tersteegen, Gerhardt, 172
Tin Pan Ally, 26
Thanksgiving (and Forefathers' Day), 138, 154-159; harvest scene in, 300
The Alcotts, 12, 197, 205-208, 210
The American Woods, 74, 86, 331
The Anti-Abolitionist Riots, 198
The Battle Cry of Freedom, 46, 145, 150-151, 152, 203, 205
The Battle Hymn of the Republic, 152
The Beautiful River, 229
The Boys are Marching, 229
The Cage, 174-175
The Campbells are Comin', 126, 129, 140
The Celestial Country,
  dating of relative to *Second Symphony*, 73; 27-30; inauthentic style, 50
The Celestial Railroad, 27, 203, 218, 225;
  text (Hawthorne), 228, 230
The Circus Band, 74
The Fisherman's Reel, 87
The Fourth of July, 140, 147-154;
  comparisons with *Fourth Symphony*, 224, 233;
  12-tone rows in, 252;

INDEX

wide leaping intervals in, 274
The girl I left behind, 152
The Good Old Summertime, Tin Pan Alley, 125
The Gong on the Hook and Ladder, 113-114, 134
The Greatest Man, 12, 162-163
The Indians, 178-180, 182, 199
The Ives Universe – a Symphonic Odyssey (Reinhard), 288, 337
The Majority (also known as *The Masses*), 10, 150, 204, 233
The Masses (also known as *Majority*), 10, 150; 12-tone row in, 253; wide leaping intervals, in, 274
The Music of Charles Ives, (Lambert), 111
The New River, 116
The One Way, 264-265
Theory of Relativity, 264
The Planets, (Holst), 276
The Pond, 112-113, 211
The Philosophy of Music: Theme and Variations, Aaron Ridley, 127-128
The Rite of Spring, Stravinsky, xiii, li, 53, 203
The Ruined River, 116
The Shining Shore, 70, 157; transformation of, 300
The See'r, 116,
The Slaves Shuffle, 203

The Unanswered Question, 93, 119, 120-125, 131, 126-127, 222
The Worms Crawl In, 129
There is a Fountain Filled with Blood, in *Third Symphony*, 101-102, 243
There's Music in the Air, 102
They are There!, 12
Third Orchestral Set, 50, 265
Third Symphony, see *Symphony No. 3*
Thirty-four Songs, 181
Thoreau, 208-212; correct interpretive approach, 189, 209
Thoreau, Henry David, xxxix, 208
Three Harvest Home Chorales, 32
Three Page Sonata, 247
Three Part Sinfonia, Bach, 75
Three Places in New England, 8, 118, 134, 205, 316
Throw out the Lifeline, 229
Timeline, for *Third Symphony*, 92
Toccata and Fugue in D minor (BWV 538), Bach, 235
Tone Roads No. 1, 339
Tone Roads No. 3, 273
Tone clusters, in *Concord Sonata*, 204
Tramp, Tramp, Tramp, 47, 117, 229, 230
Transition, 68

Transcendentalists of
  Concord, xxxiv, xliv
Transcendentalism, xx,
  in Ives' music, 92-93, 119,
  121, 174; link to quotations, 44, 79; Parker's encouragement, 44
Tristan und Isolde, Wagner, quote from, 84
Tucker, Mark, 247
Turkey in the Straw, 87, 139-140, 229, 231, 233
Town, Gown and State, 85
Twain, Mark, 77
Twelve-tone system, 53;
12-tone rows, 150, 252-253
Two Contemplations, 119
Two Little Flowers, 162, 264

U
Untermeyer, Louis, 8
Universe Symphony, xxxiii, xlv, 13, 38, 198, 245-313; advancement beyond *Concord Sonata*, 193; correct tempo, 301-302; difficulties of realization, 289-290; Earth centrism, 277; elements linking sketches to Section C, 308, 310, 341; encompassing all experiments, 266-267; extravagant descriptions, 256-257; harmonic implications for 'chordal scales', 307; innovation confirmed, 269; inspired by Adirondacks, 247, 258; instrumentation, 258; intentions to finish, 263; link to *Fourth Symphony*, 237, 249; materials rebuff Solomon, 329; in *Memos*, 271; microtones in, 286-287; 'missing' sketches, 269-270, 339-341; modernity, 226; multiple performances, 275; 'parallel listening' in 217-219; plan, 270-271, 277-278; preludes, 270-271, 302, 305; *Pulse of the Cosmos*, see separate listing; Pythagorean tuning, 286; quotations, use of in, 48; in relation to *Decoration Day*, 142; realizations, 213, 246, 266, 281-286, 299-300; Reinhard's use of pizzicato, 309; resemblance in, 184-185; rhythmic principles, 111-112; rhythmic relationships, 280; Section A, 295-301, 339; Section B, 302, 341; Section C, 306; significance, 192-193; sketch materials, 271-273, 288; sound of,

INDEX

289; tonal centers, 276; Trio in Section A, 341; 12-tone rows in, 252-253; why Ives could not finish, 254-263; wide leaps in, 116; unfinishability, 194; on verbal descriptions, 259-263

V
Variations on America, xlv, 107; polytonality in, 107
Vaughan Williams, Ralph, folk material, 49
Vernacular music, xxiv-xxv, 43-50
Vunderink, Todd, 340, 345

W
Wake Nicodemus, 81, 86
Walden; or, Life in the Woods, 208, 209
Walden Pond, 209
Walden Sounds, 209
Washington's Birthday, 136-141, 327; Ives' correction of the date, 327
Washington Post March, (Sousa), 126, 229
Watchman, tell us of the night (Bowring), 175-178, 185, 220-223
Watson, Fred, xiv, xvii
Webern, Anton, 1
Wedding March, Wagner, 207
West Redding, Connecticut, xvii, xxxiii, 134, 184
Westminster Chimes, 223, 229
What a Friend We Have in Jesus (Erie), in *Third Symphony*, 99-102
When stars are in the quiet skies, 167-168
When I Survey the Wondrous Cross, 82
When the Moon Is On the Wave, 117
Where, O Where Are the Verdant Freshmen?, 81
The White Cockade, 140
Whitehouse, Richard, 286
Whole-tone scales, 274-275
Wilson, Woodrow, 11
Woodworth (Just as I am), in *Third Symphony*, 99-100, 102-103
World War I, 36, 134, 229, 231, 254
Wordsworth, William, 183
Wright, Frank Lloyd, 54

Y
Yale University, xxvii-xxx, 2, 5, 17, 26, 31
Yaddo, 164, 178
Yankee Doodle, 153, 23